Excellent English 4
Language Skills for Success

Susannah MacKay
Mari Vargo
Pamela Vittorio

McGraw Hill

Excellent English 4, Teacher's Edition

Published by McGraw-Hill ESL/ELT, a business unit of The McGraw-Hill Companies, Inc. 1221 Avenue of the Americas, New York, NY 10020.

Book: ISBN 978–0–07–719770–4
      MHID: 0–07–719770–4
1 2 3 4 5 6 7 8 9 10 VNH 11 10 09

Series editor: Nancy Jordan
Developmental editor: Regina Velázquez
Cover designer: Witz End Design
Interior designer: NETS
Compositor: Thompson Steele

Cover photo:
  Hand: Getty
  Family with rabbit: Corbis
  Girl graduating: Getty
  Man at desk with book: McGraw-Hill
  Businessman giving presentation: Corbis
  Smiling family: Getty

Contents

Welcome to the Teacher's Edition

The *Excellent English* Teacher's Edition provides support to teachers using the *Excellent English* Student Book. Each unit of the Teacher's Edition begins with a list of the unit's lesson titles, the objective(s) for each lesson, the reading and writing strategies, and the Academic and Community Connection activities. Hundreds of additional activities are suggested throughout the Teacher's Edition to expand the use of the target grammar, vocabulary, and life skills in the Student Book.

    The *Excellent English* Teacher's Edition offers clear, step-by-step procedures for each lesson. Seasoned teachers can use the instructions as a quick refresher, while newer teachers, or substitute teachers, can use the instructions as a helpful guide for conducting the Student Book activities in the classroom.

THE TEACHER'S EDITION PROVIDES:

- Step-by-step procedural notes for each *Excellent English* Student Book activity.
- Over 200 Expansion Activities that offer creative life-skill tasks tied to the activities in each unit, including the Big Picture scenes.
- Warm-up Activities designed to activate background knowledge before each lesson.
- Big Picture Expansion Activities that focus on listening, vocabulary, conversation, reading, and writing.
- Worksheets for corresponding Big Picture Expansion Activities.
- Grammar Chart Activities that allow students to practice and explore the material presented in the grammar charts.
- Culture, Grammar, Pronunciation, and Literacy Notes.
- Literacy Development Activities for literacy students.
- Academic Connection Activities that promote academic skills.
- Community Connection Activities that encourage students to become more aware of, and interact more with, their communities.
- Achievement tests for each unit that assess listening, grammar, reading, and vocabulary skills. Listening passages for the tests are provided on the Assessment CD.
- Listening scripts for all Workbook and Unit Tests audio.
- Answer keys for the Student Book, Workbook, and Tests.

Program Overview

Excellent English: Language Skills for Success equips students with the grammar and skills they need to access community resources, while developing the foundation for long-term career and academic success.

Excellent English is a four-level, grammar-based series for English learners featuring a *Grammar Picture Dictionary* approach to vocabulary building and grammar acquisition. An accessible and predictable sequence of lessons in each unit systematically builds language and math skills around life-skill topics. *Excellent English* is tightly correlated to all of the major standards for adult instruction.

What has led the *Excellent English* team to develop this new series? The program responds to the large and growing need for a new generation of adult materials that provides a more academic alternative to existing publications. *Excellent English* is a natural response to the higher level of aspirations of today's adult learners. Stronger reading and writing skills, greater technological proficiency, and a deeper appreciation for today's global economy—increasingly, prospective employees across virtually all industries must exhibit these skill sets to be successful. Interviews with a wide range of administrators, instructors, and students underscore the need for new materials that more quickly prepare students for the vocational and academic challenges they must meet to be successful.

The Complete *Excellent English* Program

- The **Student Book** features 12 16-page units that integrate listening, speaking, reading, writing, grammar, math, and pronunciation skills with life-skill topics, critical thinking activities, and civics concepts.

- The **Student Book with Audio Highlights** provides students with audio recordings of all of the Grammar Picture Dictionary pages and conversation models in the Student Book.

- The **Workbook with Audio CD** is an essential companion to the Student Book. It provides:
  - Supplementary practice activities correlated to the Student Book.
  - Application lessons that carry vital, standards-based learning objectives through its *Family Connection*, *Community Connection*, *Career Connection*, and *Technology and You* lessons.

- Practice tests that encourage students to assess their skills in a low-stakes environment, complete with listening tasks from the Workbook CD.

- The **Teacher's Edition** with Tests provides:
  - Step-by-step procedural notes for each Student Book activity.
  - Expansion Activities for the Student Book, many of which offer creative tasks tied to the Big Picture scenes in each unit, including photocopiable worksheets.
  - Culture, Grammar, Vocabulary, and Pronunciation Notes.
  - Written test for each unit.
  - Audio scripts for audio program materials.
  - Answer keys for Student Book, Workbook, and Tests.

- The **Interactive Multimedia Program** incorporates and extends the learning goals of Student Books 1 and 2 by integrating language, literacy, and numeracy skill building with multimedia practice on the computer.
  A flexible set of activities correlated to each unit builds vocabulary, listening, reading, writing, and test–taking skills.

- The **Color Overhead Transparencies** encourage instructors to present new vocabulary and grammar in fun and meaningful ways. This component provides a full color overhead transparency for each of the Big Picture scenes, as well as transparencies of the grammar charts in each unit.

- The **Big Picture PowerPoint® CD-ROM** includes the Big Picture scenes for all four Student Books. Instructors can use this CD-ROM to project the scenes from a laptop through an LCD or data projector in class.

- The **Audio CDs and Audiocassettes** contain recordings for all listening activities in the Student Book. Listening passages for the unit test are provided on a separate Assessment CD or Cassette.

- The **EZ Test® CD-ROM Test Generator** provides a databank of assessment items from which instructors can create customized tests within minutes. The EZ Test assessment materials are also available online at www.eztestonline.com.

Student Book Overview

Consult the *Welcome to Excellent English* guide on pages xiv–xix of the Student Book. This guide offers instructors and administrators a visual tour of one Student Book unit.

Excellent English is designed to maximize accessibility and flexibility. Each unit contains the following sequence of eight two-page lessons that develop vocabulary and build language, grammar, and math skills around life-skill topics:

- Lesson 1: Grammar and Vocabulary (1)
- Lesson 2: Grammar Practice Plus
- Lesson 3: Listening and Conversation
- Lesson 4: Grammar and Vocabulary (2)
- Lesson 5: Grammar Practice Plus
- Lesson 6: Reading
- Lesson 7: Writing
- Lesson 8: Career Connection and Check Your Progress

Each lesson in *Excellent English* is designed as a two-page spread. Lessons 1 and 4 introduce new grammar points and vocabulary sets that allow students to practice the grammar in controlled and meaningful ways. Lessons 2 and 5—the Grammar Practice Plus lessons—provide more open-ended opportunities for students to use their new language productively. Lesson 3 allows students to hear a variety of listening inputs and to use their new language skills in conversation. Lesson 6 provides a new reading opportunity to reinforce and expand vocabulary and reading skills through multiple text types. In Lesson 7, students develop the more academic skills of reading and writing through explicit teaching of academic strategies and exposure to writing tasks. Each unit ends with Lesson 8, an exciting capstone that offers both *Career Connection*— compelling photographs and conversations underscoring the vocational objectives of the series—and *Check Your Progress*—a self-evaluation task.

Each lesson addresses a key adult standard, and these standards are indicated in the scope and sequence and in the footer at the bottom of the left-hand page in each lesson.

SPECIAL FEATURES IN EACH STUDENT BOOK UNIT

- **Grammar Picture Dictionary.** Lessons 1 and 4 introduce students to vocabulary and grammar through a picture dictionary approach. This context-rich approach allows students to acquire grammatical structures as they build vocabulary.

- **Grammar Charts.** In Lessons 1 and 4, new grammar points are presented in clear paradigms, providing easy reference for students and instructors alike.

- **Grammar Professor Notes.** Additional information related to key grammar points is provided at point of use through the Grammar Professor feature. A cheerful, red-haired character appears next to each of these additional grammar points, calling students' attention to learning points in an inviting and memorable way.

- **Math.** Learning basic math skills is critically important for success in school, on the job, and at home. As such, national and state standards for adult education mandate instruction in basic math skills. In each unit, a Math box is dedicated to helping students develop the functional numeracy skills they need for success with basic math.

- **Pronunciation.** This special feature has two major goals: (1) helping students hear and produce specific sounds, words, and minimal pairs of words so they become better listeners and speakers; and (2) addressing issues of stress, rhythm, and intonation so that the students' spoken English becomes more comprehensible.

- *What About You?* Throughout each unit of the Student Book, students are encouraged to apply new language to their own lives through personalization activities.

- **Big Picture Scenes.** Lesson 2 in each unit introduces a Big Picture scene. This scene serves as a springboard to a variety of activities provided in the Student Book, Teacher's Edition, Color Overhead Transparencies package and the Big Picture PowerPoint CD-ROM. In the Student Book, the Big Picture scene features key vocabulary and serves as a prompt for language activities that practice the grammar points of the unit. The scene features characters with distinct personalities for students to enjoy, respond to, and talk about.

- **Career-themed "Photo-Story."** Each unit ends with a compelling workplace conversation. These conversations highlight typical workplace situations and offer learners the opportunity to read about and discuss real events that can help them take the next step in their professional future. The engaging format provides students with role models as they pursue their own career and academic goals.

CIVICS CONCEPTS

Many institutions focus direct attention on the importance of civics instruction for English language learners. Civics instruction encourages students to become active and informed community members. The Teacher's Edition includes multiple *Community Connection* activities in each unit. These activities encourage learners to become more active and informed members of their communities.

ACADEMIC SKILL DEVELOPMENT

Many adult programs recognize the need to help students develop important academic skills that will facilitate lifelong learning. The *Excellent English* Student Book addresses this need through explicit teaching of reading and writing strategies, explicit presentation and practice of grammar, and academic notes in the Teacher's Edition. The Teacher's Edition also includes multiple *Academic Connection* activities in each unit. These activities encourage learners to become more successful in an academic environment.

CASAS, SCANS, EFF, AND OTHER STANDARDS

Instructors and administrators benchmark student progress against national and/or state standards for adult instruction. With this in mind, *Excellent English* carefully integrates instructional elements from a wide range of standards including CASAS, SCANS, EFF, TABE CLAS-E, the Florida Adult ESOL Syllabi, and the Los Angeles Unified School District Course Outlines. Unit-by-unit correlations of some of these standards appear in the Scope and Sequence on pages xv–xix. Other correlations appear in the Workbook. Here is a brief overview of our approach to meeting the key national and state standards:

- **CASAS**. Many U.S. states, including California, tie funding for adult education programs to students performance on the Comprehensive Adult Student Assessment System (CASAS). The CASAS (www.casas.org) competencies identify more than 30 essential skills that adults need in order to succeed in the classroom, workplace, and community. *Excellent English* comprehensively integrates all of the CASAS Life Skill Competencies throughout the four levels of the series.

- **SCANS**. Developed by the United States Department of Labor, SCANS is an acronym for the Secretary's Commission on Achieving Necessary Skills (wdr.doleta.gov/SCANS/). SCANS competencies are workplace skills that help people compete more effectively in today's global economy. A variety of SCANS competencies is threaded throughout the activities in each unit of *Excellent English*. The incorporation of these competencies recognizes both the intrinsic importance of teaching workplace skills and the fact that many adult students are already working members of their communities.

- **EFF**. Equipped For the Future (EFF) is a set of standards for adult literacy and lifelong learning, developed by The National Institute for Literacy (www.nifl.gov). The organizing principle of EFF is that adults assume responsibilities in three major areas of life: as workers, as parents, and as citizens. These three areas of focus are called "role maps" in the EFF

documentation. Each *Excellent English* unit addresses all three of the EFF role maps in the Student Book or Workbook.

- **Florida Adult ESOL Syllabi** provide the curriculum frameworks for all six levels of instruction: Foundations, Low Beginning, High Beginning, Low Intermediate, High Intermediate, and Advanced. The syllabi were developed by the State of Florida as a guide to include the following areas of adult literacy standards: workplace, communication (listen, speak, read, and write), technology, interpersonal communication, health and nutrition, government and community resources, consumer education, family and parenting, concepts of time and money, safety and security, and language development (grammar and pronunciation). *Excellent English* Level 4 incorporates into its instruction the vast majority of standards at the High level.

- **TABE Complete Language Assessment System— English (CLAS-E)** has been developed by CTB/McGraw-Hill and provides administrators and teachers with accurate, reliable evaluations of adult students' English language skills. TABE CLAS-E measures students' reading, listening, writing, and speaking skills at all English proficiency levels and also assesses critically important grammar standards. TABE CLAS-E scores are linked to TABE 9 and 10, providing a battery of assessment tools that offer seamless transition from English language to adult basic education assessment.

- **Los Angeles Unified School District (LAUSD) Course Outlines.** LAUSD Competency-Based Education (CBE) Course Outlines were developed to guide teachers in lesson planning and to inform students about what they will be able to do after successful completion of their course. The CBE course outlines focus on acquiring skills in listening, speaking, reading, and writing in the context of everyday life. *Excellent English* addresses all four language skills in the contexts of home, community and work, appropriately targeting adult ESL students at the High level.

TECHNOLOGY

Technology plays an increasingly important role in our lives as students, workers, family members, and citizens. Every unit in the Workbook includes a two-page lesson titled "Technology and You" that focuses on some aspect of technology in our everyday lives.

The EZ Test® CD-ROM Test Generator—and its online version, available at www.eztestonline.com—allow instructors to easily create customized tests from a digital databank of assessment items.

NUMBER OF HOURS OF INSTRUCTION

The *Excellent English* program has been designed to accommodate the needs of adult classes with 80–180 hours of classroom instruction. Here are three recommended ways in which various components in the *Excellent English* program can be combined to meet student and instructor needs:

- **80–100 hours**. Instructors are encouraged to work through all of the Student Book materials. The Color Overhead Transparencies can be used to introduce and/or review materials in each unit. Instructors should also look to the Teacher's Edition for teaching suggestions and testing materials as necessary. *Time per unit: 8–10 hours.*

- **100–140 hours**. In addition to working through all of the Student Book materials, instructors are encouraged to incorporate the Workbook activities for supplementary practice. *Time per unit: 10–14 hours.*

- **140–180 hours**. Instructors and students working in an intensive instructional setting can take advantage of the wealth of expansion activities threaded through the Teacher's Edition to supplement the Student Book and the Workbook. *Time per unit: 14–18 hours.*

Teaching Strategies

Approaches to Teaching Grammar

Some students may come from educational settings where English was taught almost exclusively through grammar and vocabulary. Other students may have acquired English through a more communicative approach. *Excellent English* is a grammar-based program that allows students from all backgrounds to feel comfortable as they acquire grammar, along with their other language skills, through *discovery*, *presentation*, *practice* and *production*.

1. DISCOVERY

- **Guided discovery.** Inductive approaches to teaching grammar encourage students to notice how grammar works in practice and figure out the rule for themselves. In *Excellent English,* students have the opportunity to see and hear the grammar structures in context as new vocabulary is presented in the Grammar Picture Dictionary. Students always begin their exposure to a new grammar point with a noticing activity, which focuses students' attention on form and function. Instructors can guide students through the rule discovery process by eliciting ideas about the rules that govern each structure. Many students may prefer that instructors begin with a presentation of the rules. Learners can be encouraged to glean rules on their own by asking questions (e.g., *When do we use an s on the end of the verb? With which pronouns?*). Guiding students through focused questioning can facilitate awareness-based understanding of grammar. When students contribute their own ideas, they can become more confident and independent learners.

2. PRESENTATION AND PRACTICE

- **Confirming rules.** Instructors can continue to reinforce grammar awareness through the more deductive approach provided by the grammar charts, which were designed to be clear and easily comprehensible. Teachers should make sure students understand how to navigate the charts in each unit of *Excellent English* and elicit reasons for the way the charts are formatted, making sure students understand that the focus structure is in a different color and the different parts of the sentence are in different columns. The charts can be used as the basis for expansion activities (suggested in the Teacher's Edition) or as a reference point for activities instructors create themselves.

- **Error correction.** When using a grammar-based approach to language learning, there is often a temptation to focus on error correction. However, research suggests that students must go through an interlanguage period, a stage in which their new language will not be perfect, but rather will reflect the transition the learner is going through. A learner may become insecure with too great of a focus on accuracy and be reluctant to take risks that would allow him or her to become more fluent. *Excellent English* is structured so that students move from very controlled practice of new structures and vocabulary, through more open-ended practice, to more personalized production. Accuracy should be the focus in the very controlled activities, such as fill-in-the-blank, and correction should be immediate and constructive. Grammar should be acquired through productive activities that ask students to use the targeted structures in a meaningful way. When students are using grammar in communicative activities, correction should be limited, or simply noted, and feedback given after the task is completed.

- **Repetition.** Language acquisition, including grammar acquisition, is facilitated through exposure to appropriate input. Research suggests that grammar acquisition is more effective when it is accompanied by vocabulary instruction. Each unit of *Excellent English* allows students to hear, see, and repeat new words and structures numerous times. Students may need more frequent repetition drills to reinforce pronunciation and word order. One way to do this is to say sentences and have the class repeat chorally. Instructors can also use the Big Picture transparency to introduce or review grammar points, along with collocational vocabulary.

3. PRODUCTION

- **Communicative tasks.** Grammar should be practiced in the context of communicative tasks. Once students have practiced the structure through controlled activities, they should be encouraged to apply the target structure in more open-ended productive tasks. Later lessons in each unit of *Excellent English* require students to integrate language skills, including grammar, to complete higher-level activities such as role playing and group projects.

Author and educator David Nunan suggests simple teaching strategies for helping students learn and retain new information:

- Emphasize inductive over deductive approaches
- Keep the work load manageable
- Recycle information
- Begin to move learners from doing reproductive activities to being creative with the language
- Personalize grammar and language
- Encourage learners to see grammar as a process

These considerations, along with sound materials for teaching English, help foster an environment for language learning success. (For more information, see *Practical English Language Teaching: Grammar* by David Nunan [McGraw-Hill].)

Approaches to Teaching Workplace and Vocational ESL

Excellent English has many features that make it an ideal text for use in workplace/VESL classrooms. The reading and writing activities, the vocabulary, the *Career Connection* dialogs, and the technology in the Workbook especially prepare students to learn and understand new work-related terms and scenarios with confidence. These activities, combined with an instructor's guidance on personalizing the vocabulary and workplace situations, will engage students and help them learn and master the content they need most. The students will become productive and satisfied employees, managers, and employers.

When customizing *Excellent English* for use in your Workplace ESL class, consider the following suggestions:

- **Personalize the vocabulary.** Encourage learners to keep a vocabulary notebook for the words and terms found in the Student Book, for words that they hear in everyday life, and for words and phrases they hear and see on the job. Invite students to bring in questions about terms and words, and then practice using the new vocabulary in sentences and in conversations. In addition, encourage students to bring in realia they see in everyday life and at their places of work. Have students practice reading and understanding all of the information in their surroundings.

- **Personalize the dialogs.** Communication is a very important skill for workplace success and safety. If there are key industries or employers in your area, use the model dialogs in the Student Book as jumping off points for conversations that might occur in certain industries or sectors.

- **Discuss common and specific work issues.** The *Career Connection* photo story at the end of each unit provides a springboard for discussion in a Workplace ESL class. The characters are in positive workplace environments and are effectively using resources to do well in their jobs and careers. Use these stories to encourage students to talk about situations they have experienced or want to experience.

- **Use all of the components of *Excellent English*.** In addition to the solid curriculum in the Student Book, it is ideal to have students use the Workbook to further strengthen their skills. The Workbook includes application lessons that carry vital, standards-based learning objectives through its *Family Connection, Community Connections, Career Connection,* and *Technology Connections lessons*.

The *Excellent English* series equips students with the grammar and skills they need to access community resources while developing the foundation for long-term career and academic success.

Additional Resources

REFERENCE TITLES AVAILABLE FROM MCGRAW–HILL:

- **Teaching Adult ESL,** Betsy Parrish
- **Practical English Language Teaching: Grammar,** David Nunan

WEBSITES FOR GRAMMAR:

- http://www.ohiou.edu/esl/english/grammar/activities.html
- http://iteslj.org/links/ESL/Grammar_and_English_Usage/
- http://www.eslcafe.com/search/Grammar/
- http://www2.gsu.edu/~wwwesl/egw/eslgract.htm
- http://w2.byuh.edu/academics/languagecenter/CNN-N/CNN-N.html

WEBSITE FOR VESL/CAREER RESOURCES

- http://eff.cls.utk.edu/fundamentals/role_map_worker.htm

Assessment

The *Excellent English* program offers instructors, students, and administrators the following wealth of resources for monitoring and assessing student progress and achievement:

- **Standardized Testing Formats.** *Excellent English* is comprehensively correlated to the CASAS competencies and all of the other major national and state standards for adult learning. Students have the opportunity to practice the types of skills that will help them succeed on the CASAS tests.

- **End-of-Unit Tests.** The *Excellent English* Teacher's Edition includes end-of-unit tests. These paper-and-pencil tests help students demonstrate how well they have learned the instructional content of the unit. Each unit test includes five CASAS-style listening comprehension questions, five reading comprehension questions, five writing questions, and ten grammar questions. Practice with these question types will help prepare students who may want to enroll in academic classes.

- **Performance-based Assessment.** *Excellent English* provides several ways to measure students' performance on productive tasks, including the Writing tasks in Lesson 7 of each Student Book unit. In addition, the Teacher's Edition suggests writing and speaking prompts that instructors can use for performance-based assessment. These prompts derive from the Big Picture scene in each unit and provide rich visual input as the basis for the speaking and writing tasks asked of the students.

- **Portfolio Assessment.** A portfolio is a collection of student work that can be used to show progress. Examples of work that the instructor or the student may submit in the portfolio include writing samples, speaking rubrics, audiotapes, videotapes, or projects.

- **Self-assessment.** Self-assessment is an important part of the overall assessment picture, as it promotes students' involvement and commitment to the learning process. When encouraged to assess themselves, students take more control of their learning and are better able to connect the instructional content with their own goals. The Student Books include *Check Your Progress* activities at the end of each unit, which allow students to assess their knowledge of vocabulary and grammar. Students can chart their mastery of the key language lessons in the unit and use this information to set new learning goals.

- **Other Linguistic and Non-linguistic Outcomes.** Traditional testing often does not account for the progress made by adult learners with limited educational experience or low literacy levels. Such learners tend to take longer and make smaller language gains, so the gains they make in other areas are often more significant. These gains may be in areas such as self-esteem; goal clarification; learning skills; and access to employment, community involvement, and further academic studies. The SCANS and EFF standards identify areas of student growth that are not necessarily language-based. *Excellent English* is correlated with both SCANS and EFF standards. Every unit in the Student Book and Workbook contains a lesson that focuses on the EFF roles of worker, family member, and community member. Like the Student Book, the Workbook includes activities that may provide documentation that can be added to a student portfolio.

- **EZ Test® CD-ROM Test Generator and EZ Test Online.** In addition to the reproducible unit tests found in the Teacher's Edition of *Excellent English,* instructors can use the EZ Test® CD-ROM Test Generator to easily create customized, paper-based tests from a digital databank of assessment items. Instructors can select question items from book-specific test banks and also augment these items with their own questions. Multiple versions of any test can be created so instructors can give different versions of the same test to different sections of students, or use these different versions within the same classroom. Answers keys are also automatically created. In addition, instructors can access *Excellent English* assessment materials through EZ Test Online (www.eztestonline.com). After registering for this testing service, instructors can create and deliver tests online and export their tests for use with course management systems such as Blackboard or save them for future use.

  EZ Test supports the use of the following question types:
  - True or False
  - Yes or No
  - Multiple Choice
  - Fill-in-the-Blank
  - Matching
  - Short Answer
  - Essay

Create EZ Tests for each Unit of Excellent English

Choose the questions.

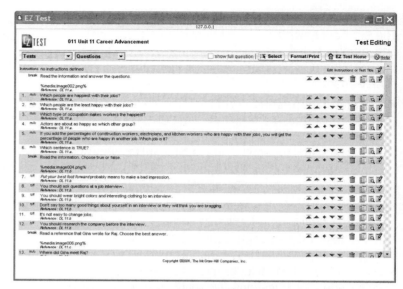

Preview the test.

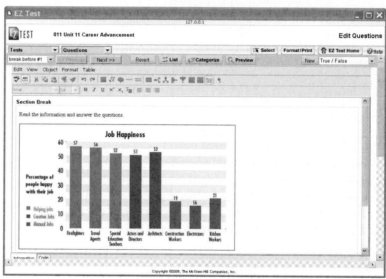

Print the test!

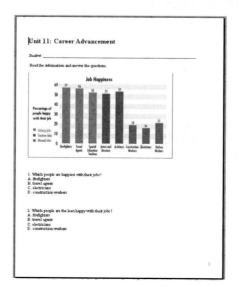

About the Student Book Authors

Susannah MacKay has taught and served as a teacher trained in community adult programs, community colleges, and secondary schools. Susannah especially enjoys her work developing materials for English instruction and has experience as both a writer and an editor of student books, teacher's editions, online learning components, and assessment tools. She has contributed to projects at all levels and in all skill areas, though she particularly enjoys literacy, reading, writing, and grammar. One of Susannah's most gratifying projects was piloting and launching a materials project for community-supported instruction centers across the Atlanta, Georgia, metropolitan area.

Mari Vargo has eleven years of experience as both a writer and an editor of English instruction materials. She has authored and edited online learning courses and components, student books, teacher's editions, workbooks, assessment tools, and CD-ROMs. Mari has developed materials for all skills, but she finds grammar and reading materials to be the most enjoyable. In addition, Mari has taught composition, research writing, and ESL at the college level.

Pamela Vittorio has over 15 years' experience teaching ESL at a variety of levels. She has been an instructor at university-level intensive English and community-based programs (as well as academic), and she has been program manager at a private English-language school. Pamela has also worked as a teacher trainer, literacy specialist, consultant, writer, and editor, often specializing in creating English language assessment, ESP, and EAP materials. She has a background in foreign languages and an M.A. from New York University. Pamela is part of the faculty at Parsons, The New School for Design, in Manhattan.

Consultants

Jan Forstrom is the EL Civics Coordinator at San Diego Community College District Continuing Education. She was recently elected to the California State CATESOL board and currently serves as assistant chair for adult–level ESL. She holds a Bachelor's degree in French and Education from Trinity College in Illinois and has 25 years' experience teaching adult ESL classes at a variety of levels. Jan is a frequent conference presenter at regional, state, and national conferences on topics related to EL Civics and assessment. Jan co-authored Contemporary English Book 2, Revised Edition (McGraw-Hill 2002).

Marta Pitt is the ESOL, ABE, and GED Department Chair at Lindsey Hopkins Technical Education Center in Miami, Florida. She has been a classroom French and ESOL instructor and Department Chair for the past 32 years. Marta is fluent in Spanish, French, and Italian.

Shirley Velasco is currently the principal for Miami Beach Adult and Community Education Center in Miami Beach, Florida. She has been involved in education for over 28 years and created a large adult ESOL program based on a curriculum developed to implement state and national standards. An author and consultant for several McGraw-Hill ESOL programs, she holds a Bachelor's degree from Barry University and a Master's degree in Educational Leadership from Nova Southeastern University.

Student Book Scope and Sequence

Unit	Grammar Point	Vocabulary	Listening/ Speaking/ Pronunciation	Reading	Writing
Pre-unit *page 2*	• Spelling • Punctuation • Verb form • Subject-verb agreement • Capitalization	• Classroom language • Appointments	• Listen to introductions • Request clarification • Answer personal information questions	• Read a daily schedule	• Complete a conversation dialog • Write a paragraph about a daily schedule
1 Education Matters *page 6*	• Simple present and present continuous • Correlative conjunctions • Expressing future time with *will, be, going to,* and the present continuous	• Adult education • Coursework • Job skills	• Listen to information about school • Express encouragement • Talk about programs and courses • Reductions with *n't* • Listen to a conversation between an employer and an employee	• Examine college transcripts • Read a career school advertisement • Read an email from a teacher	• Write statements about yourself • Make a list of programs and courses of interest to you • Write a letter to a professor
2 Aiming for Excellence *page 22*	• Past time clauses with *after, when, as soon as, before,* and *until* • Simple past and present perfect • Express similarities with *so, too, either,* and *neither*	• Feelings • Work communication • Job training	• Listen to a conversation between two coworkers • Role-play a conversation between a parent and a child	• Read a job evaluation form • Read notes from an interview • Read a letter requesting a raise	• Fill out a work schedule • List personal qualities on a chart • Write a persuasive letter
3 That's Entertainment! *page 38*	• Past perfect • Past perfect continuous	• Dating • Outings • Media	• Listen to information about a TV schedule • Listen to a dialog about a movie • Talk about activities with surprise and sympathy • Discuss your childhood	• Read a journal about a trip • Read magazine descriptions • Read an article about a politician • Read an autobiography	• Take conversation notes • Complete a personal timeline • Write an autobiography
4 Focus on Finance *page 54*	• Past modals; *should (not) / must (not) + have* + the past participle • Tag questions	• Banking • Personal finances	• Give advice about money • Talk about money mistakes • Describe a problem you have had in the past • Intonation of tag questions	• Read an online banking email message • Interpret a monthly budget • Read a credit card statement • Read an article about credit card reports • Read a letter from a hotel • Read a business letter	• Write advice about money • Write a business letter • Complete a customer survey

			Correlations		
Civics/ Lifeskills	Math	Critical Thinking	CASAS	SCANS	EFF Content Standards
• Recognize cultural differences • Keep a medical appointment and daily schedule	• Practice time on a schedule • Review dates and telephone numbers	• Observe mistakes • Manage daily tasks	• 0.1.4 • 0.1.5 • 0.2.1 • 0.1.6	• Acquires and evaluates information • Interprets and communicates information • Participates as a member of a team	• Read with understanding • Convey ideas in writing • Speak so others can understand • Listen actively
• Discuss job skills needed for a day care worker • Role-play a conversation with a parent and day care center worker	• Calculate grade point average • Scheduling classes	• Plan for future goals • Decide how to proceed based on factual information	• 1: 0.1.5 • 2: 7.4.8 • 3: 7.5.6, 0.1.4 • 4: 7.1.2 • 5: 1.1.8, 6.0.3, 6.0.4, 6.7.5, 7.1.1 • 6: 0.1.3, 2.5.5, 7.4.1 • 7: 0.1.4, 0.2.3, 4.5.5 • 8: 4.4.5, 7.1.1, 7.1.4, 7.2.3, 7.4.7	• Interprets and communicates information • Exercises leadership • Participates as a member of a team • Organizes and maintains information • Understands systems • Applies technology to task • Selects technology • Monitors and corrects performance	• Take responsibility for learning • Plan • Cooperate with others • Use math to solve problems and communicate • Reflect and evaluate • Use information and communications technology
• Read and discuss an annual benefits review • Have an active voice to initiate improvement	• Figuring salary increases • Review an annual benefits statement • Vacation time • Retirement vesting	• Compare and contrast personal qualities • Weigh options between job benefits	• 1: 4.4.1, 4.4.6 • 2: 4.6.2, 7.4.8 • 3: 0.1.4, 4.6.4, 4.7.3, 4.8.1, 7.5.6 • 4: 4.1.7, 4.4.2, 4.6.1 • 5: 4.2.1, 4.4.4, 6.1.1, 6.2.3, • 6: 4.1.7, 4.8.6 • 7: 0.1.3, 4.1.7, 4.1.9, 4.6.5, 7.2.6, 7.2.7 • 8: 4.4.3, 4.6.2, 7.1.4, 7.4.7	• Allocates time • Acquires and evaluates information • Uses computers to process information • Applies technology to task • Organizes and maintains information • Monitors and corrects performance • Allocates money • Improves and designs systems • Exercises leadership	• Read with understanding • Observe critically • Convey ideas in writing • Reflect and evaluate • Listen actively • Solve problems and make decisions • Use math to solve problems and communicate • Advocate and influence • Take responsibility for learning
• File a security report	• Calculate sales tax • Write dates on a timeline	• Discriminate types of feelings in conversations • Reflect on a past experience	• 1: 0.2.1, 0.2.4 • 2: 7.2.4, 7.2.5 • 3: 2.6.2, 2.6.3 • 4: 0.1.5, 7.5.6, 0.1.2, 0.1.3 • 5: 1.2.4, 6.0.5, 6.2.3, 6.5.1 • 6: 4.8.1, 7.2.2, 7.4.1 • 7: 0.2.3, 7.2.6, 7.4.1, 7.4.2 • 8: 4.6.2, 7.1.4, 7.4.7,	• Interprets and communicates information • Allocates human resources • Allocates money • Organizes and maintains information • Teaches others • Monitors and corrects performance	• Speak so others can understand • Observe critically • Listen actively • Use math to solve problems and communicate • Read with understanding • Solve problems and make decisions
• Guard against fraud • Make careful choices about finances	• Calculate interest earned	• Make financial decisions based on income	• 1: 1.3.1, 1.5.1 • 2: 1.8.1, 1.8.2 • 3: 1.8.5, 6.1.5, 6.4.3, 6.4.4, 6.4.5, 7.2.2, 7.3.2, 7.5.6 • 4: 0.1.6 • 5: 0.1.6, 1.3.2, 1.5.1, 1.5.3, 6.1.1 • 6: 7.2.4, 7.4.1 • 7: 1.2.5, 1.6.3, 7.2.5, 7.5.5 • 8: 1.2.5, 7.1.4, 7.3.1, 7.3.2, 7.4.7	• Allocates money • Serves clients/customers • Negotiates • Improves and designs systems • Acquires and evaluates information • Participates as a member of a team • Exercises leadership	• Solve problems and make decisions • Use math to solve problems and communicate • Resolve conflict and negotiate • Observe critically • Reflect and evaluate • Read with understanding

Unit	Grammar Point	Vocabulary	Listening/ Speaking/ Pronunciation	Reading	Writing
5 **Law and Society** *page 70*	• Active and passive voices (simple present and simple past) • *Yes/No* and information in the passive voice	• Federal government • Community services • USA holidays • Legal terms	• Listen to information about community services • Content word stress • Role-play a conversation with a partner about legal aid	• Read about branches of the government • Read a W-2 form • Read information about taxes • Read about federal holidays	• Write a list of services that are available to the public • Write personal information questions • Write about a special holiday
6 **House and Home** *page 86*	• Articles • Adjective clauses with relative pronouns as subjects • Embedded questions with *if, whether,* and other question words	• Home maintenance • Phone etiquette • Tenant rights • Rental agreement	• Talk with a partner about fixing or updating your house • Make a call to a phone company • Pronounce *a* and *an* with adjectives • Role-play a problem with a caller and a radio host	• Read about tenants' rights • Read an advice column about renting • Examine a rental agreement • Read a letter of request	• Write about a problem with household utilities • Write solutions to problems while listening to a radio program • Write a letter of complaint
7 **In the News** *page 102*	• Adjective clauses with relative pronouns as subjects • Adjective clauses with relative pronouns as objects	• News • Opinions • Reasons • Food safety	• Listen to the news • Linking with *that* • Tell your opinion to a partner • Talk about food safety • Discuss food illness experiences	• Analyze parts of a newspaper • Read a controversial article • Read a parents' news story	• Write ideas for a blog • Take notes about opinions • Write in support of an issue
8 **The World Around Us** *page 118*	• Gerunds as objects • Gerund as objects of verb + preposition	• Weather • Maps • Temperature • National disaster agencies	• Talk about the weather • Discuss weather concerns • Listen to statements about a map • Give a weather report • Link final consonant sounds with vowels	• Read a USA map • Read about national disaster agencies • Read an article about environmental issues • Read a letter from a senator	• Write about severe weather conditions • Complete a Red Cross volunteer form • Complete a chart from a TV talk show • Write a letter to a local government to assert your opinion

Correlations

Civics/ Lifeskills	Math	Critical Thinking	CASAS	SCANS	EFF Content Standards
• Discuss size of workplace and management	• Calculate refunds and taxes owed	• Research a holiday on the Internet • Communicate workplace preferences through reasoning	• 1: 5.2.1, 5.5.2, 5.5.3, 5.5.4, 5.5.8, 5.6.3 • 2: 2.5.3, 5.6.1, 5.6.2 • 3: 5.3.2, 5.3.6, 5.5.6 • 4: 5.3.1, 5.3.2, 5.3.3, 5.6.3 • 5: 5.4.1, 5.4.3, 5.4.4 • 6: 2.7.1, 2.7.3, 7.4.5 • 7: 2.7.1, 7.4.4, 7.4.5 • 8: 4.1.1, 7.1.4, 7.4.7	• Exercises leadership • Monitors and corrects performance • Organizes and maintains information • Interprets and communicates information • Works with cultural diversity • Improves and designs systems	• Listen actively • Convey ideas in writing • Speak so others can understand • Take responsibility for learning • Read with understanding • Learn through research • Observe critically • Cooperate with others • Use math to solve problems and communicate • Reflect and evaluate • Use information and communications technology
• Find errors in telephone bills • Question rental options • Use email at work	• Calculate a work estimate • Use multiplication to solve money problems	• Dispute a phone bill • Advocate to solve problems	• 1: 1.4.4, 1.7.4, 1.7.5, 2.5.1 • 2: 1.4.4, 1.4.7, 1.7.4, 1.7.5, 8.2.6, 4.7.1, 6.4.6 • 3: 2.1.4, 7.5.6 • 4: 1.4.1, 1.4.3, 1.4.5 • 5: 1.4.5, 7.3.2, 8.2.3, 8.2.4 • 6: 1.4.3, 7.4.4 • 7: 5.1.6, 7.3.1 • 8: 7.1.4, 7.4.7, 7.5.6	• Allocates human resources • Maintains and troubleshoots technology • Acquires and evaluates information • Participates as a member of a team	• Resolve conflict and negotiate • Advocate and influence • Read with understanding • Observe critically • Convey ideas in writing • Take responsibility for learning
• Listen to a food safety presentation	• Interpret a bar graph	• Locate newspaper sections • Identify opinions and reasons	• 1: 0.1.2 • 2: 5.3.7, 5.3.8 • 3: 0.1.2, 7.5.6 • 4: 1.2.5, 4.1.3 • 5: 6.7.2 • 6: 1.2.5, 7.4.1, 7.5.5 • 7: 0.1.3, 0.2.3, 1.2.5 • 8: 3.5.5, 4.3.3, 4.3.4, 7.1.4, 7.4.7	• Exercises leadership • Organizes and maintains information • Participates as a member of a team • Allocates material and facility resources • Interprets and communicates information • Acquires and evaluates information • Monitors and corrects performance	• Speak so others can understand • Convey ideas in writing • Read with understanding • Use information and communications technology • Use math to solve problems and communicate • Reflect and evaluate • Cooperate with others
• Discuss on-the-job hazards	• Convert Fahrenheit and Celsius temperature • Use multiplication and division • Percentages and sliding scales	• Decide what to do in a weather emergency	• 1: 2.3.3 • 2: 1.1.3, 2.3.3, 5.7.3 • 3: 1.1.3, 1.1.5, 6.1.2, 6.1.3, 6.1.4, 6.6.4, 6.6.7, 7.5.6 • 4: 5.7.1, 5.7.2, 5.7.4 • 5: 5.1.5, 2.5.2 • 6: 5.7.1, 7.4.1 • 7: 5.7.4, 7.5.7 • 8: 2.5.1, 3.4.2, 7.1.4, 7.4.7	• Interprets and communicates information • Organizes and maintains information • Exercises leadership • Participates as a member of a team • Monitors and corrects performance	• Use information and communications technology • Listen actively • Convey ideas in writing • Take responsibility for learning • Reflect and evaluate • Read with understanding • Cooperate with others • Solve problems and make decisions

Unit	Grammar Point	Vocabulary	Listening/ Speaking/ Pronunciation	Reading	Writing
9 **Community Crossroads** *page 134*	• Causative verbs • Causatives *get* and *have* • Verbs that take gerunds or infinitives	• Getting around • Traffic laws • Transportation • Street maps	• Discuss your childhood with a partner • Listen to statements about what people are doing • Role-play a conversation with a traffic officer • Talk about your community with a partner	• Read signs related to transportation • Locate community places on a map • Read about a small business team	• Write about what's happening in the community • Write/revise a business plan
10 **Living Well, Staying Safe** *page 150*	• Reported speech • Reported speech with *say* and *tell* • Phrasal verbs • *Used to, be used to*	• Home safety • Physical health • New Year's resolutions • Job skills	• Interview a classmate about safety devices • Listen to a talk about safety problems • Listen to a recorded message • Role-play a conversation on safety	• Read about home safety • Read an advertisement about a new prescription drug • Read a New Year's resolution	• Write reported speech using quotes • Write a plan to improve safety in your home • Write a New Year's resolution
11 **Career Advancement** *page 166*	• Real conditionals present and future • Present unreal conditional	• Career skills • Job fair • Job interview • Strengths and weaknesses	• Listen to a discussion between two managers • Rhythm of thought groups • Role-play a conversation on how to relax • Listen to interviews	• Read about careers and skills • Read about how to have a successful interview • Read a résumé from a job seeker	• Write what you would do to improve your weaknesses • Make notes about your skills, achievements, and awards • Write a résumé for yourself
12 **A Bright Future** *page 182*	• Future continuous • Infinitives of purpose • Infinitives that follow adjectives	• Future plans • Politics • Work standards • Community • Emotions	• Talk about life in a city • Listen to an interview with a candidate for mayor • Intonation and emotion • Interview classmates to discuss community problems and solutions	• Read an email from a city administrator • Read an employer's campaign to improve work conditions • Read a personal statement	• Write ideas for a city improvement plan • Write about how employees feel at work • Write notes about things you plan to change in your life • Write a paragraph with your goals for the next five years

			Correlations		
Civics/ Lifeskills	Math	Critical Thinking	CASAS	SCANS	EFF Content Standards
• Collaborate to solve a work problem	• Interpret statistical information • Work with percentages	• Devise a plan to start a business • Propose solutions to neighborhood problems	• **1:** 2.2.3, 2.5.4, 2.2.2 • **2:** 5.3.1 • **3:** 1.9.2, 2.2.2 • **4:** 1.9.2, 1.9.7, 7.5.1 • **5:** 2.3.1, 6.4.2, 6.8.1, • **6:** 0.1.2, 7.4.1 • **7:** 1.9.7, 1.9.8 • **8:** 7.1.4, 7.3.4, 7.4.7	• Interprets and communicates information • Negotiates • Understands systems • Selects technology • Applies technology to task • Acquires and evaluates information • Monitors and corrects performance	• Reflect and evaluate • Observe critically • Cooperate with others • Speak so others can understand • Use math to solve problems and communicate • Take responsibility for learning • Convey ideas in writing
• Read an online job advertisement • Plan for a safe environment	• Subtract decimals • Read a bar graph	• Examine job skills and qualifications • Make wise choices	• **1:** 1.4.8, 3.4.2 • **2:** 3.4.2, 6.1.2, 6.2.2, 6.7.2 • **3:** 3.4.2, 8.3.1 • **4:** 3.5.9 • **5:** 3.5.8, 3.5.9 • **6:** 3.4.1, 3.4.5, 7.4.1 • **7:** 0.1.3, 7.5.7 • **8:** 4.1.3, 4.4.2, 7.1.4, 7.4.7	• Understands systems • Interprets and communicates information • Allocates human resources • Teaches others • Exercises leadership • Improves and designs systems • Monitors and corrects performance	• Guide others • Plan • Observe critically • Advocate and influence • Read with understanding • Reflect and evaluate • Convey ideas in writing
• Role-play with a partner to negotiate better benefits • Observe an interview	• Read a bar graph • Work with percentages	• Self-reflect on your strengths and weaknesses • Analyze a document for detailed information	• **1:** 4.1.2 • **2:** 4.1.3, 4.1.8 • **3:** 4.4.1, 4.1.7, 7.5.6 • **4:** 4.4.5, 4.4.7 • **5:** 4.4.3, 6.4.2, 6.7.2 • **6:** 4.1.2, 4.1.3, 4.1.5, 7.4.1 • **7:** 4.1.2, 7.5.1 • **8:** 7.1.1, 7.1.2, 7.1.4, 7.4.7	• Allocates human resources • Exercises leadership • Improves and designs systems • Monitors and corrects performance • Organizes and maintains information • Selects technology • Applies technology to task • Negotiates	• Plan • Listen actively • Reflect and evaluate • Convey ideas in writing • Advocate and influence • Cooperate with others • Guide others • Observe critically • Take responsibility for learning
• Write ideas for a city improvement plan • Write about how employees feel at work • Write notes about things you plan to change in your life • Write a paragraph with your goals for the next five years	• Use the Internet to find information • Make a list of pros and cons about two job offers	• Find problems in your community, city, or country • Compare and contrast the lives and goals of others	• **1:** 0.1.5 • **2:** 5.1.4, 5.1.6, 7.2.4, 7.2.6, 7.3.1 • **3:** 4.8.1, 5.1.4, 7.3.1, 7.3.2 • **4:** 6.8.2, 7.5.7 • **5:** 4.2.4, 6.4.2, 6.7.4, 7.4.8 • **6:** 7.1.1, 7.2.1, 7.4.1 • **7:** 7.2.3, 7.2.6, 7.4.8, 7.5.5, 7.5.7 • **8:** 7.1.4, 7.2.5, 7.4.7, 7.5.5, 7.5.7	• Exercises leadership • Interprets and communicates information • Improves and designs systems • Negotiates • Acquires and evaluates information • Allocates time • Monitors and corrects performance	• Plan • Advocate and influence • Listen actively • Use math to solve problems and communicate • Read with understanding • Convey ideas in writing • Take responsibility for learning

PRE-UNIT: Language in the Classroom

WARM-UP ACTIVITY: Meeting for the first time

- In this lesson, the students will review language for greetings and introductions. Write two columns on the board: *Greetings* and *Introductions*.

- Tell the students to close their books. Elicit as many greetings as possible, such as *Hello* and *Hi*, and expressions for introductions and self-introductions, such as *My name is Jose* and *This is Alex*.

- After the board is full of words, move on to Activity 1.

 1 LISTEN. Complete the sentences with the words below.
TCD1, 2

- Read the directions to the students.

- Point out the word box to the students. Show them the three photos of students and the incomplete sentences below them.

- Make sure the students understand that they will fill in the blanks with the words from the word box.

- Play the recording and have the students complete the activity individually.

- Put the students in pairs to compare answers.

- If necessary, play the recording again.

- Go over the answers as a class.

ANSWER KEY

1. Soo-Hee is from <u>Korea</u>. She's studying English <u>to go to community college</u>.

2. Alex is from <u>Russia</u>. He's studying English <u>to take an exam</u>.

3. Marissa is from <u>Peru</u>. She's studying English <u>for her job</u>.

🎧 LISTENING SCRIPT
TCD1, 2

Soo-Hee:	Hi. My name's Soo-Hee.
Alex:	Oh, hi. My name's Alex.
Soo-Hee:	Nice to meet you, Alex. Where are you from?
Alex:	From? . . . oh, yes. I'm from Russia. How about you?
Soo-Hee:	I'm from Korea.
Alex:	I see.
Soo-Hee:	Hey, Marissa! Hi!
Marissa:	Hi, Soo-Hee! How's it going?
Soo-Hee:	Great. Marissa, this is Alex. He's from Russia.
Marissa:	Hi, Alex. Nice to meet you.
Alex:	Nice to meet you, too, Marissa. Where are you from?
Marissa:	Me? Oh, I'm from Peru.
Alex:	Oh.
Marissa:	Yeah. You're going to like it here. The class is great. The teacher is friendly . . .
Alex:	Sounds good.
Soo-Hee:	Yeah. So, why are you taking an English class, Alex?
Alex:	Oh, well. I'm getting ready to take a big exam so I can get a new job.
Soo-Hee:	Oh, I see. I'm trying to get into the community college next year.

Alex:	And how about you, Marissa?
Marissa:	I need English for my job. I have to read and write a lot of email in English now, so . . .
Marissa:	Here comes Mr. Davis. Great to have you here, Alex.
Alex:	Thanks!

2 LISTEN and read.

TCD1, 3

- Tell the students to read the sentences while they listen to the recording.
- Play the recording while the students listen and read.

3 LISTEN again and repeat. Then practice

TCD1, 4 the conversation with a partner.

- Play the recording again.
- Stop after each conversation turn and have the students repeat the sentences.
- Put the students in pairs and have them read one role. When they have finished, have them change roles and read the conversation again.

4 TALK. Introduce your partner to other students in your class.

- With their partners from Activity 3, the students should walk around the room meeting other pairs of students.
- Have them model their introductions on the conversation in Activity 2.
- Tell them to introduce themselves to at least three other pairs of students.
- Ask for pairs to volunteer to practice their conversations in front of the class.

5 COMPLETE the classroom conversations with the words below.

- Read the directions to the students.
- Point out the words in the word box and the sentences with blanks.
- Have the students do the activity individually.
- Put the students in pairs to compare answers.
- Go over the answers as a class.

ANSWER KEY

1. *A:* think; *B:* Yes, right.
2. *A:* answer, you; *B:* Actually
3. *A:* Should; *B:* I'll
4. *A:* understand; *B:* No

LANGUAGE NOTE

Explain to the students that it is extremely important for second-language learners to develop conversation management skills. They will be in many conversations and discussions where they do not understand everything. They must not be passive. Asking for clarification will communicate to their conversation partners that they need help and that they are interested in continuing the conversation. In Activity 6, important expressions for asking for clarification are underlined.

 6 LISTEN and read the conversations. They

TCD1, 5 show four things you can do in class to help you learn. Pay attention to the underlined expressions.

- Read the directions to the students.
- Point out the four short conversations.
- Play the recording while the students listen to the conversations.

TCD1, 6

7 LISTEN again and repeat the classroom expressions.

- Play the recording again.
- Stop after each conversation turn and have the students repeat the sentences.
- Put the students in pairs and have each one read one role. When they have finished, have them change roles and read the conversation again.

8 WHAT ABOUT YOU? Work with a partner. Take turns asking and answering these questions. Practice using the underlined expressions in Activity 6.

- Read the directions to the students.
- Point out the four questions below.
- Put the students in pairs. Tell them to ask each other the questions and respond with the expressions for asking for clarification from Activity 6.
- When they have finished, have the students change partners and repeat the activity.

Grammar Review

WARM-UP ACTIVITY: Review of verb forms

In this section, students will review all of the verb forms that they have studied in previous levels of *Excellent English*.

- Ask the students to give you the names of all the verb forms they know. Accept variations of names, e.g., *past tense*, *simple past*, or *past*.
- Write the names of the verb forms on the board as column heads.
- Put the students in pairs. Have each pair write a sample sentence for each verb form on the board, e.g., for the simple past, *I went to Chicago last year*.
- Have the students give you some of their sample sentences. Write them under the correct verb form names on the board.

1 COMPLETE each question. Write the missing words.

- Read the directions to the students.
- Point out the unfinished questions and the answers.
- Have a pair of students read the example question and answer.
- Have the students complete the activity individually.
- Put the students in pairs to compare answers.
- Go over the answers as a class.

ANSWER KEY

1. What time does he wake up every day?
2. Where are they taking the class?
3. When are we going to pick her up?
4. How many pieces of pizza did she eat?
5. What were you doing when the phone rang?
6. Have you ever been to Australia?
7. How long have you been studying English?
8. What will he do if he gets the job?

2 WRITE a different answer for each question in Activity 1. Write in your notebook.

- Read the directions to the students.
- Have a student read the example sentence. Make sure the students understand that this example sentence is an alternate answer to the first question in Activity 1.
- Give the students time to write their alternate answers.
- Have each student write one of their alternate answers on the board.
- Give the students feedback about the verb forms in their answers.

3 **READ** the paragraph. Correct the mistake in each sentence.

- Read the directions to the students.
- Point out the sentences and the sample correction.
- Have the students make the corrections individually.
- Put the students in pairs to compare answers.
- Go over the answers as a class.

ANSWER KEY

(1) My name's Luis Delgado. (2) I've been study**ing** English for a year and a half. (3) I really like**s** the classes here. (4) I want to take computer classes at Lincoln **C**ommunity College next year. (5) I'm looking forward to a **great** class!

4 **MATCH** each sentence in Activity 3 with the mistake below.

- Read the directions to the students.
- Point out the list of five error types with the blanks to the left.
- Show the students that the first sentence had a punctuation error, so the number *1* was written for item *b*.
- Have the students do the activity individually.
- Put the students in pairs to compare answers.
- Go over the answers as a class.

ANSWER KEY

a. 5; **b.** 1; **c.** 2; **d.** 3; **e.** 4

5 **WRITE** a paragraph about yourself in your notebook. Use the paragraph in Activity 3 as a model.

- Read the directions to the students.
- Make sure they understand that they should write a paragraph that is similar to the one in Activity 3, but with true information from their own lives.

- Give the students time to write the paragraph in class, or assign the paragraph as homework.
- Collect the paragraphs and write comments on them about spelling, punctuation, verb forms, capitalization, and grammar.
- Hand the paragraphs back to the students.

Managing Your Time

1 **READ** Alfonso's schedule and his medical appointment notice below. Then answer the questions.

- Read the directions to the students.
- Point out Alfonso's Wednesday schedule, the appointment notice from the clinic, and the questions to be answered.
- Have the students answer the questions individually.
- Put the students in pairs to compare their answers.
- Go over the answers as a class.

ANSWER KEY

1. Alfonso works from 8:00 A.M. to 2:30 P.M.
2. Alfonso has English class from 7:00 p.m. to 8:30 P.M.
3. Alfonso is also picking up his kids from daycare and paying the tuition.
4. Alfonso will need his car keys, his insurance card for the doctor, his ATM card to get money out of the bank for his co-payment for the doctor, his checkbook to pay the $600 tuition bill, and his textbook for his English class.
5. Alfonso could go to the gym in the morning from 7:00 A.M. to 8:00 A.M., in the afternoon from 2:30 P.M. to 3:30 P.M., or in the evening from 6:00 P.M. to 7:00 P.M.

2 TALK to a partner. Check your answers.

- Divide students into pairs.
- Have students discuss their answers with each other.

3 WRITE a paragraph about Alfonso's schedule today. Write in your notebook.

- Read the directions to the students.
- Have a student read the example sentences.
- Give the students time to write the paragraph in class, or assign the paragraph as homework.
- Collect the paragraphs and write comments on them about grammar.
- Hand the paragraphs back to the students.

4 WHAT ABOUT YOU? Read the questions below. Then ask and answer the questions with a partner.

- Read the directions to the students.
- Point out the three questions. Have students read the questions to the class.
- Give the students an opportunity to ask questions about anything they do not understand.
- Put the students in pairs and have them ask each other the questions.
- Go over the answers as a class. Analyze the results. What do the students do to remember their appointments? Are their methods effective or do they miss appointments?

Unit Overview

LESSON	OBJECTIVES	STUDENT BOOK	WORKBOOK
1 Grammar and Vocabulary 1	Use simple present. Use present continuous. Practice time expressions. Understand programs and courses.	p. 6	p. 6
2 Grammar Practice Plus	Use correlative conjunctions.	p. 8	p. 7
3 Listening and Conversation	Talk about schedules. Reductions with negative *n't*. Express encouragement.	p. 10	p. 8
4 Grammar and Vocabulary 2	Make college plans. Express future time with *will, be going to,* and the present continuous.	p. 12	p. 10
5 Grammar Practice Plus	Read a transcript. Calculate GPA.	p. 14	p. 11
6 Reading	Read a brochure.	p. 16	p. 12–13
7 Writing	Read and write an email.	p. 18	p. 14–15
• Career Connection	Identify work skills.	p. 20	p. 16
• Check Your Progress!	Monitor progress.	p. 21	p. 18–19

Reading/Writing Strategies

- Use prior knowledge
- Give specific details

Connection Activities

LESSON	TYPE	SKILL DEVELOPMENT
1	Academic	Learn about course requirements
2	Community	Tour a local library to gather information
3	Academic	Understand course sections
4	Community	Find out about community plans
5	Academic	Learn about transcripts
6	Community	Gather information from area schools
7	Academic	Learn about web seminars / online classes
Career Connection	Community	Interview daycare center workers

WORKSHEET #/FOCUS	TITLE	TEACHER'S EDITION
1. Listening	Verb Review	p. 305
2. Vocabulary	Vocabulary Review	p. 306
3. Reading	Name That Person	p. 307

LESSON 1: Grammar and Vocabulary

OBJECTIVES

Use simple present
Use present continuous
Practice time expressions

VOCABULARY

admissions office	placement test
continuing education course	(be a) requirement
	research
cover	submit
flexibility	test out
online course	

GRAMMAR

Simple present
Present continuous
Time expressions

COMPETENCIES

Use language for and about school
Interact in a school setting

WARM-UP ACTIVITY: Unit opener

- Put students into evenly divided teams.
- Have teams brainstorm as many course names as possible in five minutes.
- Encourage students to be specific. For example, instead of math, they might say algebra, calculus, and geometry.
- In round-robin fashion, have each team write the name of one course on the board. Teams score one point for each course they name.

TCD1, 7 SCD2 🎧 **1 GRAMMAR PICTURE DICTIONARY.**
What are the people doing at this school? Listen and read.

- Have students open their books and look at the pictures. Ask: *What do you see?* Write all the words the students say on the board.
- Say the sentences aloud or play the CD and have students repeat.
- Call on students and ask about the people in the pictures: *Why is Erika researching an online course? What is Carrie doing? Who goes to classes in the evening?*

EXPANSION ACTIVITY: Share a story

- Have volunteers look at the pictures in the Grammar Picture Dictionary.
- Ask volunteers to share personal stories that they thought of when they saw the pictures or heard what each person was doing.
- Encourage students to ask each other questions to elicit more information.

2 READ the sentences in Activity 1 with a partner.

- Put students in pairs to read the sentences.
- Call on students to read the sentences to the class.

EXPANSION ACTIVITY: Practicing vocabulary

- Put students in pairs and have them read sentences from the Grammar Picture Dictionary.
- After students have read a sentence, they should choose one of the boldfaced vocabulary words or phrases from the sentence. Have each student make up a new sentence using the word and say it to his or her partner.
- Partners can write down each other's sentences if desired and then read them back to the class.

8 NOTICE THE GRAMMAR. Circle the verbs in the simple present. Underline the verbs in the present continuous. If there is a time expression, draw a rectangle around it.

- Go over the directions.
- Have students circle the verbs in the simple present, underline the verbs in the present continuous, and draw a rectangle around each time expression.
- Elicit the verbs in each tense and write them on the board.

ANSWER KEY

1. Erika is researching an online course this semester. She needs flexibility with her schedule.
2. Tina is submitting her application to the admissions office. The admissions office accepts online applications, too.
3. Carrie is applying for financial aid. Her salary doesn't cover all of her school expenses.
4. Sam is taking history this term. The course is a requirement for his major.
5. Rick and James are taking a continuing education course. They attend classes in the evening.
6. José is taking a placement test this morning. He wants to test out of some of his required courses.

GRAMMAR CHART: Simple Present and Present Continuous Review

- Direct students' attention to the chart or project the transparency or CD.
- Go over the information in the chart and the usage notes. Read the sentences, pausing to have students repeat.
- Point out or elicit that present continuous is sometimes called present progressive.

CHART EXPANSION ACTIVITY: Grab-bag sentences

- On slips of paper, write all of the time expressions from the grammar chart. Include both present and present continuous time expressions. Put these papers in Grab-Bag 1.
- On slips of paper, write action verbs in their infinitive form such as *study, work,* and *write*. Put these papers in Grab-Bag 2.
- Have volunteers choose one slip of paper from each grab-bag and form a true sentence using the words on each slip. For example, *This evening + work = This evening, I'm not working.*

---

4 COMPLETE the paragraph. Circle the correct form of the verb.

- Go over the directions.
- Have students circle the correct form of the verb to complete the story.
- Put students in pairs to compare answers.
- Go over the answers with the class.

ANSWER KEY

1. is enrolling; 2. is taking; 3. is trying;
4. satisfies; 5. is applying

---

5 **WHAT ABOUT YOU?** Complete the sentences about yourself. Use the simple present or the present continuous.

- Go over the directions.
- Have the students complete the sentences. Point out that they can write about their schedule or about another topic.
- Call on students to tell the class one or two of the sentences they wrote.

EXPANSION ACTIVITY: Question and answer

- Have each student choose a partner and ask a question related to Activity 5. For example, Partner A might ask, *What are you doing this month?* Partner B should answer the question using the information he or she wrote in Activity 5. Encourage each pair to expand on the conversation by continuing to ask and answer questions about the topic.
- Have partners switch roles as the asker and answerer and then repeat the activity.
- Repeat the question and answer activity by having students choose new partners and pose new questions. After each round of the activity, elicit from students some of the information they learned.

ACADEMIC CONNECTION: Requirements and prerequisites

- Explain that some programs or majors have requirements that a student must fulfill to complete the program. Some courses also have prerequisites: they may require a student to complete another course first, to submit a portfolio, or to obtain the instructor's permission to enroll.
- Have students scan through course catalogs from universities or colleges to find requirements of majors and examples of classes that have prerequisites.
- Call on students to tell the class what they found out. Answer any questions that may arise.

LESSON 2: Grammar Practice Plus

OBJECTIVES

Understand programs and courses
Use correlative conjunctions

VOCABULARY

accounting
auto body repair
business
business
  management
computer
  programming
early childhood
  education

electrical work
health care
hotel and hospitality
medical assisting
nursing
restaurant
  management

GRAMMAR

Correlative conjunctions

COMPETENCIES

Interpret graphics
Recognize career interests and academic fields
  of study

WARM-UP ACTIVITY: Library "walk-through"

- Have students imagine that they are in a library. What is the first thing they do? What sections do they like to browse? What else do they do at the library? Encourage students to visualize themselves walking through the library to spark their imagination.

- Have students share what they visualized with the class.

1 TALK about the picture. What are people interested in? What are they doing?

- Elicit ideas from the students. Help them identify cue words and other clues in the picture.

 2 LISTEN and write the correct number next to each name.

- Go over the directions and the names listed.
- Play the CD and have students write the correct number next to each name.
- Put students in pairs to compare answers.
- Go over the answers with the class.

 LISTENING SCRIPT
Lesson 2, Activity 2

1. Carlos is in the business program at the community college. He is taking accounting and business management.

2. Rebecca, his wife, also attends the community college. She is in the nursing program. This semester, she is studying Medical Assisting Skills, and she's also taking Introduction to Health Care online.

3. Ana is a high school student, but she is already thinking about college. She's looking into early childhood education, restaurant management, and hotel and hospitality.

4. Luis is in middle school, but he likes to fix things. He's looking through two books—one about electrical work and one about air conditioning science.

5. Paulo is in elementary school, but he really likes cars and computers. He's looking at the pictures in a book about auto body repair. He also has a book about computer programming.

ANSWER KEY

5 Paulo; 2 Rebecca; 4 Luis; 1 Carlos 3 Ana

 3 LISTEN AGAIN. Which programs and courses are Carlos and Rebecca interested in? Check them in the box below.

- Go over the directions and the example.
- Play the CD and have students check the correct boxes.

LISTENING SCRIPT
Lesson 2, Activity 2
TCD1, 9

1. Carlos is in the business program at the community college. He is taking accounting and business management.

2. Rebecca, his wife, also attends the community college. She is in the nursing program. This semester, she is studying Medical Assisting Skills, and she's also taking Introduction to Health Care online.

ANSWER KEY

Students should check: accounting, business, business management, health care, medical assisting, and nursing.

4 **WRITE** sentences about the people in the picture. Use simple present and present continuous.

- Go over the directions and the example.
- Point out to students the kinds of missing words they will need to include to make each sentence complete.
- Have students complete the sentences.
- Put students in pairs to compare answers.
- Go over the answers with the class.

ANSWER KEY

1. Carlos is in the business program. He's taking accounting courses.

2. Rebecca is attending community college. She is in the nursing program.

3. Ana is in high school. She is looking into early childhood education.

4. Luis is in middle school. He is look through two books.

5. Paulo likes computers and cars. He is holding a book about computer programming.

EXPANSION ACTIVITY: Rewriting sentences

For advanced students, have them rewrite the sentences in Activity 4 in a different verb tense, such as future or past.

GRAMMAR CHART: Correlative Conjunctions

- Go over the information in the chart.
- Read the sample sentences and have students repeat.
- Model additional examples as needed.

CHART EXPANSION ACTIVITY: Draw a pair

- Give each student two slips of paper. Have them write down one noun on each slip.
- Put the slips of paper in a bag.
- Have volunteers draw two nouns out of the bag and try to make a sentence with them using a correlative conjunction. For example, *hat + socks = Susan wears neither hats nor socks.* Encourage students to be creative and use humor in their sentences.

5 **WRITE.** Complete the sentences about the picture in Activity 1 with either . . . or, neither . . . nor, or both . . . and.

- Go over the directions and the example.
- Have students complete the sentences.
- Go over the answers with the class.

ANSWER KEY

1. Neither Luis nor Pablo is reading about business.

2. Carlos is getting books for both business management and accounting.

3. Paulo is looking at both auto body repair and computer programming books.

4. Ana wants to study either early childhood education or restaurant management. She hasn't decided yet.

5. Neither Luis nor Ana is in college yet. They're too young.

BIG PICTURE SPEAKING/VOCABULARY EXPANSION ACTIVITY: True/False Mingle

- Have each student write three true or false statements about the Big Picture on the front of an index card. Encourage advanced students to write statements using correlative conjunctions.
- Have students mingle to ask and answer the statements. When Student A answers a statement correctly, Student B should sign the back of his or her index card.
- The mingle ends when the first student collects the signatures of six different students and reports back to the teacher.

6 WRITE sentences by putting the words in the correct order.

- Go over the directions and the example.
- Put students in pairs to complete the sentences.
- Go over the answers with the class.

ANSWER KEY

1. Alejandro is taking both management and hotel and hospitality courses.
2. Tina is studying neither electrical work nor air conditioning science.
3. Robert is looking into either health care or computer programming.
4. Neither Susan nor Berta is registering for business.
5. Both Clara and Manuel are taking medical assisting classes.

7 WHAT ABOUT YOU? Think about the programs and courses in Activity 3 on page 8. Make a list of the ones you are interested in and the ones you are not interested in. Exchange your list with a partner and write sentences about your partner's list using correlative conjunctions.

- Go over the directions and the example.
- Have partners present sentences about each other to the class.
- Prompt students to ask each other questions to determine their interests.

EXPANSION ACTIVITY: Think-Pair-Share

- Have students choose one of the programs or courses that interests them and think about why they chose it.
- Put students in pairs by finding students who chose the same program or course.
- Have partners tell the reasons they chose the program or course.
- Have pairs report their thoughts to the class, including reasons they had in common for choosing the program or course.

COMMUNITY CONNECTION: Library information tour

- Have students visit the local public library. If there are several branches, have each student choose the one most convenient to him or her. If there is only one local library, consider arranging a class field trip.
- Have students ask staff at the information desk to tell about the services the library has to offer, especially services for immigrants, second-language speakers, and people who are new to town. If possible, have students ask for a guided tour of the library and its resources.
- As an alternative, ask a librarian from a local public library to visit the class and talk about the library's services. Allow students to ask questions.
- Have students report one interesting resource or discovery to the class.

LESSON 3: Listening and Conversation

WARM-UP ACTIVITY: Days of the week

- Put students in pairs or small groups.

- Have students write out their schedules on paper. Which day of the week is busiest for them? Which day of the week is least busy? Have students give details about why these days are busy or not.

- Take a class poll to determine which day is busiest and least busy for the students.

 1 LISTEN to the question. Then listen to a husband and wife talk about schedules. Listen to the question again. Fill in the correct answer. Replay each item if necessary.
TCD1,
10–15

- Direct students' attention to the answer sheet.
- Play the CD and have students fill in the correct circles.
- Put students in pairs to compare answers.
- Go over the answers with the class.

 LISTENING SCRIPT
Lesson 3, Activities 1 and 2
TCD1,
10–15

1. Why does Linda want to talk to her husband, Tom, about schedules?
   A: Hi, Tom.
   B: Hi, honey. How was your day?
   A: It was good. I'm registering for classes this week, so we need to talk about our schedules.
   B: Sure.
   A. She's worried about being too busy.
   B. She's registering for classes.
   C. She's happy about her work schedule.

2. What is Linda signing up for?
   A: So, you're taking a continuing education course on Tuesday and Thursday afternoons, right?
   B: That's right. So you need to pick Sam up from school on Tuesdays and Thursdays.
   A: Okay. I can do that. I'm signing up for an English class that meets on Monday and Wednesday nights.
   B: That's fine.
   A. a continuing education course
   B. an English class
   C. a class that meets Tuesday and Thursday nights

3. What online course is Linda looking into?
   A: I'm also looking into an online course in American history.
   B: That sounds interesting.
   A: Yes, I'm excited about taking it. It only meets once a week, but we have lots of work online. And it satisfies the history requirement for my program.
   B: Great.
   A. an English class
   B. a class that satisfies a requirement for her program
   C. a class that sounds boring

4. What is the problem with the online course?
 B: When does the online course meet?
 A: It meets on Friday afternoons.
 B: Uh-oh. You have to take Sam to his new swim class on Friday afternoons.

  A. It meets at the same time that Linda has her English class.

  B. It meets at the same time that Linda has to work.

  C. It meets at the same time that Linda has to take Sam to swim class.

5. What is Linda's problem?
 A: Oh no! I forgot about Sam's swim class!
 B: Can you take the online class at a different time?
 A: No, I can't. I'm working a lot right now, so I don't have a lot of flexibility in my schedule.

  A. She doesn't have a lot of flexibility in her schedule.

  B. She wants to make plans for Saturdays.

  C. She can take the online course on a different day.

6. What does Tom say?
 A: Okay. I understand. Maybe Sam can take the bus to his swim class with his friends.
 B: Sure. He'll like that. Good idea.

  A. Linda needs to change her schedule.

  B. Sam can play with his friends.

  C. Sam can take the bus.

2 LISTEN to the whole conversation. Check the correct box.
TCD1, 16

- Go over the directions.
- Play the CD and have students check the answers they hear.
- Put students in pairs to check their answers.
- Go over the answers with the class.

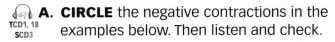

PRONUNCIATION: Reductions with Negative Contraction *n't*
TCD1, 17

Play the CD or go over the information about negative contractions.

A. CIRCLE the negative contractions in the examples below. Then listen and check.
TCD1, 18
SCD3

- Go over the directions and the example.
- Have students circle each reduced contraction.
- Play the CD again and have students check that they circled the correct letters.

B. LISTEN again and repeat.
TCD1, 19

- Go over the directions.
- Play the CD and have students repeat.

3 LISTEN and read.
TCD1, 20
SCD4

- Direct students' attention to the picture. Ask questions: *Who are the people? How do you think they feel?*
- Play the CD or read the conversation as students follow along silently.
- Play the CD or read the conversation again and have students repeat.
- Ask: *Who are the people talking about? What is he doing?*
- Put students in pairs to practice the conversation.

4 PRACTICE the conversation from Activity 3 with a partner. Use the information in the chart. For item 5, fill in the name and information for someone you know.

- Go over the directions.
- Talk about the courses in the chart.
- Have a pair of students model the activity. Have a more advanced student read Person B's lines.
- Put students in pairs to practice the conversation, making the appropriate substitutions.
- Walk around to monitor the activity and provide help as needed.
- Call on students to read the conversation to the class.

5 WHAT ABOUT YOU? Talk with a partner. Use the expressions in the Conversation Strategy box below. What classes are you taking? What new or interesting things are you doing?

- Go over the directions and the example.
- Put students in pairs to practice the example dialogue.
- Have pairs use the expressions in the Conversation Strategy box to complete the activity.
- Have volunteers present conversations in front of the class. Choose students who have not been paired together for an extra challenge.

EXPANSION ACTIVITY: Extracurricular activities

- After students have completed Activity 5, have pairs discuss their activities outside of school. Encourage them to talk about fun activities rather than duties.
- Have each student tell the class about one extracurricular activity that his or her partner enjoys. Encourage the class to respond with encouraging statements from the Conversation Strategy box.

BIG PICTURE LISTENING EXPANSION ACTIVITY: Verb Review

- Photocopy and distribute Worksheet 1: *Verb Review*
- Put the transparency for Unit 1 on the OHP or have students look at the Big Picture on page 8.
- Play the CD or read the script from Lesson 2, Activity 2, again. Have students complete Section A of the worksheet.
- Put students in pairs to compare answers.
- Go over the answers with the class.
- In Section B of the worksheet, have students write three questions to ask a partner.
- Have partners ask and answer questions, recording the answers.
- Select volunteers to read their questions and answers to the class.

WORKSHEET ANSWER KEY

A. 1. is, is taking; **2.** attends, is, is studying, 's, taking; **3.** is, is, thinking, 's looking; **4.** is, likes, 's looking; **5.** is, likes, 's looking, has
B. Answers will vary.

EXPANSION ACTIVITY: Course sections

- Distribute copies of this term's course offerings for a university or college.
- Write one full example on the board as it appears in the course offerings. Have students figure out what any abbreviations are by using the key from the course offering booklet or web page.
- Lead a discussion about the different types of sections available: daytime, evening, weekend, online, and so on.

LESSON 4: Grammar and Vocabulary

Make college plans
Express future time

VOCABULARY

contacting	organize
credits	personality test
earn	prioritize
on track	school administrator
make improvements	tasks
meet with	

GRAMMAR

Expressing future time with *will, be going to,* and the present continuous

COMPETENCIES

Learn about effective strategies for
   academic success
Make plans for the future

WARM-UP ACTIVITY: Hot potato

- Have students stand in a circle.
- Toss an object around the circle, such as an eraser or a small toy. When students catch the object, they must name one thing that they plan to do in the future.
- After everyone has had at least one turn, have students sit down. Point out sentences in which students used *will* or *be going to*.

🎧 ① GRAMMAR PICTURE DICTIONARY.
TCD1, 21
SCD5
What are these people thinking about? Listen and read.

- Have students look at the pictures. Ask: *Who are the people? What is each person doing?*
- Play the CD or read the sentences aloud as students follow along silently.

- Call on students and ask questions about the people in the picture: *When will Thomas speak with a school administrator? What improvements will Alex make?* Elicit the answers.

ACADEMIC NOTE

- Point out that in the third picture, Alex wants to improve his study skills.
- Lead a discussion about the study skills that the students in your class most rely on.
- Make a list of the study skills students suggest.
- Encourage students to copy down the list and try out a new study skill this week.

② **READ** the sentences in Activity 1 with a partner.

- Go over the directions.
- Put students in pairs to read the sentences.
- Call on students to read the sentences aloud to the class.

EXPANSION ACTIVITY: More Vocabulary Review

- Photocopy and distribute Worksheet 2: More Vocabulary Review.
- Go over the directions on the worksheet.
- Have students answer the questions.
- Put students in pairs to compare answers.
- Go over the answers with the class.

WORKSHEET ANSWER KEY

1. meet with; **2.** earn; **3.** tasks; **4.** personality test; **5.** make improvements; **6.** credit; **7.** research; **8.** prioritize; **9.** contact; **10.** organize

3 NOTICE THE GRAMMAR. Underline the verbs in present continuous in Activity 1. Circle the future verb forms with *will.* Draw a rectangle around future verb forms with *be going to.*

- Go over the directions.
- Have students underline verbs in the present continuous. Have students circle future verb forms with *will* and draw a rectangle around future verb forms with *be going to.*
- Go over the answers with the class.

ANSWER KEY

1. Gabby (will earn) three credits for taking a computer science class. She is on track for her graduation in May.
2. Thomas is contacting a school administrator tomorrow. He [is going to talk] to her about his problem with financial aid.
3. Alex [is going to make] improvements. He (will prioritize) his tasks and (organize) his time more efficiently.
4. Patricia is taking a personality test in the career center on Tuesday. Then she [is going to] meet with a career advisor.

GRAMMAR NOTE

Students may have difficulty correctly identifying the verbs using *will* in picture 3 of the Grammar Picture Dictionary. Point out that although *will* is only written once, its usage is implied twice: Alex *will prioritize* his tasks and Alex *will organize* his time more efficiently.

GRAMMAR CHART: Expressing Future Time with *Will, Be Going To,* and the Present Continuous

- Go over the information in the chart, including the Grammar Professor note.
- Read the sample sentences in the chart and have students repeat.

- Remind students of the future plans that they named during the warm-up. Have volunteers restate their plans using the language from the charts.

CHART EXPANSION ACTIVITY: Lottery winners

Have students imagine that they have won a large sum of money in the lottery. Ask what they will do tonight to celebrate. Then have them make predictions about what their classmates will do with the money.

4 COMPLETE. Circle the correct words to complete the sentences.

- Go over the directions and the example.
- Have students complete the exercise.
- Put students in pairs to check their answers.
- Go over the answers with the class.

ANSWER KEY

1. 'm going to
2. is going to rain
3. 'll
4. are you going to; 'm playing

5 WHAT ABOUT YOU? Talk with a partner about what you are going to do in the future, for example, next semester, next week, or next year. Use the verbs below.

- Go over the directions and the verbs.
- Model an example or elicit an example from students.
- Put students in pairs to complete the interviews.
- Call on students to tell about their partner to the class.

EXPANSION ACTIVITY: Timeline

- After partners have completed Activity 5, have them create a timeline that includes both of their future plans that they discussed. Have students write their plans in phrases, rather than in complete sentences. Be sure to tell students that the timeline should be anonymous; they should not indicate which one of them will be doing each activity.

- When students have completed their timelines, put two pairs together. Have Pair A ask Pair B questions based on Pair B's timeline, and vice versa. For example, one student might ask, *José, are you going to see the new movie next week?* Encourage students to refer to the grammar chart as needed to form their questions correctly.

COMMUNITY CONNECTION: Our town—Getting involved

- Put students in groups and have them discuss what will happen in the future in your town or city. Have them predict events and talk about plans related to the area.

- Have students attend a local community meeting to learn about actual plans that are being considered for your town or city. Ask them to take notes and report back to the class what they learned.

LESSON 5: Grammar Practice Plus

WARM-UP ACTIVITY: Brainstorm medical subjects

- Put students in pairs (with their books closed) to brainstorm ideas about what medical professionals study during school.
- Elicit ideas and write them on the board.

1 READ. Compare the list of required courses with Rebecca's transcript. Check the required courses that Rebecca has taken.

- Go over the directions.
- Have students put a check mark next to each course in the left-hand box that Rebecca has already taken.
- Go over the answers with the class.

 2 LISTEN to the conversation between Rebecca and her advisor. On the list of program requirements above, underline the classes you hear.

TCD1, 22

- Go over the directions.
- Have students underline the classes they hear.
- Put students in pairs to compare answers.
- Go over the answers with the class.

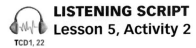

LISTENING SCRIPT
Lesson 5, Activity 2

TCD1, 22

Advisor:	Rebecca, you are doing very well in our program.
Rebecca:	Thanks, Mr. Jones. I'm really working hard.
Advisor:	I can tell! You have very good grades for many of your courses . . . in Patient Information and Medical Assisting Skills II, especially. Nice work!
Rebecca:	Thanks.
Advisor:	You still have a few more courses to take, though. Are you going to take Medical Office Procedures this summer?
Rebecca:	Yes, I'm enrolling in that course for summer, then Medical Technology in the fall.
Advisor:	Good . . . You will need those before your internship. And Mrs. Carson is teaching that this summer.
Rebecca:	Oh, great! She's my favorite professor. I'm looking forward to it.
Advisor:	Then, let's see . . . you will need Medicine Doses and your internship.
Rebecca:	Yes, I'll take Medicine Doses in the fall, too. Then I'm going to do my internship in the spring. How am I going to find my internship?
Advisor:	I'll help you with that. And it'll be your last requirement for the program!
Rebecca:	I know! I'm going to finish in only three more semesters.
Advisor:	Congratulations! You're going to really enjoy your work as a medical assistant.

ANSWER KEY

Students should underline: Patient Information, Medical Assisting Skills II, Medical Office Procedures, Medical Technology, Medicine Doses

3 **LISTEN** again. Match.

- Go over the directions and the example.
- Have students listen and match each subject with the correct predicate.
- Elicit answers from volunteers.

ANSWER KEY

1. a; **2.** d; **3.** b; **4.** c

4 **WHAT ABOUT YOU?** Think about your class(es). What plans do you have? What improvements do you want to make? Write four sentences about your plans for school. Then talk with a partner about your plans.

- Go over the directions and the example.
- Model an example of your own plans as an instructor at a school.
- Have partners share their sentences with each other.
- Have volunteers present their partners' plans to the class.

EXPANSION ACTIVITY: Setting goals

- After students have completed Activity 4, have them work individually to write step-by-step goals on how to achieve one of the improvements or plans that they discussed with their partner.
- Model an example on the board if needed.

BIG PICTURE GRAMMAR EXPANSION ACTIVITY: Future with *Will, Be Going To,* and Present Continuous

- Put the transparency for Unit 1 on the OHP or have students look at the Big Picture on page 8.
- Put students in pairs and have them write sentences about the picture, imagining what the people are going to do tomorrow or next week. Have students use *will, be going to,* and the present continuous.
- Have volunteers share their sentences with the class.

5 COMPLETE the letter from Rebecca to her friend Mari. Use the correct form of these verbs. Be prepared to say why you chose each verb tense.

- Go over the directions, explaining that students will use the word bank to fill in the blanks in the letter.
- Put students in pairs and have them read the letter aloud to each other to compare answers.
- Go over the answers with the class. Review vocabulary as needed.

EXPANSION ACTIVITY: A family affair

Have students tell about family members who are also taking classes. What school do they go to? What are they studying? Why did they choose the program or courses that they did?

6 READ the letter again. Then read each sentence below. Write *N* if it is happening now. Write *F* for something happening in the future.

- Go over the directions.
- Have students complete the exercise.
- Go over the answers with the class.

MATH: Calculating Grade Point Average (GPA)

- Go over the information and the steps shown in the reading. Show students how to calculate a GPA using the example given.
- Point out to students that GPAs are usually rounded off to the nearest tenth but sometimes extend to the nearest hundredth.
- Have students complete the charts and then check their answers with a partner.
- Go over the answers with the class.

PRONUNCIATION NOTE

Point out to students that the decimal point in a GPA is stated verbally as the word *point*. GPAs that extend to the hundredth place are generally read by saying each individual number. For example, a GPA of 3.65 would usually be read as "three point six five" rather than "three point sixty-five." Explain that decimals are typically pronounced in this way. Contrast the pronunciation of the period in GPAs and decimals ("point") with the pronunciation of the period in Internet addresses ("dot").

ACADEMIC CONNECTION: Transcripts

- Have students find out your school's policy on requesting transcripts and report their findings to the class.
- Lead a discussion about what transcripts are used for: transferring to a new school, getting into graduate school, proving knowledge of subject areas to potential employers, and so on.
- Point out that not all courses receive a letter grade. Help students understand alternative grading classifications, such as "Pass/Fail," "Satisfactory/Unsatisfactory," and designations for audited courses.

LESSON 6: Reading

WARM-UP ACTIVITY: A day in the life

- Brainstorm on the board a list of all the working people that the students encounter during a typical day (not including their coworkers). For example, students may interact with toll-booth collectors, postal office workers, doctors, teachers, administrators, store clerks, and so on.
- Choose a few of the workers listed and have students tell what kind of education or training was probably required to obtain each job.

1 THINK ABOUT IT. Discuss these questions in a group. Use your prior knowledge.

- Direct students' attention to the Reading Focus boxes. Go over the information in them.
- Go over the directions.
- Put students in small groups to answer the questions.
- Call on students to share their ideas with the class.

2 BEFORE YOU READ. Look at the brochure on the next page. Preview the brochure. Look at each heading and skim the text under it. What kind of information does each section give?

- Go over the directions.
- Have students preview the brochure.
- Put students in pairs to retell information from each section.
- Elicit ideas from the class.

3 READ the brochure on the next page. Which course is the most interesting to you?

- Go over the directions.
- Have students tell their ideas. Encourage students to ask each other questions.

EXPANSION ACTIVITY: Pros and cons

- Put students in four groups. Assign each group one of the careers highlighted in the brochure.
- Have students list the pros and cons of each job in their opinion.
- Have groups present their ideas to the class. Facilitate discussion as needed.

CIVICS NOTE

Tell students about governmental programs or benefits that are available to job seekers in your area. (You may have them research your state's website to find out about such programs.) For example, many states offer free job training to unemployed workers who wish to enter a new field of employment. Some students may also be able to deduct educational costs from their taxes.

4 AFTER YOU READ.

A. VOCABULARY. Find and circle these words in the reading. Then match the word with the definition. Use a dictionary to check your answers.

- Go over the directions.
- Have students circle the words in the brochure and complete the matching exercise.
- Put students in pairs to compare answers.
- Have students look up the words in a dictionary to check their answers.
- Go over the answers with the class.

ANSWER KEY

1. c; **2.** a; **3.** e; **4.** d; **5.** b

B. DISCUSS the questions with a partner.

- Go over the directions and the questions.
- Put students in pairs to answer the questions.
- Go over the answers with the class.

C. TALK with a partner.

- Go over the directions and the questions.
- Put students in pairs to answer the questions.
- Elicit ideas from the class.

EXPANSION ACTIVITY: Glossary

- Challenge students to write sentences using the glossary terms in new contexts. Encourage them to use a dictionary to look up multiple meanings of the words to expand their knowledge.
- Have students read their sentences to a partner, leaving out the vocabulary word (substituting the word *blank*). Partners should try to repeat the sentence using the correct missing word.

BIG PICTURE READING EXPANSION ACTIVITY: Name that person

- Photocopy and distribute Worksheet 3 *Name That Person.*
- Put the transparency for Unit 1 on the OHP or have students look at the Big Picture on page 8.
- Go over the directions on the worksheet.
- Have students read the descriptions and answer the questions.
- Put students in pairs to share their ideas.
- Go over the answers with the class.

WORKSHEET ANSWER KEY

1. Carlos; a book on business management.
2. green; 3 books
3. Rebecca; a book on medical assisting.
4. Luis; the woman carrying the books.
5. the computer science and automotive aisle.

COMMUNITY CONNECTION: Education alternatives

- Have students collect brochures and information packets from schools or education centers for adults in or near your community. If necessary, help them find schools using the telephone book, the Internet, or other resources. Encourage students to collect information from a variety of organizations: technical schools, beauty training institutes, universities, community recreation centers, and so on.
- Set up the brochures around the classroom and hold a "fair" in which students browse the information. After the fair, lead a discussion in which students ask questions and share interesting or exciting information they learned.

LESSON 7: Writing

OBJECTIVES
Read and write an email

WRITING FOCUS
Give specific details

COMPETENCIES
Understand appropriate subjects when introducing oneself Write an email to an instructor

WARM-UP ACTIVITY: The first day of class

- Tell students how you usually feel (as an instructor) before the first day of a new class.
- Divide students into pairs and have them tell each other how they feel before the first day of class. Are they nervous or excited?
- Take a class poll to see how many students experience similar feelings before the first day of class.

1 THINK ABOUT IT. What kind of personal information do you share with people when you first meet? Talk to a partner and make a list.

- Go over the questions asked for this activity.
- Model the activity by giving an example of something you would feel comfortable telling a classmate. See if students agree with your idea.
- Put students in pairs to discuss the questions.
- Have students make their lists.
- Lead a class discussion, eliciting from the class the kinds of personal information they would or would not share with someone they had just met.

2 BEFORE YOU WRITE.

A. READ this email from a teacher introducing himself to his class. Underline the details in the second paragraph.

- Direct students' attention to the Writing Focus box. Go over the information in it.
- Go over the directions.
- Have students complete the activity.
- Elicit from students the details they underlined in the second paragraph. Does everyone agree? Help students understand the difference between a main idea and a supporting detail.

B. TALK to a partner. What kinds of details does Professor Donaldson include in his email? Do you think all of these details are okay to share with students? Do you think it's okay for the professor to ask students to tell him the same kind of information?

- Go over the questions asked for this activity.
- Put students in pairs to discuss the questions.
- Elicit ideas from the class.

EXPANSION ACTIVITY: Mini-debate

- While students are completing Activity 2B, have them take notes about points they disagree on.
- Divide the class into teams and hold a mini-debate about one of the points they did not agree on as a class.
- At the end of the debate, have students tell whether they changed their opinion because of the ideas presented.

Lead a discussion about subjects that you might not want to discuss when you first meet someone in the United States. For example, some people don't like personal questions such as "Are you married?" or "How old are you?" Other people might not wish to share their political or religious views with a new acquaintance, or to discuss how much money they make or spend. Have students share their ideas about topics they probably wouldn't discuss with a new acquaintance.

C. PLAN your writing. Imagine you are writing an email to Professor Donaldson. Before you write, make notes to plan what you will say. Include details for some of your ideas. Pay attention to the verb tenses you use.

- Go over the directions.
- Have students make notes in each section.
- Elicit ideas from the class.
- Encourage students to take further notes based on the ideas elicited.

3 WRITE an email to your instructor to introduce yourself. Include a greeting, write sentences that tell the ideas and details from your notes, write a closing, and write your name.

- Direct students' attention to the Writing Focus box. Go over the information in it.
- Go over the directions. Point out that students are now writing to you, their instructor, instead of Professor Donaldson.
- Have students use their notes from Activity 2C to write paragraphs on a separate sheet of paper or in their notebooks.
- Have volunteers read their emails aloud to the class.

4 AFTER YOU WRITE.

A. EDIT your writing.

- Go over the questions.
- Have students look at their paragraphs and make changes if necessary.
- Put students in pairs to review each other's writing, answering the questions about their partner.
- Have students rewrite their letters with the necessary corrections.

BIG PICTURE WRITING EXPANSION ACTIVITY: Create a character

- Put the transparency for Unit 1 on the projector or have students look at page 8 in their books.
- Have students choose a character and imagine a new identity for him or her.
- Have students write a paragraph about the character, telling why he or she is in the library, what his or her life is like, and so on.
- Put students in pairs to read their paragraphs.
- Ask volunteers to read their paragraphs to the class.

ACADEMIC CONNECTION: Web seminars and online classes

- Have students investigate how web seminars and online classes work.
- If your school offers web seminars and online classes, arrange for one of your colleagues (an online instructor or IT specialist) to tell your students how these classes work.
- Lead a discussion about which subjects would be best for online study and which subjects would be difficult to study outside of a classroom.

Career Connection

OBJECTIVE

Identify work skills

COMPETENCIES

Know the qualifications needed to be a
  daycare worker
Communicate in a daycare setting

WARM-UP ACTIVITY: Brainstorm

- Elicit ideas from students about the kinds of
  activities that happen at a daycare center.
  Write their ideas on the board.

- Lead a discussion about what it must be like to
  work in a daycare center. Point out and explain
  important vocabulary words that come up
  during discussion.

1 THINK ABOUT IT. What qualifications or skills
do you think are important for a teacher at a
daycare center?

- Direct students' attention to the picture and
  ask questions: *Who do you see? What are they
  doing?*

- Read the directions and have students answer
  the question.

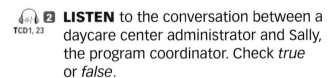

2 LISTEN to the conversation between a
daycare center administrator and Sally,
the program coordinator. Check *true*
or *false*.

TCD1, 23

- Read the directions and preview the questions
  with students.

- Play the CD and have students answer the
  questions.

- Put students in pairs to compare answers.

- Go over the answers with the class.

LISTENING SCRIPT
Career Connection, Activities 2 and 3

TCD1, 23

> *DA:* Hi, Sally. How did registration go yesterday?
>
> *Sally:* Great! But I think we're going to need
> another new teacher.
>
> *DA:* Another one?
>
> *Sally:* Yes. We had several new enrollments
> yesterday. Eight new children will start here
> on Monday.
>
> *DA:* Wow! That's great.
>
> *Sally:* Yes. Six of them are four-year-olds. And
> there were two toddlers: a one-year-old
> and a two-year old.
>
> *DA:* Oh, that's excellent news!
>
> *Sally:* I agree. But we have a problem . . .
>
> *DA:* What's that?
>
> *Sally:* Well, there aren't enough teachers for all
> the children. I just looked at the schedule.
> Jenny is going on vacation for two weeks.
>
> *DA:* Oh, yes, that's right. Well, let's see . . .
> we'll have 78 children in the program on
> Monday. We have five teachers. So we'll
> need to hire one more teacher, and we'll
> also need to find someone to cover Jenny's
> class. Any ideas?
>
> *Sally:* Hmm . . . Maybe we could ask Regina to
> cover Jenny's class?
>
> *DA:* That's one solution. Unfortunately, Regina
> doesn't have much experience with three-
> and four-year-olds. She's been here for two
> years, but she's still working on her degree.
>
> *Sally:* True. You're right, she isn't qualified yet,
> and she only has experience with toddlers.
> But she is organized and very patient. She
> could probably take care of the three- and
> four-year-olds for a couple of weeks.
>
> *DA:* Hmm . . . Is there anyone else?

Sally: Maybe Marcia. She has worked here for three years now. She's very flexible and talented. She also has a bachelor's degree in Early Childhood Education.

DA: OK. Please ask both Marcia and Regina. I'm sure one of them can help. And we still need one more new teacher.

Sally: Well, we're in luck. Two women applied here last week, and one of them seems really good. Her name is Cynthia. I put her résumé on your desk. She has a master's degree in education and five years of teaching experience. She's also creative and artistic.

DA: Wow, she sounds great! I'll call her to set up an interview.

Sally: OK, I'll speak with Marcia and Regina and see who can help take care of the three- and four-year-olds while Jenny's on vacation.

ANSWER KEY

1. T; **2.** F; **3.** T; **4.** F; **5.** T

❸ LISTEN to the conversation in Activity 2 again. Complete the chart with the words in the box.

- Go over the directions.
- Have students complete the chart with the words in the box based on information they heard during the listening from Activity 2.
- Put students in pairs to compare answers.
- Go over the answers with the class. If students have trouble completing the chart, play the CD again and have them listen for the details they need to know.

ANSWER KEY

Regina: 2 years, still in school, organized and patient; Marcia: 3 years, Bachelor's degree, flexible and talented; Cynthia: 5 years, Master's degree, creative and artistic

❹ ROLE PLAY. Imagine that you are a parent bringing your child to this daycare center. You are talking to the program coordinator. What are you going to ask? Use the information in the box. Take turns asking questions with a partner.

- Go over the directions and the example with students.
- Put students in pairs to ask and answer questions.
- Call on pairs to present some of their questions and answers.

CULTURE NOTE

In many countries, paid daycare is not a common service. Talk to students about the many reasons that people in the United States use daycare centers: financial necessity (both parents needing to work or single parents), lack of extended family nearby to care for children, other career reasons (for example, parents who both love their jobs or who do not wish to stay home full-time), developmental reasons (some parents feel the socialization of a daycare center is important for their child), and so on. Ask students to tell about how childcare may be different in their cultures or home countries.

❺ WHAT ABOUT YOU? Talk with a partner. What are your strengths in your current job? What educational goals do you have? Discuss two or three of your strengths and your educational goals.

- Go over the directions and the questions asked.
- Have students think for a few minutes about the questions, taking notes if desired.
- Put students in pairs to discuss the questions.
- Have volunteers tell the class about their partner's strengths and educational goals.

COMMUNITY CONNECTION: Daycare Center information interview

- Have students visit a daycare center in their neighborhood. Ask them to interview a teacher or administrator there about the challenges of working in such an environment. You may wish to have the students find out about the qualifications that the teachers have.

- Have students report their findings back to the class and compare their information.

CHECK YOUR PROGRESS!

- Have students circle the answers.
- Have students check whether each answer is right or wrong.
- Have students total their correct answers and fill in the chart at the bottom of the page.
- Have students create a learning plan and/or set learning goals.

ANSWER KEY

1. registers; **2.** I'm practicing; **3.** do you go; **4.** I'm taking; **5.** Will you; **6.** 'm going to; **7.** Are you looking; **8.** 's going to rain; **9.** satisfy; **10.** placement test; **11.** flexibility; **12.** cover; **13.** track; **14.** tasks; **15.** organize; **16.** earn

Unit Overview

LESSON	OBJECTIVES	STUDENT BOOK	WORKBOOK
1 Grammar and Vocabulary 1	Use work vocabulary. Use past time clauses.	p. 22	p. 20
2 Grammar Practice Plus	Use feeling words. Interpret a checklist. Compete an email.	p. 24	p. 21
3 Listening and Conversation	Use regular past tense -ed endings. Transcribe a work schedule. Role-play a work conversation.	p. 26	p. 22
4 Grammar and Vocabulary 2	Talk about job performance. Use simple past. Use present perfect.	p. 28	p. 24
5 Grammar Practice Plus	Express similarities. Read a job evaluation. Figure salary increases.	p. 30	p. 25
6 Reading	Use suffixes -able and -ive. Personal qualities. Compare job candidates.	p. 32	p. 26–27
7 Writing	List your best personal skills. Use persuasive writing.	p. 34	p. 28–29
• Career Connection	Examine job benefits.	p. 36	p. 30
• Check Your Progress	Monitor progress.	p. 37	p. 32–33

Reading/Writing Strategies

- Scan for specific information
- Persuade in writing

Connection Activities

LESSON	TYPE	SKILL DEVELOPMENT
1	Community	Interview people about office activities
2	Community	Research information on relieving stress
3	Academic	Monitor past tense pronunciation
4	Academic	Review past participles of irregular verbs
5	Community	Research types of training workshops
6	Academic	Identify common prefixes and suffixes
7	Academic	Research writing lab hours and locations
Career Connection	Community	Survey people about their work benefits

WORKSHEET #/FOCUS	TITLE	TEACHER'S EDITION
4. Reading	Today's Meeting	p. 308
5. Writing	What are they doing?	p. 309
6. Grammar	Simple Past or Present Perfect	p. 310

LESSON 1: Grammar and Vocabulary

VOCABULARY

accept	meet a deadline
ask	project
cover for	pull together
follow up	materials
join a conference	schedule
call	voicemail
make a presentation	

GRAMMAR

Past time clauses with *after*, *when*, *as soon as*, *before*, and *until*

COMPETENCIES

Use job-related language
Learn about appropriate behavior at work

WARM-UP ACTIVITY: Ordering events

- Write *before*, *after*, *as soon as*, *when*, and *until* on the board.
- Explain that these words are used to show in what order two separate actions took place. Give examples: *Before I came to school, I ate breakfast. Last night I watched TV until 11:00.*
- Point to a word on the board and ask students to use the word while explaining two events from their lives.

TCD1, 24
SCD6
1 GRAMMAR PICTURE DICTIONARY.
What are these people doing at work? Listen and read.

- Have students open their books and look at the pictures.
- Explain that the activity on the left side of each picture happened before the activity on the right side. Ask: *What two events are happening*

in each picture? Elicit answers from students for each picture.
- Say the sentences or play the CD and have students repeat.
- Call on students. Ask questions about the pictures: *What did Kristin do before she scheduled the meeting?* Elicit the answers.

EXPANSION ACTIVITY: What do you see?

- Put students into groups of three or four.
- Have each group list 15 to 20 items that they see in the pictures on page 22.
- Have each group write their lists on the board.

2 READ the sentences in Activity 1 with a partner.

- Put students in pairs to read the sentences.
- Call on students to read the sentences to the class.

EXPANSION ACTIVITY: What does that mean?

- Write the vocabulary phrases from Activity 1 on the board: *schedule a meeting, follow up with a team, join a conference call, accept an assignment, meet a deadline, complete a project, cover for someone, finish a report, listen to voicemail, make a presentation, pull together some materials.*
- Put the students into small groups.
- Have each group write definitions for the phrases.
- Tell the students that today is your first day at a new job and you do not understand what your colleagues and supervisors are saying. You need your students' help. Ask one group: *Schedule a meeting? What does* schedule a meeting *mean?*
- Continue with the other phrases until each group has answered at least once.

3 NOTICE THE GRAMMAR. Circle the words *after, when, as soon as, before,* and *until.* Underline the verb that follows these words.

- Go over the directions and the example.
- Have students circle *after, when, as soon as, before,* and *until.*
- Have students underline the verbs that follow *after, when, as soon as, before,* and *until.*
- Walk around to provide help as needed.
- Go over the answers with the class.

GRAMMAR CHART: Past Time Clauses with
After, When, As Soon As, Before,* and *Until

- Direct students' attention to the chart or project the transparency or CD.
- Go over the information in the chart and the usage notes. Read the sentences aloud, pausing to have students repeat.

CHART EXPANSION ACTIVITY:
What did they do?

- Direct students' attention to the pictures in Activity 1.
- Write the sentences for item 1 on the board: *Kristin talked to her boss before she scheduled the meeting. Then she followed up with the team.*
- Ask students what Kristin did *after* she followed up with the team. Write one answer on the board using a complete sentence: *After Kristin talked to her boss, she scheduled the meeting.* Put students into pairs. Have them write an additional sentence for each item in Activity 1 using *after, when, as soon as, before,* or *until.*

GRAMMAR NOTE

Students often confuse *until* and *by.* Both mean *any time before, but not later than.* However, *until* tells us how long a situation continues. If something happens *until* a particular time, you stop doing it at that time. If something happens *by* a particular time, it happens at or before that time.

4 COMPLETE. Circle the correct words to complete the sentences.

- Go over the directions.
- Read item 1 to the class. Elicit reasons why *after* is the correct answer.
- Have students circle the correct words.
- Put students in pairs to compare their answers.
- Go over the answers with the class.

EXPANSION ACTIVITY: Rewriting sentences

Have advanced students rewrite the sentences in Activity 4 in a different verb tense, such as future or simple present.

5 **WHAT ABOUT YOU?** Write sentences about you. Use the simple past and a time clause. Use *after, as soon as, before, until,* or *when* in your sentences. Then read your sentences to a classmate.

- Go over the directions and the example.
- Model the activity using information about what you did as soon as you got to school. Write on the board: *I unlocked the classroom as soon as I got to school.* Ask two or three students what they did as soon as they got to school.
- Have students write their sentences.
- Put students in small groups to read their sentences.

EXPANSION ACTIVITY: Is it true?

- Say one false sentence and two true sentences about your day using the past tense and a time clause.
- Tell students that one of the sentences is not true. Repeat the sentences.
- Have the class vote on which sentence is not true by raising their hands after you say the sentences again.
- Allow time for the students to write one false and two true sentences about their day using the past tense and a time clause.
- Call on students to read their sentences to the class.
- Have the class vote on which sentence is false.

COMMUNITY CONNECTION: Office activities

- Explain that you want students to interview three people who work in an office about their daily work activities.
- Brainstorm ideas on where to find office workers in your community. Write the ideas on the board: spouses, coworkers, people in the administration office at your school, friends, neighbors, etc.
- Have each student interview three office workers about their daily activities.
- Ask volunteers to report back to the class.

LESSON 2: Grammar Practice Plus

WARM-UP ACTIVITY: Describing personalities

- Ask the class for a definition of the word *personality* (e.g., a person's character or the way a person acts toward other people).
- Put students into small groups.
- Have each group write ten adjectives that describe someone's personality.
- Have each group write its list on the board. Review each list for comprehension.

❶ TALK about the picture. What do you think is going on? How does each person feel?

- Go over the directions.
- Put students in pairs to talk about the picture. Have them discuss how each person feels.
- Walk around to monitor the activity and provide help as needed.
- Elicit answers from the class.

 ❷ LISTEN. Write the number next to the correct name above.

- Go over the directions.
- Read the sentences from the script or play the CD and have students repeat.
- Go over the answers with the class.

 LISTENING SCRIPT
Lesson 2, Activity 2

1. Luke is careful with his papers and assignments. He's very organized.
2. Thomas is tired of his job. He's burned out.
3. Lorenzo has a lot of work to do. He's really overwhelmed.
4. Silvia always arrives at her meetings on time. She's very punctual.
5. Jenny often takes care of her coworkers. She's very helpful.
6. Donna has a lot of new ideas. She's very creative.

ANSWER KEY

3. Lorenzo; 4. Silvia; 5. Jenny; 6. Donna;
1. Luke; 2. Thomas

3 COMPLETE the sentences about the people in the picture. Use the words in the box below. Then match each sentence to one on the right.

- Go over the directions.
- Point to the list of adjectives in the box. Elicit definitions for the words from the students. Define words students do not know.
- Model the activity by pointing to Lorenzo in the picture. Say *Lorenzo is really...* Point to the list of adjectives. Say *Lorenzo is really overwhelmed.* Point to *b*. Explain that *b* defines *overwhelmed*.
- Have students do the activity.
- Walk around to monitor the activity and provide help as needed.
- Elicit answers from the class.

ANSWER KEY

1. overwhelmed, b; **2.** punctual, c; **3.** helpful, e;
4. creative, a; **5.** organized, f; **6.** burned out, d

BIG PICTURE CONVERSATION/ VOCABULARY EXPANSION ACTIVITY: Who am I?

- Have the students look at the Big Picture in Activity 1, or put the transparency for Unit 2 on the OHP.
- Model the activity. Choose one character from the picture and say what they might be thinking (e.g., *I can't believe that Jenny was late again. Doesn't she know that being late is rude? I don't have all day to sit here and wait for her.*).
- Elicit the name of the character who might be thinking these thoughts (*Silvia).*
- Put students in pairs or groups to practice role-playing and guessing the characters.
- Call on students to role-play to the class and elicit the name from the other students.

4 WHAT ABOUT YOU? Describe people you know by using the adjectives from Activity 1. Add a detail to explain.

- Go over the directions and the example.
- Put students in small groups to describe two people they know.

EXPANSION ACTIVITY: Tell me about a time

- Write the following sentences on the board: *Tell me about a time when you were overwhelmed. Tell me about a time when you were burned out. Tell me about a time when you were creative.*
- Model the activity. Tell the class about a time you were overwhelmed, burned out, or creative.
- Put students into pairs to discuss the questions.

5 COMPLETE Luke's email to his friend about his new job. Use the simple past tense of the verbs in the box below.

- Go over the directions.
- Direct students' attention to the words in the box.
- Have students complete the email.
- Walk around to monitor the activity and provide help as needed.

ANSWER KEY

1. arrived; **2.** listened; **3.** told; **4.** wanted;
5. began; **6.** ended; **7.** watched; **8.** discussed;
9. got; **10.** answered

6 WRITE. Choose which person in Activity 1 wrote each of the sentences below. Imagine you are one of the people. Starting with his/her sentence, write a longer email, like the one in Activity 5.

- Put the transparency for Unit 2 on the OHP or have students look at the Big Picture in their books.
- Direct students' attention to item 1. Read the sentence aloud and point to Donna in the book. Remind students that Donna is very creative and has a lot of new ideas.
- Have students choose which person in Activity 1 wrote each of the sentences.
- Go over the answers with the class.
- Have students imagine that they are one of the people in the Big Picture.
- Put students in groups to read their emails aloud. Have the other members of the group try to guess who wrote the email.

ANSWER KEY

1. Donna; **2.** Thomas; **3.** Luke; **4.** Jenny; **5.** Silvia

---

EXPANSION ACTIVITY: My day

- Have students make notes on what they did yesterday before, during, and after class.
- Direct students' attention to the body of the email in Activity 6. Point out the salutation with the comma, the pre-closing phrase (*I'd better be going*), and the closing with a comma.
- Have students write an email to a friend about what they did yesterday before, during, and after class.

---

7 WHAT ABOUT YOU? Tell a partner about your activities yesterday. Use past time clauses.

- Go over the directions.
- Model the activity orally: *Yesterday as soon as I woke up, I took a shower. Before I left my house, I . . .*

- Have students write their paragraphs on a separate piece of paper.
- Collect and correct the paragraphs.

COMMUNITY CONNECTION: Relieving stress

- Discuss how being overwhelmed or burned out can cause stress and that being stressed can often cause physical problems like high blood pressure, digestive problems, stiff muscles, etc.
- Brainstorm ideas for relieving stress (e.g., taking yoga classes, working out in a gym, going on group walks, practicing meditation, etc.).
- Have students research different community activities they can do to relieve stress. They can either survey their friends and families for techniques or search on the Internet for "stress relief strategies."
- Call on students to tell the class what they found out. Write the strategies on the board.

BIG PICTURE CONVERSATION/ VOCABULARY EXPANSION ACTIVITY: Today's Meeting

- Photocopy and distribute Worksheet 4: *Today's Meeting.*
- Put the transparency for Unit 2 on the OHP or have students look at the Big Picture in their books.
- Go over the directions.
- Have students read the letters and write the name of the character.
- Put students in pairs to compare answers.
- Go over the answers with the class.

WORKSHEET ANSWER KEY

1. Jenny; **2.** Silvia; **3.** Thomas

LESSON 3: Listening and Conversation

WARM-UP ACTIVITY: Check meaning

- Write *after, as soon as,* and *until* on the board. Check comprehension by asking students to use each word or phrase in a sentence.

- Write on the board: *When the meeting was over, I followed up with my team. (as soon as) First I'm going to go to lunch, and then I will check my voicemail. (after) She couldn't leave before she completed the project. (until)*

- Put students in pairs to rewrite the sentences using the words in parentheses.

- Call on pairs to read their sentences to the class.

 TCD1, 26–31 **1 LISTEN** to the question. Then listen to the conversation. Listen to the question again. Fill in the correct answer. Replay each item if necessary.

- Direct students' attention to the activity and the fill-in circles.

- Play the CD and have students fill in the circles.

- Go over the answers with the class.

ANSWER KEY

1. A; 2. B; 3. A; 4. A; 5. C; 6. B

 TCD1, 32 **2 LISTEN** again. Write what the person says about the time of the activity.

- Go over the directions.

- Play the CD and have students write the time of the activities.

- Replay the CD if necessary.

- Elicit the correct answers from the students.

ANSWER KEY

1. eat lunch; 2. got to the office; 3. talked to Mrs. Jones; 4. finished it; 5. left; 6. go home

LISTENING SCRIPT
Lesson 2, Activities 1 and 2
TCD1, 26–32

1. What are the people talking about?
   A: Hey, Ana.
   B: What's up, Chris?
   A: Did you complete that project for Sam this morning?
   B: No, I didn't, but I'm going to finish it after I eat lunch.
   A: Okay, thanks!
   A. a project
   B. a phone call
   C. a meeting

2. When did Natalie call Chris?
   A: Natalie, did you call Chris this morning?
   B: Yes, I did.
   A: Great, thanks. When did you call?
   B: Um . . . about 9:30 a.m. I called as soon as I got to the office.
   A: Perfect.
   A. in the evening
   B. in the morning
   C. in the afternoon

3. What does Tyler tell the speaker?
   A: Hi, Tyler. How's your day going?
   B: Just fine! What can I do for you?
   A: I was just wondering . . . did you schedule the meeting for next week?

B: Yes. I scheduled the meeting as soon as I talked to Mrs. Jones.

A: Thanks!

A. He scheduled the meeting after he talked to Mrs. Jones.

B. He scheduled the meeting before he went home.

C. He forgot to schedule the meeting.

4. Why is Natalie tired?

A: Natalie, are you okay?

B: I'm just tired.

A: Did you complete the project you were working on?

B: Yes, I did, but I didn't go to bed last night until I finished it. I went to bed at 4:00 a.m.!

A: Now you need to ask for a day off.

A. She stayed up until 4:00 working on a project.

B. She didn't finish the project.

C. She took a day off.

5. Why didn't Paul cover for his coworker?

A: Paul, did you cover for me last night?

B: I'm so sorry. No, I didn't. I got an emergency call from my sister after you left.

A: Oh, no!

B: I'm really sorry, but I had to go help her.

A: Well, I understand. It's okay.

A. He forgot.

B. He had to go to class.

C. He had to help his sister.

6. When will Lorenzo follow up with Andrew?

A: Lorenzo, did you follow up with Andrew about his assignment?

B: Um . . . no . . . What assignment?

A: The sales report?

B: Oh, right! I'm sorry. I'll call him before I go home today.

A: Thank you.

A. after he gets home

B. before he goes home

C. tomorrow

BIG PICTURE WRITING EXPANSION ACTIVITY: What were they doing?

- Photocopy and distribute Worksheet 5: *What were they doing?*

- Put the transparency for Unit 2 on the OHP or have students look at the Big Picture on page 24.

- Go over the directions.

- Have students write their sentences.

- Put students in small groups to read their sentences aloud.

EXPANSION ACTIVITY: Dictation reconstruction

- Tell students that they are going to hear one of the conversations for Activity 2 again, but that this time they should write what they hear.

- Read aloud or play the audio for item 4 in Activity 2 while students write what they hear.

- Read or play the audio once again if necessary.

- Put students into small groups to compare what they wrote.

- Have each group try to reconstruct the conversation correctly.

3 LISTEN and fill in the schedule for the things Lorenzo did in his busy day.
TCD1, 33

- Go over the directions.

- Direct students' attention to the list of activities under the directions. Explain that these are the activities they should use to fill in the schedule. Point out that there are ten blank lines on the schedule but only seven activities. Three lines will be left blank.

- Play the CD or read the script aloud and have students fill in the schedule.

- Go over the answers with the class.

LISTENING SCRIPT
Lesson 3, Activity 3

TCD1, 33

1. Lorenzo had a one-hour breakfast meeting at 8:00 A.M. He joined the conference call after his breakfast meeting.

2. Around 9:30, he pulled materials together before he went to a meeting with his supervisor at 10:00.

3. He worked with his coworker Thomas from 11:00 A.M. until they both went to lunch at 1:00 P.M.

4. As soon as he got back from lunch at 2:00, Lorenzo finished the project for Donna.

5. He covered for Silvia when she had to leave for a doctor's appointment at 4:00 P.M.

ANSWER KEY

8:00 AM had a breakfast meeting	1:00 PM ate lunch
9:00 AM joined a conference call	2:00 PM finished the project for Donna
10:00 AM met with supervisor	3:00 PM
11:00 AM worked with Thomas	4:00 PM covered for Silvia
12:00 PM	5:00 PM

EXPANSION ACTIVITY: Lorenzo's schedule

- Direct students' attention to the completed schedule in Activity 3.

- Model the activity by combining two events on the schedule using *before, after, as soon as, when,* or *until* (e.g., *Before he joined his conference call, Lorenzo had a breakfast meeting.*).

- Have students write five sentences about Lorenzo's schedule. Remind students to combine two events on the schedule and to use one of the time words from Lesson 1.

- Put students into pairs to compare and correct their sentences.

PRONUNCIATION: Regular Past Tense
TCD1, 34 *(-ed)* Endings

- Play the CD or read the explanation to the class.

PRONUNCIATION NOTE

It is often helpful to give students the three rules for past tense pronunciation for regular verbs.

1. When the verb ends in a /t/ or /ɪd/ sound, pronounce the *-ed* as an extra syllable: /ɪd/.

2. When the verb ends in a voiceless sound (/f/, /k/, /p/, /s/, /sh/, /ch/, /ks/), pronounce the *-ed* as /t/.

3. When the verb ends in a voiced sound (/b/, /g/, /j/, /m/, /n/, /ng/, /l/, /r/, /th/, /v/, /z/) or with a vowel, pronounce the *-ed* as /ɪd/.

A. PREDICT the final sound of each *-ed* ending. Write *t, d, or ɪd.* Then listen and check.
TCD1, 35
SCD7

- Go over the directions.

- Have students predict the final sound for each word.

- Play the CD or read the words. Repeat if necessary until students feel confident that they can distinguish between the endings.

- Go over the answers as a class.

ANSWER KEY

1. t; **2.** d; **3.** ɪd; **4.** d; **5.** ɪd; **6.** t

B. LISTEN again and repeat.

- Play the CD again.

- Have students practice chorally.

ACADEMIC CONNECTION: Monitoring past tense

- Point out that many English learners do not use past tense when speaking because they are confused about the pronunciation and because they are usually understood even when they do not use it (e.g., *Yesterday I work for five hours.*).

- Have students monitor their oral use of the past tense every day for the next week. Explain that monitoring is paying special attention to their language and fixing an error when it occurs.

- After a week, put students in small groups to discuss their monitoring.

TCD1, 37
SCD8

4 LISTEN to the conversation between two coworkers.

- Direct students' attention to the picture. Ask questions: *Who do you see? What's happening?*

- Play the CD or read the conversation as students follow along silently.

- Play the CD or read the conversation again and have students repeat.

- Ask: *Who did the woman call? When did she call her? When will she work on the project?*

- Put students in pairs to practice the conversation. Have each pair read the conversation twice so that each student reads Speaker A's part and Speaker B's part.

- Go around the room and monitor the activity.

5 PRACTICE the conversation from Activity 4. Speaker A, ask about things to do. Speaker B, answer using the past and future time clauses. Tell what you did do and what you will do. Make three different conversations.

- Go over the directions.

- Model the activity. Have a more advanced student read A's lines. Model how to substitute different things to do and time clauses from the chart.

- Put students into pairs to practice the conversation, making the appropriate substitutions.

- Walk around to monitor the activity and provide help as needed.

- Call on students to present the conversation to the class.

EXPANSION ACTIVITY: Things to do

- Put students in pairs.

- Have students create a conversation following the model in Activity 4, but this time their things to do should be related to things they do at home or at school.

- Ask volunteers to perform their conversations in front of the class.

6 ROLE-PLAY. Choose a situation. With a partner, create your own conversation and practice it. Then act it out for the class. Use one of the responses in the Conversation Strategy box.

- Go over the directions.
- Direct students' attention to the Conversation Strategy box. Say each phrase and have students repeat.
- Put students into pairs.
- Have students role-play at least one of the situations.
- Walk around to monitor the activity and provide help as needed.
- Call on students to act out their role-plays in front of the class.

EXPANSION ACTIVITY: Role-play swap

- Have each pair of students write their role-play conversations from Activity 6 on a separate piece of paper. Tell the students not to put their names on the paper.
- Collect the role-play conversations and redistribute so that each pair has a new conversation.
- Call on students to act out their role-play conversations in front of the class.

---

7 WHAT ABOUT YOU? Write a conversation between you and a family member or coworker. Talk about things you have to do at home.

- Go over the directions and the example in the speech bubbles.
- Have students write the conversation.
- Put students in pairs to practice their conversations.

LESSON 4: Grammar and Vocabulary

OBJECTIVES

Talk about job performance
Use simple past
Use present perfect

VOCABULARY

certification
develop
  communication
  skills
get along
maintain
  qualifications
manage time

promotion
receive positive
  performance
  reviews
show leadership
  skills
workshop

GRAMMAR

Simple past and present perfect review

COMPETENCY

Recognize qualities that lead to job retention
  and advancement

WARM-UP ACTIVITY: Annual performance reviews

- Have students close their books.
- Ask students what an annual performance review is and who in the class has had their performance reviewed by supervisors.
- Put students into small groups to list what types of things a supervisor discusses during an annual performance review.
- Have students write their lists on the board.

🎧 **1 GRAMMAR PICTURE DICTIONARY.**

TCD1, 38
SCD9
How are Josh and Kara doing at their jobs? Listen and read.

- Have students look at the pictures. Ask: *What is happening in each picture?*
- Play the CD or read the sentences aloud as students follow along silently.

- Call on students and ask questions about the people in the pictures: *Josh has received positive performance reviews. Does that mean his supervisors think he is doing a good job?* Elicit the answers.

2 READ the sentences from Activity 1 with a partner.

- Go over the directions.
- Put students in pairs to read the sentences.
- Call on students to read the sentences aloud to the class.

3 NOTICE THE GRAMMAR. Circle the verbs in simple past. Underline the verbs in present perfect.

- Go over the directions and the examples. Point out that the present perfect verbs will include two parts—*has* plus the base form of a verb—and that an adverb may be placed between the two parts.
- Have students circle the simple past verbs and underline the present perfect verbs.
- Go over the answers with the class.

ANSWER KEY

1. Josh has received positive performance reviews for the past three years at his company.
2. He has shown good leadership skills, and he has managed his time carefully.
3. He has always gotten along well with his coworkers, and he has developed good communication skills.
4. Last year, Kara attended several workshops for management and computer skills, but she hasn't finished all of her training yet.
5. She has also maintained her qualifications for her job. She has worked hard at the company.
6. She got a management certification and received a promotion last year.

EXPANSION ACTIVITY: My job performance

- Tell students that they will be writing a job performance review about themselves. If they do not currently have jobs, they can write about a job they had in the past or a job they hope to have in the future.
- Model the activity by stating three true qualities of your own job performance (e.g., *I am very punctual. I have always started class on time. I attended three workshops last year. I think I have good leadership skills. My coworkers often ask me to lead the faculty meetings.*).
- Have students write about three qualities of their job performance.
- Call on individual students to read their qualities to the class.

CULTURE NOTE

Although it may be hard for students from some cultures to show pride in their accomplishments, it is an important skill to have in the American workplace. Often job applicants and workers have to explain their job experience and personal qualities in positive terms.

GRAMMAR CHART: Simple Past and Present Perfect Review

- Go over the information and the usage notes in the chart.
- Read aloud the sample sentences in the chart and have students repeat.

CHART EXPANSION ACTIVITY: Comparing simple past and present perfect

- Ask students why items 1–3 in Activity 1 are in present perfect tense and why items are 4–6 are in past tense. Elicit the answer: in the first three items, you do not know the exact time the action took place, or the action is still true; but in the last three items, a specific time is given and the action has ended.
- Model the activity by writing the sentence for item 1 on the board: *Josh has received positive performance reviews for the past three years at his company.* Rewrite the sentence using simple past: *Josh received positive performance reviews in 2005, 2006, and 2007.*
- Have students rewrite the sentence in Activity 1. Explain that they should use the simple past for items 1–3 and present perfect for items 4–6.
- Walk around to monitor the activity and provide help as needed.
- Put students in small groups to read their sentences.

4 COMPLETE. Chris is writing to his supervisor about his team. Circle the correct form of the verb.

- Go over the directions.
- Read item 1 to the class. Elicit reasons why *got* is the correct answer.
- Have students circle the correct words.
- Put students in pairs to compare their answers.
- Go over the answers with the class.

ANSWER KEY

1. got; 2. has maintained; 3. has attended;
4. hasn't gotten along; 5. received; 6. hasn't developed

BIG PICTURE GRAMMAR EXPANSION ACTIVITY: Simple Past or Present Perfect

- Photocopy and distribute Worksheet 6: *Simple Past or Present Perfect.*
- Put the transparency for Unit 2 on the OHP or have students look at the Big Picture on page 24.
- Go over the directions.
- Have students complete the worksheet.
- Put students in pairs to compare answers.
- Go over the answers with the class.

WORKSHEET ANSWER KEY

1. has gotten, showed; **2.** pulled together, has met; **3.** has left, has already asked; **4.** thought, has not completed; **5.** has attended, has shown

5 WHAT ABOUT YOU? Write sentences about you. Use time expressions from the chart above and the verbs below.

- Go over the directions and the example.
- Model the activity using item 1. Use information about when you attended school. Write on the board: *I have worked at this school since _____.*
- Have students write their sentences.
- Walk around to monitor the activity and provide help as needed.
- Put students in small groups to read their sentences.

ACADEMIC CONNECTION: Past participles

- Point out that the perfect tense uses past participles which students may have learned as part of a verb chart, and that many past participles are irregular.
- Have students review a verb chart of irregular verbs.
- Check comprehension by saying the base form of an irregular verb and asking for the past participle (e.g., *give—given, break—broken, hear—heard*).

LESSON 5: Grammar Practice Plus

OBJECTIVES

Express similarities
Read a job evaluation
Figure salary increases

GRAMMAR

Express similarities with *so*, *too*, *either*, and *neither*

COMPETENCIES

Interpret a job evaluation form
Use math to calculate salary increases

MATH/NUMERACY

Calculate salary increases

WARM-UP ACTIVITY: Comparing

- Write *so, too, either,* and *neither* on the board.
- Explain that these words are used to compare two things.
- Write on the board *New York City and* (the name of the city or town where you are teaching).
- Compare the places using *so* (e.g., *New York City has many tall buildings, and so does* [your town].) Call on students to compare the two places using *too, either,* and *neither*.
- Write the names of two other places (countries, cities, states, etc.) and repeat the activity.

GRAMMAR CHART: Express Similarities with *So, Too, Either,* and *Neither*

- Go over the information and the usage notes in the chart.
- Read the sample sentences in the chart aloud and have students repeat.

1 MATCH the sentences.

- Go over the directions.
- Read item 1 to the class. Elicit reasons why *e* is the correct answer.
- Have students match the sentences.
- Call on students to read their answers to the class.

ANSWER KEY

1. e; **2.** c; **3.** b; **4.** d; **5.** a

CHART EXPANSION ACTIVITY: Comparing cities

- Have students compare the city where they live now with the city where they were born.
- Model the activity by writing on the board: *XX doesn't have a lot of pollution, and neither does XX.*
- Elicit a question about the sentence from a more advanced student (e.g., *Was there ever pollution in XX?*).
- Answer the question.
- Have students write four comparisons between the cities using the words *so, too, either,* and *neither*.
- Put students in pairs to read and ask questions about the sentences.

2 COMPLETE. Read the training reports to find out which training sessions each employee has attended. Then complete the sentences with the present perfect of *take* and *so, too, either,* and *neither*.

- Go over the directions. Check comprehension by asking students to define *training report*. If students do not know the definition, define it for them.

- Go over the types of training sessions in the first box. Ask: *Where do you think Ana, Lorenzo, and Donna work?* Elicit the correct answer: *A hospital or medical facility.*
- Have students complete the sentences.
- Go over the answers with the class.

COMMUNITY CONNECTION: Types of training workshops

- List the four training workshops from Activity 2 on the board—*Computer Skills, Patient Records Training, Benefits and Insurance,*and *Teams that Work*.
- Put students into small groups. Tell them that they will be researching each of the four workshops in greater detail.
- Have students research the four different workshops by calling or emailing a local hospital to see if they offer similar workshops for their employees, or have them search on the Internet for the workshop name + *workshop* (e.g., *patient records training workshop*).
- Call on students to tell the class what they found out.

ANSWER KEY

1. Ana has taken the Computer Skills session, and so has Donna.
2. Ana hasn't taken the Patient Records Training yet, and neither has Donna.
3. Lorenzo has taken the Benefits and Insurance class, and Ana has, too.
4. Donna hasn't taken Teams that Work, and Lorenzo and Ana haven't, either.

3 TALK. Change the sentences in Activity 2 into the simple past with a partner. Use simple past time expressions.

- Go over the directions and the example.
- Put students in pairs.

- Have each pair change the sentences in Activity 2 into sentences with the simple past tense.
- Walk around to monitor the activity and provide help as needed.
- Go over the answers with the class.

ANSWER KEY

1. Ana took the Computer Skills session last month, and so did Donna.
2. Ana didn't take the Patient Records Training, and neither did Donna.
3. Lorenzo took the Benefits and Insurance class, and Ana did, too.
4. Donna didn't take Teams that Work, and Lorenzo and Ana didn't, either.

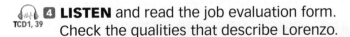

4 LISTEN and read the job evaluation form. Check the qualities that describe Lorenzo.
TCD1, 39

- Go over the directions. Emphasize to students that they are only checking the correct column. They do not need to write anything in the first column.
- Read the first exchange aloud or play it on the CD. Stop and direct students' attention to the example in the chart.
- Continue to read the sentences aloud or to play the CD as students check the qualities.
- Go over the answers with the class.

5 LISTEN again. Write the comments in the form in Activity 4.
TCD1, 39

- Go over the directions.
- Read the first exchange aloud or play it on the CD. Stop and direct students' attention to the example comment in the chart.
- Continue to read the sentences aloud or to play the CD as students write comments.
- Put students into small groups to compare answers.
- Go over the answers with the class.

LISTENING SCRIPT
Lesson 5, Activities 4 and 5

A: Lorenzo, you've done a great job here since you came to the company.

B: Thank you very much. I've worked hard and tried to manage my time well.

A: Well, you really have. In fact, your time management meets expectations nicely. Let's take a look at your evaluation form.

B: Okay.

A: You've shown good leadership skills, and you meet expectations there. Maybe you can attend a workshop on leadership.

B: Good idea. I'll look into it.

A: Great . . . especially because your teamwork has exceeded expectations. You really get along well with others and are very helpful. Your communication skills are great. They exceed expectations, too.

B: Wonderful! It's really important to me to work well with my coworkers and talk about problems.

A: You do a good job. There's one area, though, that could use improvement.

B: Okay . . . ?

A: I think your preparation has been below expectations. You do a very good job working with everyone, but you need to do a better job at pulling together materials before you need them.

B: Okay. I'll try to work on that.

ANSWER KEY

Area	Exceeds Expectations	Meets Expectations	Below Expectations
Time Management Comments: *manages time nicely*		✓	
Leadership Comments: *could attend a workshop on leadership*		✓	
Teamwork Comments: *really gets along with others and is very helpful*	✓		
Communication Comments: *great*	✓		
Preparation Comments: *should pull together materials before he needs them*			✓

EXPANSION ACTIVITY: An emotional time

- Explain that job evaluations can be very stressful because very few people like to be criticized even when the criticism is supposed to be helpful. Write *Lorenzo* and *Lorenzo's supervisor* on the board and brainstorm ideas about how both people might be feeling during the evaluation.

- Put students into pairs. Have them role-play the conversation in a way that emphasizes each person's feelings.

6 WRITE. Read about Lorenzo's coworkers. Then compare Lorenzo's performance to theirs by writing sentences with *so, too, either,* or *neither.*

- Go over the directions and the example. Point out that more than one answer can be correct. Write the example on the board and elicit another way to write the sentence: *Silvia has managed her time well, and Lorenzo has, too.*

- Have students write the sentences.

- Walk around to monitor the activity and provide help as needed.

- Ask five students to each write a sentence on the board. Correct the sentences as needed. Ask if any student wrote a sentence in a different way.

ANSWER KEY

1. Silvia has managed her time well, and so has Lorenzo.

2. Thomas has not been very prepared, and neither has Lorenzo.

3. Donna has developed good communication skills, and so has Lorenzo.

4. Luke has shown good leadership skills, and Lorenzo has, too.

5. Jenny has shown very good teamwork, and so has Lorenzo.

MATH: Figuring Salary Increases

A. READ. A salary increase is a raise in pay. It is usually a percentage of the current salary. Read the steps for figuring salary increases.

- Be sure students understand the explanation of a salary increase.
- Have students read the information about how to figure salary increases or read it aloud to the class.

B. FIGURE the new salaries with a partner.

- Go over the directions.
- Do the first item with the class. Ask: *What is Angela's salary? What is her earned increase? What's her new salary?* As students give you the answers, write them on the board: *22,000 x .03 = 660. $22,000 + $660 = $22,660. New salary = $22,660.*
- Put students in pairs to figure out the salaries.
- Call on students to read the new salaries.

ANSWER KEY

1. $22,660; **2.** $18,900; **3.** $20,800;
4. $26,500; **5.** $18,190

BIG PICTURE LISTENING EXPANSION ACTIVITY: How much?

- Have the students look at the Big Picture in Activity 1, or put the transparency for Unit 2 on the OHP.
- Dictate the sentences below.
    1. *Donna makes $63,000. She earned a 3% raise.*
    2. *Lorenzo makes $75,000. He earned a 7% raise.*
    3. *Luke makes $60,500. He earned a 5% raise.*
- Put students into pairs to compare their sentences.
- Have each pair figure out the new salary for each person.
- Go over the answers with the class ($64,890, $80,250, $63,525).

LESSON 6: Reading

WARM-UP ACTIVITY: Suffixes

- Check comprehension by asking students what suffixes are. Elicit answers.
- Put students into pairs to brainstorm as many suffixes as they can in three minutes.
- Combine pairs into small groups. Have students compare their lists of suffixes.
- Have each group write their list on the board.

1 THINK ABOUT IT. Discuss these questions in a group.

- Go over the directions.
- Put students in small groups to discuss the questions.
- Call on students to tell the class about some of the qualities they discussed. Write the qualities on the board.

2 BEFORE YOU READ.

A. SCAN. Look at the first paragraph of the article on the next page. Scan and underline the job Marsha and Felix tried to get.

- Direct students' attention to the Reading Strategy Summary. Explain what it means to scan a passage. Elicit times when scanning is a useful reading strategy: *looking up a number in the phone book, looking for the answer on a test, looking for an office number on a building directory*, etc.
- Go over the directions.
- Have students scan for the job.
- Go over the answer with the class.

B. SCAN again. Look at the whole article. Scan for adjectives that end with *-able* and *-ive*. Circle them. Underline the nouns and pronouns these adjectives describe.

- Direct students' attention to the Reading Focus box.

- Read the box aloud and ask students for other examples of adjectives ending in *-able* or *-ive* (e.g., *comfortable, manageable, extensive, selective*).

- Go over the directions.

- Have students scan the article for words ending in *-able* and *-ive*.

- Go over the answers with the class (*extensive, selective*).

ANSWER KEY

Marsha – Marsha seems very (likeable.) She'd have a great "on air" personality because she's quite (communicative,) too. She seems (capable,) but some of her job skills are (questionable.) She has never been a reporter, so we can't be sure that her work will be (suitable.) When I followed up with her references, I learned some (valuable) information. Her last employer did not think Marsha was (dependable.) Neither did her college professor. I'm not sure she'll be able to meet our deadlines, but she is ready to accept assignments starting immediately. Overall, I think our viewers would really like her youthfulness and enthusiasm, but hiring her could be a risk.

Felix – Felix has worked with a news station before. He has proven that he can complete projects on time. After I saw some of his broadcasts, I knew his work was (impressive.) However, Felix seemed a bit (aggressive) to me, so he might not be (sensitive) enough to interview people well. His last employer described him as (reliable) and (creative,) but also said that he asked for a lot of days off. Also, it seems that some co-workers weren't (comfortable) around him. It sounds like sometimes he can be (uncooperative) and (disagreeable.) Overall, I think he would a good job on camera, but he may be difficult to work with off camera.

EXPANSION ACTIVITY: Notice the tense

- Have students scan the article again. This time ask them to draw a rectangle around present perfect verbs (*has never been, has worked, has proven*).

- Put students in small groups to discuss why the present perfect was used.

- Elicit verbs and reasons from the class.

3 READ the article and think about what each word ending in *-able* or *-ive* means.

- Go over the directions.

- Have students read the article.

- Check comprehension by asking the class: *What are some of Marsha's qualities? What are some of Felix's qualities? Who do you think will get hired? Why?* Elicit answers.

4 AFTER YOU READ.

A. DISCUSS. Work with a partner. Write adjectives from the reading that describe Marsha and Felix. Discuss what each word means. Next to each adjective you write, put a (+) if you think the adjective is a positive quality or a (–) if you think it is a negative quality.

- Go over the directions and the words in the box.

- Direct students' attention to the word *likeable* in the second line of the notes on Marsha. Ask: *Is* likeable *a positive or a negative quality?* Have students write *likeable* + on the left side of the chart.

- Put students in pairs to complete the chart.

- Go over the answers with the class.

CULTURE NOTE

While the word *aggressive* usually has a negative connotation, it can be a positive quality in some careers. For example, some people may want an aggressive lawyer or an aggressive salesperson. Explain why it might be a negative characteristic for some reporting jobs.

B. TALK with your classmates and compare Felix and Marsha. What qualities do they both have? How are they different? Which candidate would you hire for TV 10 News?

- Go over the questions.
- Put students in small groups to discuss the questions.
- Elicit ideas from the class.

EXPANSION ACTIVITY: Would you be a good reporter?

- Ask students to raise their hands if they think they would be a good reporter on the local news.
- Ask a few students to explain why they would like the job or why they would not be good at the job.
- Tell students that they, too, have applied for the job at TV 10. Have them write notes that Carol may have written about their interview (e.g., *Javier seems very likeable. However, he also seems a little shy.*).
- Put students in pairs to read their notes aloud.

ACADEMIC CONNECTION: Prefixes and suffixes

- Explain to the class that one way to increase their vocabulary quickly is to learn common prefixes and suffixes.
- Write *sub-* on the board and elicit words that begin with this prefix (e.g., *subway, submarine, submerge*). Ask the students what they think *sub-* means (*under*).
- Have students write words that use the following common prefixes and suffixes: *anti-, mis-, semi-, trans-, un-, -less, -ful, -able, -ive,* and *-est.*
- Put students in small groups to compare their answers.

LESSON 7: Writing

OBJECTIVES

List your best personal skills
Use persuasive writing

WRITING FOCUS

Persuasive writing

COMPETENCIES

Write about job qualities
Use persuasive writing for career
  advancements

WARM-UP ACTIVITY: Persuade me

- Write on the board: *to convince people to change their mind about a course of action or a belief usually by giving good reasons why they should do so*.
- Ask students what word the definition defines. Elicit the answer *persuade.*
- Say that you are thinking about having everyone write a five-page essay for tomorrow's class. Have the class persuade you not to give the assignment.

❶ THINK ABOUT IT. What is your ideal job? Why would you be good at that job? What would be difficult about the job for you?

- Go over the directions.
- Direct students' attention to the questions.
- Elicit answers to the questions.

❷ BEFORE YOU WRITE.

A. READ the paragraph below. Juanita is a receptionist. She has asked her boss for a raise, so she must tell why she deserves one. Underline the adjectives that describe her qualities.

- Go over the directions.

- Read the first paragraph of Juanita's response aloud. Ask: *Which adjectives should you underline?* Elicit the response: *sensitive* and *dependable.*
- Have students read the article and underline the adjectives.
- Go over the answers by asking individual students to read a sentence from the paragraph. After they read, they should say which word should be underlined.

ANSWER KEY

Underline: sensitive, dependable, capable, and valuable.

B. BRAINSTORM. Make a list of your best personal qualities and skills. Then share your ideas with a partner.

- Review the strategy of brainstorming by asking students to define the term. If no one can define it, explain the strategy.
- Have students list their best personal qualities and skills.
- Put students in pairs to compare lists.
- Call on students to tell the class a few of their qualities or skills.

EXPANSION ACTIVITY: Things to work on

- Have students list three of their worst qualities (e.g., *sometimes unprepared, not good with details, not punctual*).
- Put students in small groups to ask for advice on how they can improve their worst qualities.

C. WRITE. Think about your own job or a job that you would like to have. Reread your list of personal qualities or skills. Which ones would help the most at this job? Write them in the chart, and give a persuasive detail about each one. Add more if needed.

- Direct students' attention to the Writing Focus box.
- Ask students what the goal of persuasive writing is.
- Read the information in the box to the class.
- Check comprehension by asking students to persuade you to end class early.
- Go over the directions and example.
- Have students fill in the chart.
- Walk around and ask questions about students' answers.

3 WRITE. Imagine that you will ask for a raise or promotion at work, or that you are applying for a job you would like to have. Write a letter that tells why you should get the raise or the promotion or why your personal qualities will be useful at the job. Give persuasive details, and give reasons.

- Go over the directions.
- Point out that the example sentence states both the person's good qualities and how those qualities will be useful for the job.
- Have students write persuasive letters.

4 AFTER YOU WRITE.

A. READ. Work with a partner. Read each other's letter and find the persuasive words and details. Discuss how you could each make your letters more persuasive.

- Go over the directions.
- Put students into pairs and have them read and comment on each other's paragraphs.
- Walk around and ask questions about students' answers.

B. EDIT your letter for spelling and grammar errors.

- Go over the directions and the questions.
- Have students edit their partner's paper, using the questions.

C. REWRITE your letter with corrections.

ACADEMIC NOTE

Many colleges have free drop-in writing labs where students can get help organizing and editing their papers. Most writing labs are connected to the English department or tutorial center.

ACADEMIC CONNECTION: Where can you find help?

- Have students research writing lab options by asking the English department at your school or by searching on the school's website.
- Ask students to know the lab hours and location by the next class.

Career Connection

WARM-UP ACTIVITY: Rank it

- Write on the board: *medical insurance, dental insurance, vision insurance, vacation time, retirement benefits*.
- Put students in small groups.
- Have each group discuss what each benefit on the board is. Ask them to rank the benefits in order of importance, with 1 being most important and 5 being least important. Explain that the group members must agree on their final ranking so that they should try to persuade each other if they disagree.
- Ask each group to write their ranking order on the board.
- Compare ranking orders.

1 THINK ABOUT IT. What are *benefits*? What is an *annual benefit review*? Have you ever had an annual benefit review? What information did you receive?

- Go over the directions and the questions.
- Put students in small groups to discuss the questions.
- Check comprehension by asking the class to list examples of benefits.

2 READ this employee's annual benefit review from human resources. As you read, circle the dates and percentages in the review.

- Go over the directions.
- Point out that some words are defined at the bottom of the review.
- Have students read the annual benefit review and circle the dates and percentages in the review.
- Go over the answers with the class.

ANSWER KEY

Human Resources Annual Benefit Review 2008
Date: (January 10, 2009)
Employee: Delgado, Josef
Department: Custodial
Date of Hire: (March 1, 2007)
Title: Janitor I

Health Benefits
Your medical and dental benefits began on (June 1, 2007.)

Retirement Benefits
You became eligible for retirement benefits on (March 1, 2008.) You currently contribute (10%) of your pay each month to your retirement fund. We match (50%) of your contributions. You will become (40%) vested in your retirement fund on (March 1, 2009.)

Vacation Benefits
You used 7 vacation days in (August 2008.) You must use your remaining 3 vacation days for 2008 before (March 1, 2009.) After that date, you will lose any vacation days you have left for 2008, and you will begin to use your 10 vacation days for 2009.

3 TALK with a partner. Answer the questions. Use Josef's benefit review and the information in the charts above to help you.

- Go over the directions.
- Put students in pairs to answer the questions.
- Walk around to monitor the activity and provide help as needed.
- Call on three students to answer the questions.

4 TALK with a partner or a group. Josef is applying to be a custodial supervisor at another company. The new job offers a higher salary, but fewer benefits. What benefits do you think he should look for? Why? Should he take the new job if he will lose some of his benefits?

- Go over the directions.
- Put students in small groups to discuss the questions.
- Ask each group to share their answers with the class.

5 WHAT ABOUT YOU? Work in a group. Discuss the questions.

- Go over the directions and the questions.
- Put students in small groups to discuss their answers.
- Call on students to share their answers with the class.

COMMUNITY CONNECTION: Survey

- Write on the board:

  Do you get benefits at work?

  What benefits do you get?

  Are you happy with your benefits? Why or why not?

  Have you had an annual benefit review?

- Have students copy the questions onto a piece of paper.
- Explain that the students should ask three people who have jobs these questions.
- Put students in small groups during the next class to compare answers.

CHECK YOUR PROGRESS!

- Have students circle the correct answers.
- Review the answers or have students check the unit to see if each answer is right or wrong.
- Have students total their correct answers and fill in the chart at the bottom of the page.
- Have students create a learning plan and/or set learning goals.

UNIT 3 That's Entertainment!

Unit Overview

LESSON	OBJECTIVES	STUDENT BOOK	WORKBOOK
1 Grammar and Vocabulary 1	Go out on a date. Use past perfect tense.	p. 38	p. 34
2 Grammar Practice Plus	Talk about a museum visit. Read a vacation journal.	p. 40	p. 35
3 Listening and Conversation	Read a television schedule. Use compound nouns vs. noun phrases.	p. 42	p. 36
4 Grammar and Vocabulary 2	Discuss surprising events. Use past perfect continuous.	p. 44	p. 38
5 Grammar Practice Plus	Use so + adjective. Read a description from a TV magazine. Calculate sales tax.	p. 46	p. 39
6 Reading	Sequence events. Read a biography.	p. 48	p. 40–41
7 Writing	Compare then and now. Complete a timeline. Write an autobiography.	p. 50	p. 42–43
• Career Connection	Learn job duties.	p. 52	p. 44
• Check Your Progress	Monitor progress.	p. 53	p. 46–47

Reading/Writing Strategies

- Scan for dates and verb forms to identify the order of events.
- Use graphic organizers to organize information before writing.

Connection Activities

LESSON	TYPE	SKILL DEVELOPMENT
1	Community	Research local events
2	Academic	Monitor your English
3	Community	Research places to see local entertainment
4	Community	Survey people on expressions of surprise and sympathy
5	Academic	Identify non-continuous verbs
6	Community	Research a U.S. politician
7	Academic	Use an encyclopedia
Career Connection	Community	Survey people about their job responsibilities

WORKSHEET #/FOCUS	TITLE	TEACHER'S EDITION
7. Graphic Organizer	Participle Review	p. 311
8. Writing	What did they do before?	p. 312
9. Reading	What a terrible day!	p. 313

LESSON 1: Grammar and Vocabulary

OBJECTIVES

Go out on a date
Use past perfect tense

VOCABULARY

auditorium	film festival
box office	fortunately
concert hall	hostess
debut performance	street vendor
reservation	unfortunately
events brochure	usher

GRAMMAR

Past perfect

COMPETENCY

Talk about leisure activities

WARM-UP ACTIVITY: Unit opener

- Have students open their books to page 38 and cover up the writing under the first row of pictures.
- Say *This is a story about Lucy and Jamie. What do you think happened on their date?*
- Elicit answers from students.
- Have students cover up the writing in the second row of pictures. Ask: *Where did they go next? What happened?* Elicit answers.

ACADEMIC NOTE

Previewing any type of assignment by looking at the pictures, charts, and tables enables readers to understand more while they are reading. After the warm-up activity, you may want to remind students that this type of previewing is an excellent reading strategy.

TCD1, 40 SCD10
1 GRAMMAR PICTURE DICTIONARY. Did Jamie and Lucy have a nice date? Listen and read.

- Have students open their books and look at the pictures. Ask: *What do you see?* Write all the words the students say on the board.
- Say the sentences or play the CD and have students repeat.
- Call on students and ask *Why didn't Lucy and Jamie see a movie? Why was the usher annoyed? Why had the hostess given their table to someone else?*

EXPANSION ACTIVITY: What do you see?

- Put students into groups of three or four.
- Have each group list 15 to 20 items that they see in the pictures on page 38.
- Have each group write their lists on the board.

2 READ the sentences in Activity 1 with a partner.

- Put students in pairs to read the sentences.
- Call on students to read the sentences to the class.

3 NOTICE THE GRAMMAR. Circle *had* + the past participle. Underline the words *before, when, by the time,* and *already*.

- Go over the directions and the example.
- Have students circle *had* + the past participle and underline the words *before, by the time,* and *already*.

GRAMMAR CHART: Past Perfect

- Direct students' attention to the chart or project the transparency or CD.

- Go over the information in the chart and the usage notes. Read the sentences, pausing to have students repeat.

GRAMMAR NOTE

You may want to point out to students that the adverb *already* is placed between *had* and the past participle. The phrases *before* and *by the time* are placed in front of the simple past tense clause.

CHART EXPANSION ACTIVITY: What did you do?

- Write on the board six things you did yesterday and the time you did them (e.g., *7:00 – made my lunch, 8:00 – drove to school*).

- Ask a more advanced student to combine two of your activities into one sentence using the past perfect with the simple past (e.g., *You had made your lunch before you drove to school.*).

- Have students write six activities they did yesterday on a piece of paper.

- Put students in pairs and have them exchange papers.

- Have each student write three sentences combining two of the activities into one sentence.

- Walk around to monitor the activity and provide help as needed.

❹ COMPLETE the sentences with the past perfect form of the verbs in parentheses. Then read the sentences with a partner.

- Go over the directions.

- Read item 1 to the class. Elicit reasons why *had closed* is the correct answer.

- Have students write the correct past perfect form of the verbs.

- Put students in pairs to compare their answers.

- Go over the answers with the class.

EXPANSION ACTIVITY: Reviewing past participles

- Put students in groups.
- Photocopy and distribute Worksheet 7: *Reviewing Past Participles.*
- Have each group complete the worksheet by writing the correct past participle and five sentences.
- Go over the answers to the first section of the worksheet with the class.
- Have each group write their sentences and questions on the board. Correct any errors as a class.

WORKSHEET ANSWER KEY

1. made; **2.** left; **3.** liked; **4.** driven; **5.** eaten; **6.** done; **7.** learned; **8.** told; **9.** drunk; **10.** given; **11.** came; **12.** forgotten; **13.** bought; **14.** written; **15.** walked

5 WHAT ABOUT YOU? What did you do for fun last week? Tell a partner. Had you done the activity before? Practice asking your partner.

- Go over the directions and the questions.
- Direct students' attention to the example. Ask two students to read the example aloud.
- Put students in pairs to discuss their answers.
- Call on students to share their answers with the class.

COMMUNITY CONNECTION: What's happening this weekend?

- Have students research weekend events happening in your city or town. They can look in the local paper, at flyers on community bulletin boards, or on local events websites.
- Have students write about the weekend events they researched.
- Call on students to tell the class what they found out. Write the options on the board.

LESSON 2: Grammar Practice Plus

OBJECTIVES

Talk about a museum visit
Read a vacation journal

VOCABULARY

amusement park   natural history
concert hall   museum
dinosaur exhibit   sidewalk café
modern art museum   theater

GRAMMAR

Use the past perfect with *never*

COMPETENCY

Draw conclusions based on evidence

WARM-UP ACTIVITY: What do you see?

- Put students into groups of three or four.
- Have each group list 15–20 items that they see in the picture on page 40.
- Have each group write their lists on the board.

❶ TALK about the picture. What are the people doing? Use the words in the vocabulary box below. What do you think happened before each of these things?

- Direct students' attention to the vocabulary box. Check comprehension by asking students what each word or phrase means. Elicit the correct definitions.
- Go over the directions and the example. Explain that they should make up what had happened before. The picture itself does not give any clues to the answers.

- Put students in pairs to talk about the picture. Have them discuss what things might have happened before other things happened.
- Walk around to monitor the activity and provide help as needed.
- Elicit answers from the class.

TCD1, 41 **❷ LISTEN** to the statements about the people in Activity 1 and write the number next to the names below.

- Go over the Grammar Professor note. Ask a few of the more advanced students for examples of things they had never done before they moved to the U.S. (e.g., *I had never eaten an avocado before I came to the U.S.*).
- Go over the directions.
- Say the sentences or play the CD and have the students write the numbers next to the names.
- Go over the answers with the class.

TCD1, 41 **LISTENING SCRIPT**
Lesson 2, Activity 2

1. The hostess had already given Uma and Rajiv menus before the server came to the table.
2. Tom and Tammy had studied dinosaurs in school before they went to the Natural History Museum.
3. Joey had never ridden a roller coaster before.
4. Andy and Amy had already picked up their tickets at the box office before they arrived at the concert hall.
5. Mark and Jill had bought tickets to the play before it sold out.
6. Tony, the usher, was still standing at the door of the auditorium because some people hadn't sat down yet.
7. Before she went to the modern art museum, Jane had already read about the exhibit in her events brochure.

BIG PICTURE CONVERSATION/ VOCABULARY EXPANSION ACTIVITY: What did they do before?

- Have the students look at the Big Picture in Activity 1, or put the transparency for Unit 3 on the OHP.
- Photocopy and distribute Worksheet 8: *What did they do before?*
- Model the activity. Choose one character from the picture and say what he or she might have been doing before each of the things in the picture (e.g., *Jane had met a friend for coffee.*). Point out that you don't actually know what Jane did, but you are guessing.
- Have students complete the worksheet.
- Walk around to monitor the activity and provide help as needed.
- Put students in pair or groups to compare their sentences.

3 **TALK** with a partner about the people in the picture. Find three things you think had never happened before.

- Go over the directions and the example.
- Put students in pairs to talk about the picture. Have them find three things they think had never happened before.
- Call on students to share their answers with the class.

4 **READ.** Henry won $1,000 and a trip to his favorite city. He took the trip last weekend. He checked into a luxury hotel Friday night. On Saturday night, he wrote about how he had spent his day. Read his journal and underline the things he did for the first time.

- Go over the directions.
- Have students underline the things Henry did for the first time.
- Put students in pairs to compare their answers.
- Go over the answers with the class.

5 **WRITE** five sentences about what Henry did. Look at the schedule in Activity 4.

- Go over the directions and the example.
- Have students do the activity.
- Ask students to read one of their sentences to the class.

6 WHAT ABOUT YOU? Tell a partner which things you had or hadn't done before you took this English course.

- Go over the directions and the questions.
- Direct students' attention to the example. Ask a student to read the example aloud.
- Put students in pairs to discuss their answers.
- Call on students to share their answers with the class.

ACADEMIC CONNECTION: Monitoring your English

- Tell the class that monitoring their English progress will help them stay motivated. If they feel their English is not improving, they may feel discouraged and not try as hard in the future.
- Model the activity by asking a few of the more advanced students for one thing they hadn't done before they started this class (e.g., *hadn't met people from other countries, didn't know how to use present perfect tense correctly,* etc.).
- Have students write 10 things they hadn't done before starting your class.
- Put students in pairs to compare their lists.
- Call on students to read their lists aloud to the class.

LESSON 3: Listening and Conversation

WARM-UP ACTIVITY: Talking about tickets

- Write on the board:
1. *When was the last time you bought tickets to an event? What was the event?* Give an example answer by discussing the last time you bought tickets.
2. *When was the last time you wanted to go to an event but it was sold out? What was the event?* Give an example answer.
3. *Have you ever lost tickets? If yes, what happened?* Give an example answer.
- Put students into groups to discuss the questions.
- Elicit answers from individual students.

 1 LISTEN to the conversation. Then listen to a question. Fill in the correct answer. Replay each item if necessary.
TCD1,42–47

- Direct students' attention to the activity and the fill-in circles.
- Point out that unlike Activity 1 in Lesson 3 of Units 1 and 2, for this listening activity students will need to listen for the best next sentence. Write on the board,

Man: *How are you?*
Woman:
   A. *I went shopping. B. OK. And you? C. It's raining.* Ask students which sentence would be the best sentence to follow the question. Elicit the correct answer (*B*).
- Play the CD and have students fill in the correct circle for each item.
- If needed, replay the CD after each item.
- Put students in pairs to compare answers.
- Go over the answers with the class.

LISTENING SCRIPT
Lesson 3, Activity 1
TCD1, 42–47

1. *A:* What did you think of the symphony's debut performance?
   B: I didn't attend the concert. By the time I arrived at the box office, the tickets had sold out.
   Which is the best response?
   A. Oh, that's too bad.
   B. Well, that's good news.
   C. Did you buy the tickets?

2. *A:* You know, I think I lost my concert tickets. I can't find them anywhere.
   B: Did you look inside the events brochure? I saw you put the tickets in the brochure.
   Which is the best response?
   A. There's nothing I want to see in that brochure.
   B. That's a good idea. I hadn't thought of looking there.
   C. I can't figure out where I put them.

3. *A:* Would you like to go to the film festival instead of renting a movie?
   B: Great idea! Can you still get tickets?
   Which is the best response?
   A. No, I sold my tickets online.
   B. I'll call the box office to find out.
   C. Okay, I'll go to the video store.

4. *A:* Mike was great in the Shakespeare
performance last night.

B: I didn't know he was an actor! Was that the
first time you'd seen him in a play?

Which is the best response?

A. No, I've read a lot of Shakespeare plays.

B. No, I've seen him play a lot of games.

C. Yes, it was. I had never seen him perform
before.

5. *A:* Would you like to go to the new Italian
restaurant for dinner tonight?

B: That sounds great. What time should we go?

Which is the best response?

A. I'll make a reservation for seven o'clock.

B. I'll talk to the usher after the show.

C. We should get there in time.

6. *A:* I took my kids to the Natural History Museum
last week.

B: That sounds great. What did you see?

Which is the best response?

A. We saw a lot of interesting modern art.

B. We saw an incredible dinosaur exhibit.

C. We heard a very nice symphony orchestra.

ANSWER KEY

1. A; **2.** B; **3.** B; **4.** C; **5.** A; **6.** B

---

2 LISTEN. Look at a TV schedule from the
newspaper. Then listen to a couple talk
about what TV shows to watch tonight. Fill
in the times that you hear.

- Go over the directions and the TV schedule.
  Point out where students need to write the
  time each show starts.
- Play the CD and have students write the time
  of the activities.
- Replay the CD if necessary.
- Elicit the correct answers from the students.

LISTENING SCRIPT
Lesson 3, Activity 2

TCD1, 48

A: Could you hand me the entertainment section
of the newspaper, please?

B: Here it is. Are we still going out tonight?

A: That's what we'd planned, right?

B: Yes, but it's 6:00 now, and we'd also talked
about staying home. Is there anything
interesting on TV tonight?

A: Hmm. There's a game show on at 7:00. What
about that?

B: Nah. You can watch it if you want.

A: Do you want to watch a history program?
There's one called the *History of the American
West* at 8:00.

B: Not really. What about that reality show I
was watching a few weeks ago . . . what's
it called . . . something about people sleep-
walking . . . ? It seemed interesting.

A: Yeah, that's on later. It's called *The Sleepover
House*! Boring!

B: Very funny. Are there any comedy shows on
tonight?

A: *Fun Times with Mr. Doozy* makes its debut
tonight at 8:30.

B: Oh, I've heard about that show. Mr. Doozy is
a children's program. I don't want to watch a
kids' show!

A: Okay. What about a drama? *Crime Scene
Detectives* is on at 9:00.

B: Forget it. Last week when I was watching it,
I realized I'd already seen that one before. It
wasn't new—it was a rerun. Ugh!

ANSWER KEY

Channel 2	Win Big Money!	7:00 p.m.
Channel 3	Crime Scene Detectives	9:00 p.m.
Channel 4	Fun Times with Mr. Doozy	8:30 p.m.
Channel 4	History of the American West	8:00 p.m.
Channel 5	Sleepover House	10:00 p.m.

🎧 **3 LISTEN** to the couple continue their
conversation. Read the movie listing and fill
in the missing information.

- Go over the directions and the movie schedule.
  Point out that this time students need to write
  either the time or the name of the movie. Play
  the CD and have students write the time or
  name of the activities.
- Replay the CD if necessary.
- Go over the answers with the class.

ANSWER KEY

Theater 1	*Jaws*	7:10 p.m.
Theater 2	*The Terminator*	10:20 p.m.
Theater 3	*E.T.*	8:10 p.m.
Theater 4	*You've Got Mail*	8:15 p.m.
Theater 5	*The Lion King*	2:20 p.m.

🎧 **4 LISTEN** to the conversation again. Read
the statements and check *True* or *False*.

- Go over the directions.
- Read aloud or play the audio for the first
  exchange. Direct students' attention to item 1.
  Ask: *Is item 1 true or false?* Elicit the correct
  answer *(false)*.
- Play the CD and have students check *true* or
  false.
- Put students into small groups to compare
  answers.
- Elicit the correct answers from the students.

LISTENING SCRIPT
Lesson 3, Activities 3 and 4

A: Well, since you didn't like anything on TV, let's
go to the movies. They're having a film festival
at the Town Theater. Ooh, I'd love to see a
thriller. *Jaws* is playing at 7:10.

B: Ew! I can't stand films about big, scary sharks.
How about an action film?

A: Let me see...Our only choice is the *Terminator*,
but 10:20 is too late for me. We can't go to
The Lion King—it was at 2:20, so it has already
ended. Um, would you like to see *E.T.*? It's
playing at 8:10.

B: Ugh! Science fiction? No way.

A: Okay. Our last choice is *You've Got Mail* at
8:15.

B: Hmm. I don't think I've ever seen *You've Got
Mail*. Isn't that the one about the woman
and guy who met online before they met in
person?

A: Oh yeah, it's so romantic. I loved that movie.

B: All right. Let's just go!

ANSWER KEY

1. False; **2.** True; **3.** False; **4.** True; **5.** True

5 WHAT ABOUT YOU? Use the information in
the box to write sentences about things you
had never seen or places you had never been
to as a child. Use *by the time* to write about
things you had seen or been to before a certain
age. Then talk with a partner.

- Direct students' attention to the vocabulary
  box. Check comprehension by asking students
  to give you an example of each word or phrase.
- Go over the directions and the examples.
- Have students write their sentences about
  things they had never seen or places they had
  never been to before a certain age.
- Walk around to monitor the activity and
  provide help as needed.
- Put students in small groups to read their
  sentences aloud.

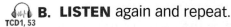

🎧 **6 LISTEN** to the conversation. Then practice with a partner.
TCD1, 50
SCD11

- Direct students' attention to the picture. Ask questions: *Who do you see? What's happening?*
- Play the CD or read the conversation as students follow along silently.
- Play the CD or read the conversation again and have students repeat along.
- Ask, *Did the man go to the film festival? What did the man do instead? Did he like the museum?*
- Put students in pairs to practice the conversation.

7 PRACTICE the conversation from Activity 6 with a partner. Use the information in the chart.

- Go over the directions.
- Model the activity. Have a more advanced student read B's lines. Model how to substitute the underlined parts of the conversation with information from the chart. Cue the student to make substitutions from the chart.
- Put students in pairs to practice the conversation, making appropriate substitutions.
- Call on students to say the conversation in front of the class.

🎧 **PRONUNCIATION: Compound Nouns vs.**
TCD1, 51 **Noun Phrases**

- Play the CD or go over the information about compound nouns and adjective plus noun phrases.

🎧 **A. LISTEN** for the stressed words in the
TCD1, 52 sentences. Circle the letter of the sentence
SCD12 you hear.

- Go over the directions.
- Play the CD or read the sentences while students listen and circle the correct stressed words in the sentences. Repeat if necessary.
- Elicit the answers from the class.
- Play the CD or read the sentences again so that students can check their understanding.

🎧 **B. LISTEN** again and repeat.
TCD1, 53

- Play the CD or read the sentences again.
- Have students repeat the sentences.

COMMUNITY CONNECTION: Reports on local places

- Write on the board: *Things to do in our city: movies, plays, concerts, nature hikes or walking tours, lectures, book readings, museum exhibits.*
- Check comprehension by asking students for an example of each activity. Ask students if they want to add any activities to the board.
- Put students in groups.
- Have each group pick a different activity from the list on the board.
- Ask each group to research their activity and to give a short report. Ask them to name three places where they could go for their activity and to give an estimate on how much it would cost.
- During the next class, have each group report on its activity.

LESSON 4: Grammar and Vocabulary

OBJECTIVES

Discuss surprising events
Use past perfect continuous

VOCABULARY

amusement park	stadium
Ferris wheel	street fair
sidewalk café	tennis match
soccer game	

GRAMMAR

Past perfect continuous

COMPETENCY

Use language to describe unexpected events

WARM-UP ACTIVITY: Preview of present perfect continuous

- Write on the board: *I had been waiting for the bus when my friend offered me a ride.*
- Draw a timeline on the board:

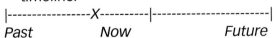

|------------------------|----------------------|

Past   *Now*   *Future*

- Ask when the action in the first clause happened. Shade in an area of the timeline between *past* and *now*. Ask when the action in the second clause happened. Mark an *X* on the timeline.

|-----------------*X*----------|----------------------|

Past   *Now*   *Future*

- Explain that present perfect continuous is used when two actions happen in the past. One action was in progress when the second action occurred.
- Elicit example sentences from several students and write them on the board.

TCD1, 54 SCD13 **❶ GRAMMAR PICTURE DICTIONARY.** Look at the pictures of some surprising events. Then read and listen to the conversations.

- Have students look at the pictures. Ask: *What do you see?*
- Play the CD or read the conversations aloud as students follow along silently.
- Call on students and ask questions about the people in the pictures: *What happened at the tennis match? Why did they leave the soccer game? Why didn't Mary go with her date to the sidewalk café? What happened to the Ferris wheel?*

❷ PRACTICE the conversations from Activity 1 with a partner.

- Go over the directions.
- Put students in pairs to read the sentences.
- Call on students to read the sentences aloud to the class.

❸ NOTICE THE GRAMMAR. Circle the past perfect continuous verb forms in the conversations above. Underline the words *when* and *for*.

- Go over the directions and the examples.
- Have students circle the past perfect continuous verb forms and underline *when* and *for*.
- Go over the answers with the class.

GRAMMAR CHART: Past Perfect Continuous

- Go over the information and the usage notes in the chart.
- You may want to read the sample sentences in the chart and have students repeat.
- Go over the information in the Grammar Professor note.

GRAMMAR NOTE

- Often past continuous is used to stress interrupted actions, and past perfect continuous is used to stress the duration of time before something happened in the past.
- If a duration of time (*for two hours, since 2005*) is used, many speakers will use the past continuous instead of the past perfect continuous.

CHART EXPANSION ACTIVITY: Creative sentences

- Put students in pairs.
- Have each pair make a list of seven activities (e.g., *work out at the gym, study English, eat an ice cream cone*).
- Model the next step by asking for one of the activities from the list (e.g., *work out at the gym*). Write a sentence using the past perfect continuous and the simple past tense (e.g., *I had been working out at the gym when I hurt my leg.*)
- Have pairs exchange lists. With their new lists, ask each pair to write seven sentences.
- Walk around the room and monitor students' progress.

4 **COMPLETE** the conversations. Use the past perfect continuous with the verbs in parentheses.

- Go over the directions.
- Direct students' attention to item 1. Read the sentences aloud. Ask: *Why is past continuous used here?* Elicit the correct answer (*They had already been sitting at their table for a long time before they got their menus.*).
- Have students complete the sentences with the past perfect continuous.
- Go over the answers with the class.

BIG PICTURE READING EXPANSION ACTIVITY: What a terrible day!

- Photocopy and distribute Worksheet 9: *What a terrible day!*
- Put the transparency for Unit 3 on the OHP or have students look at the Big Picture on page 40.
- Go over the directions.
- Have students read the story and answer the questions.
- Put students in pairs to compare answers.
- Go over the answers with the class.

5 PRACTICE the conversations in Activity 4 with a partner. Partner A, use expressions in the Conversation Strategy box to respond to Partner B.

- Go over the directions.
- Point to the Conversation Strategy box. Elicit a correct definition for *sympathy* (the feeling of being sorry for someone). Read the expressions in the strategy box and have students repeat.
- Put students in pairs to make short conversations using the sentences in Activity 4.

COMMUNITY CONNECTION: How do you express surprise and sympathy?

- Review the ways to express surprise and sympathy that were taught in Lesson 4 (*That's too bad. That's terrible. That's awful. How rude! How strange! Wow, I can't believe it. What a shame. What a waste of time.*).
- Have students survey native speakers for expressions of surprise and sympathy. Instruct students to ask five native speakers for three examples of how they express surprise and three examples of how they express sympathy.
- Call on students to tell the class what they found out. Write the expressions on the board.

LESSON 5: Grammar Practice Plus

OBJECTIVES

Use *so* + adjective
Read a description from a TV magazine
Calculate sales tax

VOCABULARY

amusement park	scary movie
cotton candy	sidewalk café
ex-boyfriend	soccer game
power	storm
racket	street fair
roller coaster	tennis match

COMPETENCIES

Talk about emotions
Use math to solve problems
Calculate sales tax

WARM-UP ACTIVITY: What does it mean?

- Direct students' attention to the vocabulary box.
- Put students in pairs. Ask students to write an example sentence for each word or phrase in the box.
- Ask each pair to write one of their sentences on the board until all the words or phrases are represented.
- Correct the sentences as needed.

1 TALK. What are these people doing? Tell a partner. Use the words in the vocabulary box below.

- Direct students' attention to the vocabulary box. Check comprehension by asking students what each word or phrase means. Elicit the correct definitions.
- Go over the directions and the example. Explain that they should use the vocabulary from the vocabulary box to answer the question.

- Put students in pairs or groups to talk about the picture. Have them discuss what the people are doing.
- Walk around to monitor the activity and provide help as needed.
- Elicit answers from the class.

 TCD1, 55 **2 LISTEN** to the conversations about the people in Activity 1. Write the number of the picture next to the correct question.

- Direct students' attention to the vocabulary box. Check comprehension by asking students what each word or phrase means. Elicit the correct definitions.
- Go over the directions.
- Play the CD and have students match the conversations with the pictures.
- Go over the answers with the class.

 TCD1, 55 **LISTENING SCRIPT**
Lesson 5, Activities 2 and 3

1. A: I gave the boys some cotton candy, but I don't think they liked it. They looked kind of sick.
   B: Well, that's because they'd been riding the roller coaster all morning at the amusement park.
   A: Oh, I see.

2. A: Hi, Suzie. Where did you go with Pete last night?
   B: We went to a great little sidewalk café.
   A: That sounds great. Did you have a good time?
   B: Well, not really. We'd only been sitting there for five minutes when it started to rain.
   A: Oh, no.

3. A: How was the street fair, Holly?
   B: Mmm. . .not so great.
   A: Really? Why?
   B: Well, I was walking around having fun, and then I saw my ex-boyfriend, Dave.
   A: That's too bad.
   B: Yeah, I know. I had been having such a good time until then.

4. A: So the boys won their soccer game?
   B: Yeah, I can't believe it.
   A: Me, neither. I know they'd been practicing really hard for the last month, but I never thought they'd win.

5. *A:* Did you win your big tennis match, Hugo?
B: No, I broke my tennis racket.
A: Really? That's too bad.
B: Yeah, and I'd been playing really well until that time. Now I have to buy a new racket.

6. *A:* Hey, Marcie. Did you hear that storm last night?
B: Yeah. My power went out. I was really scared.
A: Scared? Of a storm?
B: Well, maybe it was because I'd been watching a really scary movie on TV at the time.
A: Mmm-hmmm.

ANSWER KEY

a. 3; **b.** 1; **c.** 5; **d.** 4; **e.** 6; **f.** 2

3 WRITE. Listen again to the conversations in Activity 2. Write the answers to the questions. Tell a partner your answers.

- Play the CD again.
- Put students in pairs to answer the questions in Activity 2. Encourage students to use the past perfect continuous in their answers.
- Elicit answers from the class.

ANSWER KEY

a. Holly was upset because she ran into her ex-boyfriend.

b. The boys were sick because they had been eating cotton candy and riding the roller coaster at the amusement park all day.

c. Hugo was frustrated because he had been playing in an important tennis match when suddenly his racket broke.

d. The soccer team was happy because they had been practicing really hard, and they won their game.

e. Marcie was scared because she had been watching a really scary movie on TV when the power went out.

f. Suzie was disappointed because she and Pete had been sitting at a sidewalk café when suddenly it began to rain.

4 WRITE. Read the descriptions from a TV magazine. Then answer the questions using the past perfect continuous.

- Go over the directions.
- Have students either read the descriptions silently, or call on more advanced students to read the sentences to the class.
- Have students answer the questions using the past perfect continuous.

ANSWER KEY

Wording of answers may vary.

1. Johnny Depp had been appearing in movies for three years before he played in a TV show.

2. Tyra Banks had been acting for eleven years before she started her own talk show.

3. Clint Eastwood had been starring in films for 40 years before he directed *Million Dollar Baby*.

5 TALK with a partner. Tell your partner your answers to the questions in Activity 4.

- Go over the directions.
- Put student in pairs to tell each other their answers to Activity 4.
- Call on students to share their answers with the class.

MATH: Calculating Sales Tax

- Have students read the information about how to calculate sales tax, or read it aloud to the class.

A. READ the situation below.

- Point out that the two boxes on the right give the prices for tickets and refreshments.
- Have students read the situation.

B. ANSWER the questions.

- Have students answer the questions.
- Call on students to share their answers with the class. If students are having trouble, show on the board each step to figuring out the answers.

ANSWER KEY

1. $61.00
2. $36.00
3. $2.52
4. $0.48

BIG PICTURE LISTENING EXPANSION ACTIVITY: How much?

- Put the transparency for Unit 2 on the OHP or have the students look at the Big Picture on page 40.
- Dictate the sentences below.
1. *Uma and Rajiv's lunch was $24.50. The sales tax is 8%.*
2. *Mark and Jill's tickets to the play were $40.00 each. The sales tax is 6%.*
3. *Tom and Tammy's mom paid $10 for their tickets and $15 for her ticket. The sales tax is 7%.*
- Explain that the sales tax would be the same for each place in the Big Picture as they are in the same city, but for practice you made up different sales taxes.
- Put students in pairs.
- Have each pair figure out the amount of money spent once sales tax is added.
- Go over the answers with the class.
  (**1.** $26.46; **2.** $84.80; **3.** $37.45)

ACADEMIC CONNECTION: Non-continuous verbs

- Remind students that some verbs in English are not used in the continuous form.
- Write on the board: *I had been believing your story until you started to laugh.* Ask if this sentence is correct. Elicit the answer that it is not correct because *believe* is not used in the continuous form. Write: *I believed your story until you started to laugh.*
- Have students research other verbs that do not have a continuous form. They may use the Internet or grammar books from the library.
- During the next class, create a list of 10 non-continuous verbs on the board. The list may include: *believe, dislike, forget, hate, hear, know, like, love, need, prefer, realize, recognize, see, suppose, understand, want, wish.*

STUDENT BOOK PAGES 48–49

LESSON 6: Reading

OBJECTIVES

Sequence events
Read a biography

VOCABULARY

bodybuilding	emissions
competitions	futuristic
elected	versatility

READING FOCUS

Identify the order of event

COMPETENCIES

Read about a famous person
Put events in order

WARM-UP ACTIVITY: Who's your favorite actor?

- Ask students to choose an actor they like and know something about. Model by telling them one of your favorite actors. For example, *I really like the actor Jackie Chan.*

- Tell students they will talk about their favorite actors in groups. Each person should say at least five sentences about their favorite actor. Other group members may ask questions. Model by telling the students about your favorite actor. For example, *Jackie Chan was born in Hong Kong. He is famous for his action and comedy movies.*

- Put students in groups to discuss their favorite actors.

1 THINK ABOUT IT. Do you know of any politicians who were once in the field of entertainment? Who do you know? Talk with a partner or in a group.

- Go over the directions.

- Put students in pairs or groups to discuss the questions.

- Call on students to share their answers with the class.

2 BEFORE YOU READ. Preview the article. Do you recognize the man in the photographs? What do you know about him?

- Point out the Reading Strategy Summary box.

- Check comprehension by asking students what *use prior knowledge* and *preview an article* mean. Elicit the correct answers and examples of how to use both strategies.

- Go over the directions.

- Discuss the answers as a class.

ACADEMIC NOTE

When previewing an article or textbook chapter, students should look at the title, headings, pictures, footnotes, and glossary if one is provided. A glossary can be found at the bottom of the article (as in the article on page 49) or in the back of a textbook.

3 READ the article. As you read, circle the dates. Underline the words *before, after, when, by,* and *by the time*.

- Go over the directions.

- Have students underline the words *before, after, when, by,* and *by the time*.

- Go over the answers with the class.

ANSWER KEY

You might not recognize this man as a politician. He might be more familiar as an actor. Before Arnold Schwarzenegger became the 38th Governor of California, he had had two other exciting careers.

Arnold Schwarzenegger was born in Austria in 1947. As a child, Arnold was very athletic. In fact, he began lifting weights as a teenager. He worked hard at bodybuilding, and by the age of 20, he had become the youngest man to win the Mr. Universe title. He moved to the United States in 1968. When he first arrived in the U.S., he didn't speak much English. But he studied hard and learned English well enough to attend college. By the time he became a U.S. citizen in 1983, he had already received a degree from the University of Wisconsin (1979). In 1986, he married Maria Shriver, a famous journalist and a niece of former president John F. Kennedy.

After he stopped entering bodybuilding competitions, Arnold Schwarzenegger became an actor and a big Hollywood star. Early in his career, he starred in films such as *Hercules in New York* (1970), *Conan: The Barbarian* (1982), and futuristic action movies like *The Terminator* (1984). He later showed his versatility by appearing in several comedies, including *Twins* (1988) and *Kindergarten Cop* (1990). He last appeared in a film in 2005, *The Kid and I*.

Schwarzenegger had been interested in politics for many years before the people of California elected him governor in 2003 and again in 2007. He believed that he could do a lot for California, especially for the environment. By 2006, Schwarzenegger had already helped reduce California's greenhouse gas emissions and had started other programs to clean up the environment.

Governor Schwarzenegger set goals and achieved them. He is a man of many talents. He may be one of the most famous and successful immigrants in the United States.

❹ AFTER YOU READ.

A. SEQUENCE the events. Put the events of Arnold Schwarzenegger's life in order. Number them 1–10.

- Go over the directions.
- Direct students' attention to the example answer: *begin lifting weights.* Ask: *When did Arnold Schwarzenegger begin lifting weights?* Elicit the answer: *when he was a teenager.* Point out that this is the first event listed in Activity A, so it is number 1.
- Have students put the events of Schwarzenegger's life in order from 1 to 10.
- Put students in pairs to compare their answers.
- Go over the answers with the class.

ANSWER KEY

2 won the Mr. Universe competition

9 starred in comedy films

1 began lifting weights

3 moved to the United States

7 starred in action films

4 learned English

10 became governor

8 married Maria Shriver

5 received his college degree

6 became a U.S. citizen

B. VOCABULARY. Find and draw a rectangle around the vocabulary words in the article. Read the sentences that include the words, and the sentences before and after them so you understand the meaning of the words. Then use the words to complete the sentences below.

- Go over the directions.
- Look at the example as a class. Ask students to find the word *bodybuilding* in the article (Line 4). Have the students read the sentence before and after the sentence with *bodybuilding*. Point out that bodybuilding is defined in the sentence before the sentence that includes the word.
- Have students underline the vocabulary words in the article and then complete the sentences.
- Go over the answers with the class.

ANSWER KEY

1. bodybuilding; **2.** emissions; **3.** versatility;
4. elected; **5.** competitions; **6.** futuristic

5 TALK with a partner. Use the events in Activity 4A and the words in the Reading Focus box to talk about Arnold Schwarzenegger's life.

- Go over the directions.
- Put student in pairs to tell each other their answers to Activity 4.
- Walk around the classroom and monitor students' progress.

COMMUNITY CONNECTION: American politicians

- Have students choose an American politician to research. Ask them to give a presentation of about three to five minutes. To limit the activity, you may decide to have students research a politician from the city, state, or federal government. For a more open-ended activity, allow students to choose any politician from any country.
- Have students research their politician on the Internet, at a library, or through the local government offices.
- Call on students to give their presentations to the class.

LESSON 7: Writing

WARM-UP ACTIVITY: Tell me about yourself

- Tell students they are going to give short, 5- to 10-sentence, oral summaries of their lives.
- Model the activity by saying 5 to 10 sentences about your life. For example, *I was born in San Francisco, California. I have three sisters and no brothers. When I was 18, I went to college in New York.*
- Put students in groups to share their oral summaries.

❶ THINK ABOUT IT. Have you ever gone back to visit your hometown or your childhood friends? What was the same? What was different?

- Go over the directions.
- Direct students' attention to the questions.
- Elicit answers to the questions.

❷ BEFORE YOU WRITE.

A. TALK. Look at the picture and talk with a partner. Where are the people? What do you think they are talking about?

- Go over the directions. Tell students that a *ten-year reunion* is when people who graduated the same year get together ten years later to have a party.
- Put students in pairs to talk about the picture and the questions.
- Call on students to share their answers with the class.

 B. LISTEN to the conversation between two friends at a school reunion. Take notes in the T-charts below.

TCD1, 56

- Go over the directions.
- Direct students' attention to the T-charts. Explain that a T-chart is a good way to list and examine two facets of a topic.
- Play the CD and have students take notes in the T-charts.
- Copy the two T-charts on the board.
- Ask students to fill in the T-charts on the board.

A: Chim Doc? Is that *you*?

B: Juanita! I can't believe it's been 10 years already. Time flies!

A: I know. You look great. What have you been doing?

B: I just moved to Miami and opened another art gallery. I sell my own paintings in my art gallery.

A: Another art gallery? That's great. But I thought you were living in Los Angeles.

B: I have a gallery there too, and one in New York. I travel a lot.

A: I always knew you would be a successful painter. I'm very happy for you.

B: Thanks! Now, tell me about you. What are you doing now?

A: Oh, I'm a sixth-grade teacher. I'm also the coach of the girls' soccer team.

B: Wow, that's wonderful. It's great to see all our friends again.

A: It sure is. Hey, look! Is that Doug over there?

B: I think so! Let's go talk to him.

ANSWER KEY

Chim Doc	
Then	**Now**
Lived in Smithtown	Lives in Miami Has art galleries in Miami, Los Angeles, and New York Is a successful painter
Juanita	
Then	**Now**
Lived in Smithtown	Is a sixth-grade teacher Is coach of the girls' soccer team

ACADEMIC NOTE

Graphic organizers—such as T-charts, Venn diagrams, and idea maps—help students organize their ideas before writing. This can be an especially important step for students who are visual learners. You may want to have students organize their ideas using some type of graphic organizer before any writing assignment.

C. WHAT ABOUT YOU? Fill in the T-chart with notes about yourself. Write about important events or activities in your life now, and in the past. Talk with a partner about your information.

- Go over the directions and the questions.
- Copy the T-chart on the board. Fill in the T-chart with two examples from your life (e.g., *Then—was on the swim team. Now—exercise at the gym*). Have students ask you questions about your two activities.
- Have students fill in their T-charts about themselves.
- Put students in pairs to discuss their interests.

D. Complete Chim Doc's timeline. Then write a timeline for yourself.

- Go over the directions.
- Have students read the timeline and write a timeline with eight important events from their lives on it.
- Put students in groups to discuss their timelines.

E. READ Chim Doc's short autobiography in the Reunion Newsletter. Circle the ages and dates.

- Read the text in the Writing Focus box to students.
- Have them read Chim Doc's short autobiography and circle the ages and dates.
- Go over the answers as a class. Highlight the fact that this short paragraph includes many references to ages and dates.

3 **WRITE** a short autobiography to include in
a class reunion newsletter from your high
school.

- Go over the directions and the questions.
- Review time phrases with students by asking
  for example sentences for *before, after, by the
  time, since,* and *for.*
- Have students write short autobiographies.

4 **AFTER YOU WRITE.**

A. EDIT. Read your partner's autobiography. Ask
yourself the questions below.

- Go over the directions and the questions.
- Put students in pairs.
- Have students edit their partner's paper, using
  the questions.
- Have students rewrite their autobiographies
  with corrections.

B. DISCUSS the corrections with your partner.

- Have students discuss corrections with their
  partners and explain why they made these
  corrections.

C. REWRITE your autobiography with
corrections.

- Have students rewrite their autobiographies
  with corrections.

**ACADEMIC CONNECTION: Use an
encyclopedia**

- Ask students what an encyclopedia is (set
  of books containing articles on various
  topics, covering all branches of knowledge).
- Have students go to the library and browse
  through a set of encyclopedias looking for
  an article on an interesting person.
- Have students make timelines of the
  person's life.
- Put students in groups to compare their
  timelines.
- Call on students to give their presentations
  to the class.

Career Connection

OBJECTIVES
Learn job duties

COMPETENCIES
Use a checklist
Read and understand a security report

WARM-UP ACTIVITY: Brainstorming job responsibilities

- Write *teacher* on the board.
- Ask students what things a teacher must do and write their answers on the board. If needed, add some of your own ideas (*create materials, design assessment, etc.*).
- Point out that the things you must do for your job are called *job responsibilities.*
- Ask a student what his or her job is. Write it on the board, and as a class brainstorm job responsibilities for that job.
- Ask several students about their jobs and brainstorm job responsibilities.

❶ LOOK at the photo. What job responsibilities do security guards have?

- Direct students' attention to the photo and ask questions: *Who do you see? What do you think he is doing? What job responsibilities do security guards have?*

❷ LISTEN to the conversation between Marcel, a security guard at a museum, and Mr. Hanif, his manager. Check *True* or *False*.
TCD1, 57

- Go over the directions.
- Play the CD and have students check *true* or *false*.
- Put students into small groups to compare answers.
- Elicit the correct answers from the students.

A: Marcel, come in, Marcel.

B: This is Marcel. Go ahead.

A: Uh, yes, this is Mr. Hanif. What's your location?

B: I'm on the first floor. I was just giving directions to some patrons.

A: We've got a problem on the third floor. Can you get upstairs and check on it for me?

B: I'm on my way up now.

A: Okay, great.

B: What happened?

A: We had some kind of problem up there this afternoon. I just got Horace's report.

B: Okay, I understand. What happened?

A: Well, some curious patrons went into the restricted work area. Apparently, the warning signs had fallen down. The alarm went off after the visitors crossed the barricades.

B: Was anyone hurt?

A: No, fortunately, no one was hurt.

B: That's a relief. Was there any damage to the exhibit?

A: I'm not sure. By the time Horace got upstairs, two of the kids had already knocked over part of the dinosaur display. They didn't realize we'd put up those barricades to keep our visitors safe and protect the exhibit.

B: All right. I'll check on it. Did Horace reset the alarm system?

A: No. You'll need to reset it. Horace didn't have time to do it before his shift ended.

B: Okay. I'm here now. I see the situation. First, I will reset the alarm system. Then, I'll put the signs up again, in a better place. After that, I'll secure the barricades. When I'm done, I'll come down to your office. I should read Horace's security report and make sure all the areas are safe. I can take care of the things he didn't have time to do.

A: Great, Marcel, I knew I could count on you.

B: Always glad to help, Mr. Hanif. Talk to you later.

③ TALK. *To take the initiative* means to think of ideas for making something better on your own. How did Marcel take the initiative after talking to Mr. Hanif? Circle the things Marcel decided to do. Then tell a partner.

- Go over the directions.
- Have more advanced students read the things listed. Check comprehension by asking students questions about each thing listed (e.g., *What are patrons? What's an alarm system? What did the signs say?*).
- Have students circle the things Marcel decided to do.
- Put students in pairs and have them discuss their answers.
- Go over the correct answers as a class.

④ READ about Horace's security report and talk with a partner. What had Horace already taken care of before he left? What hadn't Horace done before he left?

- Go over the directions and the questions.
- Have students read Horace's security report.
- Put students in pairs to discuss the questions.

⑤ WHAT ABOUT YOU? What are some ways you can take the initiative at work or at home? What ideas do you have about making positive changes? Discuss your ideas with a partner.

- Go over the directions and the questions.
- Put students in small groups to discuss their answers.
- Call on students to share their answers with the class.

COMMUNITY CONNECTION: My next job

- Have students choose a job they would like in the future. It may be a job that they get from being promoted at their current place of business or a job they would like to have at a new place.
- Ask students to research the job by asking two or three people who are currently doing it. Suggest that students find people who are currently doing the job and ask them what their job responsibilities are and how they got the job.
- During the next class, have students report back on what they discovered.

CHECK YOUR PROGRESS!

- Have students circle the correct answers.
- Review the answers or have students check the unit to see if each answer is right or wrong.
- Have students total their correct answers and fill in the chart at the bottom of the page.
- Have students create a learning plan and/or set learning goals.

Unit Overview

LESSON	OBJECTIVES	STUDENT BOOK	WORKBOOK
1 Grammar and Vocabulary 1	Talk about personal finances. Use perfect modals.	p. 54	p. 48
2 Grammar Practice Plus	Discuss banking problems. Give advice for financial problems.	p. 56	p. 49
3 Listening and Conversation	Discuss investments. Calculate interest earned.	p. 58	p. 50
4 Grammar and Vocabulary 2	Understand money and budgets. Ask and answer tag questions.	p. 60	p. 52
5 Grammar Practice Plus	Intonation in tag questions. Complete a budget. Examine a credit card statement.	p. 62	p. 53
6 Reading	Read an article about a credit report.	p. 64	p. 54–55
7 Writing	Dispute a credit card bill. Write a business letter.	p. 66	p. 56–57
• Career Connection	Read a hotel memo. Write a complaint and recommendation.	p. 68	p. 58–59
• Check Your Progress	Monitor progress.	p. 69	p. 60–61

Reading/Writing Strategies

- Make inferences
- Write a business letter

Connection Activities

LESSON	TYPE	SKILL DEVELOPMENT
1	Academic	Finding courses to help manage finances
2	Community	Skimming newspapers for information
3	Academic	Learning how to finance an education
4	Community	Taking a survey
5	Academic	Learning about financial careers / education
6	Community	Examining credit advertisements
7	Academic	Formatting correspondence correctly
Career Connection	Community	Examining customer service surveys

WORKSHEET #/FOCUS	TITLE	TEACHER'S EDITION
10. Reading	I love my job!	p. 314
11. Listening	What did she say?	p. 315
12. Grammar	Roll-a-Sentence Tag Questions	p. 316

LESSON 1: Grammar and Vocabulary

OBJECTIVES

Talk about personal finances
Use perfect modals

VOCABULARY

balance a checkbook	financial advisor
certificate of deposit	interest rate
credit card	invest in
information	outrageous
debit card	overdrawn
due date	penalty

GRAMMAR

Past modals: *should (not) / must (not)* + *have* + the past participle

COMPETENCY

Use language to talk about banking and personal finances

WARM-UP ACTIVITY: Unit opener

- Have a volunteer read the title of the unit.
- Create a web on the board with the word *finance* in the center. Have students add as many subtopics and details as they can think of to the web.
- Preview any important vocabulary words that come up during the brainstorm.

TCD2, 2
SCD14

① GRAMMAR PICTURE DICTIONARY. What problems are people having with banking and personal finances? Listen and read.

- Have students open their books and look at the pictures. Ask them to describe what is happening and how the people probably feel.
- Read the sentences aloud or play the CD and have students repeat.

- Call on students and ask about the people in the pictures: *In picture 1, why was the couple's checking account overdrawn? In picture 3, how did the family pay for their dinner?*

② PRACTICE the conversations in Activity 1 with a partner.

- Put students in pairs to read the sentences.
- Call on students to read the conversations to the class.

EXPANSION ACTIVITY: Extending the conversations

- Divide the class into six groups. Assign each group one of the pictures from Activity 1.
- Have each group rewrite the conversation to include more information and more interaction between the speakers. For example, students might write what comes before or after the dialogue shown.

③ NOTICE THE GRAMMAR. Underline *should (not) have* and *must (not) have*. Circle the past participles.

- Go over the directions.
- Have students circle the past participles and underline the words indicated.
- Have students check their answers with a partner.
- Go over the answers with the class.

ANSWER KEY

1. A: Insufficient funds? It looks like our checking account is overdrawn.
   B: That's my fault. I should have (balanced) the checkbook last week.

2. A: Wow! We should have (invested) in a certificate of deposit.
   B: You're right! That's a great interest rate.

3. A: We need some cash for the bus. Did we spend it all at the restaurant?
   B: Oh, I think so. We shouldn't have (used) cash for dinner. We should've (used) our debit card.

4. A: This bill is outrageous! Why did you buy so much last month?
   B: I didn't buy all of that! Someone must have (stolen) my credit card information!

5. A. Wow! Look at that. The interest rate on that savings account is higher than ours!
   B: You're right. We should've (met) with a financial advisor.

6. A: Why do you have to pay a penalty on your credit card bill?
   B: Uh oh. I must have (paid) it after the due date.

GRAMMAR CHART: Past Modals: *Should (not) / Must (not) + have + the Past Participle*

- Direct students' attention to the chart or project the transparency or CD.
- Go over the information in the chart and the usage notes. Form sentences by putting each part together, and then have students repeat.
- Ask for volunteers to give example sentences for each intention given on the chart: regret, advice, and certainty.

PRONUNCIATION/GRAMMAR NOTE

Point out to students that phrases such as *should have, could have, would have,* and *must have* are often shortened into contractions. These contractions, when pronounced, often sound like: *should of (should've), could of (could've), would of (would've)* and *must of (must've).* Explain that although the pronunciation of *'ve* may sound the same as the word *of,* grammatically, *of* is incorrect

CHART EXPANSION ACTIVITY: It's scandalous!

- Bring to class gossip magazines or newspapers that tell about the latest drama in the lives of famous actors, musicians, politicians, and sports figures.
- Divide the class into groups and give each group one magazine or newspaper. Have the groups choose a story and write sentences about it using the modals from the chart. For example: *She should not have said that to the reporter. He must have been very angry!*
- Have groups tell the class the gist of their story and then present the sentences they wrote.

⚃ **MATCH** the statement on the left with the correct expression on the right. Then read the statements with a partner.

- Go over the directions and the example.
- Have students complete the exercise.
- Go over the answers with the class.

ANSWER KEY

1. f; 2. d; 3. b; 4. a; 5. c; 6. e

5 TALK with a partner. Take turns reading the sentences, and giving answers using *should (not) have* or *must (not) have*.

- Go over the directions and the example.
- Have students respond to the statements with a partner.
- Have volunteers model their conversations in front of the class.

6 WHAT ABOUT YOU? Have you ever made a mistake with your money or your finances? What should you have done differently? Write three sentences.

- Go over the directions and the example.
- Have students work independently to write three sentences.
- Put students in pairs to share their sentences.
- Ask volunteers to share their sentences with the class. Encourage students to respond using sentences with modals from the grammar chart.

EXPANSION ACTIVITY: Love-hate finances

- Divide the class into two groups: those who enjoy (or don't mind) keeping track of their finances and those who dislike dealing with financial issues.
- Have each group list the reasons that they enjoy or dislike working with their finances. Then have each group write three goals for themselves or recommendations for others to improve their management of personal finances. Encourage them to use modals that focus on the future: *we should, you must, we could*. For example: *You must balance your checkbook once a week. We could read a book about investing.*

ACADEMIC CONNECTION: Help with finances

- Have students research free or inexpensive classes or services that are available in your community. For example, community centers, immigration or resettlement organizations, adult education schools, and even some banks or financial institutions offer courses dealing with finances.
- Have students present the information they discovered to the class, including the time, location, and costs of any classes.
- Lead a discussion about which classes students would find most useful.

LESSON 2: Grammar Practice Plus

OBJECTIVES

Discuss banking problems
Give advice for financial problems

VOCABULARY

credit card fraud	mortgage loan
credit report	teller
deposit slip	withdrawal
insufficient funds	

GRAMMAR

Should, Must

COMPETENCIES

Discuss banking and financial problems
Give advice and make decisions about
 finances

WARM-UP ACTIVITY: Checking *vs.* savings

- On the board, create two columns and title
  them *Checking Account* and *Savings Account*.

- Have students tell everything they know about
  these two types of accounts. List details in
  each column. If possible, have students tell the
  advantages or disadvantages of each.

- Review any important vocabulary that came up
  during the activity.

- For advanced students, you may wish to add a
  column labeled *Money Market Account*.

1 TALK with a partner about the picture. What
were the people doing at the bank last Friday?
Use the words in the box below.

- Go over the directions and the question asked.

- Have students respond to the question,
  determining what each person was doing at
  the bank. Write their responses on the board.

- Go over any vocabulary from the picture that is
  unfamiliar to students.

2 LISTEN and write the correct number
next to each name.

- Go over the directions and the names listed.

- Play the CD and have students write the
  correct number next to each person's name.

- Put students in pairs to compare answers.

- Go over the answers with the class.

LISTENING SCRIPT
Lesson 2, Activity 2

1. Millie needed to cash a personal check, but she
   couldn't.

2. Tamir got in the business accounts line to make
   a withdrawal.

3. Sarah noticed unusual charges on her credit
   card, and she's worried about credit card fraud.

4. Bart wanted to make a deposit to his personal
   checking account.

5. Winnona saw a suspicious man leaving the
   bank.

6. Juan and Rosa spoke to the financial advisor
   about getting a mortgage loan.

7. Paolo got a receipt for insufficient funds in his
   checking account.

ANSWER KEY

7. Paolo; 2. Tamir; 1. Millie; 4. Bart;
6. Juan and Rosa; 5. Winnona; 3. Sarah

EXPANSION ACTIVITY: Checking
predictions

- Listen to the CD a second time.

- Have students reread the responses they
  made during Activity 1 about what people
  were doing at the bank. Were they correct?

3 TALK about what happened at the bank. Use the verb and noun phrase in parentheses to make a new sentence with *should (not) have* or *must (not) have.*

• Go over the directions and the example.
• Elicit verbal answers from the class, allowing more than one response for each item.

ANSWER KEY

Answers may vary.

1. She must have forgotten her ID.
2. He should have used a different withdrawal slip.
3. She should have spoken with a bank officer.
4. He should not have waited in line for the business accounts window.
5. They should have requested a credit report.
6. He must not have balanced his checking account.

CULTURE NOTE

Point out that Juan and Rosa were interested in getting a mortgage loan. Explain that in the United States, some home buyers do not get loans from banks. Rather, they work out financing with the owner of the property. This is called "owner financing" or "seller financing." Although it is not very common, it does allow some buyers who do not qualify for a loan to purchase a house. You may wish to have students research this concept and report what they find to the class.

4 WRITE sentences about the bank customers in Activity 1. Answer the questions with *should (not) have* or *must (not) have.*

• Go over the directions and the example.
• Put students in pairs and have them ask and answer the questions.
• Elicit ideas from the class about each situation.

ANSWER KEY

1. She should have brought her ID.
2. Tamir shouldn't have used the wrong withdrawal slip.
3. Someone must have stolen her credit card information.
4. He should have waited in the correct line.
5. They must not have requested a credit report.
6. Paolo should have balanced his checking account.
7. He must have stopped the suspicious man.

BIG PICTURE READING EXPANSION ACTIVITY: I love my job!

• Photocopy and distribute Worksheet 10: *I Love My Job!*
• Put the transparency for Unit 4 on the OHP or have students look at the Big Picture on page 56.
• Go over the directions.
• Have students read the personal statements and answer the questions.
• Put students in pairs to share their ideas.
• Go over the answers with the class.

WORKSHEET ANSWER KEY

1. It is important to keep people safe.
2. He likes to help others.
3. His family is proud of him.
4. No. She is complaining and says she isn't crazy about her job.
5. lunchtime
6. Many people come in at the same time. They glare at her.
7. first-time home buyers and people starting businesses
8. hearing their stories and talking about their hopes and plans for the future

5 **READ** the online banking email message. Then talk with a partner. Have you, or has anyone else you know ever received a message like this?

- Have students read the message and discuss it with a partner.
- Ask comprehension questions to the class to make sure that they understood the information in the message.
- Have volunteers tell about incidents that happened to them or to people they know. Encourage students to ask questions to find out more details.

6 **WRITE** sentences. Respond to each of the situations below. Use *should (not) have* or *must (not) have* and the information in Activity 5.

- Go over the directions.
- Put students in pairs to complete the sentences.
- Go over the answers with the class.

ANSWER KEY

Answers will vary. Possible answers include:

1. I should have reported the stolen card immediately.
2. I should have reported unusual charges on my credit card.
3. The email must not have been from my bank. I should have forwarded it to badmail@rainydaybank.
4. I should have called or emailed the bank to get my password.

7 **WHAT ABOUT YOU?** Tell a partner about a problem you have had with money (with a bank, a bill, a check, etc.). Then take turns giving each other advice. What should/shouldn't your partner have done?

- Go over the directions.
- Have students think silently for a minute or two about a problem or problems that they currently face.
- Put students in pairs. Have them share their problem(s) with each other and give advice using the target language.
- Call on volunteers to share the problems and advice they discussed.

EXPANSION ACTIVITY: Parenting

- Put students in groups and have them brainstorm a list of recommendations for new parents.
- Have groups write five recommendations using *should* or *must.*
- Have volunteers share their group's list with the class. Discuss how many of the rules from different groups were similar.

COMMUNITY CONNECTION: In the news

- Have students skim local newspapers for news about banks in your area. Are any of the stories about credit card or identity theft? What other banking topics made the news (e.g., changing interest rates, increase in foreclosures, and so on)?
- Lead a discussion about the topics that most interest students. Have them tell what happened in the news to start the conversation.

LESSON 3: Listening and Conversation

OBJECTIVES

Discuss investments
Calculate interest earned

MATH

Calculating interest earned

COMPETENCIES

Understand a certificate of deposit
Use math to calculate interest earned

WARM-UP ACTIVITY: Money in the bank

- Tell students that many parents in the United States open savings accounts for their children. They encourage their kids to save money and to watch the account grow.

- Have students give their ideas about why parents would do this. For example: to teach financial responsibility, to help children save for college or a car, and so on.

- Ask students if saving money is an important part of their culture(s). If so, how do people save their money and why? If not, what do people do with their money instead?

 1 LISTEN to the conversation. Then listen
TCD2, 4–9 to a question. Fill in the correct answer. Replay each item if necessary.

- Direct students' attention to the answer sheet.
- Play the CD and have students fill in the correct circle.
- Put students in pairs to compare answers.
- Go over the answers with the class.

 LISTENING SCRIPT
Lesson 3, Activity 1
TCD2, 4–9

1. *M:* Why do you look so disappointed?
   F: I just got a notice for insufficient funds in my checking account.
   Which is the best response?
   A. You should have balanced your checkbook last week.
   B. You shouldn't have used your credit card.
   C. You must have saved a lot of money.

2. *F:* You seem upset. What's wrong?
   M: We got a penalty charge on our credit card statement.
   Which is the best response?
   A. Oh. We didn't see the statement.
   B. Too bad. We need a better interest rate.
   C. You're right. We should have paid the bill on time.

3. *F:* I'm very worried. There is a lot of unusual activity on my credit card statement. I don't remember making all those purchases.
   M: Really? What do you think happened?
   Which is the best response?
   A. Maybe someone stole my credit card information.
   B. I used my credit card to buy our concert tickets.
   C. I couldn't remember my password.

4. *M:* You know, we should have talked to a financial advisor about our savings plan last year.
   F: You're right. We should have gotten a better interest rate. What should we do now?
   Which is the best response?
   A. We can't go to the bank.
   B. We had better wait.
   C. We should make an appointment.

5. *M:* Oh wow. Look at the offer in this bank brochure. We could have invested in a certificate of deposit.

   F: You're right. We could have earned more interest.

   Which is the best response?

   A. Next year, let's get a CD.

   B. This statement is outrageous.

   C. I should have opened a savings account.

6. *M:* Hello. I need to make a deposit to my personal checking account.

   F: Sorry, this is the line for business accounts. You should get in that line over there.

   Which is the best response?

   A. Oh, okay. Thanks for your help.

   B. You shouldn't tell me that.

   C. I'd better talk to you.

ANSWER KEY

1. A; 2. C; 3. A; 4. C; 5. A; 6. A

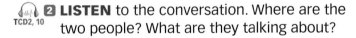 **2 LISTEN** to the conversation. Where are the two people? What are they talking about?
TCD2, 10

- Go over the directions.
- Play the CD and have students write answers to the questions.
- Put students in pairs to check their answers.
- Go over the answers with the class.

 LISTENING SCRIPT
Lesson 3, Activity 2
TCD2, 10

A: Hello. How can I help you?

B: Hi, I would like some information on investing money.

A: Well, you could get a savings account with a four percent interest rate.

B: I see. And how about a certificate of deposit? How does that earn money?

A: The CD we offer earns five percent interest over 18 months.

B: Is that a high interest rate?

A: Yes it is. It is a very good rate. I think you could earn more money with a CD.

B: I can withdraw the money whenever I want, can't I?

A: Well, you can, but with a CD there's a high penalty if you withdraw the money before 18 months.

B: Maybe I'd better open a savings account and a CD.

A: That's a good idea. Here's a brochure with more information.

B: Okay. I'll read it over. Thank you for your help.

ANSWER KEY

They are at a bank. They are talking about investing.

3 LISTEN again to the conversation. Write answers to the questions. Then discuss your answers with a partner.

- Go over the directions and the questions with the students.
- Play the CD or read the conversation.
- Have students answer the questions.
- Go over the answers with the class.

ANSWER KEY

1. four percent
2. five percent
3. She decides to open a savings account and also get a CD. She wants to be able to withdraw money but doesn't want to pay a penalty, and she wants to earn more interest.
4. Answers will vary.

BIG PICTURE LISTENING EXPANSION ACTIVITY: What did she say?

- Photocopy and distribute Worksheet 11: *What Did She Say?*
- Put the transparency for Unit 4 on the OHP or have students look at the Big Picture in their books.
- Go over the directions for the worksheet and preview the characters speaking in each conversation.
- Read aloud the listening script below for each conversation, using different voices for each character if desired.
- Have students complete the worksheet and compare their answers with a partner.
- Go over the answers with the class.

LISTENING SCRIPT/ANSWER KEY
Worksheet 11

Millie: Hi there. I'd like to cash a personal check.

Teller: Great. I'll need the check and your ID.

Millie: Just a second. I'm sure it's here somewhere. Oh dear, I must have forgotten it in the car.

Teller: If you'd like to go get it and come back, I can help you then. Just come back to my window. You don't have to stand in line again.

Millie: Thanks. I'll be right back.

* * * * * * * * * * * * * * * * * *

Loan Officer: Hello. How may I help you today?

Rosa: We're not exactly sure. We are thinking of buying a house, but we don't know where to start.

Juan: Our real estate agent said that if we get prequalified for a loan, it will be easier to buy a house.

Rosa: That's right. We wanted to ask about getting a mortgage loan here. We saw your ad in the paper, and your interest rates look very competitive.

Loan Officer: We do have great rates right now—it's a good time to buy a home! The first step you'll need to take is to request your credit report.

Juan: Oh, we already got a credit report last year when we financed our new car. We can use that one, can't we?

Loan Officer: I'm afraid not. You need a current credit report in order to apply for a mortgage here. But don't worry, it's free and it only takes a few days to get the information back.

Rosa: Well, that sounds all right. Let's get started on the paperwork.

MATH: Calculating Interest Earned

A. READ about interest.

- Go over the information in the Math box.
- Have students read the information. Make sure they understand the information in the paragraph before moving on to Part B.

B. CALCULATE interest earned.

- Have students complete the questions individually.
- Go over the answers as a class. Work the problems on the board as needed to demonstrate the steps.

ANSWER KEY

1. $25.00; 2. $80.00

EXPANSION ACTIVITY: Math practice

- Put students in groups. Give each group the financial section of your local newspaper.
- Have students find advertisements from banks that list their interest rates on CDs and savings accounts. Have each group calculate the interest they would earn in one year, given a specific amount of money. You may wish to have groups exchange work to check each other's math.
- Have each group tell the class about the best rate that they found.

4 LISTEN to the conversation. Then practice with a partner.

TCD2, 11
SCD15

- Go over the directions.
- Have a pair of students model the activity.
- Put students in pairs to practice the conversation.
- Call on students to read the conversation to the class.

5 TALK with a partner. Make new conversations with the words in the chart. Use Activity 4 as a model.

- Go over the directions. Point out that the new information will replace the underlined information in the Activity 4 dialogue.
- Put students in pairs to practice the example dialogue.
- Have volunteers present conversations in front of the class. You may wish to choose students who have not been paired together.

6 READ about Simone's day. What should Simone have done differently? What should Simone not have done? Ask and answer questions with a partner.

- Go over the directions and the example.
- Read the story as a class.

- Put students in pairs and have them ask and answer questions about the story.
- Call on volunteers to share some of their questions and answers.

EXPANSION ACTIVITY: Timeline

- Have students reread the story in Activity 6.
- On the board, construct a timeline of the events that occurred in the story.
- Have students use the timeline to retell the story by paraphrasing what happened.

7 ROLE-PLAY. Simone needs advice. Use the information in the story to form questions. Use the information in the box to respond to the advice.

- Go over the directions and the Conversation Strategy box.
- Have pairs use the expressions in the box to perform role-plays based on the story.
- Call on volunteers to present role-plays to the class. Have the class tell whether each conversation correctly used the words *should* and *must*.

ACADEMIC CONNECTION: Paying for school

- Have students visit or call the financial aid office of local universities and schools for adults.
- Have students find out the most common ways that adults pay for their education: student loans, work-study programs, scholarships, and so on.
- Have students report to the class what they discovered. If students do not mention college savings programs, be sure to tell about them. For example, a Coverdell account allows parents to save money for the costs of their children's education.

LESSON 4: Grammar and Vocabulary

OBJECTIVES

Understand money and budgets
Ask and answer tag questions

VOCABULARY

automated payment	monthly budget
credit card offers	mortgage payment
credit report	shred
credit score	spending allowance
identity theft	

GRAMMAR

Tag questions

COMPETENCIES

Discuss problems with finances
Clarify statements

WARM-UP ACTIVITY: Budget brainstorm

- Create a web with the word *budget* in the center. Have students add their ideas of words related to budgets or of items that are included in a budget.
- Go over any important vocabulary words that students suggested during the brainstorm.

🎧 **1 GRAMMAR PICTURE DICTIONARY.**
TCD2, 12
SCD16 Listen to the conversations about money and banking.

- Have students look at the pictures. Ask: *Who are the people? What is each person doing?*
- Play the CD or read the sentences aloud as students follow along silently.
- Call on students and ask questions about each situation in the pictures: *In picture 1, why should the woman shred her bills? In picture 3, what did the man get in the mail yesterday?*

EXPANSION ACTIVITY: What do we really spend?

- Challenge students to estimate how much money they spend each month for different items, such as food, gasoline, rent, utilities, and clothing. Use the word web from the warm-up activity to help students get started.
- Have students compare their estimates with their credit card statements, checkbook registers, and bank account statements to see how accurately they calculated their expenses.

2 PRACTICE the conversations in Activity 1 with a partner.

- Go over the directions.
- Put students in pairs to read the sentences.
- Call on students to read the sentences aloud to the class.

3 NOTICE THE GRAMMAR. Underline the verb in the main part of each question. Then circle the two words at the end of each question.

- Go over the directions.
- Have students underline the verb and circle the tag ending for each question.
- Go over the answers with the class.

ANSWER KEY

1. I should shred all my bills and unwanted credit card offers, shouldn't I?
2. We forgot to make our mortgage payment this month, didn't we?
3. You've requested your credit report, haven't you?
4. You haven't been following our monthly budget, have you?

GRAMMAR CHART: Tag Questions

- Go over the information in the chart, including the Grammar Professor note.
- Read the sample sentences in the chart and have students repeat.

CHART EXPANSION ACTIVITY: True and false statements

- Make a statement about a student in the class. For example: "Rania is wearing blue jeans, isn't she?" Have a volunteer use a short answer as shown in the chart to respond: "No, she's not" or "No, she isn't."
- Have the student who answered give a new statement and choose a classmate to respond. Continue in this fashion. Each person who answers a question gets to ask the next question.
- If a student answers incorrectly, the person who asked the question can choose another classmate to answer. The person who gives the correct answer then asks the next question.

CULTURE NOTE

Point out that in (informal) conversational speech, people sometimes substitute the word *right* for a tag question. For example, someone might say, "We're eating lunch together, right?" instead of "We're eating lunch together, aren't we?" Usually when people do this, they are asking for confirmation of a fact. Ask students if there is a word in their native language that serves the same function.

4 MATCH the tag question with the statement.

- Go over the directions.
- Have students complete the exercise.
- Go over the answers with the class.

ANSWER KEY

1. b; 2. d; 3. a; 4. e; 5. c

5 WHAT ABOUT YOU? Complete the sentences below with the missing tag questions. Then ask a partner the questions.

- Go over the directions and the examples.
- Put students in pairs to ask and answer questions.

ANSWER KEY

1. don't you 2. didn't you 3. don't you
4. have you 5. won't you

BIG PICTURE GRAMMAR EXPANSION ACTIVITY: Tag questions

- Photocopy and distribute Worksheet 12: *Roll-a-Sentence Tag Questions.*
- Put the transparency for Unit 4 on the OHP or display the Big Picture from the CD.
- Go over the directions. Point out that students should make sentences about the people in the Big Picture. If students roll the subject *I, we,* or *you,* they should pretend that they are one of the characters or that they are addressing one of the characters.
- Put students in pairs to take turns rolling the dice and creating questions.
- Have volunteers tell which numbers they rolled and then share the sentence they created from the subject and verb.

COMMUNITY CONNECTION: Survey

- Put students in groups and have them create a short survey to ask members of the community about basic financial needs and activities. For example: *Do you use credit cards? Do you often use a debit card for purchases? Do you have a savings account?* Instruct students not to ask for specific dollar amounts or personal information; *Yes/No* questions may be best.
- Have each student give the survey to 10 or more people in their community.
- Have groups compile the responses and share their results with the class.

LESSON 5: Grammar Practice Plus

OBJECTIVES

Intonation in tag questions
Complete a budget
Examine a credit card statement

PRONUNCIATION

Intonation in tag questions

COMPETENCIES

Clarify statements
Understand budgets
Interpret a bill

WARM-UP ACTIVITY: Over budget again!

- Ask students if they keep a budget. List on the board the categories within their budget.
- Lead a discussion about the categories in which the students tend to overspend, if any. Do they buy too many DVDs or go out to eat more often than their budgets allow?

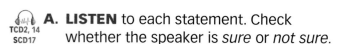 **PRONUNCIATION: Intonation in Tag Questions**
TCD2, 13

- Play the CD or go over the information about negative contractions.

A. LISTEN to each statement. Check whether the speaker is *sure* or *not sure*.
TCD2, 14
SCD17

- Go over the directions.
- Play the CD and have students put a check mark next to the correct answers.
- Go over the answers with the class.

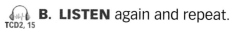 **B. LISTEN** again and repeat.
TCD2, 15

- Play the CD and have students practice repeating the statements with the proper intonation.

 LISTENING SCRIPT
Lesson 5, Pronunciation Activities A and B
TCD2, 14
SCD17

1. We didn't make the mortgage payment on time, did we? (falling intonation; sure)
2. You saw the notice for insufficient funds, didn't you? (rising intonation, not sure)
3. We won't go over our budget, will we? (falling, sure)
4. My credit score should be higher, shouldn't it? (falling, sure)
5. They charge a penalty for withdrawing money from your CD early, don't they? (rising, not sure)
6. You've never experienced identity theft, have you? (falling, sure)

ANSWER KEY

1. sure; 2. not sure; 3. sure; 4. sure; 5. not sure; 6. sure

EXPANSION ACTIVITY: Practicing short answers

- Put students in pairs and play the CD again.
- For each example, have pairs write a short response that would be appropriate considering the intonation of the question. Point out that some questions may have more than one possible answer.

ANSWER KEY

1. No, we didn't.
2. Yes, I did. / No, I didn't. / Yes, we did. / No, we didn't.
3. No, we won't.
4. Yes, it should.
5. Yes, they do. / No, they don't.
6. No, I haven't. / No, we haven't.

1 COMPLETE the conversations with the correct tag.

- Go over the directions.
- Have students complete the conversations. They will check their answers in the next activity.

2 LISTEN to the conversations in Activity 1 and check your answers.

- Go over the directions.
- Play the CD. Have students check their answers while they listen.
- Go over the answers with the class.

LISTENING SCRIPT
Lesson 5, Activities 2 and 3
TCD2, 16

1.	*Nancy:*	You didn't pay the Internet bill with the credit card, did you?
	Ian:	No, I didn't. I used the automated payment from our checking account.
2.	*Ian:*	We need to cut back on our entertainment expenses, don't we?
	Nancy:	Yes. Maybe we shouldn't have gone to the movies so often.
3.	*Ian:*	I haven't been doing a good job with the budget lately, have I?
	Nancy:	Oh, yes, you have. You've been managing it very well.
4.	*Nancy:*	We've gone over our $50 spending allowance for gas, haven't we?
	Ian:	I'm not sure. We should check our credit card statement.
5.	*Nancy:*	They charge a penalty for withdrawing money from a CD early, don't they?
	Ian:	I think so. We'd better transfer money from our savings if we want to balance our budget.

ANSWER KEY

1. did you; 2. don't we; 3. have I, you have;
4. haven't we; 5. don't they

3 LISTEN again. Check whether the first speaker is *sure* or *not sure*.

- Go over the directions.
- Play the CD. Have students answer the questions.
- Play each item one by one. Pause after each one and take a poll of the class to see which answer they chose. Decide as a class whether the speaker is sure or unsure. Replay the CD as needed.

ANSWER KEY

1. unsure 2. sure 3. sure 4. sure 5. sure

4 LISTEN to Ian and Nancy talk about their March budget. Fill in the amounts that you hear in the March column. Together, they have a total income of $3,500 and their budget is $3,000.

- Go over the directions and preview the chart with students.
- Play the CD and have students complete the chart.
- Put students in pairs to compare their answers.
- Play the CD again to have students check their answers.
- Go over the answers with the class.

LISTENING SCRIPT
Lesson 5, Activity 4
TCD2, 17

Ian:	Nancy, we should go over our budget now.
Nancy:	Good idea. Let's see . . . Our car payment is $250, but we spent $100 on gas this month. So for March, that's $350 total for car and gas expenses.
Ian:	Right. Maybe we should have made fewer trips to the supermarket and bought less. You saved our receipts, didn't you?
Nancy:	Yes. They're here. You're right. We spent $400 on food this month.
Ian:	Yep, and we also spent $200 on movies, music CDs, and dining out.

Nancy: Well, you know I love going to nice restaurants. But, maybe we could have stayed home and I could have cooked more.

Ian: With a $1,700 monthly mortgage payment we'd better stay home more often.

Nancy: I agree. Our phone bill is high this month, isn't it?

Ian: Yes. It's $165. We should have made calls on the weekends when we have free minutes.

Nancy: True, but I had to call my sister for her birthday, didn't I?

Ian: I guess so. But we could have put that extra money into the savings account. This month we don't have anything for our savings.

Nancy: Gee. I probably shouldn't have bought those new clothes.

Ian: Probably not. And I shouldn't have bought a new computer, but I needed it! Ugh! Our credit card bill is outrageous.

Nancy: We'd better transfer money from our savings account.

Ian: I think that's the best solution. We'll manage better next month, won't we?

ANSWER KEY

For March: Car payment and gas expenses, $350; Entertainment, $200; Food, $400; Phone bill, $165

PRONUNCIATION NOTE

Elicit from students how the numbers were read during the listening in Activity 4. Point out that numbers in the hundreds can be read many different ways. For example, 150 can be "one hundred fifty," "one hundred and fifty," or "one fifty." Go over numbers from the chart and tell students different ways that they can be read.

5 READ Ian and Nancy's credit card statement below. Use information in the statement to complete the budget chart in Activity 4 for April.

- Go over the directions.
- Have students complete the exercise.
- Put students in pairs to check their work.
- Go over the answers with the class.

ANSWER KEY

For April: Car payment and gas expenses, $335; Entertainment, $205; Miscellaneous, $1,035; Total, $3,975

EXPANSION ACTIVITY: Balance the budget

- Have students look at the completed budget chart from Activity 4.
- Put students in pairs and have them balance the budget by making cuts in spending. Each pair must come to an agreement.
- Take a poll of each pair to find out which expenses the class decided to cut. Write the results on the board. Which expense was considered to be the most expendable? Which expenses were not cut at all?

CULTURE NOTE

Lead a class discussion about family budgets. Explain that in the United States, many couples decide their budget together, especially if they are combining incomes from two jobs. Most family budgets include a portion for entertainment expenses, including a category for dining out. This may seem unusual to some students. Ask them to talk about typical budget decision-making in families from their respective cultures and countries.

6 WRITE short conversations about what Nancy and Ian spent in March and April. Then role-play the conversations with a partner.

- Go over the directions and the example.
- Have students write brief conversations. Discuss the topic as a class if needed before students break into pairs.
- Put students in pairs to role-play the conversations.
- Ask volunteers to present their conversations to the class.

7 WRITE advice for Ian and Nancy about what they should have done differently to stay within their budget.

- Go over the directions with students.
- Ask a volunteer to give an example of advice for Ian and Nancy.
- Have students write advice. Go over the answers in class.

8 WHAT ABOUT YOU? Who manages the finances in your family? Do you have a monthly budget? Why or why not?

- Go over the questions.
- Put students in pairs to go over the answers to the questions.
- Call on volunteers to share some of the ideas they discussed.

ACADEMIC CONNECTION: Financial education and careers

- On the board, have students brainstorm various careers related to finance. List as many as possible.
- As an out-of-class assignment, have each student find out about one career in finance, as well as the educational requirements to begin that career. Each student should list schools in your area that offer training for the career in question. Try to have each student in the class research a different career.
- Have each student present what they found out in a mock Career/Education Fair.
- As a class, create a chart or diagram that illustrates the financial careers that require the least to the most education.

LESSON 6: Reading

OBJECTIVES

Read an article about a credit report

VOCABULARY

database	denies
debts	monitor

READING FOCUS

Make inferences

COMPETENCY

Read information about credit reports

WARM-UP ACTIVITY: Internet search

- Have students do an Internet search using the words *credit score chart*.
- As a class, create a chart on the board that shows what are considered "good" and "bad" credit scores.

❶ THINK ABOUT IT.

A. Read this short questionnaire. Check *Yes* or *No.*

- Go over the directions.
- Have students answer the questions.
- Lead a discussion based on the questions.

B. TALK to a partner. Discuss your answers to the questionnaire.

- Go over the directions.
- Put students in pairs to discuss their answers.
- Have volunteers share their ideas with the class.

❷ BEFORE YOU READ. Preview the title and the subheadings. What do you think this article is about?

- Go over the directions.
- Have students read the title and subheadings.
- Elicit ideas from the class to answer the question.

❸ READ the article about credit reports. As you read, find and circle these words: *denies, database, debts, monitor.*

- Go over the directions and read the list of words. If possible, elicit definitions for each word before students read.
- After students have finished reading, have them compare the words they circled with a partner.
- Elicit definitions again for each word. Point out how seeing the words in context in the reading may have helped them understand each word more clearly.

EXPANSION ACTIVITY: Writing sentences

- Have students write sentences using the words listed in Activity 3: *denies, database, debts, monitor*.
- Put students in pairs and have them read their sentences to each other, omitting the vocabulary word and saying "blank" instead. Partners should guess which word belongs in each sentence.
- Call on volunteers to present their sentences to the class, either completed or with the vocabulary words missing. Have the class guess any missing words.

❹ AFTER YOU READ.

A. VOCABULARY. Read the sentence and circle the letter with the closest meaning. Guess the meaning of the word from the context.

- Go over the directions.
- Have students answer the questions.

- Put students in pairs to compare answers.
- Have pairs look up the words in a dictionary to check their answers.
- Go over the answers with the class.

GRAMMAR NOTE

If students have trouble finding the word *denies* in the dictionary, elicit from them the different ways to form the simple present verb tense. If students do not recall the rule about verbs that end in *y*, remind them and give an example.

ANSWER KEY

1. a; 2. b; 3. c; 4. a

B. MAKE INFERENCES, either positive or negative, about the information in the reading. Check if the statement is *True* or *False*.

- Go over the directions.
- Direct students' attention to the Reading Focus box. Go over the information in it.
- Have students complete the activity.
- Go over the answers with the class.

ANSWER KEY

1. True; 2. True; 3. False; 4. True

EXPANSION ACTIVITY: Comparing credit scores in the United States

- Have students do an Internet search for the average credit score in America and the average score for each of the 50 states. If desired, have students mark a map of the United States with the score for each state.
- Ask questions such as: "Which state has the lowest average credit score? Which state has the highest?"
- Have students identify any regional patterns concerning credit scores. Ask them what inferences they might make from any patterns they see.

BIG PICTURE WRITING EXPANSION ACTIVITY: Juan and Rosa's credit report

- Put the transparency for Unit 3 on the OHP or have students look at the Big Picture on page 56.
- Have students identify the couple applying for a mortgage loan: Juan and Rosa.
- Put students in groups. Using the information they learned in Lesson 6 about credit reports, have students create a list of fictitious actions that could affect Juan and Rosa's credit report, either positive or negative. *Rosa paid her credit card bill on time every month* (positive). *Juan defaulted on his student loan because he could not pay it* (negative). If students have trouble thinking of ideas, have them do an Internet search about what affects a person's credit rating.
- Have each group share one negative and one positive event that they imagined. You may wish to have the class vote to rank each one: Which event will affect Juan and Rosa's credit the most negatively? Which event will improve their credit score the most?

COMMUNITY CONNECTION: Credit solicitations

- For two or three days, have students keep track of every advertisement regarding credit that they see or hear in the community: billboards, television ads, credit card mailings, and so on. Have students make a detailed list or bring examples to class. They may include information on credit cards, credit score repair, credit reports, and so on.
- Take a class poll to determine the average number of sightings each student encountered.
- Lead a discussion about the results. Who seemed to be targeted by each type of ad or solicitation?

LESSON 7: Writing

Dispute a credit card bill
Write a business letter

WRITING FOCUS

Write a business letter

COMPETENCIES

Be aware of credit card fraud
Write a letter to negotiate a consumer issue

WARM-UP ACTIVITY: Credit card *vs.* cash

- Draw a T-chart on the board. Label the first column *Credit Card* and the second column *Cash*.
- Have students suggest items that they pay for exclusively by credit card or with cash. Write their ideas in the appropriate columns. Some items may be listed in both columns.
- Have students give their reasons for only paying with cash or by credit card. For example: online purchases cannot be made with cash, small purchases (such as snacks) are usually bought with cash, and so on.
- Discuss which is the most popular method of payment.

1 THINK ABOUT IT. What should you do if you find incorrect information on your credit card bill? Do you think this affects your credit report?

- Go over the questions asked for this activity.
- Put students in pairs to discuss the questions.
- Elicit ideas from the class.

2 BEFORE YOU WRITE.

A. READ about what to do if you see unusual charges on your credit card or if you think someone has stolen your credit card information. What information should you give your credit card company in a letter? Underline the information.

- Go over the directions.
- Put students in pairs to complete the activity.
- Elicit from students the information that they underlined in the first paragraph. Does everyone agree? Go over the correct answers.

ANSWER KEY

Students should underline: your credit card number, the date of the bill with the disputed or incorrect charge, a description of the charge, your reasons for the dispute

 B. LISTEN to John call the Access credit card company about his statement. Why is he calling? Check the answer.

TCD2, 18

- Go over the directions and the possible answers.
- Play the CD and have students choose the correct answer.
- Elicit the answer from the class.

 LISTENING SCRIPT
Lesson 7, Activity 2B

TCD2, 18

Ms. Suresh:	Hello. This is Access credit card company, Ms. Suresh speaking. How may I help you?
John:	Hello. I have a problem with my credit card statement. There's a charge on it for something I didn't buy.
Ms. Suresh:	Okay. What is your name?
John:	John Green.
Ms. Suresh:	And your credit card number?
John:	365 922 076.

Ms. Suresh: Thank you. And what is the date of the incorrect charge?

John: November 17. It's for $300 at Wash-Co Appliance Store. I've never bought anything there!

Ms. Suresh: Okay, don't worry. You need to send us a letter about this. Write to the billing inquiry address on your statement. The address is on the back of your statement. In your letter, include your account number and what you think the incorrect charge is. Then we'll investigate.

John: Okay.

Ms. Suresh: And make sure to pay your bill on time. You don't need to pay the disputed charge, but you do need to pay the rest.

EXPANSION ACTIVITY: Quiz time

- Divide the class into two teams. Explain that both teams will listen to the conversation from Activity 2B two more times. After listening, teams must write five questions for the other team to answer. Each team will score one point for a correctly written question (as approved by the teacher) and one point for each question they answer correctly from the other team.
- Play the listening script two more times.
- Have teams write their questions.
- Have teams alternate asking and answering questions during the quiz game.

C. READ John's letter to the credit card company. Two sentences have unimportant information. They are not needed. Cross them out.

- Go over the directions.
- Have students read the letter and complete the activity.
- Call on volunteers to tell which sentences they crossed out and why. Confirm the correct answers.

ANSWER KEY

Students should cross out: I have two other credit cards, too. I remember that I was working that day.

❸ **WRITE.** Imagine that you received a credit card statement. There is a charge for $250 at Amy's Golden Travel Agency. Write a letter to the credit card company to dispute the charge. Include the following information.

- Direct students' attention to the Writing Focus box. Go over the information in it.
- Go over the directions and the information to include.
- Have students work independently to write a first draft of their letters.
- Have volunteers read their drafts to the class.

EXPANSION ACTIVITY: Access writes back

- Have students imagine that they work at Access credit card company from Activity 2.
- Tell students that they will write a letter in response to John Green's request. They may either deny or approve the request, or they may ask for proof to substantiate his claim.
- Have students work in pairs or groups to write their letters.
- Have volunteers share their letters with the class.

Point out that while in some cultures, it may seem rude to complain or dispute a charge, it is accepted behavior in the United States. People are usually not hesitant to stand up for themselves in such cases. Ask students if they have ever heard the saying "The squeaky wheel gets the grease." Elicit what they think it means, and ask if they have a similar proverb in their own language or culture.

4 AFTER YOU WRITE.

A. CHECK YOUR WORK.

- Go over the questions.
- Have students reread their first drafts and make changes if necessary.

B. REWRITE your letter with corrections.

- Go over the directions.
- Put students in pairs to review each other's writing, answering the questions about their partner's letter.
- Have students rewrite their letters with the necessary corrections.
- Call on volunteers to share their revised draft with the class.

EXPANSION ACTIVITY: Internet search

- Have students do an Internet search for current news stories related to credit cards or for personal stories related to credit card fraud.
- Have volunteers tell what they discovered, giving their opinion as called for.

ACADEMIC CONNECTION: Letters and correspondence

- Divide students into groups and assign each group a form of correspondence: personal letter, email, invitation, postcard, and so on. You may wish to provide examples of different forms of correspondence.
- Have the group compare their form of correspondence with the business letter on page 67. Have them analyze the differences in format, information included, formality, and so on.
- Have each group report their conclusions.
- As a class, rank each form of correspondence from most to least formal. Note which types of correspondence require specific components, such as an inside address, subject line, and so on.

Career Connection

OBJECTIVES

Read a hotel memo
Write a complaint and recommendation

COMPETENCIES

Offer feedback and make suggestions to
   consumer-related businesses
Practice test-taking skills

WARM-UP ACTIVITY: One time . . .

- Have students share stories about a time they stayed in a hotel and had a particularly good or bad experience. What happened? How was the staff helpful (or *not* helpful)?

- Encourage students to ask each other questions to learn more details about each story as it is told.

- You may wish to introduce the phrase "One time . . . " as a rhetorical element of oral storytelling.

1 THINK ABOUT IT. How do hotels improve their guests' stay at the hotel? What are some ways that hotel staff can get information about their customer service and make improvements?

- Go over the questions.
- Elicit ideas from the class to answer each question. List their ideas on the board.

2 READ this memo addressed to the front desk staff at a hotel. As you read, circle these vocabulary words. Then match each word with its definition.

- Go over the directions. Point out the glossary above the memo.
- Have students read the memo and circle the designated words.
- Put students in pairs to complete the matching exercise.
- Go over the answers with the class.

ANSWER KEY

1. a; 2. f; 3. e; 4. b; 5. d; 6. c

EXPANSION ACTIVITY: Writing sentences

- Have students write sentences using the vocabulary words in Activity 2.
- Call on volunteers to share their sentences with the class.

CULTURE NOTE

Discuss the role of memos in American businesses today. Point out that memos are intended to be an impersonal or impartial way to deliver information, policy changes, or company news. Talk about which persons within a company hierarchy might send memos and which ones probably wouldn't. You may wish to review the format of a memo and have students research a list of dos and don'ts in memo writing.

CIVICS NOTE

Point out that in the memo from Activity 2, GoodNight Hotel has a company motto. Ask students if they know of any mottoes related to the United States government or governmental organizations. For example, you might have students research the following mottoes: *E Pluribus Unum,* In God We Trust, Be All That You Can Be, The Toughest Job You'll Ever Love, and so on. Have students report on their findings.

3 TALK with a partner or in a group. How will the GoodNight Hotel improve security? Do you think these new security measures will prevent future identity theft? Why or why not?

- Go over the directions and the questions.
- Put students in pairs or groups to discuss the questions.
- Elicit ideas from the class.

4 WRITE. Hotels and other service-related businesses often ask customers to fill out a feedback survey about their experience. Write two complaints that guests might have at a hotel and two possible recommendations. Then talk with a partner and compare your charts.

- Go over the directions. Remind students of the warm-up activity in which they told about problems they have had at hotels in the past.
- Have students write their two complaints and recommendations in their charts.
- Put students in pairs to compare what they wrote.
- Call on volunteers to share their writing with the class.

5 WHAT ABOUT YOU? What are some problems you have had at hotels or restaurants? Did the staff do anything to correct the problem? What should they have done differently? Talk with a partner.

- Go over the questions with students.
- Put students in pairs to discuss.
- Have volunteers share their stories and ideas with the class.

EXPANSION ACTIVITY: Cartooning

- Have students turn their stories into cartoons by illustrating frames that tell the events that happened.
- Display the cartoons in an exhibit. Encourage classmates to sign comments about each other's cartoons on designated comment sheets beneath each piece.

COMMUNITY CONNECTION: Customer service surveys

- Have students collect customer service surveys from various businesses in the community, such as hotels and restaurants.
- As a class, compare the information requested on each survey. Encourage students to categorize questions. For example, how many questions ask about staff members? How many questions ask about the product or service itself?
- Discuss the results, and have students give their opinion about whether the surveys are well-designed and useful.
- Students may also interview managers at various businesses to determine how useful their customer service surveys have been in improving their business. Have students report their findings to the class.

CHECK YOUR PROGRESS!

- Have students circle the answers.
- Go over answers with the class and have students check whether each answer is right or wrong.
- Have students total their correct answers and fill in the chart at the bottom of the page.
- Have students create a learning plan and/or set learning goals.

ANSWER KEY

1. used; 2. must; 3. have opened; 4. given;
5. don't; 6. isn't; 7. won't; 8. did;
9. checkbook; 10. payment due date;
11. deposit; 12. penalty; 13. identity theft;
14. spending allowance; 15. mortgage payment;
16. automated payments

Unit Overview

LESSON	OBJECTIVES	STUDENT BOOK	WORKBOOK
1 Grammar and Vocabulary 1	Study branches of the government. Use active and passive voices.	p. 70	p. 62
2 Grammar Practice Plus	Recognize community services.	p. 72	p. 63
3 Listening and Conversation	Use content word stress. Find online information about law services.	p. 74	p. 64
4 Grammar and Vocabulary 2	Talk about crime. Use yes/no and information questions in the passive voice.	p. 76	p. 66
5 Grammar Practice Plus	Read information about taxes. Read a W-2 form. Calculate taxes owed and refunds.	p. 78	p. 67
6 Reading	Read about federal holidays in an encyclopedia.	p. 80	p. 68–69
7 Writing	Write about Memorial Day.	p. 82	p. 70–71
• Career Connection	Read about types of workplaces.	p. 84	p. 72–73
• Check Your Progress	Monitor progress.	p. 85	p. 74–75

Reading/Writing Strategies

- Highlight important information
- Revise a paragraph

Connection Activities

LESSON	TYPE	SKILL DEVELOPMENT
1	Community	Research local government leaders
2	Academic	Review transitive and intransitive verbs
3	Community	Access legal services online
4	Community	Survey U.S. citizens about jury duty
5	Community	Tax form
6	Academic	Research what to highlight while reading
Career Connection	Academic	Defining common management styles

WORKSHEET #/FOCUS	TITLE	TEACHER'S EDITION
13. Grammar	Where's the focus?	p. 317
14. Conversation	Can you help me?	p. 318
15. Reading	Tax Form	p. 319

LESSON 1: Grammar and Vocabulary

OBJECTIVES

Study branches of the government
Use active and passive voices

VOCABULARY

approve	governor
citizen	laws
congressman	mayor
congresswoman	senator
court	

GRAMMAR

Active and passive voices (simple present and simple past)

COMPETENCY

Understand information about U.S. government

WARM-UP ACTIVITY: Schema building

- Write on the board: *the Oval Office, the Capitol building, the Supreme Court Building, president, governor, mayor.*
- Put students in groups.
- Have each group write a sentence describing each item on the board. Tell students that if they don't know anything about an item they should guess.
- Have groups share their sentences with the class.

🎧 **1 GRAMMAR PICTURE DICTIONARY.**
TCD2, 19
SCD18
There are three branches in the United States federal government: executive, legislative (Congress), and judicial. Listen and read about federal, state, and city government in the U.S.

- Have students open their books and look at the pictures. Ask: *What do you see?* Write all the words students say on the board.
- Say the sentences or play the CD and have students repeat.
- Call on students and ask *What branch of government are the president and his Cabinet part of? What does the legislative branch do? What does the judicial branch do?*

2 READ the sentences in Activity 1 with a partner.

- Put students in pairs to read the sentences.
- Call on students to read the sentences to the class.

EXPANSION ACTIVITY: Governments around the world

- Put students into groups to discuss the governmental systems in their countries.
- Prompt the discussions by writing on the board: *Who is the federal leader(s) of your native country? Are there regional leaders like governors in the U.S.? Are there local leaders like mayors in the U.S.?*
- Ask students from different countries to tell the class about the government in their countries.

3 NOTICE THE GRAMMAR.

A. UNDERLINE *is/are* + past participle in each sentence above. Circle the word *by*.

- Go over the directions and the example.
- Have students underline *is/are* + past participle and circle the word *by*.
- Elicit the answers from students.

ANSWER KEY

1. The president is a member of the executive branch and is advised (by) a group called the Cabinet.

2. New laws are written and approved (by) the legislative branch. This branch is made up of 100 senators and 435 congressmen and congresswomen.

3. The Supreme Court is part of the judicial branch. It is the highest court in the country. Laws are explained and important decisions are made (by) this branch.

4. The leaders of state governments are called governors. They are elected (by) the people of their state.

5. Mayors are responsible for city government. They are elected (by) the people of their city.

6. United States citizens are given certain rights, such as the right to vote. Citizens have the right to vote at age 18.

B. READ the words and phrases that come after *by*. Check what type of information is included after *by*.

- Go over the directions.
- Have students check the box of the type of information that is include after *by*.
- Elicit the answer.

ANSWER KEY

who or what does the action

GRAMMAR CHART: Active and Passive Voices (Simple Present and Simple Past)

- Direct students' attention to the chart or project the transparency or CD.
- Go over the information on the chart and the usage notes. Read the sentences, pausing to have students repeat.
- Read the Grammar Professor note aloud. Ask: *What information was left out of the second example?* (by the voters). Discuss why this information is not needed and was thus omitted from the sentence.

GRAMMAR NOTE

- Only transitive verbs (verbs that have an object) are used in passive sentences. Intransitive verbs (e.g., *arrive, go, sit*) cannot be used in the passive voice.

CHART EXPANSION ACTIVITY: Where's the focus?

- Read the first two sentences, which explain the use of passive voice to the class. Ask, "What's *focus*?"
- Elicit the answer that focus deals with where you want to direct the readers' attention.
- Write on the board: *Ted Lam advises the mayor. The mayor is advised by Ted Lam.* Ask for reasons why one writer may want to focus on Ted Lam while another may want to focus on the mayor.
- Photocopy and distribute Worksheet 13: *Where's the focus?*
- Go over the directions.
- Have students do the activity.
- Put students in groups to discuss their answers.
- Walk around to monitor the activity and provide help as needed.

WORKSHEET ANSWER KEY

Probable answers are:
1. B; **2.** A; **3.** B; **4.** A; **5.** A; **6.** B; **7.** B; **8.** A

4 READ the sentences. Write *A* for active sentences and *P* for passive sentences.

- Go over the directions and the example.
- Have students write *A* for active sentences and *P* for passive sentences.
- Put students in pairs to compare their answers.
- Call on students to read their answers to the class.

ANSWER KEY

1. A; **2.** P; **3.** P; **4.** A; **5.** P; **6.** P

5 REWRITE each sentence in the passive form. Use *by* + agent if that information is known, and if it is important to mention.

- Go over the directions and the example.
- Have students rewrite the sentences in passive form.
- Put students in groups to compare answers.
- Go over the answers with the class.

ANSWER KEY

1. A new president was elected this year (by the United States).
2. Important decisions are made by senators every day.
3. Many letters were sent to the governor.
4. The congressman wasn't invited to speak at the meeting.
5. A long article was written about the mayor.
6. Citizens were asked by the mayor to help clean up the parks.

6 WHAT ABOUT YOU? Complete the sentences. Use the verbs below, or your own ideas. Then talk with a partner.

- Go over the directions and use the first item as an example. Complete the sentence with information from your life (e.g., *Last year, I was invited to a friend's wedding.*). To encourage students ask at least one question for their partner's sentences, have two or three students ask you questions about your sentence (e.g., *Where was the wedding? Did you have fun?*).
- Have students complete the sentences.
- Put students in pairs to discuss their sentences.

COMMUNITY CONNECTION: Local government leaders

- Write on the board offices held by local leaders in your community (e.g., mayor, chief of police, board of supervisors, etc.).
- Put students in pairs. Have each pair research one local leader. If possible, do not have pairs research the same person. Tell students they can do their research by going to the local government building, looking at local government websites, and (if he or she is accessible) calling the local leader and asking for a short interview.
- During the next class, call on pairs to tell the class what they found out.

LESSON 2: Grammar Practice Plus

WARM-UP ACTIVITY: What do you see?

- Put the transparency for Unit 5 on the overhead projector (OHP) or have students look at the Big Picture on page 72.
- Put students in pairs or groups.
- Have each group write down 10 things that they see in the picture.
- Ask each group to write their list on the board.

1 TALK about the picture. What community services do you see?

- Put the Big Picture for Unit 5 on the overhead projector (OHP) or have students open their books to page 72.
- Read the directions aloud.
- Discuss the community services in the picture (*free health clinic, senior van, animal control, public works [trash collection], community center, public safety [police and fire fighters], local politicians [senator and mayor]*).

 2 LISTEN to the sentences. Then write the number of the correct sentence next to each verb.

TCD2, 20

- Go over the directions.
- Play item number 1 on the CD or read the sentence to the class. Point out that the sentence is about garbage collection, so a number *1* is written next to the word *collect* in the box.
- Say the sentences or play the CD and have students write the numbers next to the verbs.
- Go over the answers with the class.

 LISTENING SCRIPT
TCD2, 20 **Lesson 2, Activity 2**

1. Garbage was collected by the Public Works Department.
2. A chair was knocked over by a dog.
3. A speech was given by the mayor.
4. First aid kits were handed out by the free clinic.
5. Free bike helmets were provided by a police officer.
6. The party was sponsored by the Public Safety Department.

ANSWER KEY

6 sponsor; 5 provide; 2 knock over;
4 hand out; 1 collect; 3 give (a speech)

3 COMPLETE the article with the passive voice of the verbs in parentheses. Use the past form.

- Go over the directions. Read the example sentence aloud. Point out how the answer uses the past tense passive form of the verb. If needed, direct students to the grammar chart on page 71 to review passive form.
- Have students complete the article with the past form of the passive voice of the verbs in parentheses.
- Elicit answers from the class.

1. was not sponsored; **2.** was paid for; **3.** was organized; **4.** were welcomed; **5.** were provided; **6.** were given; **7.** were handed out; **8.** was given

4 WRITE eight new sentences about the picture in Activity 1: four affirmative and four negative. Use the passive voice in simple past. You can use the verbs and nouns in the box or other words you know. Then share your sentences with a partner.

- Go over the direction and the example.
- Check comprehension on *affirmative* and *negative* by writing on the board: *Free blood tests were not given. The mayor was invited to the park.* Ask students which sentence is an affirmative sentence and which sentence is a negative sentence.
- Have students write eight sentences using the passive voice in simple past.
- Walk around the room and monitor student progress.
- Put students in pairs to compare and edit their sentences.

BIG PICTURE LISTENING EXPANSION ACTIVITY: Dictation jigsaw

- Have students look at the Big Picture in Activity 1 or put the transparency for Unit 5 on the OHP.
- Dictate the following sentences. Do not repeat the sentences.
1. *Children under 18 were given bike helmets by the police.*
2. *The garbage was collected by the Public Works Department.*
3. *Food was provided by The Mission Community Center.*
4. *First aid kits were handed out by the free clinic.*
- Put students into groups to compare and correct their sentences.
- Check the sentences of each group.

- Have each group rewrite the dictation sentences using active voice.
- Go over the answers with the class.

ANSWER KEY

1. The police gave bike helmets to children under 18.
2. The Public Works Department collected the garbage.
3. The Mission Community Center provided food.
4. The free clinic handed out first aid kits.

5 TALK with a partner. Read the names of the community organizations below. Write the kinds of things you think each community organization provides. Share your answers with a partner.

- Go over the directions and the example. Ask: *Can you think of any other things that the Public Safety Department might do?* (sheriff's department, driver's licenses, toxic waste disposal, etc.).
- Have students write the kinds of things they think each community service provides. If you think this may be too difficult for individual students, put them in pairs or groups to make a list of services.
- Put students in pairs to compare their answers.
- Write each community service on the board and elicit from students the kinds of services each one provides. Write the services on the board.

ACADEMIC CONNECTION: Transitive and intransitive verb review

- Write on the board: *Mary drives her car every day. Mary jogs every day.*

- Ask how we would grammatically describe *her car* in the first sentence. Elicit the answer that it is a direct object.

- Ask what the direct object is in the second sentence. Elicit that the second sentence does not have a direct object.

- Review the terms *transitive* and *intransitive verbs*. Remind students that transitive verbs have a direct object that is either stated or implied, while intransitive verbs do not have a direct object. (You may wish to point out that some verbs can be either transitive or intransitive, depending on their meaning and use; e.g., *The Senate voted the question; I will vote in next week's election.*)

- Write the following list on the board: *agree, answer, close, come, do, forgive, go, help, join, laugh, miss, rain, read, share, sleep, sit, stay, talk, turn, wait*.

- Put students in pairs. Have each pair copy the list from the board and write a *T* if the verb is transitive and an *I* if the verb is intransitive.

- Go over the answers as a class.

ANSWER KEY

Transitive: answer, close, do, forgive, help, join, miss, read, share, turn
Intransitive: agree, come, go, laugh, rain, sleep, sit, stay, talk, wait

LESSON 3: Listening and Conversation

OBJECTIVES

Use content word stress
Find online information about law services

PRONUNCIATION

Content word stress

COMPETENCY

Find appropriate legal services for various situations

WARM-UP ACTIVITY: Content words

- Ask a volunteer to come to the board and write a sentence about his or her morning.
- Ask the rest of the class to identify the "important" words in the sentence. Circle them.
- Explain that the important words are content words.

PRONUNCIATION: Content Word Stress
TCD2, 21

- Play the CD or go over the information about content word stress.
- Direct students' attention to the answer sheet.
- Play the CD and have students fill in the correct circle.
- Put students in pairs to compare answers.
- Go over the answers with the class.

PRONUNCIATION NOTE

Students whose native languages are syllabic are often confused by sentence level word stress. In syllabic languages (Chinese, Korean, Spanish, etc.), each syllable has equal importance and is given an equal amount of time. In stress-timed languages (English,

Russian, German, etc.), certain words are stressed and spoken more slowly, while other words are not stressed and are spoken more quickly.

 A. UNDERLINE the content words to predict the stress patterns in the following sentences. Then listen and check.
TCD2, 22
SCD19

- Go over the directions.
- Have students underline the content words in each sentence.
- Play the CD or read the sentences. Repeat if necessary until students feel confident that they can hear the stressed content words.

EXPANSION ACTIVITY: Predict stress

- Put students in pairs.
- Have each pair write five sentences that contain at least seven words.
- Have students predict the content word stress in each sentence by underlining the content words.
- Check their predictions.
- Have students practice saying the sentences aloud.

ANSWER KEY

1. The <u>congresswoman</u> was <u>elected two years ago</u>.
2. <u>Senior citizens</u> are <u>given seats</u> at the <u>front of the room</u>.
3. The <u>votes</u> were <u>counted electronically</u>.
4. The <u>governor's speech</u> was <u>not shown</u> on <u>TV</u>.

B. LISTEN again and repeat.
TCD2, 23
- Go over the directions.
- Have students listen and repeat the sentences.
- Put students in pairs to practice content word stress in each sentence.

EXPANSION ACTIVITY: Content check

- Have students write five sentences.
- Put students in pairs.
- Have students exchange papers and correct each other's sentences.
- Have each pair underline the content words in the sentences.
- Check the sentences to make sure the correct words are underlined.
- Have students practice their sentences with the correct sentence stress.

 1 LISTEN to the conversation. Then listen to the question. Fill in the correct answer. Replay each item if necessary.
TCD2, 24–29

- Direct students' attention to the activity and the fill-in circles.
- Play the CD and have students fill in the correct circles.
- If needed, replay the CD.
- Put students in pairs to compare answers.
- Go over the answers with the class.

 LISTENING SCRIPT
Lesson 3, Activity 1
TCD2, 24–29

1. *A:* Good afternoon. Senior Services. How can I help you?
   B: Hello. My name is Bill Jones. I have a doctor's appointment at 3:00, and the van isn't here yet to take me to the doctor's office. The ride was scheduled last week by my grandson.

   Which is correct?
   A. Bill Jones is calling to schedule a ride for next week.
   B. A ride was scheduled by Bill Jones's doctor last week.
   C. Bill Jones's grandson scheduled a ride for him last week.

2. *A:* 911 operator. What is the emergency?
   B: A man was just hit by a car! I think his leg is broken. Send an ambulance to Third Street and Avenue A!

   Which is correct?
   A. A car hit a man.
   B. The caller broke his leg.
   C. The caller was in a car accident.

3. *A:* Public Works Department. How may I help you?
   B: Hi. I just moved to 578 Oak Street. Is the garbage collected on Mondays in this neighborhood?
   A: No, it isn't. It's collected every Wednesday morning.

   Which is correct?
   A. Public Works doesn't collect garbage on Oak Street.
   B. Garbage is collected on Mondays on Oak Street.
   C. Garbage is collected on Wednesdays on Oak Street.

4. *A:* Mission Community Center. How can I help you?
   B: Hi. I just signed my son up for your after-school program. Do you provide snacks for children in the program?
   A: Yes, we provide fruit, sandwiches, juice, and milk.

   Which is correct?
   A. Snacks are provided by parents.
   B. Snacks are provided by the community center.
   C. Snacks are not provided.

5. *A:* Free Clinic. How may I help you?
   B: How often is your nutrition class offered?
   A: We have a nutrition class once a month. It's always on the first Monday of every month. Would you like to sign up for the next class?

   Which is correct?
   A. The Free Clinic offers nutrition classes at the community center.
   B. The Free Clinic offers a nutrition class every month.
   C. The Free Clinic offers nutrition classes every day.

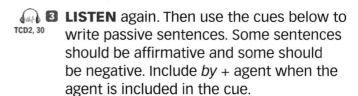

6. *A:* Good afternoon. Animal Control. What can I do for you?

   B: Hello. The bicycles in my garage were knocked over last night. I think there is an animal hiding in my garage.

   A: We'll send someone over. Can I have your address, please?

Which is correct?

   A. There is a dog in the caller's garage.

   B. Someone took bicycles out of the caller's garage.

   C. The caller wants Animal Control to help him find an animal.

ANSWER KEY

1. C; 2. A; 3. C; 4. B; 5. B; 6. C

2 LISTEN. Read the sentences and check *True* or *False*.
TCD2, 30

• Go over the directions.

• Play the CD and have students check *True* or *False*. If needed, replay the CD.

• Go over the answers with the class.

LISTENING SCRIPT
Lesson 3, Activities 2 and 3
TCD2, 30

A: Public Works. This is Erin Colby. How can I help you today?

B: I'm calling because the stop sign at the corner of Maple Street and 3rd Avenue was knocked over this morning.

A: I see. How did that happen?

B: It was hit by a car. I was standing two feet away from the sign when it happened.

A: Was anyone injured?

B: I wasn't injured, but the driver hit his head.

A: Did you talk to the driver of the car?

B: No, he drove away right after he hit the sign.

A: Did anyone else witness the accident?

B: Yes, there were three other people there. I can provide their phone numbers if you want them.

A: Thank you. We'll send someone out to talk to you and repair the sign as soon as possible.

ANSWER KEY

1. True; 2. False; 3. False; 4. False; 5. True

3 LISTEN again. Then use the cues below to write passive sentences. Some sentences should be affirmative and some should be negative. Include *by* + agent when the agent is included in the cue.

• Go over the directions and the example. Ask: *Why is* by + *agent included in the sentence?* (It's given in the cue and it's needed information.)

• Play the CD.

• Have students write passive sentences using the cues given.

• Ask individual students to write one of the sentences on the board. Check the sentences as a class.

ANSWER KEY

1. A stop sign was hit by a car.

2. The stop sign was knocked over.

3. The driver was injured.

4. The caller was not injured.

5. The accident was seen by three other people.

BIG PICTURE CONVERSATION EXPANSION ACTIVITY: Can you help me?

• Photocopy and distribute Worksheet 14: *Can you help me?*

• Put the transparency for Unit 2 on the OHP or have students look at the Big Picture in their books.

• Go over the directions.

• Have students put the exchanges in each conversation in the correct order.

• Put students in pairs to write one more conversation.

• Have each pair practice all of the conversations.

• Have a few pairs read the conversations aloud to the class.

WORKSHEET ANSWER KEY

1. 5, 1, 2, 3, 6, 4
2. 4, 6, 1, 2, 5, 3
3. Answers will vary.

TCD2, 31
SCD20 **4 LISTEN** to the conversation. Then practice with a partner.

- Direct students' attention to the picture. Ask questions: *Who do you see? Does the woman seem happy? How do you think she is feeling?*
- Play the CD or read the conversation as students follow along silently.
- Play the CD or read the conversation again and have students repeat along.
- Ask: *Why did the woman call Legal Aid Services? When is her appointment?*
- Put students in pairs to practice the conversation.

5 COMPLETE. Read the information from the website. Then complete the chart below with the correct service.

- Go over the directions. Read the website information aloud to the class. Check comprehension on difficult vocabulary such as *housing discrimination.*
- Have students complete the chart with the correct service.
- Put students in groups to compare their answers.

ANSWER KEY

1. immigration; 2. employment rights;
3. employment rights; 4. employment rights;
5. tentants' rights; 6. personal injury

6 ROLE-PLAY. Use the information in the chart in Activity 5 to practice the conversation from Activity 4 with a partner. Make up appointment times.

- Go over the directions. Model the activity with a more advanced student. Use item number 1. Have the student act as the person from the legal aid service, and you act as the person having trouble renewing your visa.
- Put students in pairs to role-play the phone conversations.
- Ask each pair to do one role-play in front of the class.

COMMUNITY CONNECTION: Free legal services

- Have students research free legal services in your area.
- Tell students they can do their research by doing an Internet search using the keywords *free legal services in (your community).*
- Ask students to write down the name and phone number of three places that offer free legal advice. For each place, they should also write down two types of legal advice given (e.g., *immigration advice, custody suits, renter's rights).* You may want to have more advanced students call the service and ask about the types of legal advice offered.
- During the next class, call on students to tell the class what they found out.

LESSON 4: Grammar and Vocabulary

<table>
<tr><td colspan="2">**OBJECTIVES**</td></tr>
<tr><td colspan="2">Talk about crime
Use *yes/no* and information questions
  in the passive voice</td></tr>
</table>

<table>
<tr><td colspan="2">**VOCABULARY**</td></tr>
<tr><td>accused of</td><td>innocent</td></tr>
<tr><td>arrested</td><td>report</td></tr>
<tr><td>attorney</td><td>serve on a jury</td></tr>
<tr><td>defendant</td><td>trial</td></tr>
<tr><td>guilty</td><td></td></tr>
</table>

<table>
<tr><td>**GRAMMAR**</td></tr>
<tr><td>*Yes/No* and information questions
  in the passive voice</td></tr>
</table>

<table>
<tr><td>**COMPETENCY**</td></tr>
<tr><td>Interpret information about the U.S. court
  system</td></tr>
</table>

WARM-UP ACTIVITY: You are under arrest

- Tell the class that you are going to tell them a story about your neighbor who was arrested for stealing cars. You saw the police come to the house and put him in handcuffs. If needed, mime the action.

- Ask: *What happens to my neighbor after the police handcuff him?* Elicit answers. At this point, do not go into specifics if students do not know the answer.

- Tell students that the police took your neighbor to the police station. Ask: *What happens at the police station?* Elicit answers.

- Tell students that your neighbor can't afford a lawyer. Ask: *What happens to my neighbor?* Elicit answers.

- Tell students that your neighbor had a trial and a jury found him guilty. Ask: *What's a jury? What does* guilty *mean?* Elicit answers.

① GRAMMAR PICTURE DICTIONARY.
TCD2, 32
SCD21   What kinds of legal issues are the people talking about? Listen and read.

- Have students look at the pictures. Ask: *What do you see?*

- Play the CD or read the conversations aloud as students follow along silently.

- Call on students and ask questions about the people in the pictures: *What did the police think the man did? How did he get a lawyer? Did the man steal the computer?* Elicit the answers.

② PRACTICE the conversations from Activity 1 with a partner.

- Go over the directions.

- Put students in pairs to practice the sentences from Activity 1.

- Call on pairs to read the sentences to the class.

③ NOTICE THE GRAMMAR. Circle the form of *be* and the past participle in each question above. Underline the subject. Which word order below is correct?

- Go over the directions and the example.

- Have students circle the form of *be* and the past participle and underline the subject.

- Go over the answers as a class.

- Have students circle the letter for the correct word order in the sentences.

ANSWER KEY

1. A: Why (was) the man (stopped) by the police?
   B: He was accused of stealing a computer.

2. A: (Are) people (required) to answer police officers' questions when they (are) (arrested)?
   B: No, they don't have to say anything. They can ask for a lawyer.

3. A: (Was) an attorney (provided) for him?
   B: Yes, he couldn't afford a lawyer, so the judge provided one.

4. A: (Is) everyone in the United States (required) to serve on a jury?
   B: Any U.S. citizen can be called to report for jury duty.

5. A: Why (are) n't you (required) to serve on the jury?
   B: Because the trial is going to start on Friday, and I have to leave for college next week.

6. A: (Was) the defendant (found) guilty?
   B: No, he wasn't. The jury decided he was innocent.

   The word order in option c. is correct.

GRAMMAR CHART: *Yes/No* and Information Questions in the Passive Voice

- Go over the information in the chart.
- Read the sample sentences in the chart aloud and have students repeat.

BIG PICTURE GRAMMAR EXPANSION ACTIVITY: Questions in the passive voice

- Have the students look at the Big Picture on page 72 or put the transparency for Unit 2 on the OHP.
- Have each student write five questions in the passive voice about things happening in the picture.
- Put students in pairs.
- Have the partners ask and answer their questions.
- Walk around the room to monitor students' progress.

4 WRITE passive *yes/no* and information questions using the cues below. Include *by* + agent when that information is available.

- Go over the directions.
- Direct students' attention to the two example sentences. Point out that because the first five sentences are in present tense and the last five sentences are in past tense, an example is given for each tense.
- Have students write passive questions using the cues.
- Walk around the room and monitor student progress.
- Have students write the sentences on the board. Correct the sentences as needed.

ANSWER KEY

1. Is Elizabeth required to serve on a jury?
2. Where are people taken after they're arrested?
3. Are attorneys provided by the court?
4. What is the defendant accused of?
5. How is the information given?
6. Was Jay Abrams found guilty?
7. When were they called to report for jury duty?
8. Why was Mark accused by the store owner?
9. How were people chosen for the jury?
10. Why were we not told about the trial?

5 WRITE three passive voice questions asking for personal information. Use the verbs in the box or other verbs. Then ask and answer questions with a partner.

- Go over the directions. Point out the speech bubble at the bottom on the page. Note how it is an example of the type of question students should write.

- Put students in pairs to ask and answer the questions.

ACADEMIC CONNECTION: Jury duty

- Ask students if they have jury duty in their countries. If they do, ask them to describe what happens when someone goes to the court house to serve.

- Write on the board: *Have you ever had jury duty? If yes, can you please tell me what happened when you went to the court house? If no, can you please tell me why not?*

- Have students copy down the questions. Tell them to ask five U.S. citizens the questions and to write down the answers.

- Call on students to tell the class what they found out.

LESSON 5: Grammar Practice Plus

OBJECTIVES

Read information about taxes
Read a W-2 form
Calculate taxes owed and refunds

VOCABULARY

federal tax	tax return
file	wages
income tax	W-2 form
state tax	withhold (taxes)

GRAMMAR

Questions in the passive voice

COMPETENCIES

Interpret information about taxes
Complete tax forms

WARM-UP ACTIVITY: Paying taxes

- Ask students what types of taxes people have to pay (e.g., income, property, sales, value added, inheritance). Put students in groups to discuss paying taxes. Write their answers on the board.

- Tell students that this lesson focuses on income tax. Check comprehension by asking what income tax is.

- Put students in groups to discuss how income tax is paid in their native countries. They should share what percent of most people's income goes to pay their income tax, when they have to pay it, and what sorts of deductions are allowed.

- Have students from different countries share their answers with the class.

1 TALK. Write answers to the questions below. Then ask and answer the questions with a partner.

- Go over the directions.
- Have students write their answers to the questions.
- Put students in pairs to discuss their answers.

ANSWER KEY

1. All citizens, residents, and non-residents need to file tax returns.

2. Taxes are due on April 15 of each year.

3. If you filed taxes last year, you will receive your tax booklets in the mail. You can also get federal booklets at www.irs.gov, at public libraries, and at post offices.

4. To file your taxes, you need W-2 forms, 1099 forms, and any other forms that show your wages.

2 READ the information about taxes. Underline each of the following words once: *file, income tax, tax return, federal tax, state tax, W-2 form, wages, withheld*. After you read, check your answers to the questions in Activity 1.

- Go over the directions.
- Have students read the information and underline *file, federal tax, income tax, state tax, tax return, W-2 form, wages, withheld*.
- Have students check their answers to the questions in Activity 1.
- Go over the answers for Activity 1 with the class.

ANSWER KEY

Who is required to file income taxes? All citizens, residents, and non-residents need to file <u>tax returns</u> if they receive more than a certain amount of money during the year. This money can come from jobs, interest from savings accounts, and unemployment pay.

To find out if you made enough money to file taxes, go to tax websites or check tax booklets. For <u>federal taxes</u> (Internal Revenue Service or IRS), go to www.irs.gov. To find the tax website for your state, go to an Internet search engine and type the name of your state and "taxes." In most states, you have to file both federal and <u>state taxes</u>.

When are taxes due? Taxes are due on April 15 of each year.

Where can I get tax booklets? If you filed taxes last year, you will receive your tax booklets in the mail. If your booklets are not mailed to you, you can get federal booklets at www.irs.gov. Some forms and booklets are provided by public libraries and post offices.

What information do I need to file my taxes? You need <u>W-2 forms</u>, 1099 forms, and any other forms that show your <u>wages</u> (how much money you made during the year). These forms also show how much money was <u>withheld</u> as <u>income tax</u>. These forms are mailed to you by your employer and usually arrive at the end of January.

Where can I get help? Call your local IRS office and ask for the Taxpayer Education Coordinator to get information about free help with your taxes. To find the phone number for your local IRS office, go to www.irs.gov and click on "Contact IRS."

❸ MATCH each word below with its definition.

- Go over the directions.
- Have students match each word with its definition.
- Elicit the correct answers from the class.

ANSWER KEY

1. d; **2.** h; **3.** b; **4.** e; **5.** f; **6.** a; **7.** c; **8.** g

❹ READ the W-2 form. What were Carlos's wages last year? Circle the amount.

- Go over the directions.
- Have students read the W-2 form and circle Carlos's wages for last year.
- Ask a student for the correct answer.

CULTURE NOTE

Income tax forms can be very confusing. You may want to point out to students that tax-payers must pay both the state and federal taxes. Money is also withheld to pay for two federal programs: social security and Medicare. The social security system provides social welfare and social insurance programs. Medicare is one of the largest programs provided by the social security system. It provides medical insurance to people who are over 65 or have special needs.

ANSWER KEY

Students should circle: $16,890.24

TCD2, 33 **❺ LISTEN.** Fill in the missing information in the W-2 form above.

- Go over the directions. Point out the five fill-in lines on the form.
- Play the CD or read the sentences while students fill in the correct information.
- Put students in pairs to compare answers.
- Go over the answers with the class.

TCD2, 33

LISTENING SCRIPT
Lesson 5, Activity 5

1. Carlos Tejada's social security number is 987-65-4320.
2. Carlos's address is 1472 South Ocean Drive.
3. Carlos's zip code is 91368.
4. The zip code for the Sunshine Catering Company is 94132.
5. $1,758 was withheld for federal taxes.

EXPANSION ACTIVITY: 1040EZ

- Make copies of a 1040EZ income tax form. (see www.irs.org.)
- Tell students that Carlos is single and has no children or dependents.
- Have students fill out the form for Carlos Tejada using the information from the W-2 form in Activities 4 and 5.
- Go over the completed form using a transparency and the OHP.

COMMUNITY CONNECTION: Tax Form

- Photocopy and distribute Worksheet 15: *Tax Form.*
- Have students read the form while you write the following information on the board.

   Mr. John Smith
   689 Main Street Apt. 4
   Lincoln, Nebraska 68464
   SSN: 003-68-9875
   John Smith is single with no dependents.
   Wages, salaries, and tips: $42,562.26
   Taxable Interest: $56.00
   Unemployment compensation: $0
   Federal tax withheld: $6809.92
   Earned Income Credit: $0
   Nontaxable combat pay election: $0

- Have students fill out the worksheet with the information from the board.
- Put students in pairs once the information is correctly on the form.
- Have each pair go to http://www.irs.gov/pub/irs-pdf/i1040tt.pdf to find out how much tax Mr. Smith should be refunded or should pay.

ANSWER KEY

Mr. Smith will get a refund of $2,342.54.

6 WRITE questions using the past passive voice. Then answer the questions with a partner.

- Go over the directions and the example. If needed, review the grammar chart at the top of page 77.
- Have students write questions using the past passive voice.
- Put students in pairs to compare their questions and then to answer the questions.
- Ask five pairs to write one of the questions on the board. Ask five other pairs to answer one of the questions on the board.

ANSWER KEY

1. Was money withheld for local income tax?
   Answer: No, there is no such thing.
2. Was Carlos assigned a Social Security number?
   Answer: Yes, it is 987-65-4320.
3. How much money was withheld by the state?
   Answer: $444.40
4. Where was Carlos employed?
   Answer: Sunshine Catering
5. How much money was withheld by the federal government?
   Answer: $1,758

MATH: Calculating Refunds and Taxes Owed

- Have students read the information about how to figure tax refunds and taxes owed or read it aloud to the class.
- Have students figure out if Carlos gets a refund of $396 or if he owes $396.
- Go over the answer with the class.

ANSWER KEY

$2,154 – $1,758 = $396
Amount he owes: $396

7 WHAT ABOUT YOU? Ask and answer the questions below with a partner.

- Go over the directions. Model the activity by giving true answers about yourself for each question.
- Put students in small groups to discuss their answers.

LESSON 6: Reading

OBJECTIVES

Read about federal holidays in an encyclopedia

READING FOCUS

Highlight important information

COMPETENCIES

Read about U.S. holidays
Use an encyclopedia

WARM-UP ACTIVITY: Holidays

- Have students close their books and not look in their books while doing this activity.
- Write the names of the 12 months on the board.
- Put students in groups to brainstorm as many holidays as they can think of for each month. Remind them that they can use holidays from both the U.S. and their native countries. If they list a holiday from their native countries, they should explain the holiday to the group.
- Ask each group for the holidays and list them on the board next to the correct month.

1 THINK ABOUT IT. Write the names of three American holidays. Are these holidays celebrated to remember a person? An event? Which ones have you celebrated before? What did you do to celebrate the holiday?

- Direct students' attention to the Reading Strategy Summary box. Check comprehension by asking what it means to use prior knowledge.
- Go over the directions.
- Have students write the names of three American holidays.

- Call on students to read their answers. For each new holiday, discuss if it commemorates a person or an event. Also, discuss which holidays students have celebrated before and how they celebrated the holiday.

2 BEFORE YOU READ.

A. READ the encyclopedia entry on the next page quickly. Which two holidays are discussed in detail? What do you already know about these holidays?

- Go over the directions. Remind students that they practiced scanning (reading something quickly to find specific information) in Unit 2.
- Give students 30 seconds to scan the reading on page 81.
- Ask the class which two holidays are discussed and what they already know about them.

ANSWER KEY

The two holidays discussed in detail are New Year's Day and Martin Luther King Jr. Day.

B. DISCUSS the highlighted information. Read only the highlighted words. Then read the whole paragraph. Why do you think each part is highlighted? Why are some parts not highlighted? Discuss with a partner.

ACADEMIC NOTE

Many students like to highlight important information in a reading or textbook. Often students who are new to this study skill will highlight too much text. Remind students that they should be selective in what they choose to highlight. Also remind them that relying on someone else's highlighting in a used textbook is not a good idea.

3 **READ** the encyclopedia entry on the next page. Highlight (or underline) the key facts in each paragraph.

- Direct students' attention to the Reading Focus box. Read the information in the box to the class. (You may want to bring in highlighting markers to show students what they are.) Ask: *"Why is highlighting information useful?"* Elicit answers from the class (e.g., Highlighting makes it easier to review a reading before a test.).
- Go over the directions.
- Have students read the entry and highlight (or underline) important facts.

4 **AFTER YOU READ.**

A. ANSWER the questions. Then discuss your answers with a partner.

- Go over the directions.
- Have students answer the questions.
- Put students in pairs to discuss their answers.
- Have pairs look up the words in a dictionary to check their answers.
- Go over the answers with the class.

ANSWER KEY

1. Ten days are federal holidays.
2. On a federal holiday, offices and banks close.
3. Answers may include having parties, counting down to midnight, making New Year's resolutions, remembering the year that has passed, and gathering in Times Square.
4. for leading the civil rights movement
5. He asked all races to live in peace.
6. peace parades; candlelight marches at night; church services; school plays and exhibits; community events such as service projects, volunteer programs, and fundraisers

B. READ the information you highlighted again. Did it help you answer the questions? Compare with a partner. Did you highlight the same information? Did you miss anything? Did you highlight too many things?

- Go over the directions.
- Have students compare the information they highlighted in the reading.
- Make a transparency of the reading. Ask advanced students to highlight the information. After each student has highlighted information, discuss whether the information really needed to be highlighted.

ACADEMIC CONNECTION: What to highlight?

- Tell students that often people new to highlighting information in a reading are confused about what they should highlight.
- Put students in groups to brainstorm at least 7 types of information they may want to highlight while reading (dates, places, key facts or events, definitions, categories, comparisons, unfamiliar words).
- Have each group ask other students in your school what they highlight in their textbooks. They might also ask teachers or research the question on the Internet.
- During the next class, have students share what they discovered.

LESSON 7: Writing

| OBJECTIVES |
Write about Memorial Day

| WRITING FOCUS |
Revise your writing

| COMPETENCY |
Read and write about holidays

WARM-UP ACTIVITY: Learning to write

- Ask: *How many people think they are very good at writing essays in English?* Have students who think they are very good at it raise their hands.
- Put students in groups to brainstorm ideas on what makes someone a good writer.
- Have each group put their ideas on the board.
- Go over the ideas with the class.

1 THINK ABOUT IT. When you write a paragraph or essay, do you go back to look for ways you could make it better? What do you look for? What changes do you make? Do you ask anyone else to help you?

- Go over the directions.
- Put students in groups to discuss the questions.
- Have a few groups share their answers with the class.

EXPANSION ACTIVITY: Revision checklist

- Put students in groups.
- Have each group create a revision checklist. Suggest that they think about what to look for organizationally and grammatically.
- Collect the checklists and make a master copy of all the relevant items to distribute to the class.

ACADEMIC NOTE

One way to help students understand the importance of revising is to explain the difference between writer-based writing and reader-based writing. Writer-based writing is when the writer is more concerned about getting his or her ideas on the paper. Reader-based writing is when the writer is concerned with engaging the reader. For example, reader-based writers will take time to consider what the reader needs to know and what to leave out. Most first drafts are writer-based. One reason we revise is to move the text from writer-based to reader-based writing.

2 BEFORE YOU WRITE.

A. READ the paragraph that a student wrote about the history of Memorial Day. Is it easy to understand?

- Direct students' attention to the Writing Focus box. Read the information in the box to the class. Mention that many writers revise their own writing and ask other people for feedback on what to revise.
- Go over the directions.
- Have students read the paragraph.

B. DISCUSS the questions with a partner. Make notes on the paragraph in Activity 2A as you discuss each question.

- Go over the directions.
- Put students in pairs to discuss the questions and to make notes on what needs to be revised in the paragraph.
- Go over the answers to the questions with the class.

❸ WRITE.

A. REWRITE. Look at the revisions you made to the paragraph on the previous page. Rewrite the paragraph. Include all of the changes that you made.

- Go over the directions.
- Have student rewrite their paragraphs.
- Walk around the room and monitor students' progress.
- Put students in groups to compare their revised paragraphs.

B. WRITE about a holiday that is special to you. Use books or the Internet to research the holiday. Write two paragraphs about the holiday. In the first paragraph, write about the history. In the second paragraph, write about how the holiday is celebrated.

- Go over the directions.
- Have students write two paragraphs about a special holiday of their choice.

❹ AFTER YOU WRITE.

A. REVISE your paragraphs. Ask yourself the questions in the Writing Focus box on page 82.

- Go over the directions.
- Have students revise their paragraphs.

B. EDIT. Check your work.

- Go over the directions.
- Have students check their paragraphs.

C. REWRITE your paragraphs with corrections.

- Go over the directions.
- Have students rewrite their paragraphs.

D. DISCUSS. Exchange papers with a partner. What interesting information did you learn from your partner's paragraphs? Discuss with your partner.

- Go over the directions.
- Put students in pairs.
- Have students exchange papers and read their partner's paragraphs.
- Have each pair discuss the question.

Career Connection

OBJECTIVES

Read about types of workplaces

COMPETENCIES

Talk about different types of workplaces
Practice test-taking skills

WARM-UP ACTIVITY: Management styles

- Write on the board or on a transparency: *Do you like teachers who only give one pass/fail test at the end of the semester? Do you like teachers who give weekly tests and a lot of homework? Do you like teachers who have you do a lot of group work? Do you like teachers who let you work alone most of the time?*

- Put students in groups to discuss their answers to the questions. Encourage students to give reasons why they prefer one teaching style over another.

- Ask students to share their answers with the class.

1 THINK ABOUT IT. Look at the photo. What kind of workplace is this? Who are the people?

- Go over the directions.
- Put students in pairs to discuss the questions.
- Ask a few pairs to share their answers with the class.

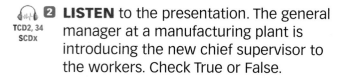

2 LISTEN to the presentation. The general manager at a manufacturing plant is introducing the new chief supervisor to the workers. Check True or False.

TCD2, 34
SCDx

- Go over the directions. To model the activity, play or read the first sentence of the audio. Read item one and ask students if it is true or false. Have them check the box under *True*.

- Play the CD and have students check *True* or *False*.

- Go over the answers with the class.

LISTENING SCRIPT
Career Connection, Activity 2

TCD2, 34
SCDx

A: As you know, Dylan Anderson is starting work here today as Chief Supervisor. This position was created because our plant is growing. With so many new employees, we need a strong leader who can step in and help manage the floor so that I can focus on administrative work. It was decided last week by a unanimous vote of the Board of Directors that Mr. Anderson is the right person for the job. And I know he's going to be a great new member of our team. Please welcome Mr. Dylan Anderson.

B: Thank you, Ms. Rivers, or should I say "boss." I'm very glad to be here with such a great group of people . . . . Well, I don't like to give speeches, so I'll just get right to business.

First of all, I want to talk about how the management here will be changing. Previously, we had three shift supervisors who oversaw operations on the floor. Last week, two more line workers were promoted to new shift supervisor positions as well. Alexis Moran and Mike Woodford, could you raise your hand? Give them a round of applause, everyone! All five shift supervisors report to me and are responsible for day-to-day operations in their department. As you know, many of you were assigned to a new shift supervisor because of this change. Updated staff charts were provided for everyone this morning, and by now you've all had a chance to meet with your new supervisors. The maintenance team was assigned to Mr. Woodford, and the warehouse team was assigned to Ms. Moran. We know that this is a big change for many of you, but it's really going to improve things around here in the long run. We hope you'll all agree.

ANSWER KEY

1. True; 2. False; 3. True; 4. True; 5. False;
6. False

3 **TALK** with a partner or in a group. Discuss the following questions.

- Go over the directions and the questions.
- Put students in pairs or groups to discuss the questions.
- Write on the board: *Good Things* and *Bad Things*. Ask students to tell you the good things that can happen when a company gets a new manager. Then ask what bad things can happen. Write the students' answers as they give them.
- Poll the class. Create two categories, *Promotion from within* and *Promotion from outside*. Ask students to raise their hands if they think it is better to promote someone from within a company. Write that number on the board. Ask people who think it's better to bring in someone from the outside to raise their hands. Write that number on the board.
- Ask a few students to share their reasoning for voting the way they did.

4 **WRITE** a conversation about the people in the picture. Who is the manager? How do you know? Write about what you think they are saying. Then read your conversations with a partner.

- Go over the directions.
- Put students in pairs to discuss their answers to the questions and to write a conversation about what the people in the photo are saying.
- Walk around the room and monitor the students' progress.
- Have each pair read their conversation to the class.

5 **WHAT ABOUT YOU?** Would you like to work in a big company with many levels of workers (such as the manufacturing plant in Activity 2), or do you prefer a small company where everyone knows each other well? Why? Discuss with a partner.

- Go over the directions.

- Ask students who have worked for big companies and small companies to talk about the benefits of each. Benefits of big companies might be factors such as job security, good benefits packages, and opportunities for advancement. Benefits of small companies might be greater camaraderie among employees, a more relaxed or less corporate atmosphere, and greater accountability for managers (both to succeed and to be kind to employees).
- Divide students into pairs and have them discuss the question.

ACADEMIC CONNECTION: Management styles

- Write on the board: *autocratic, paternalistic, democratic,* and *laissez-faire*.
- Explain to students that the words on the board are four common terms used to describe different management styles.
- Have students find brief descriptions of the four styles. Suggest to students that they look online or in an introductory business textbook.
- Put students in groups to share their research.

CHECK YOUR PROGRESS!

- Have students circle the correct answers.
- Review the answers or have students check the unit to see if each answer is right or wrong.
- Have students total their correct answers and fill in the chart at the bottom of the page.
- Have students create a learning plan and/or set learning goals.

ANSWER KEY

1. is elected; **2.** are chosen; **3.** wasn't driven; **4.** were given; **5.** asked; **6.** written; **7.** allowed; **8.** accused; **9.** laws; **10.** Mayors; **11.** court; **12.** cabinet members; **13.** accused; **14.** report to; **15.** defendant; **16.** trial

Unit Overview

LESSON	OBJECTIVES	STUDENT BOOK	WORKBOOK
1 Grammar and Vocabulary 1	Talk about people's problems. Use indefinite articles. Use the definite article.	p. 86	p. 76
2 Grammar Practice Plus	*A* and *an* with adjectives. Calculate an estimate for work time.	p. 88	p. 77
3 Listening and Conversation	Use the articles *the, a,* and *an*. Discuss errors in a phone bill.	p. 90	p. 78
4 Grammar and Vocabulary 2	Discuss rental housing. Use embedded questions with *if, whether,* and other question words.	p. 92	p. 80
5 Grammar Practice Plus	Give advice for rentals. Talk about rental problems and solutions.	p. 94	p. 81
6 Reading	Use lease vocabulary. Examine a rental agreement.	p. 96	p. 82–83
7 Writing	Read an advice column. Write a complaint to a local newspaper.	p. 98	p. 84–85
• Career Connection	Read about misunderstandings.	p. 100	p. 86–87
• Check Your Progress	Monitor progress.	p. 101	p. 88–89

Reading/Writing Strategies

- Use resources like dictionaries or the Internet to understand legal documents
- Give examples to explain a situation or problem

Connection Activities

LESSON	TYPE	SKILL DEVELOPMENT
1	Community	Getting information about service providers in the community
2	Academic	Researching college housing
3	Community	Billing mistakes by local utilities
4	Community	Rental descriptions
4	Community	Tenants and landlords in my community
4	Academic	Future academic study
6	Community	Legal information in my community

WORKSHEET #/FOCUS	TITLE	TEACHER'S EDITION
16. Grammar	Definite and Indefinite Articles	p. 320
17. Grammar	Embedded Questions	p. 321
18. Reading Comprehension	Advice Column	p. 322

LESSON 1: Grammar and Vocabulary

OBJECTIVES

Talk about people's problems
Use indefinite articles
Use the definite article

VOCABULARY

dead	out
error	power outage
gas leak	signal
losing an Internet connection	weak

GRAMMAR

Definite and indefinite articles

COMPETENCY

Learn how to order, cancel, and maintain utilities

WARM-UP ACTIVITY: Problems in my house or apartment

- Make sure the students' books are closed.
- Put the students in pairs and have them list problems that they have had in their house or apartment. Give them an example from your house or apartment to get them started (e.g., *My refrigerator broke down.*).
- Elicit the problems from the students and write them on the board.
- Give the students the opportunity to ask questions about any vocabulary or grammar that they don't understand.

1 GRAMMAR PICTURE DICTIONARY.
TLD2, 35
SCD22
What problems do these people have? Listen and read.

- Have students open their books and look at the six pictures on page 86.
- Read the sentences to the students or play the CD.
- Give the students an opportunity to ask questions about anything they do not understand.

LANGUAGE NOTE

- Explain to the students what paraphrasing is. (It is expressing an idea again with different words.)
- Tell the students that in speaking, it is often necessary to say the same thing in a different way to help their listeners understand or to show that they have understood.
- In the next activity, the students will be paraphrasing the text that accompanies the pictures to show you that they have understood the sentences.

2 READ the sentences in Activity 1 with a partner.

- Put the students in pairs and have them take turns saying the sentences to each other.
- Go through the pictures one by one, asking the students to paraphrase the problems and situations in the pictures. For example, for the first picture, a student could say, "One woman's telephone isn't working. She is going to borrow the other woman's cell phone and call the phone company."

COMMUNITY CONNECTION: Service providers and utilities in your community

- Put students into small groups.
- Explain the meaning of the phrases *service provider* and *utility*.
- Have the students list all of the utilities and service providers in your community, for example, for gas, water, electricity, telephone, and Internet service.
- Ask the students to give you the names of these utilities and write them on the board. Ask the students whether each is a private company or a government agency.
- If there is time, ask them to describe their experiences with these companies. Have they had any problems with service?

3 NOTICE THE GRAMMAR. Work with a partner. Underline *the*, and circle *a* and *an* in the sentences above. What parts of speech come after *the, a,* and *an*? Why is *an* used instead of *a* before the word *error*?

- Go over the directions with the students.
- Put the students in pairs.
- Have them underline all instances of *the* and circle all instances of *a* and *an*.
- Tell them to answer the questions about the part of speech and the word *error*.
- Check the answers as a class.

ANSWER KEY

1. The phone is dead. Do you have (a) cell phone? I need to call the phone company.
2. I keep losing my Internet connection. I need to find (a) new Internet service provider.
3. The electricity is out again! We had (a) power outage last Friday, too.
4. The signal on my cell phone is weak. I can't make (a) phone call. Do you have (a) strong signal?
5. I need to call the cable company. There's (an) error on my bill.
6. We have (a) gas leak. We have to call the gas company right away.

Nouns and adjectives come after *the, a* and *an*. *An* is used before the word *error* because *error* begins with a vowel sound.

EXPANSION ACTIVITY: Replace the word

- Give students two minutes to review the sentences in Activity 1, looking at the text under the pictures.
- Have students close their books.
- Write the sentences on the board, but leave out the articles in each sentence.
- Put the students in pairs. Have them write the articles for each sentence on a piece of paper.
- Have students open their books and confirm their answers.

LANGUAGE NOTE

- In the following explanation about articles, students will need to understand the difference between count and noncount nouns.
- Make three columns on the board with the headings *singular count nouns, plural count nouns,* and *noncount nouns*.
- Ask the students to explain to you the difference between the two kinds of nouns. Count nouns have singular and plural forms, e.g., *student* and *students*. They can have numbers as quantifiers, e.g., *one book* and *six books*. Noncount nouns cannot be preceded by a number and have no plural form, e.g., *sugar*. Noncount nouns need unit expressions, e.g., *bottles of, pounds of, pieces of,* to have numbers as quantifiers, e.g., *six pieces of paper*.
- Have the students give you examples of nouns for the three columns and write them on the board.
- For the noncount nouns, have students give you unit expressions, e.g., *glass of* for water.

GRAMMAR CHART: Articles

- Direct students' attention to the chart or project the transparency.
- Read the first section about articles to the students. Give them time to ask for clarification of anything they do not understand.
- Go over the information about indefinite articles line by line and read the examples.
- Have the students give you additional examples of the uses of indefinite articles.
- Go over the information about definite articles line by line and read the examples.
- Make sure they understand that *an* is used before words that begin with a vowel sound and that *some* is used with both plural count nouns and all noncount nouns.
- Have the students give you additional examples of the three uses of definite articles.
- Make sure the students understand the use of *the* with a noun that has already been mentioned.

CHART EXPANSION ACTIVITY: Second mention of a noun

- The concept that the definite article is used the second time a noun is mentioned is very complex, especially for students whose first language has no articles. Extra practice is needed.
- Put the students in pairs. Tell them to write a pair of sentences, similar to the example about the furnace leak in the grammar chart, in which the first sentence uses *a* or *an* + a noun and the second sentence uses *the* with the same noun.
- Have the pairs write their sentences on the board. Correct the sentences as necessary.

❹ **MATCH** each sentence or conversation with the correct rule.

- Go over the directions with the students.
- Point out the two columns that are to be matched.
- Point out the example sentence that is completed.
- Have students complete the exercise individually.
- Put students in pairs to compare answers.
- Go over the answers as a class.

ANSWER KEY

1. b; **2.** d; **3.** e; **4.** c; **5.** a

CHART EXPANSION ACTIVITY: Articles

- Copy and distribute Worksheet 16: *Definite and Indefinite Articles.*
- When the students have answered the questions individually, put them in pairs to compare their answers.
- Go over the answers as a class.

WORKSHEET ANSWER KEY

1. a, The; **2.** The; **3.** a, the; **4.** A; **5.** an; **6.** some; **7.** The; **8.** an; **9.** a; **10.** the; **11.** a; **12.** an, the; **13.** the; **14.** some; **15.** The

❺ **WHAT ABOUT YOU?** Have you ever had a problem with utilities in your home? What was the problem? What did you do? Write sentences. Then talk with a partner.

- Go over the instructions with the students.
- Point out the lines on which they will write their sentences.
- Put the students in pairs to talk about their answers. Ask them to check each other's sentences.
- Go over the answers as a class.

LESSON 2: Grammar Practice Plus

OBJECTIVES

A and *an* with adjectives
Calculate an estimate for work time

VOCABULARY

broken   peeling
cracked   stained
dripping

GRAMMAR

Definite and indefinite articles

COMPETENCIES

Communicate household repair and
    maintenance issues with landlords
Prepare a work estimate

NUMERACY

Calculating an estimate for work

WARM-UP ACTIVITY: The parts of a house or apartment

- Put the students in pairs. Tell them to brainstorm all of the vocabulary they can think of for a house or apartment. Give them one or two examples to get them started (e.g., *window*, *bathtub*).

- Have the students give you their words or expressions and write them on the board.

- Give the students an opportunity to ask questions about any words or expressions that they do not understand.

1 TALK about the picture. Who are the people? What are they talking about?

- Go over the directions.
- Point out the Big Picture and the words beneath the Big Picture. Point out the numbered items in the picture.
- Put the students in pairs and tell them to answer the two questions in the directions.
- Go over the answers as a class.

TCD2, 36

2 LISTEN to the sentences about the picture. Write the number next to the correct word.

- Play the CD and have the students write the numbers from the pictures next to the correct word.
- Put the students in pairs to check their answers.
- Go over the answers as a class.

TCD2, 36

LISTENING SCRIPT
Lesson 2, Activity 2

1. The wall in the kitchen is cracked.
2. Water is dripping from the faucet.
3. The paint is peeling from the ceiling.
4. The doorknob on the door is broken.
5. The carpet is stained.

ANSWER KEY

3 peeling; **4** broken; **1** cracked; **2** dripping
5 stained

CULTURE NOTE

In the United States, it is very common for freshmen, or first-year students, to live on campus in a dormitory. Most dormitories are still single gender, but some colleges have men and women living in the same dormitory, sometimes on separate floors. Living in a dormitory usually means that students eat in a cafeteria, so they don't have to spend a lot of time shopping for food and cooking. Many parents believe that this gives students more time to study. Each section or floor of a dormitory usually has an older student or a dormitory employee, often called a Resident Assistant (R.A.), to watch over the students. The dormitory probably has rules about noise and other factors that could disturb the students. There may also be dormitory athletic teams that a student can join. The purpose of dormitories is to provide a secure, convenient place to live for a student who may be away from home for the first time.

3 COMPLETE. Read each sentence. Complete the sentences with the words in the Activity 2.

- Read the directions to the students.
- Point out the words in the box in Activity 2 and the blanks in the sentences.
- Have the students complete the activity individually.
- Check the answers as a class.

ANSWER KEY

1. peeling; 2. dripping; 3. stained; 4. cracked
5. broken

ACADEMIC CONNECTION: College housing

- Put the students in small groups.
- Tell the students that their homework is to do research on the different kinds of housing available for students at any nearby college or university. They need to find out what housing is available on campus and off campus. They can find information in a student housing office, online, or in a library.
- Tell the students to get as much detailed information as possible, including costs, length of lease or contract, and meal plans, if any.
- Have the students report back to you with their information. Ask follow-up questions. Sample questions include: *How much does a semester in the residence hall cost? How many people live in a college apartment? How far from campus are most of the apartments?*

GRAMMAR CHART: *A* and *An* with Adjectives

- Read the grammar note to the students.
- Ask the students to give you several additional examples of the indefinite article with adjectives and nouns. Write them on the board.

4 COMPLETE the sentences with *a, an, some,* or *the*.

- Go over the directions with the students. Point out the example sentence.
- Have the students complete the activity individually.
- Go over the answers as a class.

1. an, the
2. a, the, the
3. the, the
4. some, the
5. some, a, an
6. an, the, the
7. The, a
8. an

5 WHAT ABOUT YOU? Are there any problems with your home that you would like to fix or change? Talk with a partner.

- Go over the directions with the students. Have a student read the speech bubble for the photograph.
- Put the students in pairs so that they can ask each other the question.
- Go over the answers as a class. Analyze the results. What are the most common problems that your students have in their homes?

MATH: Calculating an Estimate for Work

- Read the directions to the students.
- Give the students an opportunity to ask questions about anything they do not understand.
- Have the students make their calculations individually.
- Put the students in pairs to compare their answers.
- Go over the answers as a class.

ANSWER KEY

rate $350 x days 6 = $2,100
paint $378 + brushes $72 = $450
                ESTIMATE = $2,550

BIG PICTURE GRAMMAR EXPANSION ACTIVITY: Sentences with definite and indefinite articles

- Put students into pairs.
- Have them look at the Big Picture on page 88.
- Tell each pair to write five new sentences with definite and indefinite articles. Tell them that they must have at least one sentence with each of the words they have studied: *a, an, the,* and *some*.
- Have each pair write one or two of their sentences on the board. Comment on the correctness of their articles.

Expansion Activity: My ideal apartment or house

- Tell the students that they must describe their ideal house or apartment. They will have to make notes to describe their ideal house or apartment to the class.
- Give the students a short sample presentation about your ideal house or apartment. A few sentences will be enough to give the students a good idea of what they are to do. For example, you can say, *My ideal house has four bedrooms, three bathrooms, and a very large kitchen. The kitchen has a large kitchen table for the family to eat together. It has some big windows, so it is very bright inside. It has a large backyard and a two-car garage.*
- Emphasize to the students that they must be careful with the articles that they use.
- Have each student give a brief presentation to the class about their ideal house or apartment.

LESSON 3: Listening and Conversation

OBJECTIVES

Use the articles *the, a,* and *an*
Discuss errors in a phone bill

COMPETENCIES

Use strategies to state the reason for a
  phone call
Dispute errors in utility bills

WARM-UP ACTIVITY: Billing mistakes

- Explain that in this lesson the students will
  talk about mistakes that utilities and service
  providers make when they send a bill.

- On the board, write the question, *Do your
  utilities sometimes make billing mistakes?*

- Give the students an opportunity to ask for
  clarification of the question.

- Elicit one or two examples of billing mistakes
  from the class. Ask the students what they did
  when there was a mistake. Did they just pay
  the bill or did they complain?

PRONUNCIATION: The Articles *The, A,*
TCD2, 37 **and *An***

- Read the first paragraph about articles
  and stress to the students. Give them an
  opportunity to ask for clarification of anything
  they do not understand.

A. LISTEN to the examples. Then repeat.
TCD2, 38
SCD23

- Read the directions to the students. Point
  out the two examples and the **sounds like**
  column. Point out the schwa symbol in the first
  example. Explain that it sounds like "uh."

- Make sure the students understand that in the
  second example, there is no schwa symbol
  because the word *the* is in front of a vowel, the
  "i" of the word *Internet*.

- Play the two phrases on the CD. Have the
  students repeat the phrases as a class.

- Read the sentences about stress and the
  articles *a* and *an* to the students. Give them an
  opportunity to ask for clarification of anything
  that they do not understand.

B. LISTEN to the examples. Then repeat.
TCD2, 39
SCD24

- Read the directions to the students. Point out
  the two examples and the **sounds like** column.
  Point out the schwa symbols in the examples.

- Play the two phrases on the CD. Have the
  students repeat the phrases as a class.

C. PRACTICE saying the phrases below.

- Play the phrases on the CD one by one, having
  the students repeat the phrase after each.

- Give the students feedback on their
  pronunciation.

**BIG PICTURE LISTENING EXPANSION
ACTIVITY: Listening for reduced articles**

- Have the students look at the Big Picture
  on page 88.

- Put the students in pairs. Tell the students
  to take turns reading sentences from the
  dialogue in Activity 3 about the problems in
  the apartment.

- One student will read a sentence. The other
  will listen to see whether the student read
  the articles with the proper reduction,
  using the schwa sound. The listening
  student should give feedback to the
  speaking student, for example, *Yes, that's
  right.* or *I'm not sure that's the correct
  pronunciation. Could you read it again?*

- Walk around the room helping the students
  pronounce the words correctly.

- When they have finished, ask for volunteers
  to read the sentences for the class.

TCD2, 40–45

❶ LISTEN to the conversation. Then listen to the question. Fill in the correct answer. Replay each item if necessary.

- Read the directions to the students.

- Explain that they will hear about a billing problem. They will hear a short piece of a conversation and then a question. Point out the circles they will fill in.

- Tell the students to answer the questions while the CD is playing. Play the recording, pausing the CD after each question to give the students time to answer.

- Put the students in pairs to compare answers.

- If necessary, play the CD again.

- As a class, go over the answers.

LISTENING SCRIPT
Lesson 3, Activity 1

TCD2, 40–45

1.

    A: Union Bell Telephone Company. May I have your name and home phone number please?

    B: Hello. My name is Sara Lopez, and my phone number is 818-555-8747.

Which is correct?

    A. Sara's phone number is 818-555-8747.

    B. Sara is calling 818-555-8747.

    C. The number for the telephone company is 818-555-8747.

2.

    A: How may I help you?

    B: I'm calling because there are some errors on my telephone bill.

    A: I'm sorry about that. Were the errors on this month's bill?

    B: Yes, they were.

Which is correct?

    A. Sara didn't receive her most recent bill.

    B. Sara made some errors on her most recent bill.

    C. The phone company made some errors on her bill.

3.

    A: Okay. I have your bill on my computer screen. What is the first error?

    B: I was charged for a call to New York on March 3. But I didn't call New York.

Which is correct?

    A. Sara called New York.

    B. Sara was in New York.

    C. Sara didn't call New York.

4.

    A: Is it possible that someone else in your home called New York?

    B: No, I live alone.

Which is correct?

    A. Sara lives by herself.

    B. Sara lives with one roommate.

    C. Sara's roommate made the phone call to New York.

5.

    A: All right. Is there anything else?

    B: Yes. There's a charge for a call to Los Angeles on March 8, but I didn't make that call. I was out of town that day.

Which is correct?

    A. Sara was in Los Angeles on March 8.

    B. Sara wasn't home on March 8.

    C. Sara got a voicemail message from Los Angeles.

6.

    A: Hold one moment, please, while I check your call history. Thank you for holding, Ms. Lopez. I apologize for the errors. I've taken the charges off of your bill. You will receive an updated bill in a couple of days.

    B: Thank you very much.

Which is correct?

    A. The phone company will not take the charges off the bill.

    B. The phone company is going to send Sara a new bill.

    C. Sara has to pay for the changes to her bill.

ANSWER KEY

1. A; **2.** C; **3.** C; **4.** A; **5.** B; **6.** B

ANSWER KEY

Students should circle Call #1 and Call #3 in the table.

EXPANSION ACTIVITY: Customer service in the real world

- Put the students in small groups.
- Tell the students that in the dialogue they just heard, the utility quickly fixed the mistake.
- Write the phrase *Customer Service* on the board. Ask the students to explain what it means.
- Ask the students to discuss whether or not utilities admit and fix their mistakes that quickly in real life. What has their experience been with utilities and service providers? Which utilities have good customer service or bad customer service?
- Give the students five minutes to discuss the questions in their groups.
- As a class, go over the answers. Analyze the results. Which utilities do the students think have good customer service? Which ones have bad customer service?

 2 LISTEN again. Circle the incorrect charges
TCD2, 46   on the phone bill below.

- Read the directions to the students. Make sure they understand they will be hearing the same conversation from Activity 1.
- Point out the table with the details of Sara's phone calls.
- Play the recording and have the students circle the incorrect charges.
- Put the students in pairs to compare their answers.
- If necessary, play the recording again.
- As a class, go over the answers.

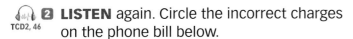 **3 LISTEN** to the conversation. Then practice
TCD2, 47   with a partner.
SCD25

- Go over the directions with the students.
- Point out the underlined phrase, *I'm calling because there are*. Explain that it is important to state the reason for a telephone call.
- Play the recording.
- Give the students an opportunity to ask for clarification of anything they don't understand.

LANGUAGE NOTE

- In the conversation that the students have just heard, there are many phrases used to show respect or courtesy to the other person, especially in a customer service situation.
- Put the students in pairs and have them circle any words or phrases that they think are very polite.
- Go over the conversation with them. They should have circled the following:
- *How can I help you?*
- *I'm sorry about that.*
- *Can you tell me . . .*
- *Please*
- *Thank you*

COMMUNITY CONNECTION: Billing mistakes by local utilities

- For homework, have students interview other students or people they know in the community. Tell them to ask those people what kinds of billing mistakes they have had to deal with.

- Tell the students to list the name of the utility or service provider and make a note about the type and seriousness of the mistakes.

- When the students are back in class, ask them to tell the class about the mistakes they found. Make a list of the utilities in columns on the board. Mark off the number of mistakes the students found for each utility. Analyze the results. Which utility had the most billing mistakes? Which had the fewest?

CONVERSATION STRATEGY: Stating reason for a phone call

- Point out the Conversation Strategy box with the three expressions.

- Have three students read the three phrases in the box.

- Make sure the students understand that the meaning of the three expressions is the same, but that the grammar for using them is different.

- Elicit from the students complete sentences using the three phrases. Write the sentences on the board.

- Put the students in pairs. Have each pair write one new sentence with each of the three phrases for stating a reason for a phone call.

- Ask for volunteers to read their sentences to the class.

4 **PRACTICE** the conversation from Activity 3 with a partner. Use the expressions in the Conversation Strategy box.

- Read the directions to the students.

- Put the students in pairs to read the dialogue.

- Tell the students to use one of the expressions from the Conversation Strategy box for the sentence about the two billing errors.

- Tell the students to change roles and read the dialogue a second time.

5 **ROLE-PLAY.** Discuss the errors in the phone bills below. Write a conversation with a partner. Take turns being a customer and a representative from the phone company.

- Go over the directions with the students. Point out the two charts with the notes about billing errors. Make sure the students understand that one student will be the customer for the first chart and one will be the customer for the second chart.

- Put students in pairs to do the role-plays.

- Walk around to monitor the activity and provide help as needed.

- Ask for volunteers to do the role-plays for the class.

- Have the students write down their conversations and turn them in so that you can check them.

BIG PICTURE SPEAKING EXPANSION ACTIVITY: Problems in my apartment

- Have the students go back to page 88 and look at the characters in the Big Picture.

- Put the students in pairs. Explain that one of them will role-play the part of the son and the other will be the landlord.

- Have the son call the landlord to describe the problems in the apartment. Tell the landlords that they should use polite language and agree to fix the problems.

- When the pairs have finished the conversation, have them switch roles and do the role-play a second time.

- Ask for volunteers to do the role-play for the class.

LESSON 4: Grammar and Vocabulary

OBJECTIVES

Discuss rental housing
Use embedded questions with *if, whether,*
and other question words

VOCABULARY

break my lease	discriminate against
condition	file a complaint
consent	policy

GRAMMAR

Past, present, and future tenses

COMPETENCIES

Understand tenant and landlord obligations
Talk about different kinds of housing

WARM-UP ACTIVITY: Leases

- Ask the students to raise their hands if they rent an apartment or house.

- Write the word *lease* on the board. Ask the renting students whether they have a lease. Have these students explain to the rest of the class what a lease is.

- Ask the students to tell the class what information is in the lease. What can they do? What can't they do?

- Write their information on the board. Give all of the students the opportunity to ask for clarification of anything that they do not understand.

🎧 1 GRAMMAR PICTURE DICTIONARY.

TCD2, 48
SCD4
What do people want to know about an apartment? Listen and read.

- Have students open their books and look at the six pictures.

- Tell them to read the mini-dialogues.

- Give the students an opportunity to ask questions about anything they do not understand. Some of the words, like *discriminate*, will take some time to explain. Some students may have to look some words up in a monolingual dictionary.

- Play the CD and have students repeat the sentences.

- Call on students and ask questions about the people in the pictures: *Who are the people who are talking? Who is the man that the women on the phone are talking about?* Elicit the answers.

CULTURE NOTE

In the United States, it is illegal to refuse to rent an apartment or house to someone because of their race, religion, national origin, age, gender, or family status. It is also illegal to discriminate against handicapped people. The basic federal law that covers these issues is the Civil Rights Act of 1968 and later amendments to that law. Landlords are only allowed to refuse prospective tenants on the basis of income, amount of savings, credit history, previous rental record, and any other financial or behavioral criteria that affect the tenant's ability and willingness to pay the rent and take care of the property.

COMMUNITY CONNECTION: Rental descriptions

- Tell the students that for homework they must find advertisements for apartment and house rentals. They may look in newspapers, on the Internet, or on bulletin boards near their school.
- Students will check the advertisements for the landlords' requirements. They should make notes about what the landlords are asking for.
- When the students have finished this task, have them report on their findings to the class. Analyze their findings. Did they find any requirements that are evidence of discrimination? Do any of their advertisements state a desired age or race?

2 PRACTICE the conversations from Activity 1 with a partner.

- Go over the directions with the students.
- Put the students in pairs. Have them read the conversations in Activity 1.
- Choose pairs to read the conversations to the class. Help the students with any words that are difficult to pronounce.

3 NOTICE THE GRAMMAR. Circle *if*, *whether*, and *wh*-question words in the sentences above. Then underline the sentences where these words appear.

- Read the directions to the students.
- Have them circle the key words and underline the sentences.
- As a class, go over the answers.

ANSWER KEY

1. *A:* I don't know why I didn't get the apartment. Maybe I'm too old.
   B: Landlords can't discriminate against people because of their age.

2. *A:* My landlord comes into my apartment without my permission. Do you know if that's illegal?
   B: Yes, it definitely is! He can't come in without your consent.

3. *A:* Can you tell me how I can file a complaint against my landlord?
   B: Yes, you can start by filling out this form.

4. *A:* Could you tell me what your pet policy is?
   B: Yes. We allow cats and small dogs only.

5. *A:* Before you rent the apartment, check to see whether it's in good condition.
   B: I checked it yesterday. It's clean, and nothing is broken or damaged.

6. *A:* I want to move, but I signed a one-year lease. Do you know how I can break my lease?
   B: No, I don't. You should call the legal aid office for advice.

EXPANSION ACTIVITY: Paraphrasing

- If necessary, explain the importance of paraphrasing to the students again. Use the language note from Lesson 1.
- Ask the students to paraphrase the problem in the first conversation with you. A sample might be: *A landlord didn't rent an apartment to an older man. He thinks his age might be the reason.*
- Put the students in pairs. Have them paraphrase the remaining conversations.
- Ask for volunteers to read their paraphrases to the class.

COMMUNITY CONNECTION: Tenants and landlords in my community

- Tell the students that they are going to research laws about renting property in their community. They can use the Internet, a library, or go to a local tenants' rights organization.
- Students should cover all of the issues from the conversations, including discrimination, a landlord's right to enter a unit, breaking a lease, and filing a complaint.
- Put the students in small groups and tell the groups to brainstorm strategies for getting this information.
- Give the groups time to go over their information with each other. Then, have the students tell you about the laws in your community governing property rental.

GRAMMAR CHART: Embedded questions with *if, whether,* and other question words

- Direct students' attention to the chart or project the transparency or CD.
- Read the paragraph at the top of the chart. Give the students an opportunity to ask for clarification of anything that they do not understand.
- Point out the column for direct questions and the columns with their embedded equivalents.
- Go over the examples one by one. Make sure the students notice that because the first and fifth questions are about events in the past, the embedded questions must have a past tense verb.

CHART EXPANSION ACTIVITY: Additional embedded questions

- Put the students in pairs.
- Tell each pair to come up with one additional embedded question for each of the main clauses listed in Activity 1, starting with *I wonder* and going through

Can you tell me. Tell the students that they must have at least one sentence with *if* or *whether* and a *wh*-question.
- When they have finished writing the embedded questions, go through the main clauses and elicit examples from the students. Write their sentences on the board.

4 REWRITE each question as a sentence (ending with a period) containing an embedded question.

- Go over the directions with the students.
- Have students rewrite the direct questions as embedded questions.
- Put students in pairs to compare answers.
- Go over the answers with the class.

ANSWER KEY

Answers will vary. Possible answers are below.
1. I don't know if the house is in good condition.
2. I'd like to know what the lateness policy is.
3. I'm not sure where I can file a complaint.
4. I don't know why they discriminated against Tom.
5. I wonder whether he gave his consent.
6. I'm not sure how I can break my lease.

EXPANSION ACTIVITY: Additional practice with embedded questions

- Photocopy and distribute Worksheet 17: *Embedded Questions.*
- Go over the directions.
- Have students complete the worksheet.
- Put students in pairs to compare their answers.
- Go over the answers with the class.

WORKSHEET ANSWER KEY

A. 1. if; 2. where; 3. how; 4. if; 5. whether

B. Answers will vary. Possible answers are below.

1. I wonder if she is coming to the party tonight.
2. I don't know what her name is.
3. I'd like to know whether the landlord fixed the problem.
4. I'm not sure why he came home so late.
5. I wonder if I should ask the teacher for help.

5 WRITE each of your sentences in Activity 4 as a question containing an embedded question.

- Go over the directions with the students.
- Go over the sample sentence and point out its relation to the sample sentence in Activity 4.
- Have the students rewrite their sentences as questions.
- Put the students in pairs to compare answers.
- Go over the answers as a class.

ANSWER KEY

Answers will vary. Possible answers are below.

1. Do you know if the house is in good condition?
2. Can you tell me what the lateness policy is?
3. Do you know where I can file a complaint?
4. Can you tell me why they discriminated against Tom?
5. Do you know whether he gave his consent?
6. Can you tell me how I can break my lease?

6 WHAT ABOUT YOU? Think of three questions to ask your partner. Use embedded questions.

- Go over the directions with the students.
- Give the students ten minutes to write three questions with embedded questions.
- Put students into pairs to ask each other the questions.
- As a class, go over the answers. Analyze the results. What information did the students find out about each other?

BIG PICTURE WRITING EXPANSION ACTIVITY: Embedded questions

- Project the Big Picture or have students turn to page 88.
- Put the students in pairs. Tell the pairs to write three sentences with embedded questions for the situation in the Big Picture. They should specify which character is saying or thinking the sentence. Tell the students to use their imagination.
- Possible sentences include: Father: *I wonder if we can break the lease.* Mother: *I'd like to know whether a lawyer can help us.*
- Have the students write their sentences on the board.

ACADEMIC CONNECTION: Future academic study

- Tell the students that they must talk to someone at their school about their future academic study. The person can be a teacher, a counselor, a librarian, another staff member, or an undergraduate or graduate student.
- To prepare for the conversation, the student must write down at least three sentences with embedded questions and give them to you as homework.
- Examples of sentences are: *Can you tell me where I could study nursing? I wonder if I should stay at this school for my B.A. I'm not sure what the best school is for me.*
- When you have read and corrected the sentences, help the students find someone to talk to. You can give them the names of counselors or other teachers who are willing to talk to the students.
- When the students have finished their interviews, go over their answers as a class. Analyze the results. What did the students learn about academic study?

LESSON 5: Grammar Practice Plus

VOCABULARY
current   notice
evict   sublet

GRAMMAR
Embedded questions

COMPETENCY
Identify solutions to rental problems

WARM-UP ACTIVITY: Advice columns

- Have the students look at the reading in Activity 1. Explain that it is common in English-speaking countries to see these kinds of advice columns in newspapers and on the Internet. People write a description of a problem that they have in a letter or an email. An advisor writes suggestions for the person with the problem.

- Ask the students if these kinds of columns are common in their countries. Where do they find advice columns? What kinds of subjects are covered? Are there some advisors who are extremely famous?

❶ READ the advice column. Underline the two embedded questions.

- Read the directions to the students.
- Have the students read the letters and circle the two embedded questions.
- Put the students in pairs to compare their answers.
- As a class, go over the answers.

ANSWER KEY
The two embedded questions are: *Can you tell me when I have to tell my landlord that I want to move out?*   *Do you know what I can do to keep my apartment?*

❷ MATCH the words from the advice column to their definitions.

- Go over the directions with the students.
- Point out the blanks and words on the left and the letters and definitions on the right.
- Have the students do the activity individually.
- Go over the answers as a class.

ANSWER KEY
1. b; 2. d; 3. c; 4. a

❸ WRITE each sentence in the correct order.

- Read the directions to the students.
- Point out the sentences in incorrect order.
- Show the students the sample sentence.
- Have the students unscramble the sentences individually.
- Put the students in pairs to compare answers.
- Go over the answers as a class.

ANSWER KEY
1. Do you know when I have to give notice to my landlord that I'm moving out?
2. Can you tell me the current phone number for the tenants' rights organization?
3. I'm not sure what I have to do if my landlord evicts me.
4. Do you know who I should call if I have a problem with my landlord?
5. I wonder if the other tenants are coming to the meeting.
6. I don't know whether I can sublet my apartment.

EXPANSION ACTIVITY: Additional practice with the advice column

- Photocopy and distribute Worksheet 18: *Reading Practice.*
- Go over the directions.
- Have students complete the worksheet.
- Put students in pairs to compare their answers.
- Go over the answers with the class.

WORKSHEET ANSWER KEY

1. b; **2.** a; **3.** d; **4.** b; **5.** d; **6.** c

4 **WRITE** each of your sentences in Activity 3 as a direct question.

- Read the directions to the students.
- Point out the example sentence to the students.
- Have the students complete the activity individually.
- Put students in pairs to compare their answers.
- Go over the answers with the class.

ANSWER KEY

Answers will vary. Possible answers include

1. When do I have to give notice to my landlord that I'm moving out?
2. What is the current phone number for the tenants' rights organization?
3. What do I have to do if my landlord evicts me?
4. Who should I call if I have a problem with my landlord?
5. Are the other tenants coming to the meeting?
6. Can I sublet my apartment?

EXPANSION ACTIVITY: My future

- Tell the students that they are going to write three sentences with embedded questions about their future.
- Write a sentence with an embedded question about your own future to get them started. For example, you could write, *I wonder whether I'll be a teacher next year,* or *I'd like to know if I'll move to another city.*
- Give the students some time to write their sentences.
- Put the students in pairs to share their sentences.
- Have each student write one of their sentences on the board. Analyze the results. What are the most common themes for questions? Future employment? Marital status? Income? Place of residence?

TCD2, 49 **5** **LISTEN** to the radio program. Look at the list of problems below. Check the problems that you hear. Then listen again, and write the suggested solution.

- Go over the directions with the students carefully. This is a fairly complex activity, so be sure students understand what they are supposed to do.
- Point out the chart with the column for checking problems that they hear and the column for writing in suggested solutions.
- Tell the students to fill out the chart while they are listening to the recording.
- Play the recording. Give the students some time to finish the chart.
- Put the students in pairs to compare their answers.
- If necessary, play the recording again.
- Go over the answers as a class.

LISTENING SCRIPT
Lesson 5, Activity 5
TCD2, 49

A: Hello, and thanks for calling the Renter's Rights Radio Show. What's the problem?

B: Hi. Well, I'm having a problem with one of my neighbors. Every time he does his laundry, he spills soap all over the floor and doesn't clean it up. He's not very friendly, so I'm afraid to talk to him about it. Can you tell me what I should do?

A: You should ask your landlord or your apartment manager to talk to your neighbor about the problem. If your neighbor doesn't start cleaning up his mess, your landlord should make sure that the laundry room is clean.

B: Okay. Thank you.

A: Let's have another call. Hi there. What's the problem?

C: Hi. My problem is with my landlord. He says he is going to evict me for paying my rent late. It's due on the first of each month, and I paid it on the third. That's only two days late! Then he changed the locks so I can't get into my apartment. I don't know what I should do.

A: Your landlord doesn't have the right to evict you for paying your rent two days late. You should call a lawyer. This is a serious issue.

C: Okay, I will. Thank you.

A: We have time for one more call. Hello, caller. What's the problem?

D: Well, there are cockroaches in my apartment. I told my landlord about them two weeks ago, but he still hasn't done anything about them.

A: Because this is an important health issue, your landlord should have taken care of this problem right away. Write him a letter and keep a copy of the letter for yourself. It's best if you send the letter by certified mail so you have proof that he received it. In the letter, tell your landlord that you are going to call a health inspector to file a complaint. If he still doesn't take care of the issue, file a complaint with a health inspector.

ANSWER KEY

Problem	Solution
1. Not mentioned	
2. Another tenant makes a mess.	Have the landlord talk to the messy tenant.
3. Not mentioned	
4. The landlord is evicting a tenant for a late payment.	Get a lawyer. This is a serious problem.
5. Cockroaches in the apartment	Write a certified letter to the landlord about the problem. Tell the landlord that you will complain to a health inspector. If the landlord doesn't do anything, complain to a health inspector.

6 TALK with a partner. Think of other possible solutions for the problems in Activity 5 that you didn't hear on the radio program. Write your ideas with the other solutions in the chart above.

- Go over the directions with the students. Make sure they understand that they are to come up with new solutions.
- Put the students in pairs to come up with new solutions.
- As a class, go over their answers.

7 ROLE-PLAY. Look at the list of problems in Activity 5. Role-play with a partner. Take turns being the caller and the radio program host.

- Read the directions to the students.
- Put the students in pairs.
- Point out the example dialogue and have the pairs read it.
- Have each pair decide who will be the radio host first.

- Write the radio host's first sentence on the board to get them started: *Hello, and thanks for calling the Renter's Rights Radio Show. What's the problem?*
- Have the students start the role-plays.
- Walk around the room helping students with difficult language.
- Remind the students to take turns doing the two roles.
- Ask for volunteers to perform the role-plays for the class.

8 WHAT ABOUT YOU? Have you ever had a problem with a landlord, an apartment manager, or a neighbor? What happened? Talk with a partner.

- Go over the directions with the students.
- Put the students in small groups to discuss the questions.
- Go over the answers as a class. Analyze the results. What were the most common problems your students had?

EXPANSION ACTIVITY: A new radio advice program

- Tell the students that they are going to create a new radio program that gives advice.
- Put the students in pairs. Tell each pair to answer the following questions about their program:
  1. What is the name of their radio advice program?
  2. What topic will they give advice on?
  3. What are four possible problems that listeners would ask for help with?
  4. What solutions would they suggest for the problems?
- Give the students time to answer the questions.
- Have each pair give a brief presentation about their radio program.

LESSON 6: Reading

VOCABULARY

access	parties
deposit	tenant
landlord	term
obligations	utilities

COMPETENCY

Interpret a rental agreement

WARM-UP ACTIVITY: Rental agreements

- Before the students open their books and look at the rental agreement, tell them that they are going to look at a sample of one in this activity.
- Ask the students to guess what information rental agreements typically contain.
- Write the categories of their guesses on the board, e.g., *Name*, *Address*, *Period of Time*, *Rental Amount*, and *Dates*.

1 THINK ABOUT IT. Have you ever rented an apartment? Did you have to sign a lease? What were the rules in the lease? Did you have any problems with the apartment? What happened? Who fixed the problem?

- Go over the directions with the students.
- Put the students in small groups and tell them to discuss the questions.
- Go over the answers as a class. Analyze the results. What rules are common in leases? What were common problems that your students had?

2 BEFORE YOU READ. Preview the rental agreement on the next page. Read each word in boldface. What do you think each section will be about?

- Go over the instructions with the students.
- Give them time to preview the rental agreement.
- As a class, go over the bolded subheadings and have the students explain what they mean, e.g., *Tenant's obligations are things that the renter has to do*.

READING FOCUS: Use resources

- Go over the information in the strategy box with the students.
- Ask the students to give examples of legal words in the rental agreement that they did not understand.
- Ask the students where they could find the meaning of the words that they didn't understand.

COMMUNITY CONNECTION: Legal information in my community

- Tell the students that they are going to research what resources are available in their community for understanding legal documents like the rental agreement in this lesson.
- Put the students in small groups and tell each group to make a list of legal resources available to them. They can look on the Internet, go to a library, or go to a community organization. Legal resources might include renter's rights associations, government offices, and legal services in a local college or university.
- Give the students a few days to gather the information. When they have finished, have each group make a brief presentation of their findings. Write the resources on the board.

3 READ the rental agreement on the next page. Put a check next to two sections that you want to learn more about.

- Go over the instructions with the students.
- Point out the glossary at the bottom of the page and go over the four words defined there.
- Give them time to read the rental agreement and check two sections.
- Put the students in small groups. Have students tell the group what sections they checked and why they chose those sections.
- As a class, go over the answers. Analyze the results. What sections were checked most often?

④ AFTER YOU READ.

A. VOCABULARY. Find the words in the vocabulary box in the reading on page 97 and circle them. Then read each definition and fill in the blanks with the correct words.

- Go over the directions with the students.
- Give the students ten minutes to circle the words in the reading and fill in the blanks.
- Put the students in pairs to share their answers.
- Go over the answers as a class.

ANSWER KEY

1. tenant; **2.** landlord; **3.** parties; **4.** deposit; **5.** term; **6.** obligations; **7.** utilities; **8.** access

BIG PICTURE SPEAKING EXPANSION ACTIVITY: The rental agreement

- Have the students go to page 88 and look at the characters in the Big Picture.
- Put students into pairs.
- Tell them to guess what the terms of the son's rental agreement are. The students should use their imagination to speculate about the rent, the length of the lease, the deposit, etc.
- As a class, go over the students' guesses.

B. REREAD the two sections that you put a checkmark next to. Circle any words that you don't know. Reread each sentence, then guess the meaning of each word. Next, use a dictionary or the Internet to look up the new words. Were your guesses correct?

- Go over the directions with the students.
- Give the students the opportunity to ask questions about anything they do not understand.
- Give the students time to reread their two sections and look up their words.
- Ask the students how accurate their guesses were. Ask them what strategies they used to guess the meanings of the words.
- As a class, go over the words that the students didn't know. Analyze the results. What were the most common words that they didn't know? Were they legal words?

C. TALK with a partner. Answer the questions.

- Go over the directions with the students.
- Point out the eight questions.
- Have the students answer the questions individually.
- Put the students in pairs to compare their answers.
- Go over the answers as a class.

ANSWER KEY

1. One, only Richard
2. 12 months
3. It becomes a month-to-month agreement.
4. $10 per day
5. The tenant will receive a security deposit refund, but any damage caused by negligence will be deducted from the deposit.
6. None
7. The landlord
8. No

LESSON 7: Writing

OBJECTIVES

Read an advice column
Write a complaint to a local newspaper

WRITING FOCUS: GIVE EXAMPLES

Give examples

COMPETENCIES

Write to express problems with housing
Advocate for better housing

WARM-UP ACTIVITY: Complaints

- Write on the board, *What do you do when you have a complaint?*
- Put the students in small groups. Ask them to answer the question on the board. Explain that a complaint can be a problem with a product, a company, an individual, and so on. Do they complain directly to a person? Do they ask someone to help them? Do they remain silent?
- As a class, discuss the strategies that the students use to deal with a complaint.

1 THINK ABOUT IT. Have you ever written a letter of complaint? What was the letter about? What happened after you wrote the letter? If you haven't ever written a letter of complaint, have you ever wanted to? Why?

- Go over the directions with the students.
- Put the students in small groups. Tell them to discuss the questions.
- Have each group give a brief report on the opinions in their group.
- Analyze the results. How many students have written a letter of complaint? What were the most common complaints?

BIG PICTURE WRITING EXPANSION ACTIVITY: What would they say?

- Have the students look at the Big Picture on page 88.
- Write the words *Mother*, *Father*, and *Son* on the board.
- Give the students some common expressions for complaining, e.g., *Why did they have to . . .* , *I can't believe that he . . .* and *Why don't they understand that . . .*
- Tell the students to write one complaint for each character.
- Have the students do the activity individually.
- Put the students in pairs to compare their answers.
- As a class, go over the answers.

2 BEFORE YOU WRITE.

A. SCAN the letter below. What is the main problem?

- Go over the directions with the students.
- Point out the letter and the photo of the man with the lease.
- Remind students that *scan* means to look quickly through something for a specific piece of information.
- Give the students one minute to scan for the answer to the question.
- Put students in pairs to compare their answers.
- Go over the answer with the class.

ANSWER KEY

The main problem is that the landlord is illegally trying to get "Frustrated in Phoenix" to move out.

EXPANSION ACTIVITY: True/False quiz

- Put students into pairs. Tell them they are going to be making *true/false* quizzes for each other.
- Have students write five true or false statements about the information in the article, e.g., *"Frustrated in Phoenix" damaged the apartment.*
- Have students trade papers and mark each others' statements as *true* or *false*.
- Have the pairs of students go over their answers.
- Ask students to read some of their sentences aloud and have the class judge them *true* or *false*.

WRITING FOCUS: Give examples

- Go over the strategy with the students.
- Give the students an opportunity to ask for clarification of anything they do not understand.

B. READ this letter to an advice column. Circle the examples.

- Go over the directions with the students.
- Give the students five minutes to circle the examples.
- Put the students in pairs to compare their answers.
- Go over the answers as a class.

ANSWER KEY

Students should circle: *The toilet leaks and he won't fix it. He has entered my apartment three times without my consent and with no notice.*

C. WRITE. Imagine you are having a serious problem with your apartment or house. Answer these questions and make notes about the problem.

- Go over the directions with the students. Point out the blank letter on page 99.
- Make sure they understand that their notes from this activity will be used to fill in the letter in the next activity.
- Give the students ten minutes to answer the questions.

D. DISCUSS your problem with a partner. Can you add more details to your notes?

- Put the students in pairs.
- Have the students go over their notes with each other. Tell them to count the number of examples that their partner wrote and make suggestions for additional examples.

3 WRITE. Using your notes, write a letter about a housing problem to an advice columnist at a local newspaper. Be sure to sign your letter with a creative anonymous name (like *Frustrated in Phoenix*)!

- Go over the instructions with the students.
- Point out the lines for the letter.
- Remind the students to use the information that they wrote down in the last activity.
- Before the students begin writing, go over the editing guidelines in Activity 4B. Give the students an opportunity to ask for clarification of anything they do not understand.
- Give the students 15 minutes in class to write their paragraph or assign it as homework.

4 AFTER YOU WRITE.

A. DISCUSS. Exchange letters with your partner. Read your partner's letter. Then talk with your partner and answer his or her letter.

- Go over the directions with the students.
- Put the students in pairs.

- Have the students exchange letters and read their partner's letter. Tell the students to comment on anything in their partner's letter that is unclear.

- Have the students take the role of advice columnist and write a detailed answer to their partner's letter telling them what to do about their problem.

B. EDIT. Check your letter. Ask yourself these questions.

- Have the students go through the editing guidelines.

- Tell them to make notes on their paragraphs as they answer the questions.

C. REWRITE your letter with corrections.

- Give the students overnight to rewrite their paragraphs using their partner's comments and the editing guidelines.

- Collect the paragraphs and write comments on them, using the editing guidelines as your guide.

- Return the paragraphs to the students.

D. ROLE-PLAY. Choose one of the letters that you and your partner wrote. With your partner, role-play the situation for the class. For example, if the problem is between you and a neighbor, act out a scene in which you ask the neighbor to fix the problem.

- Read the directions to the students.

- Have the pairs role-play one of their letters.

- Ask for volunteers to do their role-plays in front of the class.

BIG PICTURE WRITING EXPANSION ACTIVITY: Goals

- Have the students go to page 88 to look at the Big Picture.

- Tell the students to take the role of the son and write a letter to an advice columnist about the terrible state of his apartment. Have them ask for advice on what to do.

- Have the students exchange letters and read their partner's letter. Tell the students to comment on anything in their partner's letter that is unclear.

- Have the students take the role of advice columnist and write a detailed answer to their partner's letter telling the son what to do about his apartment problem.

Career Connection

OBJECTIVES

Read about misunderstandings

COMPETENCY

Recognize strategies to improve communication and avoid errors

WARM-UP ACTIVITY: Communication problems

- Ask the students if they have ever had communication problems, either in their native language or in English. Did they misunderstand something a teacher said? Did they have a problem understanding a friend? Did they have a hard time explaining what they wanted in a store?

- Put the students in small groups. Have them come up with as many examples of communication problems as they can. Tell them to explain what they did when they realized that there was a problem. Were they able to resolve the problem?

- As a class, ask the students to discuss their communication problems.

1 THINK ABOUT IT. In what kinds of situations do you write email, talk on the phone, send a text message, or speak face-to-face with people as part of your job? What are the advantages of each way of communicating? Are there situations in which one or more of these ways do not work well? Explain.

- Go over the directions with the students.
- Put the students in small groups to answer the questions.
- As a class, go over the answers to the questions.

2 READ the series of email messages between Jack, a building contractor, and Carl, the foreman at a construction site. What are the two things that Carl misunderstood in Jack's first message?

- Go over the directions with the students.
- Tell the students to read the emails individually.
- Put students into pairs to answer the question.
- As a class, go over the answer.

ANSWER KEY

The two mistakes are:
Jack typed *fax* when he meant *fix*. Carl misunderstood the word *plans*. Jack didn't mean the architectural plans for the building; he meant the plans for the schedule.

3 MATCH the word from the reading in Activity 2 with its definition.

- Go over the directions with the students.
- Point out the words at the top of the activity and the sentences with blanks in front of them below. Show the students the example sentence that has been done and explain that they are to write the letter next to the word from the list in the blank next to the correct definition.
- Have the students do the activity individually.
- As a class, go over the answers.

ANSWER KEY

1. a; 2. d; 3. e; 4. b; 5. c

4 WRITE answers to the questions. Then discuss your answers with a partner.

- Go over the directions with the students.
- Point out the questions below.
- Have the students answer the questions individually.
- As a class, go over the answers.

ANSWER KEY

1. Jack just wants Carl to tell the site engineers that there has been a change in the schedule. He doesn't want him to tell them to stop working.

2. Carl sends Jack his fax number because he thinks that Jack is going to fax him a change in plans.

3. "Change of plans" means that the schedule will change, not that the architectural drawings for the site will change.

4. Carl asks for a text message because the building site is noisy and he won't hear his phone ring.

5 WHAT ABOUT YOU? Have you had an experience when there was a misunderstanding in email or on the phone, but you did not ask for clarification? What happened? Talk to a partner.

- Go over the directions with the students.
- Put the students in small groups to answer the questions.
- As a class, go over the answers to the questions.

CHECK YOUR PROGRESS!

- Have students circle the answers.
- Have students check whether each answer is right or wrong.
- Have students total their correct answers and fill in the chart at the bottom of the page.
- Have students create a learning plan and/or set learning goals.

ANSWER KEY

1. a; 2. a; 3. the; 4. The; 5. if; 6. who the landlord is; 7. what the rent is; 8. whether I should; 9. connection; 10. outage; 11. weak; 12. bill; 13. against; 14. condition; 15. complaint; 16. policy

Unit Overview

LESSON	OBJECTIVES	STUDENT BOOK	WORKBOOK
1 Grammar and Vocabulary 1	Use adjective clauses with subject relative pronouns. Talk about the news.	p. 102	p. 90
2 Grammar Practice Plus	Use adjective clauses. Talk about crimes.	p. 104	p. 91
3 Listening and Conversation	Pronunciation: Linking with *that*. Talk about current events.	p. 106	p. 92
4 Grammar and Vocabulary 2	Use adjective clauses and object relative pronouns. Talk about news media.	p. 108	p. 94
5 Grammar Practice Plus	Talk about news stories and blogs. Math: Reading bar graphs.	p. 110	p. 95
6 Reading	Read an article to identify key information. Identify opinions and reasons.	p. 112	p. 96–97
7 Writing	Express and support an opinion.	p. 114	p. 98–99
• Career Connection	Understand food safety and health codes.	p. 116	p. 100–101
• Check Your Progress	Monitor progress.	p. 117	p. 102–103

Reading/Writing Strategies

• Identify key information   • Identify opinions and reasons   • Express and support an opinion

Connection Activities

LESSON	TYPE	SKILL DEVELOPMENT
1	Community	Using the Internet to find information
2	Academic	Identifying and using scientific vocabulary
3	Community	Interviewing and reporting
4	Academic	Researching school policies and blogging
5	Community	Interviewing and reporting
6	Academic	Debating
7	Community	Taking a poll
Career Connection	Academic	Researching and comparing educational programs

WORKSHEET #/FOCUS	TITLE	TEACHER'S EDITION
19. Conversation/Vocabulary	Vocabulary Poll	p. 323
20. Reading/Comprehension	A Funny Thing Happened . . .	p. 324
21. Listening	Mr. Lee's Dilemma	p. 325

LESSON 1: Grammar and Vocabulary

Use adjective clauses with subject relative
  pronouns
Talk about the news

VOCABULARY

collision	epidemic
commit a crime	investigate
demonstration	rescue
demonstrators	role model
donate	

GRAMMAR

Adjective clauses with relative pronouns
  as subjects

COMPETENCY

Use language to communicate information

WARM-UP ACTIVITY: Telephone game

- Have students stand in a circle. Whisper a
  secret to the first student, beginning with the
  phrase "Did you hear . . ."
- The first student should whisper it to the next
  student, and so on, until the secret makes it
  around the circle.
- Have the last student tell the secret that he or
  she heard. Was it the same as the secret you
  began with, or did the information change?

1 GRAMMAR PICTURE DICTIONARY.
TCD3, 2   What stories are in the news? Listen and
SCD27   read.

- Have students open their books and look at
  the pictures. Ask: *What is happening in each
  picture?*
- Say the sentences aloud or play the CD and
  have students repeat.
- Call on students and ask about the people

in the pictures: *How many cars were in the
accident? Why are people demonstrating? How
is the firefighter doing?*

2 PRACTICE the conversations in Activity 1 with
a partner.

- Put the students in pairs and have them take
  turns saying the sentences to each other.
- Go through the pictures one by one, asking
  the students to paraphrase the problems and
  situations in the pictures. For example, for the
  first picture, a student could say, *The children
  look up to the man who gave money to the
  community center. They can learn from him.*

**EXPANSION ACTIVITY: Extend the
dialogues**

- Put students in groups. Assign each group
  one of the pictures from the Grammar
  Picture Dictionary.
- Have each group write additional lines of
  dialogue for their picture.
- Have volunteers present their completed
  dialogue to the class.

3 NOTICE THE GRAMMAR. Underline the
pronouns *who* and *that* in the sentences
above. Then check the correct lines below.

- Go over the directions.
- Have students underline *who* and *that* in the
  sentences.
- Put students in pairs to check their answers.
- Elicit the answers to the questions and have
  students point out examples of *who* and *that*
  used as indicated.

ANSWER KEY

1. *A:* Did you hear about the man <u>who</u> donated
      money to our community center?

   B: Yes, I did. He's a great role model for
      children. They want to be like him.

ANSWER KEY

2. *A:* Did you hear about the five-car collision <u>that</u> happened on the freeway?
   B: No, I didn't. When did it happen?

3. *A:* Did you hear about the demonstration <u>that</u> was held outside City Hall today?
   B: Yes. The demonstrators want the mayor to make the city safer.

4. *A:* How is the firefighter <u>who</u> rescued the little boy?
   B: He's in the hospital, but he's ok.

5. *A:* Did you talk to the officers <u>who</u> are investigating the robbery?
   B: Yes, I did. I was a witness, so I described the person <u>that</u> committed the crime.

6. *A:* I read there might be a flu epidemic this winter. A lot of people might get sick.
   B: I read that, too. Fortunately, people <u>who</u> are over 65 can get free flu vaccinations.

1. <u>who</u> Used for People
2. <u>that</u> Used for Places and Things

GRAMMAR CHART: Adjective Clauses with Relative Pronouns as Subjects

- Direct students' attention to the chart or project the transparency or CD.
- Go over the information on the chart and the usage notes. Read the sentences, pausing to have students repeat.
- Go over the information in the Grammar Professor note.

CHART EXPANSION ACTIVITY: Around the room

- Choose an object or person in the room. Make up a sentence about this person or object using an adjective clause as shown in the chart.
- State your sentence as a clue, and have students guess the object or person you've described. For example: *This is the person who sits next to Janet.*

EXPANSION ACTIVITY: The house that Jack built

- Read a part or all of the nursery rhyme "This Is the House That Jack Built."
- Have students identify the noun that each adjective clause refers to.
- Assign each student one phrase. Read the poem aloud by having each student recite their phrase at the correct time.

ANSWER KEY

1. Did you hear about the man (who) rescued the girl from the river?
2. I read about an epidemic (that) is happening in South America.
3. Politicians (who) are honest and hardworking are good role models for citizens.
4. The woman (who) donated money to the hospital was a patient there two years ago.
5. The police officer (that) investigated the crime got a promotion.

5 **WRITE** sentences in your notebook. Put the words in the correct order.

- Go over the directions and the example.
- Have the students complete the sentences.
- Call on volunteers to write sentences on the board.
- Go over the answers with the class.

ANSWER KEY

1. I met a woman who works at the police station downtown.
2. The men who committed the crime were punished.
3. Were you stuck in the traffic jam that happened after the collision?
4. Musicians who have healthy lifestyles are positive role models for children.
5. Did you hear about the little boy that rescued his sister from a burning house?

EXPANSION ACTIVITY: Write a conversation

- Divide the class into groups.
- Assign each group item 3 or item 5 from Activity 5.
- Have groups read the question and write a conversation that answers the question. Encourage groups to add follow-up questions and details that tell the whole story.
- Have groups present their conversations to the class. Did students come up with similar stories or vastly different ones?

6 **WHAT ABOUT YOU?** Complete the sentences below. Then talk with a partner.

- Go over the directions.
- Have the students complete the sentences and share with a partner.
- Call on students to tell the class one of the sentences they wrote.

COMMUNITY CONNECTION: Accident reports

- Show students a website that gives real-time traffic reports for your city or town, such as Traffic.com or Maps.google.com.
- Have students find information about accidents and road closings around the city.
- Have students write sentences using adjective clauses to describe the road conditions. For example, *The construction that is on Highway 1 causes long delays.*

LESSON 2: Grammar Practice Plus

OBJECTIVES

Use adjective clauses
Talk about crimes

VOCABULARY

evidence	suspect
identify	theory

GRAMMAR

Adjective clauses

COMPETENCY

Understand small crimes: infractions, reporting, consequences

WARM-UP ACTIVITY: On the big screen

- Ask students if they enjoy watching movies or television shows about police solving crimes.
- Have volunteers tell about their favorite movies or shows in this genre.
- Lead a discussion about whether the class thinks these shows are realistic or just for entertainment.

1 VOCABULARY. Read the definitions. Then complete the sentences with the correct forms of the words.

- Go over the directions and the example.
- Have students complete the exercise.
- Go over the answers with the class.

ANSWER KEY

1. identified; 2. theory; 3. evidence;
4. suspects

EXPANSION ACTIVITY: Video vocabulary

- Show students an episode or clips of a television show or movie about a crime scene or trial.
- Put students in groups. Have them write a summary of the video, using the vocabulary words from Activity 1.
- Have groups share their summaries and reconstruct the complete plot of the video as a class.
- Replay the video so students can check to confirm that no major events or important details were missed.

2 READ the sentences. Circle the words that correctly complete each sentence.

- Go over the directions.
- Have students circle the correct answer for each item.
- Put students in pairs to compare answers.
- Go over the answers with the class.

ANSWER KEY

1. who lives; 2. that proves; 3. who rescued;
4. who works; 5. who are

EXPANSION ACTIVITY: Writing sentences

- Put students in pairs.
- Have each pair write follow-up sentences for the statements and questions from Activity 2. Students may write further details, answer a question, or ask a question in return.
- Have pairs volunteer to role-play the original sentence and the follow-up they wrote. Have several pairs present the same item and ask the class to tell whether their responses were similar or different.

3 WRITE. Combine each pair of sentences to make one sentence.

- Go over the directions and the example.
- Have students write the sentences and compare with a partner.
- Call on volunteers to write the sentences on the board.
- Go over the answers with the class.

1. John thanked the firefighter who helped him.
2. The police are looking at the evidence that was in the apartment.
3. A woman who is in my class has a theory about the missing tests.
4. The witness who identified a suspect saw everything.
5. A woman who graduated 30 years ago donated a million dollars to her university.
6. The witnesses who were inside the bank during the robbery identified the suspect.
7. A reporter who interviewed several witnesses wrote a story about the crime.

4 TALK about the picture. Then listen and write the correct number next to each name.

- Go over the directions.
- Play the CD and have students write the correct number next to each name.
- Go over the answers with the class.

LISTENING SCRIPT
Lesson 2, Activity 4
TCD3, 3

1. Officer King is the person who is talking to the owner of the butcher shop.
2. Officer Dill is the person who has a theory about the robbery.
3. Robin Gale is the person who looks surprised.
4. Tina Ruiz is the person who identified the thieves.
5. Tom Lee is the person who owns the butcher shop.
6. Lee West is the person who is looking for his dog.

ANSWER KEY

3. Robin Gale; 1. Officer King; 6. Lee West;
4. Tina Ruiz; 2. Officer Dill; 5. Tom Lee

BIG PICTURE CONVERSATION/ VOCABULARY EXPANSION ACTIVITY: Vocabulary poll

- Photocopy and distribute copies of the Big Picture and Worksheet 19: *Vocabulary Poll* for each student.
- Have students show the Big Picture to people in their neighborhood or community. Students should explain that they are studying English and trying to learn vocabulary. Have students ask participants to describe what they see in the picture.
- When students hear an unfamiliar word, they should write it in the chart and ask for an explanation of the word. Then they should write a definition or translation of the word in the chart.
- After the chart is complete, have students check their definitions with a dictionary.
- Put the transparency for Unit 7 on the OHP and have volunteers present new words that they learned while pointing them out on the picture.

5 WRITE. Complete the article with the adjective clauses in the box below.

- Go over the directions.
- Put students in pairs and have them complete the story.
- Have volunteers read each line aloud to go over the answers.

Unit 7 159

ANSWER KEY

1. that were behind the window
2. who arrived at the scene
3. who were in the butcher shop
4. that was walking by
5. who stole the steaks
6. that led to the park

BIG PICTURE READING EXPANSION ACTIVITY: A Funny Thing Happened . . .

- Photocopy and distribute Worksheet 20: *A Funny Thing Happened . . .*
- Put the transparency for Unit 7 on the OHP or have students look at the Big Picture on page 105.
- Go over the directions.
- Have students read the email and answer the questions.
- Go over the answers with the class.

WORKSHEET ANSWER KEY

1. because the steaks that were stolen were very expensive
2. the officer who was on duty
3. to take a look around the neighborhood
4. laughing and pointing at something
5. were not punished for a crime

ACADEMIC CONNECTION: Scientific vocabulary

- Have students look again at the vocabulary listed on page 104: *evidence, suspect, theory, identify*.
- If possible, have students tell how these words can be used in scientific studies. Give examples as needed, such as these: *There is no evidence that genetic factors cause the disease. Scientists suspect that the environment may be to blame. One theory states that pollution contributes to the disease, but nobody can identify its true cause as yet.*
- Have students browse through academic periodicals online or in a library to look for examples of these words used in a scientific context. Have students copy down one sentence for each word.
- Ask volunteers to write their sentences on the board and examine the language as a class. How is academic writing different from other types of writing?

LESSON 3: Listening and Conversation

OBJECTIVES

Pronunciation: Linking with *that*.
Talk about current events.

PRONUNCIATION

Linking with *that*

COMPETENCY

Interpret and communicate information
from a news story

WARM-UP ACTIVITY: Review

- Divide the class into two teams.
- Challenge each team to make up sentences using adjective clauses with *who* and *that*.
- Have the opposing team tell whether each sentence is correct or not.
- For each correct sentence, award the team a point. For each incorrect sentence, award the opposite team a point if they can correct the sentence.

PRONUNCIATION: Linking with *That*
TCD3, 4

- Play the CD or go over the information about adjective clauses.

A. DRAW marks to predict the linking in the adjective clauses. Then listen and check.
TCD3, 5
SCD28

- Go over the directions and the example.
- Have students draw a link in each sentence.
- Play the CD and have students check their answers.
- Go over the answers with the class.

ANSWER KEY

1. The woman that is in my class
2. the crimes that are common
3. the officer that arrived late
4. the people that asked about the suspect
5. the photographs that are lost
6. the witness that offered to help

EXPANSION ACTIVITY: Writing sentences

- Have students write sentences using the clauses in Activity A.
- Call on volunteers to share their sentences with the class.

B. LISTEN again and repeat.
TCD3, 6

- Go over the directions.
- Play the CD and have students repeat.

❶ LISTEN to the conversation. Then listen to the question. Fill in the correct answer. Replay each item if necessary.
TCD3, 7–10

- Direct students' attention to the answer sheet.
- Play the CD and have students fill in the correct circle.
- Put students in pairs to compare answers.
- Go over the answers with the class.

**LISTENING SCRIPT
Lesson 3, Activity 1**
TCD3, 7–10

1. *A*: Did you read about the man who found 500 coins in the walls of his house?

   B: Yeah, I did! The coins are 200 years old!

   Which is correct?

   A. A man found 200 coins in his house.

   B. A man found 500 coins in his house.

   C. A man found coins that are 500 years old.

TCD3, 11 2. *A*: Did you read about the bus drivers who are demonstrating?

   B: Yes, I did. They've been demonstrating for two weeks. They're asking for higher pay and better health care.

   Which is correct?

   A. Bus drivers want higher salaries and better health insurance.

   B. Health care workers have been demonstrating for two weeks.

   C. Bus drivers demonstrated two weeks ago.

3. *A*: Did you hear about the 20-car collision that happened this morning?

   B: No, I didn't. What happened?

   A: Someone's car broke down on the freeway. The driver who was behind that car didn't see it, so he hit it. Then 18 more cars crashed.

   B: Oh, that's terrible!

   Which is correct?

   A. Eighteen cars crashed on the freeway this morning.

   B. A driver of a car that broke down caused a 20-car collision.

   C. Twenty cars broke down on the freeway this morning and caused a collision.

4. *A*: Hi, Bill. Are you going to get a flu vaccination this year?

TCD3, 12 *B*: Yes, I am. I heard there might be a flu epidemic. My doctor told me about it.

   A: Let's get our vaccinations together. I know about a hospital that offers free vaccinations.

   Which is correct?

   A. Bill is going to visit a doctor because there may be a flu epidemic.

   B. Bill visited a doctor because he wanted to get a flu vaccination.

A: Did you read the article about the couple that got married at the airport last month?

B: No, I didn't. What happened?

A: Well, they met each other 30 years ago at the airport gift shop, but they didn't speak again after that. They both married different people, and years later, they both got divorced. But they never forgot each other. Then, last year,

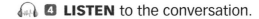

 2 LISTEN to the conversations again. Write the number of each conversation next to the correct headline.

- Go over the directions.
- Play the CD and have students answer the questions.
- Put students in pairs to check their answers.
- Go over the answers with the class.

CIVICS NOTE

Remind students that the third item of conversation they heard tells about a big car crash that happened. Explain to students the legal requirements and ramifications of being involved in a car crash in the United States: reporting the accident to the police, having insurance to cover accidents, giving a statement as a witness, etc. You may wish to have students research the penalties for hit-and-run accidents, for not carrying insurance, and so on.

 3 LISTEN to the conversation. Then read the sentences and check *True* or *False*.

- Play the CD or read the conversation.
- Have students circle *True* or *False* for each statement.
- Go over answers with the class.

LISTENING SCRIPT
Lesson 3, Activity 3

TCD3, 12

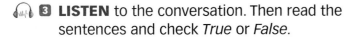

they saw each other at a restaurant that's next to the same gift shop!

B: Really? And they recognized each other?

A: Yeah. They remembered each other, so they said hello. They started dating, and now they're married!

B: I can't believe it!

A: It's true!

 4 LISTEN to the conversation.

- Go over the directions.
- Play the CD or read the conversation.

5 PRACTICE the conversation from Activity 4 with a partner. Use the expressions below.

EXPANSION ACTIVITY: Creative writing and presentations

- Put students in small groups.
- Have each group brainstorm ideas and write a short fictional story about an animal that did something extraordinary or unusual.
- Have groups present their stories to the class. Encourage them to use lively narration to entertain their peers.

COMMUNITY CONNECTION: Amazing animals

- Remind students that in the article from Activity 6, a dog saved a man's life.
- Have students interview people in the community to find an interesting story about an animal.
- Have students report the story they heard to the class. Encourage students to use *who* and *that* clauses when they tell the story.

6 TALK with a partner. Make up a conversation about the news story below. Student A, read the news story below. Underline the interesting points. Then tell your partner about the story. Student B, ask your partner questions about the story.

- Go over the directions and the example.
- Put students in pairs and assign Student A and

LESSON 4: Grammar and Vocabulary

OBJECTIVES

Use adjective clauses and object
  relative pronouns
Talk about news media

VOCABULARY

blog	human-interest
classified ads	local
column	top story
columnist	URL
front page	website address
headline	

GRAMMAR

Adjective clauses with relative pronouns as objects

COMPETENCY

Identify sections of a newspaper

WARM-UP ACTIVITY: Newspaper shuffle

- Pass out different sections of newspapers to the class.
- Have each person hold up their section of the newspaper and tell why they like or dislike it (or whether they are indifferent).
- If possible, elicit reasons that use the target grammar, adjective clauses. For example: *You can read about people who do interesting things. You can buy things that are for sale.*

🎧 **1** GRAMMAR PICTURE DICTIONARY.

TCD3, 14
SCD30
What kinds of news items are the people talking about? Listen and read.

- Have students look at the pictures. Have students read any words in the picture and make predictions about what each conversation will be about.
- Play the CD or read the sentences aloud as students follow along silently.

- Call on students and ask questions about the people in the picture: *Who found the missing woman? What does Carly Baker do? What kind of information is on Edward's blog?* Elicit the answers.

EXPANSION ACTIVITY: Vocabulary blanks

- Put students in pairs and have each pair write two sentences using vocabulary words from the Grammar Picture Dictionary.
- Have students write their sentences on slips of paper, putting a blank line where the vocabulary word belongs. Have them write the missing word in parentheses at the end of the sentence. For example, *The ___ today was about the tornado. (top story)* Note that some sentences may have more than one logical answer, such as *column, headline, blog,* or *front page* in the preceding example.
- Put the papers in a bag and draw them out one at a time. Read each sentence and have students guess the answer. Discuss whether each one could have more than one answer.

BIG PICTURE WRITING EXPANSION ACTIVITY: In the news

- Put the transparency for Unit 7 on the OHP or display the Big Picture from the CD.
- Put students in four groups and assign each group one of the following: front page story/headline; column; human-interest story; blog.
- Have each group write a story about the Big Picture in the style that they were assigned. For example, the "column" group might write an opinion column on the great work the police force has done this year in solving crimes.
- Put students' stories together and publish them as a newspaper.

2 PRACTICE the conversations in Activity 1 with a partner.

- Put students in pairs and have them practice the conversations.
- Ask volunteers to model the conversations for the class.

3 NOTICE THE GRAMMAR

A. CIRCLE the relative pronoun in each adjective clause above. Underline the subject and verb that come after each relative pronoun.

- Go over the directions.
- Put students in pairs to circle each relative pronoun and underline the subjects and verbs.
- Go over the answers with the class.

ANSWER KEY

1. (that) you told
2. (who) hikers rescued
3. (that) Carly Baker writes
4. (who) Karen told
5. (that) I had
6. (that) you write

B. READ the adjective clauses in the grammar chart on page 103. Find each relative pronoun and look at the word after it. What part of speech is the word after the relative pronoun?

- Go over the directions.
- Put students in pairs to read the sentences.
- Call on students to read the sentences aloud to the class.

ANSWER KEY

verb

GRAMMAR CHART: Adjective Clauses with Relative Pronouns as Objects

- Go over the information in the charts, including the Grammar Professor note.

- Read the sample sentences in the charts and have students repeat.
- Elicit further examples of adjective clauses from students.

CHART EXPANSION ACTIVITY: Classmates

- Put students in groups. Have students describe their classmates by writing sentences that use adjective clauses. For example, *The shirt that Rosa is wearing is pink.*
- Have students write about the people in another group. For example, students from Group 1 will write about the students from Group 2.
- Have each group read their sentences aloud to the class.

4 WRITE. Combine each pair of sentences to make one sentence. Include an adjective clause with a relative pronoun as the object.

- Go over the directions.
- Have students combine sentences using adjective clauses.
- Put students in pairs to check their answers.
- Go over the answers with the class.

ANSWER KEY

1. This is the human-interest story that I told you about.
2. The column that Janice wrote was entertaining.
3. The photo that I was looking for was in the local section.
4. The doctor that I met writes a medical blog.
5. The URL for the blog that Lisa writes is www.drlisablog.com.

5 READ. Put parentheses around the relative pronouns in the sentences you wrote in Activity 4. Read the sentences with a partner. First read them with the relative pronoun, then read them without the relative pronoun.

- Go over the directions.
- Be sure they understand that they are to use their answers from Activity 4 to find the relative pronouns.
- Divide students into pairs.
- Have them read the sentences to each other with and without relative pronouns.

ANSWER KEY

1. This is the human-interest story (that) I told you about.
2. The column (that) Janice wrote was entertaining.
3. The photo (that) I was looking for was in the local section.
4. The doctor (that) I met writes a medical blog.
5. The URL for the blog (that) Lisa writes is www.drlisablog.com.

EXPANSION ACTIVITY: Classified ads

- Put students in groups and give each group a page from the classified ads.
- Have groups scan the page to find ads that they can write sentences about using adjective clauses with relative pronouns as objects. For example, *The house that is for sale in my neighborhood is very expensive. The person who gets the job will have to take a training course.*

6 WHAT ABOUT YOU? Complete the sentences with your own ideas.

- Go over the directions and the sentence starters.
- Model an example or elicit an example from students.
- Have students complete the sentences.
- Call on volunteers to read the sentences they wrote.

ACADEMIC CONNECTION: Blogs

- Have students find out whether your school or schools in your community have blogs. Have them find out how the blogs are regulated and if any rules apply to posting on the blogs.
- Lead a discussion about what students discovered, pointing out that many schools or school districts have blog policies to regulate faculty, staff, and student blogs.
- Have students add a post to your school's blog if possible.

LESSON 5: Grammar Practice Plus

OBJECTIVES
Talk about news stories and blogs Math: Reading bar graphs

VOCABULARY
Bar graph

MATH
Reading bar graphs

COMPETENCY
Interpret a bar graph

WARM-UP ACTIVITY: How healthy do we eat?

- Bring to class several circulars from local supermarkets.

- Have each student cut out one picture of a food that he or she eats frequently. Have students tape their picture to the blank side of an index card.

- Scatter the cards on a table in random order. On the board, make a two-column chart labeled *Healthy* and *Unhealthy.*

- Have each student choose one card and tape it in the column in which he or she thinks it belongs.

- When all cards have been categorized, lead a discussion about whether students agree with each placement. Talk about how healthy the choices were that the class made as a whole.

- Save the index cards for use in a later activity.

1 **COMPLETE** the article. Write the correct relative pronoun in each sentence below. Then circle the subject relative pronouns.

- Go over the directions.
- Have students complete the exercise.
- Put students in pairs to compare their answers.
- Go over the answers with the class.

ANSWER KEY

Childhood obesity is an important issue (1) (that) is currently affecting many children. Some even call it an epidemic. According to researchers, about 15 percent of children (2) (who/that) live in the United States and more than 20 percent of Australian children are dangerously overweight.

There are several factors (3) (that) may be responsible for this problem. First, many of these children eat fast food or junk food instead of nutritious meals (4) (that) are prepared at home. The food (5) that they eat is full of fat and sugar and doesn't contain the vitamins and nutrients (6) that they need.

Second, children (7) (who/that) spend all their time in front of a television, a computer, or a video game don't get enough exercise. They don't do activities (8) (that) burn calories, such as playing sports or simply playing outside. If children don't burn off the calories (9) that they consume, they gain weight.

EXPANSION ACTIVITY: Eating well at school

- Have students search the Internet for articles about school food programs. How have these programs changed in recent years because of the concern about childhood obesity?
- Ask each student to select a different article and write a short summary of its main points. Have each student present these points to the class.
- Alternatively, have students prepare a poster or display that includes the original article, an illustration, and a student-written summary or opinion piece.

BIG PICTURE GRAMMAR EXPANSION ACTIVITY: Adjective clauses

- Put the transparency for Unit 7 on the OHP or display the Big Picture from the CD.
- As a class, name the foods that are shown in the Big Picture and brainstorm other foods that are found in a butcher shop or in the meat department of a supermarket. Write the list of foods on the board.
- Put students in pairs.
- Have pairs write three sentences that tell healthy and unhealthy ways to prepare the foods listed on the board. For example, *Chicken that is fried is unhealthy.*
- Have pairs share their sentences aloud. Ask the class to tell whether each one is formed correctly and whether they agree that it is a true statement.

2 WRITE. Combine each pair of sentences to make one sentence. If a relative pronoun is the object of the relative clause, put it in parentheses to show it can be omitted.

- Go over the directions.
- Have students combine the sentences as directed.

- Put students in pairs to compare answers.
- Call on volunteers to read their sentences and check answers with the class.

ANSWER KEY

1. Many activities (that) children do outdoors are fun and good exercise.
2. Many parents who worry about what their kids eat at school pack nutritious lunches for their children.
3. Children who have computers in their bedrooms spend more time online.
4. Health groups provide programs that teach children how to choose nutritious foods.
5. Junk food (that) children buy at school is full of fat and sugar.
6. Video games (that) children play keep them indoors.
7. Playing outside is an activity (that) children can do to stay healthy.

MATH: Reading Bar Graphs

- Go over the direction and the labels on the bar graph.
- Have students answer the questions with a partner.
- Go over the answers with the class.

ANSWER KEY

1. ages 6–11; 2. ages 2–5; 3. ages 6–11

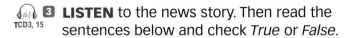 **3 LISTEN** to the news story. Then read the sentences below and check *True* or *False*.
TCD3, 15

- Go over the directions.
- Have students listen to the story and answer each question.
- Elicit answers from volunteers.

LISTENING SCRIPT
Lesson 5, Activity 3
TCD3, 15

Mike Jennings of Plainfield, Illinois, had a problem. He was overweight, dangerously overweight. And, he spent too much time on the computer. His doctor said he needed to get out of the house and exercise more, but Jennings didn't do it.

"I had gotten used to spending all of my free time in front of the computer, surfing the Net. It was hard to just stop doing it," he explained. Then one day Jennings found a website that quickly changed his mind and his health.

"I like to read blogs, so I decided to look for some health blogs. I found some really interesting stuff. There are some great blogs out there that are written for people like me." Jennings is talking about a growing number of health-related blogs that include tips for losing weight, eating right, and preparing easy and healthful meals.

"I started to read tips and ideas from people who were trying to lose weight, like I am. I tried the exercises and recipes I read about. Before I knew it, I had lost ten pounds. I felt great. Now I spend a lot less time on the Internet. But when I am surfing the Net, I read health blogs. I told my doctor about the blogs, and she's going to tell her other patients about them."

For people like Mike, blogs can be a good source of information and support for the difficult tasks of losing weight and staying healthy.

ANSWER KEY

1. True; 2. False; 3. False; 4. False; 5. True; 6. False; 7. True

EXPANSION ACTIVITY: Recreate the story

- Have students listen again to the story from Activity 3. Tell them to take notes as they listen and try to write down all the important points of the story.
- Put students in groups and have them compare notes.
- Have each group rewrite the story from memory as much as possible, using only their notes.

- Have each group read its version of the story to the class. Did they remember all of the important points? Were the events in the correct order? Is the information accurate?

4 **WHAT ABOUT YOU?** Think of an idea for your own blog and ideas you would like to share on it. Use the phrases below to write your sentences. Then share your ideas with a partner.

- Go over the directions.
- Have students write their ideas and share them with a partner.
- Have students give feedback on each idea.

COMMUNITY CONNECTION: At the supermarket

- Have students take the index cards they created in the warm-up activity to their local supermarket.
- Have students find the item pictured on their card. On the lined side of the card, students should copy down the nutritional information for the product.
- At the store, have each student interview three or four shoppers. The student should show his or her product and its nutritional information, asking the shopper if the item is healthy or unhealthy, and why.
- Have students share their results.

EXPANSION ACTIVITY: Food chart

- Have students create a whole-class chart or diagram that compares the nutritional information for the products they researched at the supermarket. For example, for each product, have students list the calories and/or grams of fat, sugar, protein, and fiber.
- Have students ask and answer questions about the chart in pairs.
- Lead a discussion with the class about the results that the chart reveals.

LESSON 6: Reading

OBJECTIVES

Read an article to identify key information
Identify opinions and reasons

VOCABULARY

big business
opinion
reason

READING FOCUS

Skim the text
Identify key information
Identify opinions and reasons

COMPETENCIES

Read a newspaper article about a consumer-
   related issue
Recognize opinions and supporting reasons

WARM-UP ACTIVITY: Our city

• Ask students if they can think of new
  construction and developments that have
  happened in your city or town within the last
  few years. Write their ideas on the board.

• Lead a discussion about the new
  developments. Have they improved the city or
  detracted from its appeal? Why were the new
  developments built? Was there community
  support for them or protest against them?

1 THINK ABOUT IT. Do you like to shop at big
corporate stores or small privately owned
stores? Why? With a partner, list the names
of several large corporate stores and several
small independent stores that you know.
Discuss the benefits of shopping at both kinds
of stores.

• Go over the directions and the questions.

• Put students in pairs to answer the questions.

• Call on students to share their ideas with the
  class.

2 BEFORE YOU READ. Read the title of the
newspaper article on the next page. What do
you already know about "big business"? Can
you give an example of a "big business"? Skim
the text by reading the first sentence of each
paragraph. What is the article about?

• Go over the directions.

• Direct students' attention to the first Reading
  Focus box. Go over the information in it.

• Have students skim the article as directed.
  Point out the definition of *big business* in the
  glossary.

• Elicit ideas from the class to predict what the
  article will be about.

3 READ the article. Underline the details that
answer *who, what, where, when, why,* and
how.

• Go over the directions.

• Direct students' attention to the second
  Reading Focus box. Go over the information
  in it.

• Have students read the article and underline
  the appropriate information.

• Put students in pairs to compare what they
  underlined.

• Elicit ideas from the class and write them on
  the board. Discuss any differences in opinion
  on which details could be considered "key"
  information.

**EXPANSION ACTIVITY: Vocabulary
practice**

• Go over the vocabulary in the glossary on
  page 113.

• Have students write sentences using the
  vocabulary words.

• Call on volunteers to share their sentences
  with the class, omitting the vocabulary
  word. Have students guess the correct
  word to complete each sentence.

EXPANSION ACTIVITY: Role-Play

- Have students look at the picture on page 113 and describe the man and his daughter.
- Put students into pairs.
- Have pairs role-play a scene between the father and a reporter who is interviewing him. The reporter asks his opinion about the proposed BigMart.
- After students have finished role-playing, take a poll to see how many of the "fathers" opposed the BigMart. Why? Discuss.

CULTURE NOTE

Discuss with students the city revitalization movements that have happened around the country in the past several years. Point out that many cities make great efforts to preserve their historic buildings and businesses. You may wish to tell students about the National Register of Historic Places and other organizations dedicated to preserving places of historical interest. Students may also be interested to learn about historical reenactments of important past events and about preserved and reconstructed villages such as Colonial Williamsburg.

❹ AFTER YOU READ.

A. DISCUSS the questions with a partner. Look at what you underlined in the article on page 113.

- Go over the directions.
- Put students in new pairs to talk about the questions.
- Go over the answers with the class.

ANSWER KEY

1. Davidson Park
2. They want to build a store where the park is now.
3. Kathy Jones
4. They could walk to the store to buy things they need.
5. Jonas Wilson. He thinks the store will drive smaller stores out of business.
6. They can attend the town council meeting.

B. COMPLETE the chart with the names of people in the article and the reasons for their opinions.

- Go over the directions, the chart, and the example.
- Direct students' attention to the third Reading Focus box. Go over the information in it.
- Put students in pairs to complete the chart.
- Go over the answers with the class.

ANSWER KEY

BigMart will be good for downtown.	BigMart will not be good for downtown.
Kathy Jones – more jobs Miles Morris – the people who live downtown need a place nearby to shop	Jonas Wilson – it will drive stores out of business Lacey Briggs – does not want to lose the park Denny Peters – the store would be ugly and would ruin the neighborhood

BIG PICTURE LISTENING EXPANSION ACTIVITY: Mr. Lee's Dilemma

- Photocopy and distribute Worksheet 21: *Mr. Lee's Dilemma.*

- Put the transparency for Unit 7 on the OHP or have students look at the Big Picture on page 105.

- Go over the directions for the worksheet and preview the characters.

- Read the listening script, using different voices for each character if desired.

- Have students complete the worksheet and compare their answers with a partner.

- Go over the answers with the class.

WORKSHEET LISTENING SCRIPT / ANSWER KEY

Mr. Lee: I'm so tired of all the <u>crime</u> downtown. My butcher shop has been broken into <u>three</u> times this year!

Mrs. Lee: That's true, but crime isn't much better here in <u>Glendale</u>. And besides, the police downtown have always been so <u>helpful</u> when you needed them. Officer King always does a great job, and Officer Dill is so nice.

Mr. Lee: I know, I can't complain about the police. But what bothers me is that I've had to pay to replace nearly <u>$1,000</u> worth of food that was stolen.

Mrs. Lee: Hmm, that is a lot of money. On the other hand, the <u>rent</u> on a shop here would be much <u>higher</u> than it is downtown. You might end up losing money if you move the business here.

Mr. Lee: What about the money I'd save on commuting? If I worked here in Glendale, I could <u>walk to work</u> instead of driving.

Mrs. Lee: Well, you may have a point. But wouldn't you miss all the friends you've made over the years? People come into the shop every day just to <u>chat</u> with you. If you move, you probably won't see them anymore. You might get <u>lonely</u> in a new shop.

Mr. Lee: I don't think so. So many of my old <u>customers</u> have moved to the suburbs anyway. Nobody wants to shop downtown anymore. Everyone wants to go to the <u>superstores</u> in the suburbs.

Mrs. Lee: If that's the case, how do you think you can <u>compete</u> against the superstores here in Glendale?

Mr. Lee: I'm not sure, to be honest. I guess I need to <u>study</u> the market more before I make such a big decision.

Mrs. Lee: That sounds like a good idea.

ACADEMIC CONNECTION: Debate

- Divide the class into two debate teams.

- Have students research a controversial new development in your town or in the world in preparation for a formal debate. One team will represent the supporters and the other will represent the opponents of the development.

- Review the rules of debating with students, holding a short mock debate on another topic as a model if needed.

- Decide whether the debate will have a winning team, and if so, how the winner will be determined.

- Hold the debate, having each student participate during discussion.

- After the debate, discuss what was difficult or interesting about the debate format, and whether students felt comfortable using it.

LESSON 7: Writing

WRITING FOCUS

Express and support an opinion

COMPETENCY

Write a letter to express opinion and
influence readers

WARM-UP ACTIVITY: News poll

- Take a class poll about the news. Ask students
how frequently they check the news: Daily?
More than once a day? A few times a week?
Then ask students how they prefer to check
the news: newspaper, television, Internet, or
some other method?
- Chart students' answers in a graph or other
chart. Discuss the results.

1 THINK ABOUT IT. List three recent news
stories in the newspaper or on television that
were interesting to you.

- Go over the directions.
- Have students make their lists.
- Ask volunteers to share the news stories that
they listed.

2 BEFORE YOU WRITE.

A. WRITE ideas. Look at the stories you listed
in Activity 1. Which one do you have the
strongest opinion about? Write your opinion
about the story you chose.

- Direct students' attention to the Writing Focus
box. Go over the information in it.
- Go over the directions.
- Have students complete the activity.

- Call on students to share what they wrote.
If any students wrote about the same topic,
discuss whether they shared the same opinion.

EXPANSION ACTIVITY: Newspaper search

- Put students in groups. Give each group a
copy of a current newspaper.
- Have students scan the newspaper for
articles about their topic from Activity 2A.
- Have students read the articles and
compare their opinions and information
with what is in the newspaper.
- Ask students to evaluate whether each
article is an opinion piece or a factual
article. If an opinion piece, have them circle
the main opinion and underline a few
sentences that support it.

B. READ the paragraph that a parent wrote about
a news story. Find the sentence that tells the
parent's opinion. Circle it.

- Go over the directions and point out the
paragraph at the bottom of the page.
- Have students read the paragraph and
underline the opinion.
- Elicit from students which sentence should be
circled.

ANSWER KEY

Students should circle: *In my opinion, our school
district should not make students pay to play
sports this year.*

C. READ again. What reasons does the parent
give for the opinion? Find three reasons.
Underline them.

- Go over the directions.
- Put students in pairs to complete the activity.
- Go over the answers with the class.

- Students should underline: *Kids who can't afford to pay won't be allowed to play, and that isn't fair.*
- *Also, we pay taxes for our school's sports program, so kids shouldn't need to pay even more.*
- *Finally, we might lose some of our best student athletes if their parents don't have the extra money.*

D. WRITE your ideas about a current issue in the news. Fill in the chart below with complete sentences. Use adjective clauses with *who* and *that*. Follow these steps.

- Go over the directions and the chart.
- Have students make notes in each section.
- Elicit ideas from the class.
- Encourage students to take further notes based on the ideas elicited.

3 WRITE a paragraph about the issue you chose. Use the information in the chart above. Add details and supporting information.

- Direct students' attention to the Writing Focus box again and reinforce the information in it.
- Go over the directions.
- Have students use their notes from the chart to write a paragraph on a separate sheet of paper or in their notebooks.
- Have volunteers read their paragraphs aloud to the class.

EXPANSION ACTIVITY: Slogans and promotions

- Have students create a slogan that expresses their opinion from Activity 3 in one short phrase or sentence.
- Have students create a design for a bumper sticker, poster, or other promotional material using their slogan, as if they were going to distribute it around the community to raise awareness and support for their issue.

- Post students' promotional materials on a display board in the classroom or elsewhere in your school.

4 AFTER YOU WRITE.

A. EDIT your work. Ask yourself these questions.

- Go over the directions and the questions.
- Have students look at their paragraphs and make changes if necessary.
- Put students in pairs to review each other's writing, answering the questions about their partner.

B. REWRITE your paragraph with corrections.

- Go over the directions.
- Have students rewrite their paragraphs.

C. DISCUSS these questions with a partner.

- Go over the directions and the questions.
- Put students in pairs to discuss the questions.
- Have volunteers tell the class what they discussed. Encourage students to ask questions.

EXPANSION ACTIVITY: Video case study

- Search the Internet for articles and video clips from a well-publicized, controversial media event (either from today or from the recent past): high-profile trials, heated political debates, environmental protests, and so on.
- Have students review the materials and outline the major points of argument on each side of the topic at hand.
- Ask students to analyze whether the video clips presented were impartial or biased. Why do they think so?

CIVICS NOTE

Point out that when public opinion on a court case becomes too volatile or influential, the court may order a change of venue. Explain how a change of venue helps ensure a fair trial. Have students search the Internet to find examples of cases in which a change of venue was needed. Discuss a few of the cases as a class.

COMMUNITY CONNECTION: Poll

- Have students take an opinion poll in their neighborhood or community. Have them tell people about the issue they wrote about in this lesson and ask for their opinions.

- Have volunteers tell the class the results of their poll, as well as any particularly interesting conversations that they had.

Career Connection

OBJECTIVES

Understand food safety and health codes

VOCABULARY

contagious	plastic gloves
food poisoning	temperatures
outbreak	thoroughly

COMPETENCIES

Identify safe and clean food handling
   practices
Practice test-taking skills

WARM-UP ACTIVITY: What's for dinner?

• Take an informal poll about restaurants
and fast food. How many students eat out
frequently? Do they prefer fast food or more
formal restaurants? Are there any restaurants
that they refuse to go to? Why?

• Lead a class discussion about the information
students shared.

❶ THINK ABOUT IT. Look at the photo. What
food safety rules do you think restaurant
employees have to follow?

• Direct students' attention to the photo and
ask questions: *Who do you see? What are they
doing?*

• Discuss food safety rules, eliciting students'
ideas.

❷ LISTEN to the presentation. A trainer
is talking to a group of employees in a
restaurant. Check *True* or *False.*

• Go over the directions.

• Play the CD. Have students check the correct
answers.

• Put students in pairs to compare their
responses.

• Go over the answers with the class.

LISTENING SCRIPT
Career Connection, Activity 2

TCD3, 16

Trainer: Welcome to the food education and safety
training session. At least once a year,
local Health Inspectors visit restaurants
to make sure employees are following the
health codes. As you know from recent
news stories, a few restaurants have been
shut down because their customers got
sick from the food.

First of all, it's important for *all* employees
to wash their hands after using the
restroom. Employees who don't wash
thoroughly might spread germs and
bacteria, such as E. coli. You've all heard
of E. coli, right?

B: Yeah. E. coli can give people food
poisoning.

Trainer: Right. E. coli is a type of bacteria that
causes food poisoning. You can get
abdominal cramps, fever, and an upset
stomach. E. coli is very contagious. It can
cause an epidemic because it spreads
easily from person to person. Does
anyone know how E. coli spreads?

C: I do. E. coli can spread if you have the
bacteria on your hands and then touch
food or another person.

Trainer: That's right. If you have bacteria on your
hands and don't wash properly, you
can contaminate anyone or anything
you touch. You can also spread E. coli
by handling raw food or unwashed
vegetables and touching clean food. Did
you know that foods like raw eggs and
uncooked meat, chicken, or shellfish
contain bacteria? Well, it's true. Both
cooked food and uncooked food that
haven't been stored at the correct
temperatures can contain E. coli and
other types of bacteria. So that's why
proper refrigeration is very important!
Fruits and vegetables may also contain
bacteria, so cleaning them properly
can help prevent the spread of food
poisoning.

B: Is E. coli the same thing as salmonella?

Trainer: Good question. They're both bacteria and cause similar symptoms. Like E. coli, salmonella can cause abdominal cramps, fever, and vomiting. People can also spread salmonella by the improper handling of food. That's why it's important to follow the health codes. Thoroughly wash your hands, cooking utensils, and food preparation surfaces. Also, all food preparation staff must wear plastic gloves while handling food. Employees who have long hair must wear a hair net in the kitchen. This helps prevent food contamination and the spreading of illnesses. Remember: You can help prevent food poisoning outbreaks by following these health codes! We want to keep all of you and the customers safe and happy! That's it for today. Thanks for your participation.

ANSWER KEY

1. True; 2. True; 3. True; 4. False; 5. False

EXPANSION ACTIVITY: Pronunciation practice

- Put students in pairs.
- Give each pair a copy of the listening script for Activity 2.
- Have partners read the script twice, switching roles.
- Encourage students to read the script as fluently as possible, moving on if they pause or stumble over difficult words.
- You may wish to practice difficult words or sentences chorally with the group, modeling proper intonation, stress, and rhythm.

3 COMPLETE the sentences with the correct vocabulary word from the presentation.

- Go over the directions.
- Have students complete the exercise.
- Call on volunteers to read the completed sentences

ANSWER KEY

1. food poisoning; 2. thoroughly; 3. contagious; 4. temperature; 5. plastic gloves; 6. outbreak

EXPANSION ACTIVITY: Vocabulary practice

- Put students in six groups and assign each group one vocabulary word from Activity 3.
- Have each group think of five one-word clues to describe their vocabulary word.
- Have each group reveal one word at a time to the class. The class must guess which word is being described.

4 WRITE three things that employees must do to protect themselves and customers from food poisoning.

- Go over the directions.
- Put students in small groups to discuss the topic.
- Lead a class discussion, eliciting a list of rules that employees should follow. Write student ideas on the board.

EXPANSION ACTIVITY: At the cafeteria

- Arrange to have your class visit the school's cafeteria or a nearby restaurant.
- Tour the cafeteria's kitchen and have students take note of health precautions that are used, including informative signs and posters.
- If possible, have students hold a question and answer session with the manager of the cafeteria. Have them prepare questions to ask in advance.

5 TALK with a partner or in a group. What could happen if employees do not follow the health codes? Can you think of other places in the community where health or food safety codes are important to follow?

- Go over the directions and the questions.
- Put students in small groups or pairs to talk about the questions.
- Call on volunteers to present their ideas to the class. List on the board other places in the community that follow health or food safety codes.

EXPANSION ACTIVITY: The restaurant business

- Put students in small groups.
- Have groups discuss whether they would like to own or manage a restaurant. Why or why not? What type of restaurant would they choose?
- Have groups list the positives and negatives of owning or managing a restaurant, including information about public health and food safety as appropriate.
- Poll the class to find out people's opinions.
- Have volunteers tell what their group talked about. Discuss any particularly interesting points as a class.

6 WHAT ABOUT YOU? Have you heard any news stories about illnesses caused by foods in local fast-food restaurants? Have you ever been sick from something that you ate? Describe what happened.

- Go over the directions and the questions.
- Lead a class discussion about fast-food illnesses.
- Have volunteers share personal experiences, asking them to describe the situation. Where were they? What had they eaten? You may wish to preface the discussion by telling students not to include details of the physical symptoms they experienced.

ACADEMIC CONNECTION: Education investigation

- Have students research food service education programs in your area, whether at public schools, community colleges, culinary arts programs, or other venues.
- Have students present the information they find to the class. Encourage students to ask questions.
- Lead a discussion on how food service education programs are different from other educational programs. How are they similar?

CHECK YOUR PROGRESS!

- Have students circle the answers.
- Have students check whether each answer is right or wrong.
- Have students total their correct answers and fill in the chart at the bottom of the page.
- Have students create a learning plan and/or set learning goals.

ANSWER KEY

1. who lives; 2. that was; 3. that arrested; 4. that caused; 5. that I read; 6. I told you about; 7. she wrote; 8. we know; 9. collision; 10. investigating; 11. committed; 12. role model; 13. classified; 14. URL; 15. top; 16. column

Unit Overview

LESSON	OBJECTIVES	STUDENT BOOK	WORKBOOK
1 Grammar and Vocabulary 1	Talk about the weather. Gerunds as objects of prepositions.	p. 118	p. 104
2 Grammar Practice Plus	Read a map. Write about disasters.	p. 120	p. 105
3 Listening and Conversation	Listen to a weather report. Convert Fahrenheit to Celsius.	p. 122	p. 106
4 Grammar and Vocabulary 2	Learn about disaster organizations. Gerunds as objects of verb + preposition.	p. 124	p. 108
5 Grammar Practice Plus	Match emergency organizations to text. Pronounce linking final consonant sounds.	p. 126	p. 109
6 Reading	Learn about the environment.	p. 128	p. 110–111
7 Writing	Write about environmental issues.	p. 130	p. 112–113
• Career Connection	Natural disaster preparedness.	p. 132	p. 114
• Check Your Progress	Monitor progress.	p. 133	p. 116–117

Reading/Writing Strategies

- Scan for Specific Information
- Use Parallel Structure

Connection Activities

LESSON	TYPE	SKILL DEVELOPMENT
1	Community	Extreme weather in my community
2	Academic	A famous natural disaster
3	Community	Disaster preparedness
4	Academic	Campus organizations
6	Community	Publicity from government

WORKSHEET #/FOCUS	TITLE	TEACHER'S EDITION
22. Grammar	Gerunds as Objects of Prepositions	p. 326
23. Grammar	Gerunds as Objects of a Verb + Preposition	p. 327
24. Listening	Four Problems	p. 328

LESSON 1: Grammar and Vocabulary

OBJECTIVES

Talk about the weather
Gerunds as objects of prepositions

VOCABULARY

air quality	severe thunderstorm
extreme heat alert	warning
forecast	smog advisory
gust of wind	tornado
issued	torrential rain
precautions	

GRAMMAR

Gerunds as objects of prepositions

COMPETENCY

Learn about weather conditions

WARM-UP ACTIVITY: Weather vocabulary

- In this lesson, the students will learn very advanced words and expressions for talking about extreme weather, e.g., *extreme heat alert*. It will be very helpful for them to review more basic words and expressions for weather, including words for extreme weather.
- Make sure that the students' books are closed.
- Write the word *Weather* on the board in large letters.
- Tell the students that you want them to call out every word about weather that they can think of. This may include words like *sunny*, *rainy*, and *cloudy*. After the usual words are on the board, try to lead them toward extreme weather words. If they have given you the word *windy*, for example, you can ask them what a really strong wind that can knock down a house is.

- After the board is full of words, give the students the opportunity to ask questions about any of the words or phrases that they don't understand.

❶ GRAMMAR PICTURE DICTIONARY.
TCD3, 17
SCD31
What is happening with the weather? How do the people feel about it? Listen and read.

- Have students open their books and look at the four pictures on page 118.
- Read the sentences to the students or play the CD.
- Give the students an opportunity to ask questions about anything that they do not understand.
- Put the students in pairs to answer the two questions about each picture.
- Go over the answers as a class.

❷ PRACTICE the conversations from Activity 1 with a partner.

- Put the students in pairs and have them read the mini-conversations in Activity 1. Tell them to change roles so that they have the opportunity to read both parts in each picture.
- Walk around the room helping students with pronunciation.

COMMUNITY CONNECTION: Extreme weather in my community

- Put the students into small groups.
- Ask them to list any types of extreme weather that sometimes occur in their community. What damage has there been in their community from storms or other extreme weather? What has been their personal experience with extreme weather? Has anyone seen a tornado or hurricane?

- Have each group report their findings to the class. Analyze the results. What are the most common types of extreme weather in the community?

❸ NOTICE THE GRAMMAR. Underline adjective + preposition combinations. Circle the gerunds (verb + *ing*) that follow them.

- Go over the directions with the students.
- Put the students in pairs. Show them the example sentence with *nervous about* underlined and *driving* circled.
- Have them complete the exercise individually.
- Put the students in pairs to compare answers.
- Check the answers as a class.

ANSWER KEY

1. *A:* I didn't hear the forecast. Is there a severe thunderstorm warning today?
   B: I don't know. But I'm nervous about (driving) in torrential rain.
   A: So am I. We'd better take the train instead.
2. *A:* The air quality is really terrible! There isn't a smog advisory today, is there?
   B: I don't know. But I'm concerned about (running) outdoors.
   A: So am I. Maybe we should exercise at the gym instead.
3. *A:* Uh-oh! We just had another power outage!
   B: Right. I'm not surprised because there's an extreme heat alert today.
   A: I'm worried about (keeping) our food cold.
4. *A:* Wow! What a strong gust of wind!
   B: I know. The National Weather Service issued a tornado warning. They're serious about (taking) precautions.
   A: Let's get out of here and find shelter right away!

GRAMMAR CHART: Gerunds as objects of prepositions

- Direct students' attention to the chart or project the transparency.

- Ask the students for an example of a sentence with a gerund. Make sure they understand that gerunds are the only verb form that can follow a preposition.
- Point out the grammar chart.
- Go over the five example sentences.
- Point out the Grammar Professor box. Read the "Correct" and "Incorrect" examples of verb forms after a preposition.
- Have the students give you additional examples of sentences with gerunds as objects of prepositions.

EXPANSION ACTIVITY: Fill in the blanks

- Give students two minutes to review the sentences in Activity 1, looking at the text under the pictures.
- Have students close their books.
- Write the sentences on the board, but leave out the boldfaced words in each sentence. As an alternative, you can type up the conversations, leaving the boldfaced words out, and give each student a printed copy.
- Put the students in pairs. Have them fill in the blanks on a piece of paper or on an activity sheet that you give them.
- Have students open their books and confirm their answers.

TIP

Advisory, Watch, Alert or Warning, Emergency

- Point out the vocabulary chart in the Tip box under the grammar chart.
- Show the students how the level of danger increases as you go down the column to the left.

CHART EXPANSION ACTIVITY: Questions with gerunds as objects of prepositions

- Write the following on the board:
  1. What are you afraid of?
  2. What kinds of sports are you interested in?
- Put the students in pairs.
- Have each pair write three questions with the adjectives and prepositions that they studied in the grammar chart.
- Walk around the room helping students form grammatically correct sentences.
- When the students are finished, have each pair write one of their sentences on the board.
- As a class, go over and answer the questions.

④ COMPLETE the sentences with the correct forms of the words in parentheses. Use the present or past form of *be*.

- Go over the directions with the students.
- Point out the sentences with blanks and the words in parentheses.
- Point out the example sentence that is completed.
- Have students complete the exercise individually.
- Put students in pairs to compare answers.
- Go over the answers as a class.

ANSWER KEY

1. was nervous about driving
2. was serious about taking
3. is not concerned about exercising
4. were not worried about playing
5. was excited about playing
6. are/were nervous about having

CHART EXPANSION ACTIVITY: Gerunds as objects of prepositions

- Tell students to turn to Worksheet 22: *Gerunds as Objects of Prepositions.*
- When the students have answered the questions individually, put them in pairs to compare their answers.
- Go over the answers as a class.

WORKSHEET ANSWER KEY

A. 1. about; 2. serious; 3. driving; 4. about; 5. keeping; 6. excited; 7. worried; 8. warning
B. 1. I'm worried about exercising outdoors today.
   2. They were excited about visiting their parents.
   3. She was serious about taking shelter during the storm.
   4. We are concerned about driving in this torrential rain.
   5. Martin was nervous about having a power outage.

⑤ WHAT ABOUT YOU? Answer the questions below with your own information. Complete the sentences. Then talk about them with a partner.

- Go over the instructions with the students.
- Put the students in pairs to complete the sentences.
- Go over the answers as a class.

LESSON 2: Grammar Practice Plus

OBJECTIVES

Read a map
Write about disasters

VOCABULARY

blizzard	hurricane
drought	mudslide
earthquake	tornado
extreme heat	wildfire
flash flood	

GRAMMAR

Gerunds as objects of prepositions

COMPETENCY

Interpret a weather map

WARM-UP ACTIVITY: Natural disasters

- Tell the students to close their books.
- Write the words *Natural Disasters* on the board.
- Ask the students to explain what a natural disaster is. Elicit from the students a list of natural disasters.
- Ask the students what kind of natural disasters, if any, their home country sometimes has.

LANGUAGE NOTE

Cyclone (or *tropical cyclone*) is the general term for huge rotating storms that have a low pressure area in their center. They originate over large bodies of water and often move onto land. They bring torrential rain and storm surges, or giant waves that crash against the shore. They often cause terrible flooding.

These storms are called *hurricanes* in the Atlantic Ocean and *typhoons* in the Pacific or Indian Ocean. In the Northern Hemisphere, they rotate counter-clockwise; in the Southern Hemisphere, they rotate clockwise. Tornadoes are also rotating storms, but they do not have to originate over water. They are smaller than cyclones but can cause more damage in a limited area. The United States has more tornadoes than any other country.

 ① LISTEN to the statements and look at the
TCD3, 18   map. Write the number in the box next to the area where the situation is happening.

- Go over the directions. Make sure the students understand that they will hear listening passages with numbers. They must listen for the number and write it on the map next to the icon it describes.
- Point out the Big Picture and the words in the box below. Give the students the opportunity to ask questions about any of the words that they do not understand.
- Play the recording. Pause after the first listening segment and make sure that the students are writing the number "1" next to an icon. Play the recording through to the end.
- Have the students complete the activity individually.
- Refer to answer key for Activity 2 for correct answers.

LISTENING SCRIPT
Lesson 2, Activity 2

TCD3, 18

1. Residents have been concerned about returning to their homes after lightning started a fire in the area. It has taken firefighters three days to control the intense fire.

2. There has been a drought with no rain or snow and low water levels for over four months. State government officials are serious about reducing water use. They are asking citizens to conserve water.

3. People in the area are nervous about traveling on highways in the heavy snowstorms and freezing temperatures. If you have to drive today, drive very slowly and carefully or wait until the blizzard ends.

4. There have been torrential rains in the northern part of the state this week, especially on the coast. The local government is asking residents to leave the area if the ground starts to move and there is a mudslide.

5. Residents of the coast are worried about experiencing sudden, high levels of water near their homes. Local government officials are asking residents to take precautions and leave the area because they think there might be flash floods.

6. Because of the tornado warning, people should be serious about finding shelter or a safe place in their homes immediately. The weather service reports that there are extremely high winds in several parts of the state.

7. There were three small earthquakes today in the southern area of the state. Scientists think there is a small possibility of another one later today. Take precautions if you feel the ground begin to shake. For example, you can wait under a strong table or desk until the shaking is finished.

8. Today's forecast is for 100 degrees with poor air quality. People should be cautious about spending time outdoors. We are advising people to stay inside and drink plenty of water.

9. Severe thunderstorms and extremely high wind gusts have been reported in the area today. A hurricane warning has been issued. Many residents are concerned about protecting their homes from the high winds and torrential rain.

2 **TALK** to a partner. Check your answers to Activity 1. Then write the numbers from the picture next to the words below.

- Put the students in pairs to check their answers.
- Go over the answers as a class.
- Put the students in pairs to compare their answers.
- Play the recording one more time.
- Have the students write the numbers from the recording next to the words in the vocabulary box.
- Go over the answers as a class.

ANSWER KEY

a. 3 blizzard; **b.** 2 drought; **c.** 7 earthquake; **d.** 8 extreme heat; **e.** 5 flash flood; **f.** 9 hurricane; **g.** 4 mudslide; **h.** 6 tornado; **i.** 1 wildfire

BIG PICTURE SPEAKING EXPANSION ACTIVITY: Natural disasters in the United States

- The goal of this activity is for the students to practice speaking and to learn about the different regions of the United States.
- Put the students in small groups.
- Have the students look at the Big Picture again.
- Tell the students to try to name all of the states that the icons are in. (1. Colorado, 2. Arizona, 3. Washington, 4. California, 5. New Jersey, 6. Wisconsin, 7. California, 8. Texas, 9. Florida)
- Ask the groups to list areas of the United States that have particular natural disasters. Which area of the United States is sometimes hit by hurricanes? Which areas have the most tornadoes? Where is drought or extremely hot weather often a problem?
- Go over the students' answers as a class.

LESSON 3: Listening and Conversation

OBJECTIVES

Listen to a weather report
Convert Fahrenheit to Celsius

COMPETENCIES

Interpret a weather map
Identify safe procedures in a weather
 emergency
Use math to convert Fahrenheit and Celsius
 temperatures

WARM-UP ACTIVITY: Temperatures in my city

- On the board, write the questions: *What is the hottest temperature in your city? What is the coldest temperature in your city?*

- Give the students an opportunity to ask for clarification of the questions. Make sure they understand that they are to give temperatures in their native city.

- Put the students in pairs and have them answer the questions.

- Go over the answers as a class. Be prepared to deal with the differences between Fahrenheit temperatures and Celsius. (See the Math Skills box on page 123.)

 TCD3,19–24 **1 LISTEN** to the conversation. Then listen to the question. Fill in the correct answer. Replay each item if necessary.

- Read the directions to the students. Point out the answer sheet.

- Make sure students understand that at the end of each short conversation, there will be a question. They will hear three possible answers and must choose the best one.

- Play the recording and have the students do the activity individually.

- Put the students in pairs to compare answers.

- Play the recording again if necessary.

- Go over the answers as a class.

LISTENING SCRIPT
Lesson 3, Activity 1
TCD3, 19–24

1.
 A: What's the weather forecast for today?
 B: I'm not sure. I heard that there might be a severe thunderstorm.
 A: Uh-oh. I'm worried about driving to Boston in the rain.
Which is the best response?
 A. Maybe you should take the train.
 B. You should go to the airport and wait.
 C. You should find shelter immediately.

2.
 A: How was your trip to Wisconsin?
 B: There was a tornado when I was there. It was scary!
 A: Wow! I saw a tornado there last year too. I'd never seen one before.
Which is the best response?
 A. Neither had I.
 B. So had I.
 C. I did too.

3.
 A: In New York City, we had a power outage for five hours.
 B: I heard about that. There were power outages all over the state.
 A: Well, now people are cautious about using energy during the extreme heat.
Which is the best response?
 A. Droughts happen all the time.
 B. People should use less electricity when it is so hot.
 C. Everyone should turn the air conditioning on high.

4.
 A: There was a drought in Atlanta last year.
 B: I didn't know about that. What happened?
Which is the best response?
 A. Atlanta had torrential rain.
 B. They had no rain for six months.
 C. People had to evacuate.

5.
    A: It's really snowing a lot now.
    B: I hate driving in snow. It's hard to see, and the roads are bad.
    A: The weather report said we should be cautious about traveling in this blizzard.

Which is the best response?
    A. I heard that, too. We should be cautious of flash floods.
    B. I heard that, too. We should drive slowly with the lights on.
    C. I heard that, too. We should prepare for a hurricane.

6.
    A: There isn't a smog advisory today, is there?
    B: Yes, I think there is. Why do you ask?
    A: I'm worried about exercising outdoors, but I want to go running.

Which is the best response?
    A. You should exercise at the gym.
    B. You shouldn't drive in bad weather.
    C. You should go running in the park.

ANSWER KEY

1. A; 2. A; 3. B; 4. B; 5. B; 6. A

 2 LISTEN to an announcer give a national weather report. What does she say about weather in an area near you, or an area you are familiar with?

- Read the directions to the students.
- Tell the students to take notes while they are listening.
- Play the recording.
- Put the students in pairs to compare notes.
- Go over the answers as a class. Which regions are having what problems?

Hello, I'm Mary Armstrong with your national weather and emergency preparedness report. In the Northeast, residents have been concerned about flash floods because of the severe thunderstorms that moved through the area yesterday. Government officials recommend getting to higher ground right away if you live on the coast or near the rivers because of the very high water levels.

In the Southeast, there is a hurricane warning in effect. As always, residents are advised to protect their homes from the high winds and find a safe place on the first floor in preparation for the possible hurricane.

Throughout the Midwest there has been a tornado advisory today. We have reports of wind gusts of up to 100 miles per hour. The weather service recommends finding shelter as soon as possible if there are tornadoes in the area.

In the Northwest, the torrential rains last week have caused extremely wet, shifting ground. Residents should be prepared to leave the area quickly if there are mudslides.

Finally, due to the extremely dry temperatures in the Southwest, forest rangers and firefighters have been on alert. They have been concerned about fighting the wildfires that have spread across the region. Government officials have told residents to evacuate the area immediately until the fires are completely under control and it is safe to return. Tune in tonight at 6:00 p.m. for an update.

 3 LISTEN again. Write the letters of the precautions on the lines. Then check your answers with a partner.

- Read the directions to the students. Point out the two columns that are to be matched.
- Have the students complete the activity individually.
- Put the students in pairs to compare their answers.
- Go over the answers as a class.

ANSWER KEY

1. c; 2. e; 3. d; 4. a; 5. b

BIG PICTURE SPEAKING EXPANSION ACTIVITY: Preparations and precautions

- Have the students look at the Big Picture on page 120.
- Write the words *blizzard, drought, earthquake*, and *extreme heat* as column headings on the board. These are the conditions that were not mentioned in Activities 2 and 3.
- Put the students in pairs. Have them list actions that people can take to prepare for the disasters listed on the board, e.g., keep two days' worth of food and water in their home in case of an earthquake. Have the students also discuss actions that they can take after one of the disasters on the board happens, e.g., staying at home during a blizzard.
- Have the students tell you their items and write them in the columns on the board. Analyze the results. Which disasters are the easiest to deal with? Which are the most difficult to prepare for?

4 TALK with a partner. Take turns giving weather reports using the map and the information in the chart below.

- Read the directions to the students.
- Point out the map to the right and make sure students understand that the red areas are very hot and the blue areas are cold.
- Go over the language in the chart below.
- Have a student read the example weather report.
- Put the students in pairs and have them give weather reports to each other.
- Ask for volunteers to do weather reports for the class.

5 ROLE-PLAY. Imagine you and your partner are listening to one of the weather reports from Activity 4. Discuss what you are concerned about, and decide what you should do.

- Read the directions to the students.
- Point out the map and chart from Activity 4. Be sure students understand the terms in the chart and know what they should do in any of these weather conditions.
- Put the students in pairs and tell them to take the role of people listening to a weather report. They may use one of their own weather reports from Activity 4 or exchange reports with another pair. Pairs must express their concerns and decide what action to take.
- Ask for volunteers to do their role-plays for the class.

EXPANSION ACTIVITY: Weather report for a city

- Tell the students that they must each choose one city in the world. It can be a city from the United States or another country.
- Tell them to use a weather site on the Internet, e.g., www.weather.com, to find information about the current weather in the city.
- Give each student a few minutes to present the information to the class.

6 LISTEN to the conversation.

TCD3, 27
SCD32

- Read the directions to the students.
- Play the recording while they read the conversation.

7 PRACTICE the conversation from Activity 6 with a partner. Then make new conversations with the information below.

- Go over the directions with the students.
- Put the students in pairs. Tell the students to read the original conversation.
- After the students have finished practicing the original conversation, have them read it again, substituting the language from the chart. Point out that the recommendations for hurricanes will go in Pat's first conversation turn.

LANGUAGE NOTE

- Since gerunds are the major grammar focus for this unit, have the students circle all of the gerunds in the conversation in Activity 6 (*practicing, pressing, practicing, responding*).
- Ask the students in each case whether the gerund is being used as a subject or an object.

COMMUNITY CONNECTION: Disaster preparedness

- For homework, have students do research on disaster preparation in your community. Write the following questions on the board.
  1. What organizations in this community help people prepare for disasters?
  2. What kinds of disasters do the organizations prepare for?
  3. What specific actions do the organizations take?
- Tell the students that they can do their research in a library or on the Internet.
- After the students finish their research, put them in small groups to share their information.
- As a class, list the organizations in your community. Under their names, give details of what each organization does.
- Analyze the results. Ask the students whether they think that the disaster precautions are sufficient. If not, what additional measures do your students think are necessary to prepare your community for disasters?

Math Skills: Converting Fahrenheit and Celsius temperatures

- Point out the Math Skills box.
- Go through the three steps with the students.
- Have the students do the math problems individually.
- Put the students in pairs to compare their answers.

ANSWER KEY

1. 36.67
2. 21.11
3. 12.77
4. −6.67

8 TALK with a partner. In the U.S., we often use weather to make "small talk." Use the conversation strategies to talk with your partner about the weather today. Then discuss weather in your native country. How hot does it get in the summer? How cold does the temperature usually get in the winter?

- Read the directions to the students.
- Point out the Conversation Strategy box.
- Have two students read the example sentences.
- Put the students in pairs and tell them to talk about today's weather using the expressions in the box. Walk around the room helping the students with their conversations.
- Then have the students answer the two questions about their country.
- Analyze the results as a class. Who comes from the hottest country? Who comes from the coldest?

BIG PICTURE SPEAKING EXPANSION ACTIVITY: Temperatures

- Have the students go back to page 120 and look at the places in the Big Picture.
- Put the students in pairs. Tell them to discuss what weather "small talk" would be appropriate for some of the places, e.g., where would people be saying, "It's freezing today, isn't it?"
- Go over the answers as a class. In the places for which there may be no good expressions from the box, ask the class what you could say. For example, for the flash flood, you could say, "It's really terrible about the flood, isn't it? So many people have had to leave their homes!"

LESSON 4: Grammar and Vocabulary

OBJECTIVES

Learn about disaster organizations
Gerunds as objects of verb + preposition

VOCABULARY

believe in	global warming
crisis	natural disasters
disaster relief	resources
evacuating victims	toxic waste
focus on	

GRAMMAR

Gerunds as objects of a verb + preposition

COMPETENCY

Interpret information about environmental and disaster relief organizations

WARM-UP ACTIVITY: Disaster-relief organization

- Write the phrase *disaster-relief organization* on the board.
- Ask the students to explain or guess what it means.
- Elicit from the students the names of organizations that do this kind of work (*Red Cross, Doctors Without Borders, Oxfam,* etc.).
- Write the names of the organizations on the board.

🎧 **1 GRAMMAR PICTURE DICTIONARY.** Who helps when there is a disaster? Listen and read.

TCD3, 28
SCD33

- Have students open their books and look at the four pictures.
- Tell them to read the mini-dialogues.
- Give the students an opportunity to ask questions about anything they do not understand. Some of the words, like *toxic*, will take some time to explain. Some students may have to look up words in a monolingual dictionary.
- Play the CD and have students listen.

2 READ the sentences from Activity 1 with a partner.

- Go over the directions with the students.
- Put the students in pairs. Have them read the sentences in Activity 1.

ACADEMIC CONNECTION: Campus organizations

- Tell the students that on most college and university campuses, there are student organizations that act as advocates for protecting the environment and helping people who have suffered from a disaster.
- Put the students in pairs. Tell them to go to a nearby college or university and get information about one student organization that helps with disaster relief or with environmental causes. This research must involve going to an office and talking with someone. It cannot be done in a library or on the Internet.
- When the students have finished their research, give them some time to organize their information for a short presentation to the class. They should focus on the following questions:
  1. What is the name of the organization?
  2. What issues are the members concerned about?
  3. What are examples of a positive actions the organization has taken in the last year?
  4. What is your overall opinion of the organization?
- Tell the pairs that both members must have active speaking parts in the presentation.

- Have the students do their presentations in front of the class.
- Analyze the information that they found. Which organizations did the students think are doing the most to help the world?

3 NOTICE THE GRAMMAR. Underline the verb + preposition combinations. Circle the gerunds.

- Read the directions to the students.
- Have them do the activity individually.
- Put the students in pairs to compare their answers.
- As a class, go over the answers.

ANSWER KEY

1. The Federal Emergency Management Agency (FEMA) is a government organization that helps with evacuating victims of natural disasters. FEMA also helps victims after a crisis.

2. The American Red Cross is a volunteer organization that helps people during emergencies. They focus on providing disaster relief to victims all over the world.

3. The Environmental Protection Agency (EPA) works on removing toxic waste from the rivers and streams. This government group believes in keeping water clean and the environment safe.

4. The Natural Resources Defense Council (NRDC) focuses on protecting the Earth and its resources. It works on finding solutions to global warming.

EXPANSION ACTIVITY: Relief organizations

- Write the names of the four organizations described in Activity 1 on the board.
- Tell the students to close their books.
- Write the following phrases in a column: *focuses on*, *works on, believes in*, and *helps with*.
- Put the students in small groups. Have them write down as many details about the organizations as they can remember.

- As a class, elicit the information about the organizations from the students and write it under the name of the organizations. Tell the students that they must give you complete sentences about the organizations.

COMMUNITY CONNECTION: The environment in my community

- Tell the students that they are each going to interview one person from the community about environmental issues.
- Have them ask the following questions:
  1. What is the most serious environmental problem in this community?
  2. Why is it the most serious?
  3. What should environmental organizations do about the problem?
- Give the students several days to complete their interview. If necessary, help them find a member of the community to interview.
- Have each student give a short presentation to the class. They should describe the person whom they interviewed and summarize his or her opinions.
- Analyze the results. Did many of the interviewees name the same environmental problem? What are the most serious problems in the community?

GRAMMAR CHART: Gerunds as objects of a verb + preposition

- Direct students' attention to the chart or project the transparency or CD.
- Read the sentence about a gerund following a verb + preposition.
- Point out the columns for *Subject*, *Verb + Preposition*, and *Gerund + Phrase*.
- Choose different students to read the example sentences.

CHART EXPANSION ACTIVITY: Additional gerunds as objects of a verb + preposition

- Put the students in pairs.
- Tell each pair to write down three additional sentences like the example sentences in the grammar chart. Tell the students that the sentences must have true information from their lives.
- When they have finished writing the sentences, have each pair write one of their sentences on the board. Tell them to underline the verb + preposition and circle the gerund.

4 READ the information about the American Red Cross volunteers. Fill in the correct form of the verb + preposition + gerund.

- Go over the directions with the students.
- Point out the blanks and the words in parentheses.
- Have a student read the example sentence.
- Have the students do the activity individually.
- Go over the answers with the class.

ANSWER KEY

1. help with setting up
2. supplying
3. works on sending
4. care about making
5. help with feeding
6. handing out
7. focus on providing

EXPANSION ACTIVITY: Additional practice with gerunds as objects of a verb + preposition

- Photocopy and distribute Worksheet 23: *Gerunds as Objects of a Verb + Preposition*.
- Go over the directions.
- Have students complete the worksheet.
- Put students in pairs to compare their answers.
- Go over the answers with the class.

WORKSHEET ANSWER KEY

A. 1. focuses; 2. in; 3. care; 4. on; 5. volunteering; 6. help

B. 1. removing; 2. in; 3. focusing; 4. with; 5. works; 6. about

5 WRITE sentences to answer the questions about the organizations described in Activity 1. Use a verb + preposition + gerund.

- Go over the directions with the students.
- Point out the five blanks for students to write their answers.
- Have the students answer the questions individually.
- Put the students in pairs to compare answers.
- Go over the answers as a class.

ANSWER KEY

Answers may vary. Possible answers are below.

1. The NRDC focuses on saving the environment.
2. FEMA works on helping victims of natural disasters.
3. The American Red Cross helps with providing disaster relief.
4. The EPA focuses on removing toxic waste from rivers and streams.
5. The NRDC believes in finding solutions to global warming.

BIG PICTURE SPEAKING EXPANSION ACTIVITY: Disaster agencies

- Project the Big Picture or have students turn to page 120.

- Put the students in pairs. Tell the pairs to look at each of the nine disasters in the Big Picture and decide which of the four agencies that they have read about could help, e.g., *The American Red Cross provides disaster relief, so they could help the victims of the mudslides.* Have them also decide which agencies could help reduce the underlying cause of the problem, e.g., *The NRDC fights global warming, so they may be able to help stop droughts and forest fires.*

- Go over the answers as a class.

ACADEMIC CONNECTION: Careers in disaster relief and environmental science

- Tell the students that they must do some research on the requirements for jobs in disaster relief and environmental science.

- Put the students in small groups. Each group must choose one of the organizations in Activity 1. They must go to the organization's website or call someone at the organization to get information to answer the following questions:

  1. What kinds of people does this organization hire?
  2. What experience does it want?
  3. What kind of certification or degree does it want?
  4. Where in your area can you get the required certification or degree?

- When the groups have finished their research, have each group summarize their findings for the class. Analyze the results. What kinds of degrees or certifications are required by the different organizations?

LESSON 5: Grammar Practice Plus

WARM-UP ACTIVITY: Volunteerism

- Explain that it is common in the United States for people to volunteer their time for good causes. Many high school students volunteer for nonprofit organizations because they know that colleges and universities want students who believe in volunteerism and have shown that they are willing to help others.
- Ask the students if volunteerism is common in their countries. What kinds of organizations can they volunteer for?
- Write the names of the organizations in their country on the board.

🎧 TCD3, 29 **1 LISTEN** to the statements. As you listen, match the statement with the photo below. Then take turns reading the sentences with a partner.

- Read the directions to the students.
- Point out the statements with the blanks to the left.
- Point out the six photos with the captions.
- Have students read the photo captions to the class. Give them an opportunity to ask for clarification of anything that they do not understand.
- Have the students match the photos and the statements individually.

- Put the students in pairs to compare their answers.
- As a class, go over the answers.

ANSWER KEY

1. B; **2.** A; **3.** D; **4.** F; **5.** C; **6.** E

2 TALK with a partner about the organizations in Activity 1. Who do you think are government workers? How do you know? Who are the volunteer workers? Which organizations are you already familiar with?

- Go over the directions with the students.
- Put the students in pairs to discuss the questions.
- Go over the answers as a class. Analyze the results. Which workers did they think were volunteers? Which organizations were the best known?

🎧 TCD3, 30 **Pronunciation: Linking final consonants with vowels**

- Read the title of the activity to the students.
- Briefly review consonants and vowels. Ask the students to give you examples of each and write them on the board.
- Read the explanation at the top of the box.
- Play the recording of the example sentences.
- Ask several students to pronounce the sentences with linking.

🎧 TCD3, 31 SCD34 **A. DRAW** marks to predict the linking. Then listen and check.

- Read the directions to the students.
- Put the students in pairs. Have them predict linking for the six sentences in the activity.
- Play the recording so that the students can check their answers.

ANSWER KEY

1. focuses on; **2.** work on; **3.** believe in; **4.** count on; **5.** care about; **6.** believes in

B. LISTEN again and repeat.

TCD3, 32

- Read the directions to the students.
- Play the six sentences one by one. Have the students repeat them as a class.
- Ask selected students to read the six sentences with linking.

3 LISTEN to an interview on a TV talk show. Listen for the four problems the guest talks about and write them in the correct column in the chart.

TCD3, 33

- Read the directions to the students.
- Point out the chart with the four columns for the problems and the help that the organizations gave. Make sure they understand that in this activity they are only filling in the second column.
- Play the recording and have the students fill in the second column individually.
- Put the students in pairs to compare answers.
- Go over the answers as a class.

**LISTENING SCRIPT
Lesson 5, Activities 3 and 4**

TCD3, 33

Juan: This is Juan Perez and you're watching "The Solutions Hour." Today, I'm happy to welcome Ms. Eva Erickson, an expert on natural disaster preparedness. Eva, thank you for being here. Tell us about environmental and disaster relief organizations and what they do.

Eva: Thanks, Juan. First, I'll talk about the National Resources Defense Council. They've really focused on improving the environment after Hurricane Katrina. They've also been cleaning up the neighborhoods and making sure the water is safe to drink. They try to keep areas where children play free from toxic waste.

Juan: I see. There were wildfires in Northern California a few years ago. Who usually helps during this type of disaster?

Eva: Well Juan, the U.S. Department of Agriculture is concerned about protecting our wildlife, and they are also concerned about preventing wildfires. The USDA may also investigate the causes of the fires and take precautions to prevent them, especially during extreme heat or drought conditions.

Juan: That's great information to know. Now, I remember that one year, Wisconsin had more than 60 tornadoes. Who helps people rebuild their homes after this type of disaster?

Eva: Habitat for Humanity is an organization that goes to many areas of the country to help build homes for victims of natural disasters. Several teams of volunteers in Wisconsin built houses for people after their homes were destroyed by tornadoes.

Juan: In 2003, New York had a serious problem with the power outages. Who helped and what did they do?

Eva: During the power outages, the city's food supply was in danger. So the American Red Cross made sure that residents had water and food. Volunteers were on the streets of New York during the crisis, giving out bottles of water and meals to the residents.

Juan: That's all the time we have for today. Thanks for being here with us today, Eva, and giving us some important information about these groups.

ANSWER KEY

Where was the problem?	What was the problem?	Who helped solve the problem?	How did they help?
Louisiana	Hurricane Katrina	The National Resources Defense Council	improved the environment after the hurricane
Northern California	Wildfires	U.S. Department of Agriculture	investigates causes of fires, takes precautions to prevent them during drought or extreme heat
Wisconsin	Tornadoes	Habitat for Humanity	built homes for victims of natural disasters
New York	Power Outages	American Red Cross	gave out bottles of water and meals

4 LISTEN again and fill in the rest of the chart. Then talk with a partner or in a group about the situations from the interviews. Can you remember how each organization helped?

- Read the directions to the students.
- Make sure students understand that they will fill in the last two columns of the chart.
- Play the recording again.
- Put the students in pairs or small groups to compare their answers.
- If necessary, play the recording again.
- As a class, go over the answers.

ANSWER KEY

See chart in Activity 3.

EXPANSION ACTIVITY: Listening for details about the four problems

- Photocopy and distribute Worksheet 24: *Reading Practice.*
- The purpose of this activity is to provide practice listening for details. The students know the big ideas of the listening passage. Now they will listen for the details.
- Go over the directions.
- Play the recording from Activity 3 once or twice more.
- Have students complete the worksheet.
- Put students in pairs to compare their answers.
- Go over the answers with the class.

WORKSHEET ANSWER KEY

1. c; 2. b; 3. d; 4. b; 5. c; 6. a

5 WRITE. Check your answers in Activity 4 with a partner. Write sentences about what each organization is and what they do after a natural disaster.

- Read the directions to the students.
- Have a student read the example sentence.
- Put the students in pairs.
- Have them write down one sentence about each organization and what they do. Make sure they understand that the sentences must have a verb + preposition + gerund structure.
- Have each pair write one sentence on the board.

EXPANSION ACTIVITY: My beliefs

- Write the following phrases on the board:
  I am focusing on . . .
  I plan on . . .
  I care about . . .
  I believe in . . .
  I help with . . .
- Have the students write down complete sentences with the phrases. Make sure they understand that they must have a gerund after the verb + preposition.
- Put the students in pairs and have them read their sentences to each other.
- Have each student read one of his or her sentences to the class.

6 WHAT ABOUT YOU? Volunteers give their time without payment. Why do you think people volunteer? What organization are you interested in volunteering for? Talk with a partner.

- Go over the directions with the students.
- Put the students in pairs to discuss the questions.
- Go over their answers as a class. Analyze the results. Are there any organizations that many students want to volunteer for? Why do they like that organization?

LESSON 6: Reading

<table>
<tr><td>

OBJECTIVES

Learn about the environment

VOCABULARY

activism	raise awareness
activist	spokesperson
participants	
public service campaign	

COMPETENCIES

Read about environmental issues
Use scanning as a study strategy

</td></tr>
</table>

WARM-UP ACTIVITY: Publicity campaigns

- Before the students open their books and look at the article about raising public consciousness about environmental issues, have them talk about publicity campaigns that they have heard about. They can talk about ads for a product or efforts by the government to gain support for a policy.

- Write the word *Publicity* on the board. Ask students to explain what it is. (It is an effort to get the public to be aware of something or someone.) Ask students who wants publicity. They may come up with movie stars, companies, or a campaign by a government agency.

- Ask the students what kinds of publicity campaigns they find effective. They may mention posters, celebrity endorsements, the use of animated characters, or TV advertisements. Ask for specific examples of publicity campaigns that they have seen or heard.

- Write the examples on the board. Analyze the results. What media are considered most effective by your students? Is the Internet an effective medium? Do they go to websites like YouTube to watch promotional videos?

1 **THINK ABOUT IT.** What things do people do to hurt the environment? What things do companies do to hurt the environment?

- Go over the directions with the students.
- Put the students in small groups and tell them to discuss the questions.
- Go over the answers as a class. Write the students' answers on the board in two columns, one for people and one for companies. Analyze the result. What were the most common things listed that hurt the environment?

2 **BEFORE YOU READ.**

A. PREVIEW. Read the title and look at the picture.

- Go over the directions and the information in the Reading Focus box with the students.
- Have the students read the title and look at the poster and the photo in the article.
- Ask them if they understand the poster. Ask them who the man is in the photo.

B. SKIM the article. Read the first sentence of each paragraph. Then read the questions below. Next, scan to find the answers to the questions. Which paragraph is each answer in?

- Read the directions.
- Have the students skim by reading the first sentences. Ask the students to tell you what the general idea of the article is. (Over a long period of time, a variety of public organizations worked to publicize environmental problems.)
- Point out the three questions. Have the students individually scan the article for the answers.

C. SCAN the article and write the answers to the questions in Activity 2B.

- Read the directions.

- Point out the questions in Activity 2B and the Reading Strategies Summary. Remind them how to scan for specific information.
- Have students write answers to the questions.

3 READ the article. Check the answers you wrote in Activity 2C with a partner.

- Read the directions to the students.
- Tell the students to read the entire article.
- Put the students in pairs to check their answers to the three questions in Activity 2B.
- Go over the answers as a class.

ANSWER KEY

1. Smokey the Bear
2. April 22, 1970
3. Gore made a film, *An Inconvenient Truth.*

COMMUNITY CONNECTION: Publicity from government

- Tell the students that for a few days, they must check local newspapers, look at billboards, the sides of buses, TV ads, and any other medium available to them for evidence that the local, state, or national government is trying to influence their opinions on a topic.
- After a few days, put the students in small groups and have them compare their findings. In what ways does the government try to inform or persuade them? On what issues does the government spend money for publicity?
- Open up the discussion to the class. Analyze the results. Did the different groups find the same information?

4 AFTER YOU READ.

A. VOCABULARY. Find these words in the text. Match them with their meanings.

- Go over the directions with the students.

- Point out the two columns that are to be matched.
- Have the students do the activity individually.
- Put the students in pairs to share their answers.
- Go over the answers as a class.

ANSWER KEY

1. e; 2. d; 3. b; 4. c; 5. a

B. WRITE answers to the questions below.

- Read the directions to the students.
- Point out the four questions.
- Have the students answer the questions individually.
- Put the students in small groups to check their answers.
- Go over the answers as a class.

ANSWER KEY

1. To raise awareness of environmental issues
2. People engaged in a variety of activities that helped the environment. The EPA was created. The U.S. Congress passed laws that helped clean up the environment.
3. To persuade people not to pollute the water and air
4. Two things resulted from Gore's activism: a Nobel Peace Prize for Gore and the film *An Inconvenient Truth.*

EXPANSION ACTIVITY: Environmental activists

- Put students into small groups.
- Tell the students to list as many environmental activists as they can. For each activist, tell them to give as many details as possible about what issues they addressed and what results they achieved. If your class comes from many different countries, expect a diverse range of answers.
- As a class, go over the students' answers.

LESSON 7: Writing

OBJECTIVES
Write about environmental issues

WRITING FOCUS
Use parallel structure

COMPETENCY
Write a letter to encourage change

WARM-UP ACTIVITY: Letters to government officials

- Write on the board, *What do you do when you want your government to change a law or policy?*
- Put the students in small groups. Ask them to answer the question on the board. Do they talk with friends? Do they go to a government office and try to meet an official? Do they remain silent?
- As a class, discuss the strategies that the students use to deal with this situation.

❶ THINK ABOUT IT. Talk about these questions with your class.

- Go over the directions with the students.
- Put the students in small groups. Tell them to discuss the questions.
- Have each group give a brief report on the opinions in their group.
- Analyze the results. What are the most common things cited that we can do to help protect the environment? What does "green" mean?

❷ BEFORE YOU WRITE.

A. DISCUSS. Look at the pictures with a partner. What do you think each group does? Why do you think they are called "green groups"?

- Go over the directions with the students.
- Point out the questions and the three photos with captions.
- Put the students in small groups. Tell them to discuss the questions.

EXPANSION ACTIVITY: Green groups

- In Activity 2, students saw three examples of green groups. Ask the students what other organizations could be called green.
- Put the students into small groups to list additional green groups.
- As a class, list the groups on the board. Possibilities include Friends of the Earth and the World Wide Fund for Nature.

 B. LISTEN to a talk about green groups. Read the statements and check *True* or *False*.
TCD3, 34

- Read the directions to the students.
- Point out the statements and the *True* and *False* boxes to the right.
- Play the recording and have the students check the boxes.
- Put the students in pairs to compare their answers.
- Play the recording again.
- Go over the answers as a class.

 LISTENING SCRIPT
Lesson 7, Activity 2B
TCD3, 34

What do you know about green groups? Today we're going to talk about three green groups that support finding solutions to global warming, protecting our wildlife, and saving our environment. The first group is Greenpeace. Greenpeace activists often have demonstrations against the government. They want politicians and government leaders to pay attention to the issue of global warming and other environmental problems.

The Nature Conservancy is another well-known green organization. They're against extreme logging and cutting down trees in our forests. They also support helping our forests by planting trees after wildfires. Like Greenpeace, the Nature Conservancy is also concerned with solving our problems with global warming.

Another group that you might have heard of is The National Wildlife Federation. This organization cares about protecting wildlife. They believe in protecting nature for the children's future. They're against killing wildlife that are endangered, or at risk. The National Wildlife Federation supports protecting wild animals such as elephants, polar bears, and tigers. They are also interested in finding solutions to global warming.

These groups are important to our society. You can make a donation to one of these groups or register to volunteer by visiting their websites.

ANSWER KEY

1. T; 2. F; 3. T; 4. F; 5. T; 6. F

C. **TALK** in a group. Which environmental issues are you worried about? Why?

- Read the directions to the class.
- Put the students in small groups and have them answer the questions.
- Go over the answers as a class. Analyze the results. Which environmental issues came up most often?

WRITING FOCUS: State your purpose

- Go over the strategy with the students.
- Explain to students that many public officials and corporate leaders don't have time to read letters from individuals. They often have staff members who do this for them. A clear statement of purpose in the beginning of the letter can help ensure that the rest of the letter is read and taken seriously.
- Ask a student to read the example sentence.
- Discuss why this statement is clear and direct.

- Direct students to their answers from Activity 2C. Tell them to imagine that they are writing letters to government officials about environmental issues that concern them. As a class, practice writing statements of purpose to open their letters.

D. **READ** the letter to a senator from a green group's website. Underline the places where the writer did the following:

1. stated his purpose
2. said what the problem is
3. explained why it is important
4. gave reasons to support his opinion

- Go over the directions with the students.
- Give the students five minutes to underline the writer's purpose, the problem, the reason why it is important, and reasons to support his argument.
- Put the students in pairs to compare their answers.
- Go over the answers as a class.

ANSWER KEY

Students should underline the following:
(statement of purpose) to request your support of the Beach Protection Act

(problem) Because of toxic waste, our nation's beach waters have become contaminated.

(importance) We are concerned about toxic waste harming swimmers, destroying the environment, and damaging the coasts.

(reasons to support opinion) This Act would give money to programs in states and local communities. It would help identify and clean up the sources of pollution.

3 **WRITE** a letter to your local government official or your state senator explaining what you would like to change in your community or state.

- Go over the directions and the information in the Tip box with the students. Point out and read the four steps that the students must follow.
- Give the students this assignment as homework so that they can think about the problem and the recipient of the letter.

4 **AFTER YOU WRITE.**

A. EDIT your letter. Ask yourself these questions.

- Read the directions to the students.
- Have the students go over the checklist questions.
- Put the students in pairs and have them read their letters to their partners.
- Tell the partners to give feedback on anything that is missing in the letters.

B. REWRITE your letter with corrections.

- Go over the directions.
- Give the students overnight to rewrite their letters using their partner's comments and the editing guidelines.
- Collect the paragraphs and write comments on them, using the editing guidelines as your guide.
- Return the paragraphs to the students.

BIG PICTURE SPEAKING EXPANSION ACTIVITY: Letters to government officials

- Have the students go to page 120 to look at the Big Picture.
- Put the students in pairs.
- Tell the students to take the role of a resident of each of the nine different areas. For each area, tell the students to describe a letter that they would write to a government official. Each pair will end up with plans for nine letters.
- Go over the students' responses as a class. Analyze the results. What do they think the government could do to help the residents in the different areas?

Career Connection

Natural disaster preparedness

COMPETENCIES

Identify safety precautions on the job
Practice test-taking skills

CULTURE NOTE

In the next activity, students will be asked what to do during an earthquake. The following are suggestions from the Centers for Disease Control and Prevention, part of the Department of Health and Human Services of the United States government.

- If you are in a building during an earthquake, try to take cover under a heavy desk or table. It can provide you with protection from falling objects and air space if the building collapses. If the table moves, try to move with it.
- Inner walls or door frames may shield you against falling objects. Go to an inner corner or doorway, away from windows or glass panels.
- Stay away from glass, hanging objects, bookcases, china cabinets, or other large furniture that could fall. Watch for falling objects, such as bricks from fireplaces and chimneys, light fixtures, wall hangings, high shelves, and cabinets with doors that could swing open.
- Grab something to shield your head and face from falling debris and broken glass.
- Earthquakes sometimes cause gas leaks. If there is a power failure, use a battery-operated flashlight. Do not use candles, matches, or lighters during or after the earthquake.
- If you are in the kitchen, quickly turn off the stove and take cover at the first sign of shaking.

1 THINK ABOUT IT. How can companies be sure that their employees stay safe during a natural disaster? What do you know about how to stay safe in an earthquake?

- Read the directions to the students.
- Put the students in small groups.
- Have the students discuss the two questions.
- As a class, go over the answers. Analyze the results. How effective do you think that their strategies would be in an earthquake?

2 READ the following company memo on updated emergency evacuation procedures for earthquakes. What precautions have they taken? What can employees do to stay safe during and after an earthquake?

- Read the directions to the students. Point out the company memo. Show the students the four words that are defined at the bottom.
- Give the students time to read the memo.
- Put the students in pairs. Have them write down answers to the two questions.
- As a class, go over the answers.

ANSWER KEY

1. What the company has done:
- secured/tied down cabinets, bookcases, and heavy objects that could fall over or move around during an earthquake
- installed first-aid kits near elevators and in the kitchen on each floor
- stocked the kitchens with emergency water and food

2. Guidelines for earthquakes
During an earthquake:
- Get under a desk or table and stay there even if it moves.
- Stay away from windows, bookcases, filing cabinets, hanging plants, and other heavy objects that could fall.

- If you aren't near a desk or table, move next to an indoor wall and use your arms to cover your head.
- Don't use the elevators.
- If you are outside, move as far as possible away from the building.

After an earthquake:

- Stay calm.
- Expect aftershocks, small earthquake tremors.
- Plan a safe place to go during aftershocks.
- Check for injuries in your workplace. Take care of yourself before you try to help others.
- Put out any small fires that you see.
- Use the telephone only for emergency calls.
- Remember to eat and drink water.

3 COMPLETE. Circle the correct answer to complete each sentence. Then compare your answers with a partner's.

- Read the directions to the students. Point out the four sentences that they will complete.
- Have the students complete the activity individually.
- Put the students in pairs to compare answers.
- Go over the answers as a class.

ANSWER KEY

1. c; 2. b; 3. a; 4. c

4 WHAT ABOUT YOU? What precautions have you taken for earthquakes? Are there other natural disasters in your area, such as tornadoes, hurricanes, or blizzards? What precautions can you take for them?

- Read the directions to the students.
- Put the students in small groups to discuss the questions.
- Go over the answers as a class. Make a list of precautions that the students can take for natural disasters in their area.

EXPANSION ACTIVITY: Precautions for natural disasters in this area

- Put the students in pairs. Tell the students that they must do research on precautions for whatever natural disasters could happen in their area. They can go to a library, talk to local emergency organizations, or find information on the Internet.
- Give the students one or two days to do their research. Tell them that they must come up with a list of precautions. For example, for hurricanes, they may find out that they should evacuate their homes because they are in a flood zone.
- As a class, go over the information that they find. Analyze the results. Did all of the pairs agree with each other about what precautions to take?

CHECK YOUR PROGRESS!

- Have students circle the answers.
- Have students check whether each answer is right or wrong.
- Have students total their correct answers and fill in the chart at the bottom of the page.
- Have students create a learning plan and/or set learning goals.

ANSWER KEY

1. flying; 2. providing; 3. getting; 4. driving
5. with building; 6. on getting; 7. work on;
8. care about; 9. earthquake; 10. tornadoes;
11. advisory; 12. mudslide; 13. offering emergency assistance; 14. preventing wildfires
15. protecting the environment; 16. Hazardous Materials worker

UNIT 9 Community Crossroads

Unit Overview

LESSON	OBJECTIVES	STUDENT BOOK	WORKBOOK
1. Grammar and Vocabulary 1	Getting around town. Causative verbs.	p. 134	p. 118
2. Grammar Practice Plus	Recognize traffic laws. Causatives *get* and *have*.	p. 136	p. 119
3. Listening and Conversation	Read traffic signs. Pronounce reduced *To*.	p. 138	p. 120
4. Grammar and Vocabulary 2	Discuss transportation information. Verbs with gerunds or infinitives.	p. 140	p. 122
5. Grammar Practice Plus	Read a town map. Interpret statistical information.	p. 142	p. 123
6. Reading	Read about a small business.	p. 144	p. 124–125
7. Writing	Fill out an insurance claim form.	p. 146	p. 126–127
• Career Connection	Solve a problem at work.	p. 148	p. 128
• Check Your Progress	Monitor progress.	p. 149	p. 130–131

Reading/Writing Strategies

- Identify the main idea
- Use the layout of a business plan

Connection Activities

LESSON	TYPE	SKILL DEVELOPMENT
1	Community	Compare and contrast cultural expectations
2	Community	Access community services
3	Community	Understand problems in the news
4	Academic	Understand a "Dear John" letter
5	Academic	Interpret statistical information
6	Community	Learn what to do following an accident
7	Community	Compare car insurance
Career Connection	Academic	Solve problems

WORKSHEET #/FOCUS	TITLE	TEACHER'S EDITION
25. Listening	What Were They Thinking?	p. 329
26. Grammar	Try and Regret	p. 330
27. Reading	A Fender Bender	p. 331

LESSON 1: Grammar and Vocabulary

OBJECTIVES

Getting around town
Causative verbs

VOCABULARY

crossing guard	rush hour
driver education	school zone
guide dog	visually impaired
handicapped passenger	person
pedestrian	wheelchair lift

GRAMMAR

Causative verbs

COMPETENCY

Use language to talk about traffic and
transportation

WARM-UP ACTIVITY: Unit opener

- Tell students to think about all the things they have helped other people to do in the past week or that other people have helped them do.
- Put students in pairs to list all the activities they have given or received help with.
- Set a time limit of three minutes. Elicit activities and write them on the board.

❶ GRAMMAR PICTURE DICTIONARY.
TCD3, 35
SCD35   What's happening around town? Listen and read.

- Have students open their books to page 134 and look at the pictures.
- Ask: *What is happening around town?*
- Write what the students say on the board.
- Say the sentences or play the CD and have students follow along silently.
- Play the CD again and pause so students can repeat.

- Call on students and ask questions, such as: *What do traffic laws require drivers to do? What does a crossing guard do?*

CULTURE NOTE

- Point out that traffic laws and traffic signs differ from country to country.
- Find out from students which traffic laws they do not have in their countries that the U.S. has, and vice versa.
- Have students come up to the board and draw traffic signs that exist in their countries, but not here, or signs that look different, but have the same meaning as a U.S. sign. (You might want to have colored chalk for this.)

❷ READ the sentences from Activity 1 with a partner.

- Put students in pairs to read the sentences.
- Call on students to read the sentences to the class.

❸ NOTICE THE GRAMMAR. Circle the verbs. Underline the infinitives or base forms that follow objects.

- Go over the directions.
- Have students circle the verbs and underline the infinitives/base forms.
- Elicit the causative verbs and write them on the board.
- Elicit the different object + verb structures that can follow causative verbs and write examples on the board.

ANSWER KEY

1. The crossing guard (allows) pedestrians to cross the street safely.
2. The traffic rule (doesn't permit) drivers to turn left during rush hour.
3. Traffic laws (require) all drivers to drive slowly in a school zone.
4. A guide dog (helps) a visually impaired person cross the street more confidently.
5. A wheelchair lift (allows) handicapped passengers to get on a bus easily.
6. The driver education teacher (helped) his students study for the learner's permit exam.

GRAMMAR CHART: Causative Verbs

- Direct students' attention to the chart or project the transparency.
- Go over the information on the chart, emphasizing the two object + verb structure patterns that can follow causative verbs.
- Go over the information in the Grammar Professor box.

CHART EXPANSION ACTIVITY: Rewrite using a different causative

- Have students rewrite the first four sentences from the chart using a different causative verb and changing the form of the verb that follows accordingly, but keeping the same basic meaning (e.g., *The teacher makes his students study for an hour every day.*).
- Put students in pairs to compare sentences.
- Have students write their new sentences on the board.

4 COMPLETE. Circle the infinitive or the base verb to complete the sentences.

- Go over the directions.
- Have students circle the correct verb form.
- Put students in pairs to compare answers.
- Go over the answers with the class.

ANSWER KEY

1. to drive; 2. cross; 3. check; 4. to bring; 5. hold; 6. to get on

EXPANSION ACTIVITY: Listen and correct

- Have students close their books.
- Tell students you are going to read the sentences from Activity 1, but you have forgotten your reading glasses, so you might not read them all correctly. Have students raise their hands when they hear a mistake (e.g., *The crossing guard allows pedestrians cross the street safely.*), and call on a student to give the correct version.

5 COMPLETE the sentences with the correct form of the verb.

- Have students reopen their books to page 135.
- Go over the directions and the example.
- Have students complete the sentences.
- Put students in pairs to compare answers.
- Go over the answers with the class.

ANSWER KEY

1. allows, to turn; 2. helped, practice; 3. help, cross; 4. had, lower; 5. makes, hold

6 WHAT ABOUT YOU? Talk with a partner. What did your parents make you do when you were a child? What did they let you do?

- Go over the directions and the example.
- Put students in pairs or small groups to talk about what their parents made them do and let them do as children.

COMMUNITY CONNECTION: Compare and contrast cultural expectations

- As an out-of-class assignment, have students interview a native speaker about certain cultural expectations: what he or she was (not) allowed to do in school, is (not) required to do for work, helped her/his parents do as a child, lets/does not let her/his children do. Tell students to take along a notebook so they can take notes.

- Have students write a few paragraphs comparing and contrasting themselves with their interviewees in terms of these cultural expectations.

- Put students in pairs or small groups to share their findings and discuss their interviews. Have them compare their interviewees' responses to see if there are expectations that seem distinctly American.

- Call on students to talk about their interviews and the similarities and differences in cultural expectations that they found between themselves and the people they interviewed.

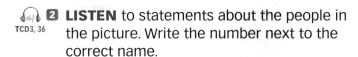

LESSON 2: Grammar Practice Plus

OBJECTIVES

Recognize traffic laws
Causatives *get* and *have*

VOCABULARY

fire hydrant	tow-away zone
parking meter	wheelchair access
road construction	ramp

GRAMMAR

Passive causatives with *get* and *have*

COMPETENCIES

Identify traffic signs
Understand traffic laws

WARM-UP ACTIVITY: What do you know?

- Put students in pairs and ask them to list different places and things found on a typical city street (e.g., bus stop, café, telephone pole).
- Set a time limit of two minutes.
- Call on students to come up to the board and jot down one or two things from their lists.

1 TALK with a partner. What are people doing? Use the words in the box to talk about the picture.

- Have students look at the picture on page 136 and discuss with a partner what the various people are doing.
- Call on students to tell what different people in the picture are doing.

2 LISTEN to statements about the people in the picture. Write the number next to the correct name.

TCD3, 36

- Go over the directions.
- Play the CD and have students write the numbers next to the correct names.
- Put students in pairs to compare answers. If necessary, play the CD again.
- Go over the answers with the class.

LISTENING SCRIPT
Lesson 2, Activity 2

TCD3, 36

1. A guide dog helps Rita cross the street.
2. Luz is a driver education teacher. She is making her student practice parking at a parking meter.
3. The traffic rule does not allow Tony to turn left at the intersection during rush hour.
4. Carla is a traffic officer. She made Sue pay a fine for parking in a tow-away zone.
5. Martina is letting her son Ben ride the bus by himself today.
6. Lina is helping Ralph go around the road construction.
7. The wheelchair access ramp allows Tom to get to his classes on time.
8. The traffic law does not permit Howie to park so close to a fire hydrant.

ANSWER KEY

8 Howie; 2 Luz; 5 Martina and Ben; 1 Rita;
6 Lina and Ralph; 7 Tom; 4 Carla and Sue;
3 Tony

BIG PICTURE LISTENING EXPANSION ACTIVITY: What Are They Thinking?

- Photocopy and distribute Worksheet 25: *What Are They Thinking?*

- Go over the directions. Tell students that when identifying the thinkers, they can put the person's name if they know it from the previous activity (e.g., *Luz*) or just describe them (e.g., *the girl giving out menus*).

- Put the transparency for Unit 9 on the OHP or have students look at the Big Picture on page 136.

- Read the Listening Script below, and have students fill in the blanks in the sentences.

- Read the script again if necessary and have students identify who in the picture is thinking each thought.

- Put students in pairs to compare answers.

- Go over the answers with the class.

WORKSHEET LISTENING SCRIPT

1. "Boy, I'll be glad when this road construction is finished. I'm never going to get to work on time!"

2. "I really hope I pass my driving test this time!"

3. "Oh, dear, I hope Carla will let me go without giving me a ticket! I was only out of the car for a few minutes."

4. "I hope he's okay all by himself."

5. "Great! I finally found a place to park!"

6. "Hm—that parking space looks awfully small. I don't know if we really can park there."

ANSWER KEY

1. road construction; get/work; Ralph; **2.** hope/pass/driving; the student driver; **3.** Carla/go/giving; Sue; **4.** all/himself; Martina; **5.** finally/place/park; Howie; **6.** parking space/small; Luz, or the student driver

BIG PICTURE CONVERSATION/ VOCABULARY EXPANSION ACTIVITY: Role-play

- Put students in pairs. Assign each pair a character from the Big Picture. Then assign each pair a situation (*character calling his boss to say he'll be late for work due to traffic, character giving driving instructions and advice, character hoping to avoid a parking ticket, etc.*).

- Have students create conversations for their character and the other person for that situation.

- Have volunteers perform their conversations for the class.

3 WRITE sentences about the people in Activity 2. Use the causative verbs with the verbs on the right to make new sentences.

- Go over the directions and the example sentence.

- Have the students write sentences on their own first.

- Put students in pairs to compare their sentences.

- Call on students to read out their sentences. Write them on the board. Elicit any necessary corrections from the class.

ANSWER KEY

1. The mother let her son take the bus by himself.
2. The traffic officer helped pedestrians go around the road construction.
3. The driver education teacher made her student practice parking at the parking meter.
4. The wheelchair access ramp enabled the handicapped student to enter the school.
5. The guide dog helped the visually impaired woman (to) cross the street.
6. The traffic officer made Sue pay a fine for parking in a tow-away zone.
7. The traffic law does not allow Tony to turn left at the intersection during rush hour.
8. The traffic officer made Howie pay a fine for parking near the fire hydrant.

GRAMMAR CHART: Passive Causatives *Get* and *Have*

- Go over the chart.
- Point out that *get* and *have* are used to show that someone has caused something to be done by someone else.
- Draw students' attention to the fact that it is the *past participle* of the verb that follows the passive causative + object.

4 COMPLETE the sentences with the past participle of the verbs in parentheses.

- Go over the directions and the example.
- Have students complete the sentences.
- Call on students to read sentences to the class.

ANSWER KEY

1. fixed; 2. done; 3. lowered; 4. repaired;
5. cut; 6. checked

GRAMMAR EXPANSION ACTIVITY: The last thing I had done

- Have students write a paragraph describing the last thing they had done for them by someone else: *I had my hair cut and colored by Eduardo at the Shear Beauty Salon. It was my first time there and I was nervous, but . . .*
- Put students in small groups and have them read their paragraphs to the group.
- Call on a few students to share their paragraphs with the whole class.

5 WRITE sentences with the words below.

- Go over the directions and the example: *I / have / computer / fix / last week = I had my computer fixed last week.*
- Have students work on their own to write sentences from the prompts.
- Pair students to compare sentences.
- Call on students to read their sentences. Write them on the board yourself or ask a student volunteer to do it.
- Make any necessary corrections.

ANSWER KEY

1. I had my computer fixed last week.
2. He got his hair cut yesterday.
3. He had the kitchen sink repaired last month.
4. We got the car repaired yesterday.
5. She had her hair done last night.

VOCABULARY NOTE

Point out that *get something done* is less formal than *have something done,* and that students may hear *get something done* more frequently from native speakers.

GRAMMAR NOTE

- Point out that the verb *allow* is often used in the passive voice: *You're not allowed to park there. We are allowed to turn right on red lights.*
- *Allow* is a synonym for *permit* and *let*.

6 COMPLETE the sentences with the correct form of *be + allowed*.

- Before beginning this exercise, go over the Grammar Note above.
- Go over the directions and example sentence.
- Have students complete the sentences on their own and then check answers with a partner.
- Go over the answers with the whole class.

ANSWER KEY

1. are not allowed to park; **2.** are not allowed to turn; **3.** is allowed to drive; **4.** are not allowed to cross; **5.** is allowed to ride; **6.** are not allowed to smoke

7 WHAT ABOUT YOU? Write sentences with *allow* about your community, work, or family. Example: *We're not allowed to use cell phones in the library.*

- Go over the directions and example sentence. You might want to provide a few more examples or have the class brainstorm some things they are/are not allowed to do if they seem to be having trouble getting started.
- Have students work individually to write their sentences, and then get into small groups to share them.
- Call on students to read their sentences to the class.

COMMUNITY CONNECTION: Access community services

- Point out that there are many businesses in the community that offer services that students might find useful.
- Bring in several phone books with advertising (yellow pages) in the back.
- Put students in pairs and have them look through the phone books, listing all the different services on offer (*moving companies, accountants, veterinarians, etc.*).
- Make a master list on the board of all the services students found.
- Lead a discussion about how these services differ from community services featured in the Big Picture such as public works, animal control, etc.

LESSON 3: Listening and Conversation

OBJECTIVES

Read traffic signs
Pronounce reduced *To*

COMPETENCY

Interpret traffic signs

WARM-UP ACTIVITY: Problems you've had

- Put students in pairs or small groups.
- Set a time limit of two minutes. Have students discuss small problems they have had with things (such as cars) and how they fixed them.
- Elicit the problems and solutions.

TCD3, 37–42

1 LISTEN to the question. Then listen to the conversation. Listen to the question again. Fill in the correct answer. Replay each item if necessary.

- Go over the directions with the students.
- Play the CD and have students fill in the correct circles.
- Put students in pairs to compare answers.
- Go over the answers with the class.

TCD3
37–42

LISTENING SCRIPT
Lesson 3, Activity 1

1. What did the woman tell the man?
   A: Excuse me. You're not allowed to park here.
   B. Oh really?
   A: Well, there's a wheelchair access ramp here.
   B. Oh, I'm sorry. I didn't see the ramp.

What did the woman tell the man?
   A. He is not handicapped.
   B. He can't park there.
   C. He's allowed to park there.

2. What happened to the man's car?
   A: Could you drive me to work in the morning?
   B: Sure. Where's your car?
   A: It broke down while I was driving home yesterday. Last night I had to take it to a mechanic to get it fixed. It will be ready this afternoon.

What happened to the man's car?
   A. It is at his home.
   B. He has to take it to a mechanic.
   C. The mechanic is fixing it.

3. What is the teacher helping the man do?
   A: Did you take your learner's permit exam?
   B: Yes, I passed it weeks ago! Since then, I've been practicing for my driver's test.
   A: That's great. What have you been doing in your driving class?
   B: Well, the teacher has been helping me practice parking on the street.

What is the teacher helping the man do?
   A. Practice parking on the street
   B. Practice parking in a parking lot
   C. Practice for the learner's permit exam

4. Why was the woman late?
   A: Hey, where have you been? I've been waiting here at the restaurant for half an hour.
   B: There was road construction, so there was a big traffic jam.
   A: Well, I already ordered some soup because I was very hungry.
   B: That's okay. I should have called but I left my cell phone at home.

Why was the woman late?
   A. Because her car broke down
   B. Because she forgot her cell phone
   C. Because there was road construction and a traffic jam

5. What is the man's new job?
   A: Ok. Here are some tips about your new job. The first thing is to get the drivers to slow down in the school zone.
   B: Right.
   A: Also, I usually make the children hold hands before they cross the street. And, I have

What is the man's new job?

    A. He's a bus driver.

    B. He's a crossing guard.

    C. He's a driver education teacher.

6. What is the woman going to do?

    A: Ugh! I can't stand driving in rush hour traffic.

    B: I know that, but you have to be patient. Just stay calm.

    A: Let's listen to the radio. The music makes me feel better.

    B: Good idea. Since you're nervous about driving, I'll let you listen to your favorite music.

What is the woman going to do?

    A. Drive the car

    B. Listen to music she likes

    C. Let the man listen to music that he likes

ANSWER KEY

1. B; **2.** C ; **3.** A; **4.** C; **5.** B; **6.** C

EXPANSION ACTIVITY: Listen for specific information

- Write questions on the board for each conversation:

    1. Why isn't the man allowed to park there?

    2. When did the man's car break down?

    3. When did the man pass his learner's permit exam?

    4. Where and how long has the man been waiting?

    5. What two things does the woman require the children to do?

    6. Why is the man upset?

- Play the CD for Activity 1 again and have students take notes.

- Have students answer the questions on the board.

- Put students in pairs to compare answers.

- Go over the answers with the class.

ANSWER KEY

1. Because there's a wheelchair access ramp there and he isn't handicapped

2. While he was driving home yesterday

3. Weeks ago

4. At a restaurant for half an hour

5. She makes them hold hands before they cross the street, and she has them walk, not run.

6. He hates driving in rush hour traffic.

 2 **LISTEN** to the conversation. Read the statement and check *True* or *False*.
TCD3, 43

- Go over the directions and read the statements.

- Play the CD and have students check *True* or *False*.

- Put students in pairs to compare answers.

- Go over the answers with the class.

 LISTENING SCRIPT
Lesson 3, Activities 2 and 3
TCD3, 43

A: Hi. Where have you been? I thought you'd be home at 3:30.

B: Oh, you won't believe this. There was an accident at the intersection of Main Street and South Street.

A: That must have been a bad traffic jam!

B: Yeah, it was! But that's not all. It was 3:00, so all the school buses were on the roads. I was behind a bus, so of course, we had to stop and wait every time it stopped.

A: Well, I can understand that.

B: Oh, but that's not the worst part. My car broke down. I had to have it towed to the gas station. Then I had the mechanic drive me here.

A: That's terrible. You know, my hair appointment was for 4:00. I had to cancel it because you weren't here with the car.

B: Sorry about that.

A: Well, I won't get my hair done before the party tonight!

B: Don't worry. You'll still look great.

ANSWER KEY

1. True; 2. False; 3. False; 4. False; 5. True

3 LISTEN again and write answers to the questions. Then tell a partner.

- Go over the directions and questions.
- Play the CD and have students answer the questions.
- Call on students to give their answers.

ANSWER KEY

1. There was an accident at the intersection of Main and South Streets; he was behind school buses and kept having to stop and wait every time they stopped; his car broke down and he had to have it towed to a gas station.
2. His car broke down and he had it towed there.
3. They're going to a party tonight.

CULTURE NOTE

- Point out that drivers on both sides of the road are required by law to stop behind school buses that are flashing red lights.
- Ask if there are similar laws in students' native countries.
- Discuss the reasons for this law and what kinds of problems students think it might cause or solve.

4 ROLE-PLAY. Imagine that you are a traffic officer. Your partner is a new resident in town. Make a dialogue about each sign.

- Go over the directions and make sure students know what each sign means.
- Put students in pairs to make a dialogue about each sign.
- Have pairs come up to the front of the class and perform their role-plays.

🎧 **5 LISTEN** to the conversation.
TCD3, 44
SCD36

- Direct students' attention to the picture and ask what they think the relationship is between the two people.
- Play the CD or read the conversation as students follow along silently.
- Play the CD or read the conversation again and have students repeat out loud.
- Ask: *What problem did the man have? How did he solve the problem?*

6 PRACTICE the conversation from Activity 5 with a partner. Use the information in the chart to make new conversations.

- Go over the directions.
- Model the activity. Have a more advanced student read the woman's lines. Model how to substitute a problem.
- Put students in pairs to practice the conversation, making the appropriate substitutions.
- Walk around the room to monitor the activity and provide help as needed.
- Call on students to read their conversation to the class.

EXPANSION ACTIVITY: Realia

- Bring in pictures of a variety of things with which one might have a problem: kitchen sink or faucet, motorcycle, television, portable music player, computer, sewing machine, etc.
- Put students in pairs and give each pair a picture.
- Draw a chart on the board:

Situation	Problem	What you did	Solution

- Have students work with their partners to create charts to map out problems and solutions for the various objects.
- Set a time limit of three minutes per picture, and then have students pass their picture on to the next pair so that everyone gets to come up with at least three problems and solutions.
- Have pairs create a conversation about one of their objects.
- Let the pairs share their conversations with the class.

PRONUNCIATION: Reduction of *To*
TCD3, 45

A. CIRCLE the word *to* in each sentence below. Then listen to the sentences.
TCD3, 46
SCD37

- Go over the directions with the students.
- Play the CD for Activity A and have students listen for the reduction of *to*.

B. LISTEN again and repeat.
TCD3, 47

- Play the CD for Activity B and have students repeat after each sentence, paying special attention to reducing *to*.

ANSWER KEY

1. You're not allowed (to) turn left here.
2. Only students 16 and older are permitted (to) take the driving class.
3. The laws require drivers (to) drive slowly.
4. The wheelchair lift allows passengers in wheelchairs (to) get on the bus.

7 WHAT ABOUT YOU? Think about problems in your community or neighborhood. Use the conversation strategies to propose solutions to your partner.

- Go over the directions, example, and conversation strategies.
- Have students work in pairs to think of problems and propose solutions.
- Call on students to role-play their problems and solutions for the class.

COMMUNITY CONNECTION: Understand problems in the news

- Bring in several copies of a local newspaper or have students go online to the news website for your local paper.
- Distribute sections (avoid sports and arts) of the newspapers to students.
- Have students look through their section to find problems going on in the area (or statewide or nationally) and make a list.
- Put students in pairs and have them choose one problem from their lists.
- Have pairs discuss ways of solving the problem.
- Call on pairs to share their problem and proposed solutions with the class.

LESSON 4: Grammar and Vocabulary

OBJECTIVES

Discuss transportation information
Verbs with gerunds or infinitives

VOCABULARY

change of address	tow truck
convenience store	Town Hall
engine trouble	Visitor Information
proof of insurance	Center
road test	

GRAMMAR

Verbs that take gerunds or infinitives

COMPETENCIES

Identify steps to obtain a driver's license
Talk about transportation problems

WARM-UP ACTIVITY: New in town

- Ask a student who is usually quiet to come up to the board to be the secretary.
- Have students brainstorm a list of things that need to be done before or when you move to a new place (*find an apartment, find a job, get a new driver's license, sign up for various utilities*).
- Have the student write the list on the board.

🎧 ① GRAMMAR PICTURE DICTIONARY.
TCD3, 48 What are these people talking about?
SCD38 Listen and read.

- Have students look at the pictures. Ask: *What do you see?*
- Play the CD or read the conversations aloud as students follow along silently.
- Call on students and ask questions about the people in the pictures: *What does A in the first picture need to do? What did A forget to do?*

② PRACTICE the conversations in Activity 1 with a partner.

- Go over the directions.
- Put students in pairs to practice the conversations.
- Call on students to read the conversations in front of the class.

EXPANSION ACTIVITY: I forgot to bring my suitcase

- Model making up a conversation similar to those in Activity 1, but about travel. Example:
  A: Passport, please.
  B: Oh, my goodness! I forgot to bring my passport!
  A: Well, I'm afraid I can't let you through security.
- Put students in pairs to make up their own conversations.
- Have students share their conversations with the class.

③ NOTICE THE GRAMMAR. Find the verbs that are followed by gerunds or infinitives. Circle the gerunds. Underline the infinitives.

- Go over the directions.
- Have students circle the gerunds and underline the infinitives.
- Go over the answers with the class.

ANSWER KEY

1. *A:* I need to renew my car registration.
   B: Did you remember to bring proof of insurance?
   A: Yes, but I forgot to bring my registration card.
2. *A:* Hi. I just moved and I haven't gotten any mail lately.
   B: Do you remember filling out a change of address form?
   A: No, I don't remember doing that.

3. A: I still remember (taking) my road test. I was so nervous.
   B: Well, I'll never forget (riding) with you for the first time. I was terrified!

4. A: Uh-oh. We've got engine trouble.
   B: We'd better stop to call a tow truck. That gas station is closed.

5. A: Excuse me. We need to find the Visitor Information Center. Do you know where it is?
   B: It's on that corner. You can stop to pick up a map while you're there.

6. A: Excuse me. Could you tell us where Town Hall is?
   B: Sorry, I can't stop (running!) Ask someone at that convenience store.

GRAMMAR NOTE

- Point out that some verbs take only gerunds (e.g., *enjoy, mind, finish, keep, discuss, consider*) or only infinitives (e.g., *plan, decide, promise, offer, seem, pretend, ask, expect*).
- Point out that other verbs can take a gerund or an infinitive with no change in meaning (e.g., *begin, start, continue, like, love, hate*).

GRAMMAR CHART: Verbs That Take Gerunds or Infinitives

- Go over the information and the usage notes in the chart.
- Read the sample sentences in the chart and their meanings and have students repeat.
- In your explanations of meaning changes, be very expressive and mime things like stopping to look for traffic or forgetting something (a light smack to the forehead, for example).

CHART EXPANSION ACTIVITY: Picture this!

- Hand out blank sheets of paper.
- Using the board, model for students a simple stick-figure illustration of forgetting or remembering something (use thought bubbles). For example, to illustrate *I remember mailing the letters*, you could draw a stick person with a thought bubble with letters, a mailbox, and a check mark inside. Or to show *I forgot to mail the letters*, draw the same thing, but this time instead of a check mark, there would be an X over the whole thought bubble.
- Elicit from students the correct caption for your drawing.
- Emphasize to students that they don't need to draw well, just do something quick and simple.
- Put students into pairs.
- Have students fold their papers in half and draw one illustration on each half and a line below the illustration where their partner will write a forget/remember caption for the picture.
- Have students exchange drawings and write the captions suggested by their partner's illustrations.

4 COMPLETE the conversations with a gerund or an infinitive. Then practice reading the conversations with a partner.

- Go over the directions and example.
- Have students complete the conversations with gerunds and infinitives.
- Go over the answers with the class.
- Put students in pairs to read the conversations.

ANSWER KEY

1. to bring; 2. driving; 3. to take; 4. to call;
5. putting; 6. eating

EXPANSION ACTIVITY: *Try* and *regret*

- Make copies of Worksheet 26: *Try and Regret*.
- Explain that *try* and *regret* are two other verbs that change meaning slightly depending on whether they are followed by a gerund or an infinitive.
- Write on the board or on a transparency:

1. *try* + infinitive = to attempt to do something: *Henry's trying to fix the plumbing.*

2. *try* + gerund = to experiment with different ways of doing something: *I've tried using more eggs and I've tried baking it longer, but the cake just doesn't come out right.*

3. *regret* + infinitive = to inform someone of bad news: *We regret to inform you that your application for a loan has been denied.*

4. *regret* + gerund = to be sorry to have done that thing in the past: *I regret giving the salesperson my phone number because now he calls me every day.*

- Distribute the worksheet and go over the directions.
- Have students write in the correct form of the verb.
- Put students in pairs to compare answers.
- Go over the answers.

WORKSHEET ANSWER KEY

1. lending; **2.** to do; **3.** telling **4.** telling, to make; **5.** to learn; **6.** fixing, taking, buying; **7.** to inform

5 WRITE three sentences with the verb *remember* + gerund. Then write three sentences with *never forget* + gerund.

- Go over the directions and the example.
- Have students write the six sentences.
- Put students in pairs to share their sentences.
- Call on students to read out their sentences.

6 WHAT ABOUT YOU? Think of things in your home that you sometimes forget to do, usually remember to do, and always remember to do. Talk with a partner.

- Go over the directions and example with students.
- Model the activity. Tell the class what you forget or remember to do at home: *I always forget to take out the garbage, but I usually remember to put away the milk.*
- Put students in pairs to talk about what they remember and forget to do at home.
- Call on students to share what their partners always forget or remember with the class.

ACADEMIC CONNECTION: Understand a "Dear John" letter

- Explain to students that a "Dear John" letter is a rejection letter. It can be a letter from a woman telling her boyfriend ("John") she is breaking up with him or a letter telling you that you did not get something you wanted, such as admission to the college of your choice or a job you had applied or interviewed for.
- With students, decide which kind of "Dear John" letter to write.
- On the board, draw a chart with four columns and four headings: *(Always) Remember, (Never) Forget, Try,* and *Regret*.
- Have students brainstorm actions for each category, and tell them it's fine to be a little exaggerated:

(Always) remember	(Never) forget	Try	Regret
being together in Rome in the spring	*seeing you for the first time at the coffee shop*	*to forgive me for breaking your heart*	*to tell you that I've found someone else*

- Using a blank transparency, lead the students in writing a "Dear John" letter. Incorporate the suggestions from the chart.

LESSON 5: Grammar Practice Plus

OBJECTIVES

Read a town map
Interpret statistical information

VOCABULARY

Chamber of Commerce
Department of Motor Vehicles
hardware store
moving van rental service
post office

GRAMMAR

Verbs that take gerunds or infinitives

NUMERACY

Interpreting statistical information

COMPETENCY

Understand percentages in interpreting
  statistical information

WARM-UP ACTIVITY: Moving to a new apartment

- Put students in pairs (with their books closed) to list tasks that have to be done when you move into a new apartment.
- Elicit tasks and write them on the board.

 1 LISTEN to the conversations. Sam is
TCD3, 49 moving to a new apartment and has to get things done today! Match the letter in the map with the name of each place Sam went.

- Go over the directions and the places on the map.
- Play the CD and have students do the activity.

- Put students in pairs to compare answers.
- Go over the answers with the class.

 LISTENING SCRIPT
Lesson 5, Activity 1
TCD3, 49

1. A: Hi Jack. I have to buy paint supplies and light fixtures. Do you know where the hardware store is?

   B: Sure, Sam, it's on the west side of town. Take Main Street and turn left on North. Go past the Stardust Hotel and you'll see it on the corner of North Street and West Street.

   A: Thanks!

   B: You're welcome.

2. A: Excuse me. Do you know where the post office is?

   B: Sure. Go up Main Street and around the statue. Its on the corner of First Street and State Street. It should be on your right.

3. A: Hello. I need to get my car registration renewed. Is there a Department of Motor Vehicles near here?

   B: Yes. It's on South Street between Elm Street and West Street.

   A: Oh, thanks.

   B: Don't mention it.

4. A: Excuse me, is there a parking lot around here?

   B: Sure. Go up Main Street and turn right on Pine. It's across the street from the shopping mall.

   A: Thanks for your help.

   B: No problem!

5. A: Excuse me. Is there a moving van rental service near here?

   B: Yes. Just go up Main Street and take a left on First Street. It's across the street from the auto repair shop.

   A: Thanks!

6. *A:* Excuse me. I need to get information about a business license. Do you know where I should go for that?

   B: Yes, I do. You can get advice at the Chamber of Commerce. It's located at the corner of Main and Hope Streets. The entrance is in front of the statue.

7. *A:* Excuse me. Do you know where I can find a convenience store around here?

   B: I remember seeing one near the school on State Street. Go straight up Main Street and turn right on Pine. Go past the shopping mall, and I think it is on State Street across from the school.

ANSWER KEY

1. C; **2.** A; **3.** B; **4.** G; **5.** E; **6.** D; **7.** F

BIG PICTURE GRAMMAR EXPANSION ACTIVITY: Gerunds and infinitives

- Have students look at the Big Picture on page 136.
- Put students in pairs to write conversations about what they have remembered or forgotten to do/doing at various places around town.
- Have students role-play their conversations.
- Call on pairs to perform their role-plays for the class.

2 WRITE. Read Sam's "to-do" list. Write sentences to say where Sam needs to go to do each of the things on his list.

- Go over the directions and the example.
- Have students write sentences based on the "to-do" list. If necessary, play the CD again.
- Put students in pairs to compare "to-do" lists.
- Go over the answers with the class.

ANSWER KEY

Sam needs to go to the hardware store to buy paint and light fixtures.
He needs to go to the convenience store to pick up milk, bread, and coffee.
He needs to go to the post office to fill out a change-of-address form.
He needs to go to the moving van rental service to reserve a moving van.
He needs to go to the auto repair shop to drop off his car for a tune-up and new tires.
He needs to go to the Chamber of Commerce, to get information about a business license.
He needs to go to the Department of Motor Vehicles to renew his vehicle registration.

3 ROLE-PLAY. Take turns asking and answering the questions. Use the map in Activity 1.

- Go over the directions, example, and Conversation Strategy box.
- Put students in pairs to do the role-plays.
- Walk around monitoring role-plays.
- Have volunteers come up and perform their role-plays for the class.

EXPANSION ACTIVITY: New resident information

- Find your city or town's website of information for visitors and new residents.
- Put students in pairs and have them go on the Internet to your city or town's website of information for visitors and new residents.
- Have students find and write down the names, addresses, and telephone numbers of a realtor, an elementary school, a bank, a shopping mall, the Department of Motor Vehicles, a moving service, a post office, and the local Chamber of Commerce.
- Have pairs share the information they gathered with the class.

4 **LISTEN** to the conversation. As you listen, put a check under Sam or Mrs. Peterson.
TCD3, 50

- Go over the directions and the list of activities in the chart.
- Play the CD and have students check off the things that apply to Sam or Mrs. Peterson.
- Go over the answers.

 LISTENING SCRIPT
Lesson 5, Activity 4
TCD3, 50

A: Hi, Mrs. Peterson.

B: Hello Sam. It looks like you're really getting things done today.

A: Yes, but I forgot to do some things this morning.

B: Oh, well. I always forget things. This morning I forgot to take my keys with me. I had to call my son at work and get him to bring his set of keys.

A: Oh. Yesterday, I went to the Department of Motor Vehicles and forgot to bring my proof of insurance. I had to go all the way back to my apartment to get it.

B: Oh, we're quite the pair! What else do you have to do today?

A: Well, I forgot to buy a winter coat before I moved here. Do you know where I can find a nice coat?

B: Hmm. I remember seeing sale signs at the shopping mall. There's a good department store there.

A: Thanks. I also need some information about a business license. Do you know where I can get that?

B: Oh, yes. Go to the Chamber of Commerce. It has a lot of information about small businesses. Then, stop at Town Hall to pick up the application. Town Hall is such a beautiful building. I remember getting my marriage license there 40 years ago.

A: Wow, you've really lived here a long time, haven't you?

B: Yes. I remember seeing this town for the first time when I was 20 years old. I thought the houses were so beautiful. Now I only see the town by bus because I stopped driving last year. You probably have a car, don't you?

A: Well, yes, but my car is getting fixed at the auto shop. I have to remember to call the mechanic this afternoon. I should add that to my to-do list.

ANSWER KEY

1. Mrs. Peterson; **2.** Sam; **3.** Sam; **4.** Mrs. Peterson; **5.** Sam; **6.** Mrs. Peterson; **7.** Mrs. Peterson **8.** Sam

5 **WRITE** five sentences from the information in Activity 5 about what Sam and Mrs. Peterson forgot or remembered, and where they stopped.

- Go over the directions with students.
- Have students work on their own first, and then put them in pairs to compare sentences with a partner.
- Call on volunteers to read their sentences to the class.

6 **TALK** to a partner. Ask and answer questions about the conversation.

- Go over the directions with students.
- Put students into pairs and have them practice asking and answering questions about the conversation in Activity 4.

ANSWER KEY

1. He forgot to do some things.
2. She stopped driving last year.
3. Because she got her marriage license there 40 years ago.
4. He needs to remember to call the mechanic about his car.

MATH: Interpret Statistical Information

- Direct students' attention to the chart.

A. **READ** the statistics about transportation in Sam's new town. Note: a *household* is usually a family.

- Go over the directions and the note.
- Tell students the number of people in your household and ask them how many people live in theirs.
- Have students practice reading the numbers in the chart.

B. CALCULATE the answers.

- Go over the directions and the formulas.
- Make sure students understand how to use each formula.
- Have students solve the three problems.
- Go over the answers with the class.

ANSWER KEY

1. 3; **2.** 179,928 **3.** 69,854.4

EXPANSION ACTIVITY: Class statistics

- Bring a calculator to class.
- Prepare a large version of the statistical chart on page 143 (adding more columns), but leave all headings blank except the first one. Write "Total Number of Students" in the first heading and the number of students in your class below.
- Have students brainstorm a list of activities and characteristics, such as *have dark hair, have children, exercise regularly, have a car, speak French*. Write them on the board.
- Have students choose the activities/ characteristics they want to gather statistical information about and head the columns accordingly.
- Choose a student to come up to the front and count (in the case of things you can see, such as dark hair) or poll everyone on each of the statistical categories. Have him or her jot down the total number of students in each category.
- Have different students use the calculator to figure out what percentage of students belong in each category using this formula: divide the number of students in a given category by the total number of students, and convert the decimal into a percentage (7 out of 12 students = 0.58333 = 58%).
- Write the percentage in the correct category.

7 WHAT ABOUT YOU? Talk to a partner about your community. Where do you go in your community when you need to get things done? Where do you go shopping? Where do you get your hair cut? Do you take public transportation or do you drive?

- Put students into pairs and have them discuss where and how they get things done in their native country.
- Walk around monitoring their conversations and offering help when necessary.
- After about five minutes, bring the whole class back together again. Call on students to answer the questions.

ACADEMIC CONNECTION: Interpret statistical information

- Bring in examples of articles that contain statistical information. (Check news magazines such as *Time* and *Newsweek*.)
- Talk about the articles with the class. Elicit why the statistics might be helpful or misleading, and why they were included in the articles.
- Have students bring in articles containing statistics.
- Discuss why the statistics were included in the articles.

LESSON 6: Reading

OBJECTIVES

Read about a traffic accident

VOCABULARY

authorities	parking lot
fatalities	responders
jackknifed	vehicles

READING FOCUS

Identify main idea

COMPETENCY

Use language to interpret and convey information

WARM-UP ACTIVITY: Types of vehicles

- Write the word *vehicle* on the board and elicit its meaning from students.
- Elicit from students all the different types of land vehicles they know and add in ones they don't come up with: cars, trucks, motorcycles, mopeds, convertibles, bicycles, rickshaws, carriages, semis, 18-wheelers, ambulances, hearses, sedans, coupes, vans, RVs/motorhomes, etc.

1 THINK ABOUT IT. Have you ever been in an accident? What happened? Did the police come?

- Put students in pairs to answer the questions.
- Call on students to describe car accidents they have been in.

EXPANSION ACTIVITY: Prior knowledge

- Put students in pairs.
- Set a time limit of two minutes. Have students brainstorm a list of all the information they should write down in the event of an accident: the details of the accident; the other driver's full name, telephone number, address, and car insurance information; the license plate number of the other car; the names and badge numbers of any police officers or other emergency workers who are on the scene.
- List the information students came up with on the board, and add any important information that they miss.

2 BEFORE YOU READ. Preview the article on the next page. Look at the title and the pictures. What is the article about?

- Go over the directions.
- Have students preview the article.
- Elicit the main idea of the article.

ANSWER KEY

The article is about a huge car accident on Interstate 70.

3 READ the article. What happened? What was the cause of the accident?

- Go over the directions and the questions.
- Have students read the article through once.
- Have students reread the article and use a highlighter to highlight the cause and basic events of the accident.
- Put students in pairs to discuss their answers.
- Discuss the answers as a class.

ANSWER KEY

The cause isn't clear, but police think a semi truck jackknifed on the highway and then, due to slippery snow on the road, other vehicles were unable to brake in time and crashed into the truck and each other.

EXPANSION ACTIVITY: How can different weather conditions contribute to car accidents?

- Put students in pairs or small groups to discuss and list various weather conditions (snow, rain, sleet, ice, sun glare, fog) and the ways they can cause car accidents.
- Call on students to share their group's ideas.

4 AFTER YOU READ.

A. VOCABULARY. Underline each word or phrase in the article. Read the paragraph again. Then match the word or phrase with its meaning.

- Go over the directions.
- Have students underline the vocabulary words in the article and do the matching.
- Go over where the words are found in the article and the answers to the matching activity.

ANSWER KEY

1. C; 2. E; 3. D; 4. A; 5. B

READING FOCUS: Identify the main idea

- Go over the information in the Reading Focus box carefully with the students.
- Remind students that main ideas are frequently found in the first sentence of a paragraph.

B. READ the article again. What is the main idea of each paragraph? Discuss with a partner.

- Go over the directions.
- Put students in pairs and have them find, underline, and discuss the main idea of each paragraph.
- Go over the answers with the class.

ANSWER KEY

Paragraph 1: Interstate 70 was reopened this morning after a 60-car accident yesterday forced it to close.
Paragraph 2: Police and emergency responders worked throughout the night helping victims of the crash and cleaning up the highway.
Paragraph 3: The exact cause of the crash is unclear, but police think it was started by a jackknifed truck that other cars ran into.
Paragraph 4: An eyewitness reported that it was a terrible series of crashes involving numerous vehicles.
Paragraph 5: The injuries were few and minor considering what a big accident it was.
Paragraph 6: You shouldn't drive during a snowstorm, but if you have to, drive slowly.

EXPANSION ACTIVITY: Find supporting details

- Have students circle the details given in each paragraph that support its main idea.
- Put students in pairs to share the supporting details they identified.

C. SCAN the article to answer the following questions.

- Have students answer the questions on their own.
- Put students in pairs to compare answers with a partner.
- Go over the answers with the class.

ANSWER KEY

1. During Friday afternoon rush hour
2. Snowy
3. 60
4. A semi truck jackknifed in the road initially, and then other cars could not stop in time to avoid the crash since the roadway was slippery with snow.
5. Twelve people were injured. They had broken bones, bruises, and scrapes. They went to a local hospital and were treated, and released. There were no fatalities.

EXPANSION ACTIVITY: Role-play

- Divide students into groups of four or more. The core roles are two drivers, a police officer, and a witness. Additional roles could be passengers, other (conflicting) witnesses, emergency workers, or reporters, depending on how elaborate you want to get.
- Have each group devise a car accident, detail what happened (including the cause), and then make up a role-play based on their ideas.
- Set a time limit for each role-play, such as three minutes.
- Give groups time to practice their role-plays.
- Have groups perform their role-plays for the class.

BIG PICTURE READING EXPANSION ACTIVITY: A Fender Bender

- Photocopy and distribute Worksheet 27: *A Fender Bender.*
- You may wish to create a diagram of the accident and draw it on the blackboard or create and project a transparency.
- Put the transparency for Unit 9 on the OHP or have students look at the Big Picture on page 136.

- Have students discuss which cars are the most likely to have an accident.
- Go over the directions and questions on the worksheet.
- Read aloud the transcript for the students.
- Have students read the transcript and answer the questions.
- Go over the answers with the class.

WORKSHEET ANSWER KEY

1. At the intersection of Third Street and Rodney Boulevard; 2. Two; a blue car and a red car 3. The blue car stopped suddenly and the red car ran into it; also, both drivers were on cell phones and one was eating; 4. No, a fender bender is not a serious accident, and you can tell because no one was really hurt and the red car only hit the bumper of the blue one; 5. the drivers were taken to and released from the hospital.

COMMUNITY CONNECTION: What to do following an accident

- Put students in pairs and have the pairs brainstorm a list of actions to take after a car accident.
- Have the student partners go online to research steps they should take following an accident.
- Have the pairs of students note the steps they missed in their lists.

LESSON 7: Writing

OBJECTIVES
Fill out an insurance claim form

WRITING FOCUS
Make a numbered list to sequence an event

COMPETENCIES
Understand information about automobile insurance Learn procedures to follow after an auto accident

WARM-UP ACTIVITY: Car insurance

- Put students in pairs and have them come up with reasons why it's useful to have car insurance.
- Make a master list of reasons on the board.

1 THINK ABOUT IT. How do car insurance companies help people who have been in an accident? What do people have to do after they have an accident to get help from their insurance companies?

- Give students a minute or two to think about the questions on their own and maybe jot down answers.
- Put students in pairs or small groups to talk about their answers.
- Call on students to share their answers with the class.

2 BEFORE YOU WRITE.

A. DISCUSS. Look at the picture on page 145 with a partner. Describe what happened.

- Go over the directions.
- Put students in pairs to discuss the picture.

B. LISTEN to a conversation about another car accident. Read the statements and check *True* or *False*.

- Go over the directions.
- Play the CD and have students check *True* or *False*.
- Go over the answers with the class.

LISTENING SCRIPT
Lesson 7, Activity 2B

TCD3, 51

> A: Hello?
>
> B: Hi, Mom. It's Tom. I just got in a car accident.
>
> A: Oh, no! Are you okay?
>
> B: Yes, I'm okay, don't worry.
>
> A: How many people were in the other car? Is anyone else hurt?
>
> B: Well, there was a woman driving and her two children in the back seat. The kids were scared, but they stopped crying once they were out of the car. Luckily everyone is okay.
>
> A: Oh, thank goodness! What happened?
>
> B: Well, I just got out of school and was driving to work. It was almost 3:30, so I was worried I was going to be late. I was sitting at a stoplight behind another car. The light turned green and she started to go. But then she saw a pedestrian in the cross-walk and stopped suddenly. I put on my brakes but wasn't able to stop in time. I hit her from behind. We both pulled over, and like I said, her kids were crying, but we are all okay.
>
> A: Did you get her name and contact information?
>
> B: Yeah—after she calmed her kids down, we exchanged names and insurance information. Her name is Maria Chang. I got her phone number and email address but forgot to get her home address.
>
> A: Did the police come?
>
> B: Yes, an officer from the Miami Police Department came. He took a report and had us move our cars off the road.
>
> A: Is your car okay?

B: No, actually, the whole front of my car is dented in. I'm having it towed to Pete's Body Shop on Main Street.

A: Well, the most important thing is that you are okay. We can fill out an insurance claim when you get home.

B: Okay, Mom. See you soon.

A: Bye.

ANSWER KEY

1. False; **2.** True; **3.** False; **4.** False

WRITING FOCUS: Make a numbered list to sequence an event

• Go over the information in the Writing Focus box.

• Direct students' attention to the numbered list on the insurance form they are going to fill out.

C. COMPLETE. Read the insurance form that Tom filled out and fill in any missing details. Then listen again to check your answers.

• Go over the directions.

• Have students read the insurance form and fill in the missing information.

• Play the CD again and have students check their answers.

• Go over the answers with the class.

ANSWER KEY

Time of the accident: 3:30 p.m.
General description of what happened:
1. stoplight; 2. green, pedestrian; 3. stop;
4. behind
Location where your vehicle was towed: Main Street
Contact information for the other people involved: Maria Chang

3 WRITE. Imagine you were one of the cars in the accident described in the reading on page 145. Fill out the insurance form. Be sure to make a numbered list to describe what happened.

• Go over the directions and tell students to make up any information not included in the reading (such as, "Location where your vehicle was towed").

• Have students complete the form on their own.

ANSWER KEY

State where the accident occurred: **Colorado**

Date and time of the accident: **January 21, 2010 at 5:30 p.m.** (The newspaper article came out the morning after the accident).

General description of what happened: **Answers will vary.** Possible response:
1. **A semi truck jackknifed on Interstate 70.**
2. **The cars in front of me started braking and kept sliding forward.**
3. **I tried to stop, too, but the road was slippery with snow and I couldn't stop.**
4. **I ran into the car in front of me.**

Location where your vehicle was towed: **Answers will vary.**

Police department involved (if any) and accident report number: **Colorado State Troopers** and **answers will vary.**

Contact information for the other people involved (name, address, phone number, email address: **Answers will vary and may include names of classmates.**

License plate numbers for the other vehicles involved: **Answers will vary.**

Insurance information for the other vehicles involved: **Answers will vary**

❹ AFTER YOU WRITE.

A. DISCUSS. Share your insurance claim with a partner. What questions does your partner have about the accident? How can you improve your insurance claim form?

- Have students exchange claim forms with a partner.
- Ask students to read their partner's claim form and, on a separate sheet of paper, write questions or comments about it.
- Have students return the claim forms along with questions and comments to their partners.

B. EDIT your insurance claim form. Ask yourself these questions:

- Go over the directions and questions.
- Advise students to also use their partner's questions and comments to help them edit their claim forms.

C. REWRITE your insurance claim form, making corrections.

- Go over the directions.
- Have students rewrite their insurance claim forms, making the necessary corrections.

BIG PICTURE WRITING EXPANSION ACTIVITY: Describe the accident

- Have students look at the Big Picture on page 136 in their books.
- Have students write a numbered list sequencing the events in the accident described on Worksheet 27: *A Fender Bender.*
- Put students in pairs to read each other's lists.
- Ask a volunteer to read his/her list to the class.

COMMUNITY CONNECTION: Comparing car insurance

- To prepare for this activity, use the Internet to get an insurance quote comparison so that you can note the types of information students will be asked to provide, along with any vocabulary they will need to know. Tell them they can make up information and do not have to give their real names, etc.
- Tell students that with a partner, they are going to do online research to find car insurance.
- Put students in pairs.
- Have the pairs go online to find a website that allows you to compare car insurance rates.
- Have the pairs select one of the insurance companies and give the class their reasons for choosing that company.

Career Connection

OBJECTIVES

Solve a problem at work

COMPETENCIES

Use problem-solving strategies
Collaborate to solve a problem
Practice test-taking skills

WARM-UP ACTIVITY: Two heads are better than one

- Draw a T-chart on the board. Label one side *One Head* and the other *Two Heads*.

- Explain that sometimes it's better to solve a problem or make a decision by yourself, and other times it's better to resolve problems or make decisions with a partner or group.

- Give a couple of examples: *Parents should make decisions that concern their children together. If you're unhappy in your present job, you can solve that yourself by figuring out what you want in a job and looking for a new one.*

- Elicit examples for both sides from students and write them in the T-chart.

1 THINK ABOUT IT. Look at the picture. What are the workers doing to solve their problem? What does *collaborate* mean?

- Direct students' attention to the picture and ask questions: *Where are these people? What are they doing? What do you think just happened?*

- Elicit the meaning of *collaborate* from students. (Direct their attention to the people in the picture.)

 2 LISTEN to a discussion among engineers and line workers at an auto plant. What problem are they discussing? Choose the correct answer.

TCD3, 52

- Go over the directions and possible answers.
- Play the CD and have students choose an answer.
- Go over the correct answer.

 LISTENING SCRIPT
Career Connection, Activities 2 and 3

TCD3, 52

Carl: Ray, what's going on? Where are those car parts? I needed them 15 minutes ago.

Ray: Yeah, hey, Carl, we've got a machine that's broken down on the production line.

Carl: Oh, no. I need the parts for this shipment.

Ray: But we only have three completed here, Carl.

Carl: But I need ten . . .

Ray: Well, I don't know what to say. It's broken. We just have to wait for an engineer to come fix the machine.

Carl: But that could take over an hour! We have to get this machine working again right away. I need to get this shipment of parts out by six o'clock tonight . . . Let's ask Nancy. I think she knows how to fix this machine . . . Nancy, do you know how to fix this thing?

Nancy: I don't know, guys. I worked on this machine a long time ago. I'm not sure if I remember how to fix it. I guess I could try, but . . .

Ray: If you don't want to wait for an engineer, let's ask the supervisor if we can call Gary. Gary's the lead engineer on this machine. He can definitely tell us how to fix it. Let's ask the supervisor for Gary's number . . .

Nancy: But Gary's in Germany. He's on vacation. Remember? It's kind of late to call him there now. I don't want to wake him up . . .

Carl: Aw, c'mon, Nancy, can't you just try to fix the machine?

Ray: Listen, Carl, I don't think it's a good idea for Nancy to work on the machine. What happens if she can't fix it? Then no one can help us, and your order won't go out on time. Let's just call Gary. He said we can call him any time.

Carl: Well, if we're going to call him, let's do it now. If we wait until later, it'll really be too late to call him. I'll get his number.

ANSWER KEY

They are discussing a broken machine.

3 LISTEN again. Pay attention to the names of the speakers. Then complete the sentences with the correct name.

- Go over the directions and example sentence.
- Play the CD again and have students fill in the answers.
- Put students in pairs to compare answers.
- Go over the answers.

ANSWER KEY

1. Carl; 2. Ray; 3. Nancy; 4. Ray; 5. Nancy;
6. Carl

4 DISCUSS. How did Carl, Ray, and Nancy decide to solve their problem? How were they different in how they tried to do it? Discuss with a partner.

- Go over the directions and questions.
- Put students in pairs to discuss the questions.
- Discuss the questions as a class.

EXPANSION ACTIVITY: Your problem-solving style

- Call on various students to tell whose style (Carl's, Nancy's, or Ray's) is closest to theirs and why.
- Ask students if they have family members whose problem-solving style is like any of the workers'. Have them explain why.
- Share with students which of the workers' styles is closest to yours and why.

5 TALK with a partner about the ways that people try to solve problems. When there's a problem at work, do you think it's best to collaborate in a group, work as individuals, or wait for a supervisor's decision?

- Go over the directions and questions.
- Put students in pairs or small groups to discuss the questions.
- Discuss the questions as a class.

6 WHAT ABOUT YOU? Think about a situation where you had a problem in your job. How did you solve the problem? Can you think of any other ways you could have solved the problem?

- Go over the directions and questions.
- Have students work on their own for a few minutes, jotting down a past work problem, how they solved it, and other ways they could have solved it.
- Put students in pairs to discuss past problems, solutions, and alternative solutions.

ACADEMIC CONNECTION: Solve problems

- Remind students that sometimes they might run into problems with classes, teachers, or the administration.
- Put students into small groups to discuss strategies and available resources for dealing with and solving these types of problems.
- Have the groups share their strategies and resources with the class.

CHECK YOUR PROGRESS!

- Have students circle the correct answers.
- Review the answers or have students check the unit to see if each answer is right or wrong.
- Have students total their correct answers and fill in the chart at the bottom of the page.
- Have students create a learning plan and/or set learning goals.

ANSWER KEY

1. to have; 2. cross; 3. hold; 4. fix;
5. to go; 6. eating; 7. going; 8. to see;
9. disabled; 10. fire hydrant; 11. road construction; 12. school zone; 13. change-of-address; 14. road test; 15. trouble; 16. visitor information center

Unit Overview

LESSON	OBJECTIVES	STUDENT BOOK	WORKBOOK
1 Grammar and Vocabulary 1	Read about home safety. Practice reported speech.	p. 150	p. 132
2 Grammar Practice Plus	Discuss home safety. Reported speech with *say* and *tell*.	p. 152	p. 133
3 Listening and Conversation	Take a phone message. Role-play a conversation.	p. 154	p. 134
4 Grammar and Vocabulary 2	Read about health concerns. Phrasal verbs.	p. 156	p. 136
5 Grammar Practice Plus	Write and pronounce *used to* and *be + used to*.	p. 158	p. 137
6 Reading	Read and write specific medical information.	p. 160	p. 138–139
7 Writing	Write a New Year's resolution.	p. 162	p. 140–141
• Career Connection	Read an online application.	p. 164	p. 142
• Check Your Progress	Monitor progress.	p. 165	p. 144–145

Reading/Writing Strategies

- Use context to guess the meaning of new words
- Use the layout of a business plan

Connection Activities

LESSON	TYPE	SKILL DEVELOPMENT
1	Academic	Listening to presentations and lectures
2	Community	Researching home safety programs
3	Academic	Learning about school safety
4	Community	Interviewing at athletic clubs and gyms
5	Academic	Examining curriculum and learning
6	Community	Interviewing at pharmacies
7	Academic	Analyzing persuasive essays
Career Connection	Community	Showing appreciation in the community

WORKSHEET #/FOCUS	TITLE	TEACHER'S EDITION
28. Reading/Comprehension	At the Community Center	p. 332
29. Vocabulary	Vocabulary Practice	p. 333
30. Listening/Graphic Organizer	Winter Safety	p. 334

LESSON 1: Grammar and Vocabulary

Read about home safety
Practice reported speech

VOCABULARY

carbon monoxide detectors	handrails
	outlet covers
child-safety locks	safety devices
fire drill	smoke detectors

GRAMMAR

Reported speech

COMPETENCY

Use language to talk about home safety

WARM-UP ACTIVITY: Unit opener

- Have a volunteer read the title of the unit. Have students predict what will be in the unit.
- Divide the class into two teams and give each team a piece of chart paper and markers.
- Have each team create a web on their chart paper. One team should write the word *Health* in the center and the other team should write the word *Safety.* Have students add as many subtopics and details as they can think of to their web.
- Have each group present and explain their web to the other group.
- Preview any important vocabulary words that come up during the brainstorm.

🎧 **1 GRAMMAR PICTURE DICTIONARY.**
TCD4,2
SCD39
What did the instructor say about home safety? Listen and read.

- Have students open their books and look at the pictures. Ask: *What do you see?* Write all the words the students say on the board.

- Say the sentences aloud or play the CD and have students repeat.
- Call on students and ask about the people in the pictures: *What is the woman pointing to? What is she holding?*

2 PRACTICE the conversations in Activity 1 with a partner.

- Put students in pairs to read the sentences.
- Call on students to read the sentences to the class.

3 NOTICE THE GRAMMAR. Look at the blue parts of the sentences above. Then look at what the teacher says. How are the sentences different? Then circle the differences in speaker B's sentences.

- Go over the directions and the example. Have students name the verb tense used by each speaker. Have them point out any pronouns that change.
- Have students circle Speaker B's words that are different from what the instructor in the picture says.
- Elicit answers and write them on the board. Have students name the verb tenses and changed pronouns for each sentence.

ANSWER KEY

1. She said we needed handrails on all of our stairways.
2. She said we needed to have an emergency escape plan, and the whole family needed to practice once a year.
3. She said carbon monoxide was a deadly gas that collects when fuels like kerosene are burned.
4. Yes, she said we could keep our children safe by using outlet covers and child-safety locks.

GRAMMAR CHART: Reported speech

- Go over the information in the chart and the Grammar Professor note.
- Read the sentences, pausing to have students repeat.

CHART EXPANSION ACTIVITY: Pair playoffs

- Put students in pairs.
- Give each pair two index cards. Pairs must write one direct quotation on the front of each card and the reported speech version of the sentence on the back. Quotes may come from news articles, stories, students' imagination, or elsewhere.
- Put pairs together to form groups of four. Have pairs exchange index cards face-up, so students can only see the direct quotations. Pairs must then race to write the correct reported speech for the two sentences they received. Students may write on the index card fronts or on a separate sheet of paper.
- When Pair A thinks they have the correct answer, they must put their pencils down and both pairs must stop writing. Pair A may then check the back of the index cards to confirm their answers. If they are correct, they win the round. If they are incorrect, Pair B gets the opportunity to finish and check their own sentences. If both pairs are incorrect, they may play against each other in the next round.
- Continue play by pairing up new groups of four. You may wish to form elimination brackets on the board to make the game exciting. Award the winning team a prize. Eliminated teams may continue to play against other eliminated teams to see who can win the most rounds for a consolation prize.

EXPANSION ACTIVITY: News report

- Find a video clip on the Internet in which the reporters use reported speech to tell the news.
- Have students listen to the clip and write down the reported speech they hear.
- Have partners compare what they wrote.
- As a class, evaluate whether the reporter used correct reported speech. Point out that it is not uncommon for people to use reported speech incorrectly in spoken English.
- Alternatively, have students listen to a news report delivered in direct speech and write a summary of what the reporter said, using reported speech.

CULTURE NOTE

Explain to students that sometimes people do not follow the rules for reported speech when they want to emphasize specific information. As an example, write the following two sentences on the board and explain the difference in meaning to students: *Mark said that he had a tent but we couldn't borrow it. John said that he has a tent we can borrow next weekend.* In the second sentence, the emphasis is on the fact that John's tent is available now and can be borrowed in the future. Point out that technically, the sentence should read *John said that he had a tent*, as reported speech requires the past tense in this case.

4 WRITE reported speech for each direct quotation.

- Go over the directions.
- Have students write the reported speech in their notebooks.
- Put students in pairs to compare answers.

ANSWER KEY

1. Susan said (that) she was installing child-safety locks on their kitchen cabinets.

2. Terry said (that) they had a fire drill twice a year at their house.

3. He said (that) he hadn't bought a carbon monoxide detector.

4. Chuck said (that) he was building a handrail for their stairs.

5. Sarah said (that) she had never used outlet covers before.

6. Aaron said (that) his medicine cabinet had a child-safety lock on it.

5 WHAT ABOUT YOU? Interview a classmate and ask the questions below. Write down your classmate's answers as direct quotations. Then share the information with the class using reported speech.

- Go over the directions and the example.
- Have the students interview each other and write direct quotations.
- Call on students to tell the class what they discovered, using reported speech to tell about their partner.

EXPANSION ACTIVITY: It's a secret!

- Have each student write down a fact or a secret (real or imaginary) to share with the class.
- Have students do a class mingle. Students should exchange secrets by whispering to one another. Each student who hears a secret should write it down using reported speech: *Maria said that she would eat pizza for lunch today.*
- After a set time limit or after the first student reports to the teacher with five secrets written down, have students take their seats.
- Go around the class, asking about each student's secret: "What did Maria say?"

ACADEMIC CONNECTION: Presentations and lectures

- Have students listen to presentations by peers or lectures by teachers. Ask them to take notes about what they hear.
- Have each student report to the class some of the facts that he or she learned from the presentation or lecture, using reported speech.
- Encourage the class to ask questions about what the presenter or lecturer said: "Did Mr. Miller say which painting he likes best?" Have the student reporting back answer using reported speech, allowing classmates to help him or her form difficult sentences if needed.

LESSON 2: Grammar Practice Plus

OBJECTIVES

Discuss home safety
Reported speech with *say* and *tell*

VOCABULARY

burn hazard	electrical cord
child-safety gate	electrical outlet
choking hazard	toxic cleansers

GRAMMAR

Reported speech with *say* and *tell*

MATH

Subtracting decimals

COMPETENCIES

Identify safe practices in the home
Use math to interpret a bar graph
Subtract decimals

WARM-UP ACTIVITY: How safe is it?

- Bring in a common small appliance from home, such as an iron, a toaster, or a food processor.

- Have students identify the names of as many parts of the appliance as possible: *cord, plug, knob, blade,* etc. Write the words on the board and go over new vocabulary as needed.

- After eliciting vocabulary, ask students whether they think the appliance is safe for children to use or not. Have them give reasons to support their opinion.

1 TALK about the safety problems in the picture.

- Elicit ideas from the students. Help them identify unknown words and objects from the picture. If appropriate, refer to the list of words written on the board during the warm-up activity.

2 LISTEN to the conversation. Then write the correct number next to each word below.

TCD4, 3

- Go over the directions and the words listed.
- Play the CD and have students write the correct number next to each word.
- Go over the answers with the class.

LISTENING SCRIPT
Lesson 2, Activity 2
TCD4, 3

1. A: Please don't leave this bowl of candy on the table.
   B: Why not?
   A: Jimmy can get up on the chair and reach these. Didn't I tell you they're a choking hazard?
   B: Oh yeah, you did.

2. A: Whoa! Who left this toy on the stairs?
   B: Oh, I bet one of the boys did that.
   A: We need to put these child-safety gates up. And please tell them to keep their toys off the stairs.
   B: All right.

3. A: Wow. You have too many electrical cords plugged in here!
   B: Do you think so?
   A: Yeah. I heard we shouldn't have more than two plugged in at one time. You've got four things plugged in here! It could start a fire.
   B: Oh, okay. I'll take care of it.

4. A: Miriam, did you say you bought new locks for the cabinet doors?
   B: Yes, they're in the living room.
   A: We need to lock these cabinets. There are toxic cleansers inside, and I don't want the boys to get in there.

5. A: Who left these pans on the stove like this?
   B: I did. Why?
   C: I told you last time you need to turn the handles toward the wall. It's a real burn hazard if the boys pull these pans off the stove.

> 6. *A:* Billy, stay away from that outlet. Susan—they said we have to put covers on the electrical outlets. It's dangerous if they're not covered, especially if the children can reach it easily.
>
> *B:* Okay, I'll get some more covers for the outlets.

ANSWER KEY

5 burn hazard; 3 electrical cord;
6 electrical outlet; 2 child-safety gate;
4 toxic cleansers; 1 choking hazard

3 COMPLETE each sentence with a vocabulary word from Activity 2.

- Go over the directions and the example. Explain to students that some words may need to be plural in order to complete the sentences.
- Have students complete the exercise.
- Put students in pairs to compare their answers.
- Go over the answers with the class.

ANSWER KEY

1. choking hazard; 2. child-safety gates;
3. burn hazard; 4. toxic cleansers;
5. electrical cords, electrical outlet

GRAMMAR CHART: Reported speech with *say* and *tell*

- Direct students' attention to the chart.
- Go over the information in the chart and the usage notes. Read the sentences and have volunteers repeat each one.
- Have students compare the new information with what they learned in the Grammar Chart from Lesson 1, pointing out any similarities and differences.

CHART EXPANSION ACTIVITY: It's a secret! Part 2

- Remind students of the game they played in Lesson 1, in which they reported facts or secrets their classmates told them.

- Play the game again, using the new grammar structures. Add complexity to the game by following this pattern: Student A tells a secret to Student B. Student B uses reported speech with *said* to tell the class the secret (*Becky said that . . .*). Student C uses reported speech with *told* to tell the class what Student A told Student B (*Becky told Luis that . . .*).

4 WRITE. Use the information from Activity 3 to write six things that Doris told Mia. Use reported speech. Write 3 sentences with *said*, and 3 sentences with *told*.

- Go over the directions and the example.
- Have students write the sentences.
- Ask volunteers to share the sentences they wrote.
- Have the class tell whether each statement is accurate. If not, encourage peer correction of information and grammar.

ANSWER KEY

Answers will vary. Possible responses:

1. Doris said, "Turn the handles toward the wall."
2. Doris said, "It's a real burn hazard if the boys pull these pans off the stove."
3. Doris said the pans were a burn hazard.
4. Doris told Mia to turn the handles toward the wall.
5. Doris told Mia that the pans were a burn hazard.
6. Doris told her that the pans were a burn hazard.

BIG PICTURE GRAMMAR EXPANSION ACTIVITY: Listen and report

- Play the CD from Activity 2 again.
- Pause after each conversation and ask questions such as, "What did she say? What did the man tell her?"
- Have students answer verbally using reported speech with *say* and *tell*.

EXPANSION ACTIVITY: The latest gossip

- Bring in copies of popular entertainment magazines that track the lives of celebrities.
- Put students into groups. Give each group one of the magazines.
- Have groups write reported speech statements about the goings-on of the stars. For example, *Madonna told the reporter that the rumors were false.*
- Call on students to share their sentences with the class, displaying the article in which they found the information. Encourage the class to ask follow-up questions about each celebrity.

5 TALK with a partner. Look at the sentences in Activity 3. What should Mia do to fix each problem? Write your partner's answers. Then tell another classmate what your partner said.

- Go over the directions and the example.
- Put students in pairs to discuss how to fix the problems.
- Have students tell their partner's ideas to another classmate.
- Go over solutions to each problem as a class.

MATH: Subtracting Decimals

A. READ the chart below. It shows that in Westfield accidents decreased from 1988 to 2008 because of new technologies and safety measures. Calculate the decrease from 1988. Subtract the 2008 number for each category.

- Go over the directions, example, and chart.
- Have students complete the questions individually.
- Go over the answers as a class. Work the problems on the board as needed to demonstrate the steps.

ANSWER KEY

1. 0.60; **2.** 3.56; **3.** 0.06; **4.** 3.99; **5.** 0.40

B. CALCULATE. Which category had the largest decrease?

- Go over the directions.
- Have students answer the question.

ANSWER KEY

Burns from Fire

EXPANSION ACTIVITY: Math practice

- Have students write an amount of money under 100 dollars, including change, on slips of paper.
- Put the slips of paper into a paper bag.
- Have students draw out two slips of paper and create a subtraction problem based on the two numbers. Write each unsolved problem on the board.
- Have students solve the problems individually.
- Go over the answers as a class.

COMMUNITY CONNECTION: Home safety programs

- Have students find out about organizations in the community that help people learn about home safety. Students may wish to do an Internet search to find such groups or organizations.
- Have students visit an organization to find out about the information it offers to the community. What audience does each organization target and why?
- Have students report back to the class, showing any brochures or other information they obtained while explaining what the organization does to improve home safety in the community.

LESSON 3: Listening and Conversation

OBJECTIVES

Take a phone message
Role-play a conversation

COMPETENCY

Take steps to prevent accidents in the home

WARM-UP ACTIVITY: Fire drill!

- Have students discuss the building where your class takes place. If there were a fire, what would be the safest route out of the building? What features could help or hinder people trying to exit the building? List students' ideas on the board.

- Have students search the building to find out whether evacuation routes are posted in the event of fire or other emergencies. Discuss whether the routes they proposed matched those of the evacuation plan. What was different? Did students forget any important information when planning their route?

 1 **LISTEN** to the conversation. Then listen
TCD4, to the question. Fill in the correct answer.
4–9 Replay each item if necessary.

- Direct students' attention to the answer sheet.
- Play the CD and have students fill in the correct circle for each item.
- Put students in pairs to compare answers.
- Go over the answers with the class.

 LISTENING SCRIPT
Lesson 3, Activity 1
TCD1, 11

1. *A:* Do you have electric heat in your house?
   B: No, we use a kerosene heater.
   A: You need a carbon monoxide detector.

Which is correct?
   A. She told him he needed a smoke detector.
   B. He told her he had a carbon monoxide detector.
   C. She said he needed a carbon monoxide detector.

2. *A:* Does your family practice fire drills?
   B: Yes, we practice twice a year.

Which is correct?
   A. She told him her family practiced twice a year.
   B. He told her she needed to practice fire drills.
   C. She told him he needed to practice fire drills twice a year.

3. *A:* Did you buy some cabinet locks?
   B: No, I didn't have time. I'll buy them tomorrow.

Which is correct?
   A. He told her she needed to buy cabinet locks tomorrow.
   B. He told her he'd buy cabinet locks tomorrow.
   C. She told him she would buy cabinet locks tomorrow.

4. *A:* I think the smoke detector is broken.
   B: No, it isn't. It just needs a new battery.

Which is correct?
   A. He told her that he had to put a new battery in the smoke detector.
   B. She told him that the smoke detector needed a new battery.
   C. She told him that the smoke detector was broken.

5. *A:* I can't find the bathroom cleanser. Did you move it?
   B: I put all the toxic cleansers in a high cabinet.
   A: Oh, that's a good idea.

Which is correct?
   A. She told him she put the bathroom cleanser in a high cabinet.
   B. He told her he put the toxic cleansers in a high cabinet.
   C. He told her she should move the toxic cleansers.

6. *A:* We need a new child-safety gate.
   B: I can buy one tomorrow on my way home from work.
   A: That would be great. Thanks.

Which is correct?

   A. She told him that they needed a new child-safety gate.

   B. He told her that he bought a child-safety gate.

   C. She told him that she could buy a child-safety gate tomorrow.

ANSWER KEY

1. C;   2. A;   3. B;   4. B;   5. B;   6. C

 2 LISTEN to the conversation. Then circle the correct words to complete the message slip.

- Go over the directions.
- Play the CD and have students circle the answers they hear.
- Put students in pairs to check their answers.
- Go over the answers with the class.

 LISTENING SCRIPT
Lesson 3, Activities 2 and 3

Laura: Brown and Miller. This is Laura speaking.

Jack: Hi, Laura. It's Jack.

Laura: Hi, Jack. Are you coming to work today?

Jack: No, I'm not. That's why I'm calling. I fell this morning and broke my ankle.

Laura: Oh no! How did you fall?

Jack: I tripped on some toys on the stairs.

Laura: That's terrible. Are you feeling okay?

Jack: It hurts a lot, but I'll be fine.

Laura: Are you at home now? Do you need a ride to the hospital?

Jack: No, I'm at the hospital now. Mia drove me here. Will you let Stan know what happened?

Laura: Sure, I'll give him the message. Well, take it easy, and I'll call you later to find out how you're doing.

ANSWER KEY

1. Stan;   2. Jack;   3. isn't coming to work;
4. broke;   5. the hospital;   6. call

EXPANSION ACTIVITY: Take a message

- Distribute one message sheet (like the one pictured in Activity 2) to each student in the class.
- Have students role-play, following the model they heard in Activity 2. Partner A should make up new reasons that he or she will be late or will miss class. Partner B should write a message to the teacher on the memo.
- Have students switch roles and do the exercise a second time.
- Call on volunteers to report what their partner said.

3 LISTEN again to the conversation between Laura and Jack. Then complete the following conversation between Laura and her boss, Stan.

- Go over the directions and the example. Point out that students may need to supply more words than just the verbs in parentheses.
- Play the CD and have students complete the exercise.
- Put students in pairs to check their answers.
- Call on volunteers to read their completed sentences.

ANSWER KEY

1. wasn't coming;   2. fell and broke;   3. tripped;
4. was;   5. drove;   6. would call

EXPANSION ACTIVITY: At the hospital

- Have students imagine that they are Jack. He is at the hospital with Mia.
- Put students in pairs. Ask each pair to write a dialogue between Jack and Mia. In the dialogue, Jack should tell Mia about his phone conversation with Laura.
- Have each pair present their dialogue to the class.

4 LISTEN to the conversation.

TCD4, 11
SCD40

- Play the CD or read the conversation to the class.
- Answer any questions students may have about vocabulary from the conversation.

5 ROLE-PLAY. Imagine that you had these conversations with Linda and Jack. Then work with two classmates. Take turns telling each other what Linda and Jack said to you. Use the conversation in Activity 4 as a model.

- Go over the directions with students.
- Put students in pairs to practice the conversations.
- Have volunteers present conversations in front of the class.

6 WHAT ABOUT YOU? Talk with a partner. Tell each other three things you want to do to improve your home safety. Take notes about your partner's ideas.

- Go over the directions and the example.
- Put students in pairs and have them discuss their ideas and take notes.
- Have each student summarize their partner's ideas to make sure their information is correct.

7 TALK with a different partner and tell him or her what your partner in Activity 6 said. Use reported speech.

- Go over the directions and the example.
- Put students in new pairs to discuss what they learned in Activity 6.
- Have volunteers tell what they learned about their classmates.

EXPANSION ACTIVITY: Listening and speaking practice

- Put students in groups.
- Have each group imagine they are taking a tour of someone's home or apartment. Have students tell each other the safety hazards they "see" around the house. To increase participation, assign each student of the group a particular area of the house to report on (kitchen, garage, living room, etc.).
- Have one group member take notes on the safety hazards.
- Discuss with the class the different safety hazards that people imagined. Were there any unusual hazards?

ACADEMIC CONNECTION: School safety

- Have an administrator from your school visit the classroom to tell your students about safety precautions that are in place at the school. Record the discussion on video or audiotape if possible. Encourage students to ask questions.
- After the administrator has finished speaking, put students in groups to write questions about what they heard. For example, *What did Ms. Hunt say about the elevator?*
- Have groups exchange papers and answer each other's questions.
- Go over the answers as a class. Play back the video or audiotape to check answers as needed.

CULTURE NOTE

Tell students about laws that ensure public safety in your school and your community. Some topics you may wish to discuss are fire safety, prohibition of firearms, traffic laws, and so forth.

LESSON 4: Grammar and Vocabulary

OBJECTIVES

Read about health concerns
Phrasal verbs

VOCABULARY

find out about	pay off
follow through with	sign up
give up	think over

GRAMMAR

Phrasal verbs

COMPETENCIES

Talk about healthy practices
Make wise decisions

WARM-UP ACTIVITY: At the gym

- Have students brainstorm a list of activities that people do at the gym. Write their ideas on the board.
- Go over each activity and take a poll of how many students enjoy or do the activity regularly. Find out which activity is most popular and which activities nobody has tried.

🎧 **1 GRAMMAR PICTURE DICTIONARY.**
TCD4,12
SCD41   What did this man do for his health? Listen and read.

- Have students look at the pictures. Ask: *Who are the people? What is each person doing?*
- Play the CD or read the sentences aloud as students follow along silently.
- Call on students and ask questions about the people in the picture: *Where is the man? How does the man probably feel? What are the other people in the picture doing?* If appropriate, encourage students to use the list on the board from the warm-up activity.

2 READ the sentences in Activity 1 with a partner.

- Go over the directions.
- Put students in pairs to read the sentences.
- Call on students to read the sentences aloud to the class.

3 NOTICE THE GRAMMAR. Match the phrasal verbs with the words that have the same meaning.

- Go over the directions.
- Have students complete the exercise.
- Go over the answers with the class.

ANSWER KEY

1. d; 2. f; 3. b; 4. c; 5. a; 6. e

BIG PICTURE READING EXPANSION ACTIVITY: At the Community Center

- Photocopy and distribute Worksheet 28: *At the Community Center.*
- Put the transparency for Unit 10 on the OHP or have students look at the Big Picture on page 152.
- Have students read the dialogue and complete the questions.
- Put students in pairs to compare their answers.
- Go over the answers with the class.

WORKSHEET ANSWER KEY

1. The Home Safety course is on Saturday.
2. Rick thinks his home is safe enough, and he wants to relax on Saturday.
3. "right at that moment"; "right there"
4. Doris suggests that Rick bring his kids to the pool at the community center.

ACADEMIC NOTE

Explain to students that some phrasal verbs are used more in conversation than in writing and would not be appropriate for a formal document such as a business letter or an academic paper. For example, a business invitation would not invite participants to "show up" at 10:00; it would invite them to "arrive" at 10:00. If desired, review the list of phrasal verbs from this lesson and discuss whether each one should be used formally, informally, or in either context.

GRAMMAR CHART: Phrasal verbs

- Go over the information in the chart.
- Read the sample sentences in the charts and have students repeat.

CHART EXPANSION ACTIVITY: Writing sentences

- Challenge students in pairs to write a new sentence for each phrasal verb listed in the chart.
- Have volunteers present examples of each phrasal verb. Have the class decide whether each sentence used the phrasal verb correctly in terms of both meaning and mechanics.

4 COMPLETE. Read the sentences. Then complete each sentence with the words in parentheses and the correct particle. Pay attention to word order. When you are finished, ask and answer the questions with a partner.

- Go over the directions and the example.
- Have students complete the exercise using the cues provided.
- Put students in pairs to check their work. Tell students that they will ask and answer questions in the next activity.
- Go over the answers as a class.

ANSWER KEY

1. talked you into; **2.** look up phone numbers/ look phone numbers up; **3.** count on your friends; **4.** find out about events; **5.** fallen for a story

5 WHAT ABOUT YOU? Ask and answer the questions in Activity 4 with a partner.

- Go over the directions. Give an example from personal experience if needed.
- Have partners ask and answer the questions from Activity 4.
- Have volunteers tell about their partner's responses to the questions.

COMMUNITY CONNECTION: At the gym, Part 2

- Have students visit an athletic club, gym, or community center in their neighborhood.
- Students should prepare in advance 3 to 5 questions they want to ask, such as: *How many people can sign up for each class? Where can I find out about how to lift weights safely? Why do people have trouble following through with their exercise goals?* Encourage students to use phrasal verbs in their questions.
- Have students use their questions to interview a person who works at the gym, such as an administrator, a personal trainer, or a class instructor. Instruct students to take notes during the interview.
- Have students report what they learned to the class. Encourage discussion about interesting topics that may arise.

LESSON 5: Grammar Practice Plus

OBJECTIVES

Write and pronounce *used to* and
  be + used to

VOCABULARY

be used to   look forward to
drop out   miss out on
grow up   turn down

GRAMMAR

Used to, be used to

PRONUNCIATION

Used to and *be used to*

COMPETENCY

Understand information about health
  management

WARM-UP ACTIVITY: I used to . . .

- On the board, write the following phrase: *When I was a kid, I used to . . .*

- Have students form a circle. Begin by stating the phrase and completing it, using an activity from your childhood. For example: *When I was a kid, I used to fly kites.*

- The next student should complete the phrase and add to it the response that you gave: *When I was a kid, I used to play baseball. (Teacher's name) used to fly kites.* Continue around the circle, with each student completing the phrase and adding on all of the phrases that came before. See if the class can make it all the way around the circle and remember everyone's contribution. For larger classes, you may wish to have students say only their own statement and that of the previous person.

GRAMMAR CHART: *Used to, be used to*

- Go over the information in the chart, including the Grammar Professor note.

- Read the sample sentences in the charts and have students repeat.

CHART EXPANSION ACTIVITY: That's not right!

- Based on the information you learned in the warm-up activity, make an incorrect statement about a student in the class. For example: "Ricardo used to play basketball."

- Have volunteers correct each statement by responding in this manner: "That's not right! Ricardo used to play baseball."

- Alternatively, volunteers can make statements for their peers to correct. Whoever corrects a statement gets to give the next statement to the class.

GRAMMAR NOTE

Point out to students that people often substitute *would* for *used to* when referring to a specific time in the past. For example: "When Ricardo was a kid, he would play basketball every afternoon."

1 READ the paragraphs below. Fill in each blank with *used to, didn't use to, be + used to,* or *be + not used to*.

- Go over the directions.
- Have students complete the exercise.
- Put students in pairs to compare their answers.
- Go over the answers with the class.

ANSWER KEY

used to; didn't use to; used to; used to; wasn't used to; used to; am used to

EXPANSION ACTIVITY: We're used to it

- Follow the same procedure used in the warm-up activity to play a new version of the circle game. On the board, write: *I don't like _____, but I'm used to it.*
- Complete the phrase using a personal example, such as *I don't like getting up at 6:00, but I'm used to it.*
- Have the next student complete the phrase and add your response, altering the language like this: *I don't like studying calculus, and (teacher's name) doesn't like getting up at 6:00, but we're used to it.*

2 VOCABULARY. Find and underline the phrasal verbs below in the paragraph in Activity 1. Then match each phrasal verb with the correct definition.

- Go over the directions.
- Have students underline the phrasal verbs and complete the matching exercise.
- Put students in pairs to compare answers.
- Go over the answers with the class.

ANSWER KEY

Students should underline the phrasal verbs *miss out on, drop out, grow up, turn down,* and *look forward to* in the paragraph from Activity 1.
1. d.; **2.** e; **3.** b; **4.** c; **5.** a

3 WRITE each phrasal verb from Activity 1 in the correct place in the chart below.

- Go over the directions.
- Have students complete the chart.
- Elicit answers from volunteers.

ANSWER KEY

Separable: talked (me) into, signed (someone) up, turn (it) down
Inseparable: missed out on, dropped out, found out, grow up, look forward to

 PRONUNCIATION: *Used to* and *be used to*

- Go over the information and examples in the box.

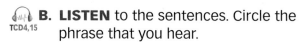 **A.**

- Read the information for Activity A.
- Play the CD. Have students listen and repeat each phrase.

B. LISTEN to the sentences. Circle the phrase that you hear.

- Go over the directions.
- Play the CD. Have students complete the exercise.
- Go over the answers as a class.

ANSWER KEY

1. I'm not used to; **2.** I used to; **3.** I didn't use to; **4.** I'm used to; **5.** I used to; **6.** I'm not used to

 LISTENING SCRIPT
Lesson 5, Pronunciation Activity B

1. I'm not used to my new job yet.
2. I used to drink four cups of coffee a day, but now I have only one cup a day.
3. I didn't use to like vegetables when I was young.
4. I'm used to getting up early because I have a two-year-old son.
5. I used to take a walk at lunch every day when I worked downtown.
6. I'm not used to cooking for myself. I usually eat out.

4 LISTEN and complete the chart below. Check the correct column for each item.

- Go over the directions and the example.
- Play the CD and have students complete the chart.
- Have partners compare their answers with each other.
- Go over the answers as a class.

LISTENING SCRIPT
Lesson 5, Activity 4

TCD4, 16

When I was in college, I used to exercise every day. I went to the gym every morning, and my friends could always count on me to play basketball or soccer with them in the afternoons. I used to be in really great shape. But now, I'm about 30 pounds overweight. I'm not used to taking care of myself anymore. Instead, I'm used to eating fast food for dinner and watching TV every night. I started a diet three months ago, but I didn't follow through with it. I gave up after a week. I tried to go jogging last week, but I'm not used to exercising anymore. I got tired after three minutes! I used to be able to run five miles without getting tired! I need to get back in shape. I just signed up with the gym in my neighborhood, and I'm going to start exercising three days a week starting tomorrow. Well, maybe I'll start next Monday.

ANSWER KEY

1. Past; **2.** Past; **3.** Past; **4.** Present;
5. Present; **6.** Past; **7.** Present

5 **WHAT ABOUT YOU?** Complete the sentences below with *used to, didn't use to, am used to,* or *am not used to* to make them true about yourself.

- Go over the directions and model an example if needed.
- Have students complete the sentences.
- Have volunteers share their sentences with the class.

EXPANSION ACTIVITY: Compare and contrast

- Put students in pairs and groups.
- Have groups create two lists related to their current schoolwork: what it was like before their classes began (past), and what their situation is like now (present).

- Encourage groups to write statements similar to what they heard in Activity 4, such as: *Before I started taking night classes, I used to watch TV every night. Now I don't have the time. I'm not used to giving up my favorite shows!*
- Have volunteers share their writing with the class. Discuss whether groups came up with similar ideas or different ones.

ACADEMIC CONNECTION: Today's curriculum

- Bring to class a variety of outdated textbooks for learning English. Many of these can be found in the reference section of the library, or you may have some of your own that you can bring from home.
- Lead a discussion about the students' second-language learning experiences as children in school. How were language classes taught differently many years ago compared to how they are taught today? Write students' ideas on the board.
- Put students in pairs and ask each pair to compare one of the outdated textbooks with their current textbook. Have pairs analyze what has changed about the nature of teaching and learning English, based on their comparison of the books.
- Have volunteers present their ideas to the class and compare what they discovered to the list of ideas brainstormed on the board.
- Have each student write a reflective paragraph or essay about whether new teaching and learning techniques have helped him or her. What practices have helped the most? What practices from earlier years are still valid today?

LESSON 6: Reading

OBJECTIVES

Read and write specific medical information

READING FOCUS

Use context to guess the meaning of new words

VOCABULARY

advertisement

COMPETENCIES

Identify problems related to smoking
Understand product safety labels

WARM-UP ACTIVITY: Medications

- Have students brainstorm common medications that they know about or have at home. List their ideas on the board.

- Discuss what side effects the medications have. If students are unsure, have them find out and report this information in the next class.

1 THINK ABOUT IT. When your doctor gives you a new medication, what questions do you ask him or her? Write your ideas here.

- Go over the directions.

- Have students write their ideas on the lines.

- Ask volunteers to share their ideas with the class. Lead a discussion about interesting points that arise.

EXPANSION ACTIVITY: Medication versus natural remedies

- Ask students their opinion on taking medications versus using homeopathic remedies to cure their ills. Have students give examples of natural remedies that are used in their home countries or cultures.

- Have students do Internet research about the natural remedies they've suggested to find out if there is any scientific basis behind each one.

- Ask volunteers to present what they discovered in their research.

2 BEFORE YOU READ. Preview the advertisement. Look at the picture and the different parts of the advertisement. What product is advertised?

- Go over the directions and point out the Reading Strategy Summary box.

- Have students preview the brochure.

- Put students in pairs to tell their ideas to one another.

- Elicit ideas from the class.

3 READ the advertisement on the next page. Did you correctly guess what the advertisement is about?

- Direct students' attention to the Reading Focus box. Go over the information in it.

- Go over the directions. Point out that starred words are defined in the glossary below the article.

- Have students read the selection.

- Discuss whether students correctly predicted what the advertisement was about.

EXPANSION ACTIVITY: Glossary words

- Have volunteers read aloud the words and definitions in the glossary below the advertisement. Explain unclear words.

- Have students write sentences using the new words.

- Ask volunteers to read their sentences, replacing each glossary word with a nonsense word such as *blork*. Have the class guess from the context which glossary word completes the sentence.

❹ AFTER YOU READ.

A. ANSWER the questions with a partner.

- Go over the directions.
- Have partners answer the questions, referring to the advertisement as needed.
- Go over the answers with the class.

ANSWER KEY

1. Fumenol; **2.** quitting smoking; **3.** He had a heart attack.; **4.** He should try Fumenol.; **5.** three times per day; **6.** nausea, dizziness, or tiredness; **7.** rash, itching, swelling, and shortness of breath

B. REREAD the advertisement and underline any words you do not know. With a partner, choose five words from the advertisement. Write them below, and use the context to guess the meaning of each word. Write your guesses below. Then use a dictionary to look up the word and find out if you were correct.

- Go over the directions. Point out that students should not choose words that are glossed below the advertisement.
- Have partners complete the exercise and use a dictionary to check their work.
- Ask volunteers to tell about the words they chose and whether they correctly guessed the meaning using context from the advertisement.

EXPANSION ACTIVITY: Medicines in the news

- Have students perform an Internet search on medications that have recently made the headlines, either for positive or negative reasons. Have names of medications ready to suggest in case students have difficulty with the task.

- Have students print out articles about the medications. Put students in groups and give each group one article to review.
- Have each group present what they learned from the article to the class. Lead a discussion of interesting points.

BIG PICTURE VOCABULARY EXPANSION ACTIVITY: Vocabulary Practice

- Photocopy and distribute Worksheet 29: *Vocabulary Practice* and go over the directions.
- Put the transparency for Unit 10 on the OHP or have students look at the Big Picture on page 152.
- Have students complete the worksheet.
- Put students in pairs to compare their answers.
- Go over the answers with the class.

WORKSHEET ANSWER KEY

1. dozen; **2.** rash; **3.** dizziness; **4.** swelling; **5.** advice; **6.** lifestyle

COMMUNITY CONNECTION: At the pharmacy

- Have students set up a brief interview with a pharmacist in their neighborhood.
- Before the interview, have students prepare 3 to 5 questions about medications that they would like to ask the pharmacist. For example, *What common mistakes do people make when taking medication? Why don't people take medications the way they are supposed to?* Help students create questions as needed.
- Have students report to the class what they learned from the pharmacists. Discuss any important or interesting issues that are brought up.

LESSON 7: Writing

WRITING FOCUS

Identify problems and solutions

COMPETENCIES

Use language to give advice
Identify positive ways of changing habits

❶ **WARM UP.** Every January, people make New Year's resolutions, or promises to themselves. These promises are often about a healthier lifestyle. Have you ever made a New Year's resolution about your health? What was it?

- Go over the questions asked for this activity.
- Have students discuss the questions and tell about resolutions they have made in the past.

❷ **BEFORE YOU WRITE.**

A. THINK about health habits that people often want to change. Make notes about ways that people can improve their health.

- Go over the directions, the column headers, and the examples.
- Have students complete the chart.
- Put students in pairs to share their ideas.
- Have volunteers talk about the ideas they wrote down. If students disagree, have them support their opinion.

B. WRITE. Imagine that a friend (or family member) wants to live a healthier lifestyle. He or she asks for your advice. Write your ideas in the chart. Give several suggestions.

- Go over the directions, the column headers, and the examples. Point out that the examples are written as if the person is speaking to his or her friend.
- Have students fill out the chart. Encourage them to write additional ideas and advice in their notebooks.
- Call on students to share what they wrote with the class.

C. READ the New Year's resolution that Victor wrote. Underline the sentences that answer these questions: What? Why? How?

- Go over the directions.
- Have students read the selection and underline the appropriate sentences.
- Put students in pairs to compare what they underlined.
- Go over the answers as a class.

ANSWER KEY

Students should underline the following:

What: This year, I must exercise more.

Why: I can't do all the things I used to do.

How: My doctor said that I should sign up for the gym.

❸ **WRITE** three New Year's resolutions about your own health. Follow the steps below.

- Direct students' attention to the Writing Focus box. Go over the information in it.
- Go over the directions and the column headers. Point out to students that they can use the chart from Activity 2 as a model if needed.
- Have students complete the chart. For students who do not wish to write about their personal health, allow them to choose a different topic for writing their resolutions.

Tell students that discussing health problems can be a sticky issue in American society. In many places (especially the workplace), discussing health problems may be taboo or even prohibited. As an example, tell students that potential employers are not allowed to ask questions about a person's health status during an interview. Among friends and acquaintances, however, it is common to discuss health problems—sometimes to a degree of detail that may make your students feel uncomfortable if they are not used to hearing such things discussed openly. Give advice on the types of health questions students should ask friends and acquaintances, and point out that even if someone asks, one is never obliged to discuss his or her private health concerns.

EXPANSION ACTIVITY: World resolutions

• Have students imagine that they could write resolutions for the entire world population. Ask them to think about what resolutions they would like to see come true, and then have them make notes. For example: *We (the people of the world) resolve to stop developing nuclear weapons.*

• Call on volunteers to share the resolutions they wrote with the class. How many students wrote similar resolutions?

4 AFTER YOU WRITE.

A. EDIT your paragraphs. Ask yourself these questions.

• Go over the questions.
• Have students look at their writing and make changes if necessary.
• Put students in pairs to review each other's paragraphs, answering the questions about their partner's writing.

B. REWRITE your paragraphs with corrections.

• Have students rewrite their paragraphs with the necessary corrections.

C. DISCUSS your work with a partner. Read each other's resolutions. Then ask and answer questions about each other's ideas.

• Go over the directions.
• Put students in pairs with a new partner.
• Have students discuss the resolutions they wrote.
• Ask volunteers to share what they wrote and discussed. Lead a class discussion about interesting topics that arise.

EXPANSION ACTIVITY: Internet research

• Lead a discussion about the kinds of resolutions students have discussed during the lessons of Unit 10.

• Have students do an Internet search on the most popular resolutions that people make. Are there any resolutions that the class didn't think of? Examples: volunteer more, get out of debt, spend more time with family, and so on.

• Have each student present one hope or goal that they would like to achieve in the upcoming year.

ACADEMIC CONNECTION: Persuasive writing

- Remind students that the Writing Focus for Unit 10 is identifying problems and solutions. Point out that in persuasive essays and speeches, the problem-solution structure is often used to sway the audience to the author's point of view.

- Put students in small groups. Give each group an example of a persuasive essay that uses the problem-solution structure.

- Have groups analyze the essay by identifying each problem and solution, circling transition words or conjunctions that join the two together, and so on. Have students rate how effective the essay's argument is based on whether the problems are factual (versus a matter of opinion) and whether the solutions are realistic and well-explained. Does each solution offer enough detail to persuade the reader?

- Pair up groups in a Writing Workshop. Have each group tell the other about their essay and its strengths and flaws.

- As a class, discuss the general strengths and flaws that students discovered in the essays. What were the traits of an effective essay?

BIG PICTURE WRITING EXPANSION ACTIVITY: Poison control

- Put the transparency for Unit 10 on the OHP or have students look at the Big Picture on page 152.

- Remind students that in the picture, the children are able to reach the toxic cleansers under the sink.

- Divide students into groups. Have groups research on the Internet information about poison control. Topics to assign may include: poison prevention; common poisonous substances in the home; what to do if a person accidentally ingests a toxic substance such as those in household cleansers; statistics on household poisonings; and so on.

- Have groups create a brochure that tells what to do in the event of accidental poisoning. Direct groups to use a problem-solution structure to present their information.

- Allow groups to present their brochures to the class, and then display them in a prominent place. You may wish to have students publish and distribute their brochures in the community.

Career Connection

OBJECTIVES

Read an online application

COMPETENCIES

Interpret an online job application
Identify job skills
Practice test-taking skills

WARM-UP ACTIVITY: Around the hospital

- Have students brainstorm things and people that you see at a hospital. Ask questions to elicit the names of different departments, if possible. List student responses on the board.
- Have students choose a word from the board and make a sentence that tells how that person or thing makes them feel. For example, *An emergency room makes me nervous.*

1 THINK ABOUT IT. What kinds of things do nurses do at a hospital? What kinds of skills do you think a nurse has that can transfer to other departments in a hospital or private doctor's office?

- Go over the questions with the students.
- Have students name and discuss the skills that nurses have.
- Lead a discussion about how these skills might transfer to other settings.

BIG PICTURE LISTENING EXPANSION ACTIVITY: Winter safety

- Photocopy and distribute Worksheet 30: *Winter Safety.*
- Put the transparency for Unit 10 on the OHP or have students look at the Big Picture on page 152.
- Have students look at the Big Picture and predict what kind of hazards the family might face during the winter.

- Go over the directions and the graphic organizer on the worksheet. Tell students that they are going to hear a nurse talking about winter safety hazards around the home.
- Read the script for the worksheet. Have students fill out the graphic organizer using information from the listening.
- Put students in pairs to compare their answers.
- Reread the script to have students check their work. Go over the answers with the class.

LISTENING SCRIPT
Worksheet 30

In a typical family home, there are many safety hazards for you, your children, and your pets. I'm sure most of you know about using child safety gates, keeping toxic cleansers away from children, and using electrical outlets safely. But there are many other safety hazards to look out for during the winter—especially during the holidays.

It may be surprising to think about, but food can be a big safety hazard around the home. If you have a holiday party, make sure to refrigerate leftovers immediately, especially meats and foods that contain dairy products. Foods that aren't properly stored may harbor bacteria that can make you very sick. If you've ever had food poisoning, you know it isn't pleasant: nausea, abdominal cramps, vomiting, and diarrhea are only some of the symptoms caused by food poisoning. Beyond proper food storage, be aware that holiday treats such as nuts and candies may be choking hazards for children, so keep them out of reach.

Holiday decorations can be a hazard, too. Decorated trees can be lovely, but make sure kids and pets can't reach your decorations. Tinsel and icicles are choking hazards. Ornaments and lights can easily break and might cut your children or pets.

How many of you love filling your house with holiday plants? I know I do! But be careful that holiday plants are kept out of the reach of children and pets. Holly and mistletoe are both poisonous, especially mistletoe berries. Kids who eat mistletoe may get blurry vision, throw up, have diarrhea, or even have convulsions.

Don't forget to take care of man's best friend during the holidays, too. We all leave out dishes of treats during the holidays—like chocolate. But make sure your kids know not to feed any chocolate to your dog. Chocolate can be toxic for dogs. For a small dog, as little as two ounces of baker's chocolate can cause serious harm. Chocolate can cause vomiting, diarrhea, and increased heart rate, and it can make your dog overexcited. Put chocolates out of reach of children and pets, and be sure to put away chocolate supplies after you've finished baking those holiday cookies.

WORKSHEET ANSWER KEY

Safety Hazard	Problems it can cause	How to prevent problems
Food	Nausea, abdominal cramps, vomiting, diarrhea	Refrigerate foods after eating; keep treats out of children's reach
Decorations	Choking, cuts	Keep decorations out of reach of kids and pets
Plants	Blurry vision, throwing up, diarrhea, convulsions	Keep plants out of reach of kids and pets
Chocolate	In dogs: vomiting, diarrhea, increased heart rate, excitability	Tell children not to give dogs chocolate; keep chocolate out of reach

2 READ this online job advertisement and application form. Nina is applying for a case manager's position at Children's Hospital. As you read, match the numbered words to the correct definition.

- Go over the directions.
- Have students read the job advertisement and complete the matching exercise.
- Put students in pairs to compare answers.
- Go over the answers with the class.

ANSWER KEY

4 A.; 1 B.; 2 C.; 3 D.; 5 E.

EXPANSION ACTIVITY: Online applications

- Have students use the Internet to find and print out online applications for various jobs.
- Post the applications in the classroom and have students circulate to look at the different applications.
- Lead a discussion about the format of each application. Which fields are common to all applications? Which fields are specific only to certain kinds of jobs?
- Point out to students that many online job search sites allow users to complete and save their application information. This information can then be sent easily to any job postings from the website that students may wish to apply for.

3 WRITE. Compare three things from Nina's experience and qualifications to the job description in the advertisement. Do you think Nina's qualifications match those asked for in the job description?

- Go over the directions.
- Have students work in pairs or groups to complete the exercise. Have them write their ideas in their notebook.

- Call on students to tell which facts they wrote in their chart. Discuss whether the class thought Nina was qualified for the job.

4 ROLE-PLAY a scene between Nina and the hiring supervisor at Children's Hospital. Interview Nina. Ask her how her qualifications will transfer to this job.

- Go over the directions.
- Put students in pairs to practice the role-play. For students who find the role-play difficult, have them write down dialogue first and then practice it.
- Ask volunteers to present their role-plays to the class.

EXPANSION ACTIVITY: Watch and discuss
Record, rent, or borrow a video from an episode of a popular medical drama or a film that takes place in a hospital or other medical setting.

- Tell students that they will watch clips from the video.
- Preview vocabulary that students will hear in the video and write the names of the characters on the board as an aid to students.
- Play the video. Ask comprehension questions that prompt students to tell about the main events and characters.
- Play the video a second time so that students have a chance to deepen their understanding of what they've viewed.
- Lead a discussion about the video. Was the plot realistic? Would students have acted differently than the characters did?

EXPANSION ACTIVITY: Creative writing

- After discussing the video from the previous Expansion Activity, put students in groups.
- Have each group write a creative piece that follows up on the video. Students may write a narrative, a screenplay, or a piece in another format of their choice. Encourage students to write about what the characters might do next or what events might happen.
- Have each group present or act out their creative writing for the enjoyment of the class.

5 WHAT ABOUT YOU? What skills do you have from your previous experience or from your educational background that could transfer easily to a job you would like to have? Talk with a partner.

- Go over the questions.
- Put students in pairs to discuss the questions.
- Call on students to share their ideas with the class.

COMMUNITY CONNECTION: Nurse appreciation day

- Have students create greeting cards or posters that illustrate the important things that nurses do in their work. Have students write a paragraph on each card that tells why they appreciate nurses.

- Have students deliver their card or poster in person to a nurse that they know, or arrange a visit to a hospital, nursing facility, or other medical venue. As a class, present the cards and posters to the nurses who work there. Encourage students to give short speeches to the nurses, and if possible, arrange a question and answer session in which students can ask the nurses about their daily work. Be sure to take photos to document your Nurse Appreciation Day!

CHECK YOUR PROGRESS!

- Have students circle the answers.
- Have students check whether each answer is right or wrong.
- Have students total their correct answers and fill in the chart at the bottom of the page.
- Have students create a learning plan and/or set learning goals.

ANSWER KEY

1. had; 2. hadn't seen; 3. he; 4. my; 5. you into; 6. it up; 7. the exercises over; 8. on her; 9. handrails; 10. Outlet covers; 11. gas; 12. devices; 13. about; 14. up; 15. off; 16. follow through with

Unit Overview

LESSON	OBJECTIVES	STUDENT BOOK	WORKBOOK
1 Grammar and Vocabulary 1	Practice career communication. Real conditionals: Present and future.	p. 166	p. 146
2 Grammar Practice Plus	Talk about a job fair. Compare strengths and weaknesses.	p. 168	p. 147
3 Listening and Conversation	Rhythm of thought groups. Expressing agreement.	p. 170	p. 148
4 Grammar and Vocabulary 2	Listen to descriptions about careers. Present unreal conditional.	p. 172	p. 150
5 Grammar Practice Plus	Listen to communication about a job interview. Read a bar graph about job satisfaction.	p. 174	p. 151
6 Reading	Read tips on successful interviews. Make a T-chart to solve job problems.	p. 176	p. 152–153
7 Writing	Write notes about your past job achievements. Write a résumé.	p. 178	p. 154–155
• Career Connection	Listen to job interviews. Check your progress.	p. 180	p. 156
• Check Your Progress	Monitor progress.	p. 181	p. 158–159

Reading/Writing Strategies

• Identify problems and solutions   • Give specific details   • Use résumé style

Connection Activities

LESSON	TYPE	SKILL DEVELOPMENT
1	Academic	Understanding rhetoric
2	Community	Finding resources for job preparation
3	Academic	Reviewing educational goals
4	Community	Giving advice
5	Academic	Creating bar graphs
6	Community	Researching local businesses
7	Academic	Writing résumés
Career Connection	Community	Q&A with a guest speaker

WORKSHEET #/FOCUS	TITLE	TEACHER'S EDITION
31. Listening	The Interview	p. 335
32. Reading/Comprehension	An Unhappy Employee	p. 336
33. Grammar	Unreal Conditionals	p. 337

LESSON 1: Grammar and Vocabulary

VOCABULARY

build a stronger résumé	opportunities
conduct a job search	professional development
cover the costs	pursue
evaluate credentials	take steps
feedback	take the initiative
identify strengths and weaknesses	update a résumé

GRAMMAR

Real conditionals: present and future

COMPETENCIES

Use language to talk about careers
Understand the steps in applying for a job

WARM-UP ACTIVITY: Unit opener

- On the board, brainstorm with students a list of as many careers as they can think of. Circle five very different careers, such as *lawyer, police officer, bus driver, teacher,* and *landscaper*.

- Have students copy the circled careers and rank the jobs, according to which they would most and least like to do. Have them take notes telling why they would or wouldn't like the job.

- Lead a class discussion about the ranking results. Which career was most popular and why? Which was least popular and why?

1 GRAMMAR PICTURE DICTIONARY.
TCD4, 17
SCD43
What are people doing for their careers? Listen and read.

- Have students open their books and look at the pictures. Ask: *What do you see?* Write all the words the students say on the board.

- Say the sentences aloud or play the CD and have students repeat.

- Call on students and ask about the people in the pictures: *Where are the people? What is Carlos looking at? What are the man and woman doing?*

EXPANSION ACTIVITY: Vocabulary practice

- Review the vocabulary from the Grammar Picture Dictionary.

- Put students in pairs to write sentences using the vocabulary. Encourage students to use the vocabulary in different contexts if possible. For example: *The basketball player worked with the coach to identify her strengths and weaknesses.*

- Have volunteers share their sentences with the class.

2 PRACTICE the conversations in Activity 1 with a partner.

- Put students in pairs to read the sentences.

- Call on students to read the sentences to the class.

3 NOTICE THE GRAMMAR. Circle *if* and underline the clause that follows. What form is the verb: past, present, or future?

- Go over the directions.

- Have students circle *if* and underline the clauses.

- Put students in pairs to check their work.

- Go over the answers with the class.

1. (if) you look on some job websites
2. (if) he gets the résumé done tonight
3. (if) you bring your résumé to the career advisor
4. (if) I tell my boss about my idea; you tell her
5. (if) I identify my strengths and weaknesses
6. (if) I save money carefully

Verb form: present

GRAMMAR CHART: Real Conditionals: Present and Future

- Direct students' attention to the chart or project the transparency or play the CD.
- Go over the information, including the usage notes.
- Read the sentences, pausing to have students repeat.

CHART EXPANSION ACTIVITY: Reverse sentences

- Have students rewrite the sentences in the chart in the reverse order: main clause first, *if*-clause last. Note that students will need to change the subjects of some clauses. (Melissa *finishes her tasks quickly if* she *works hard.*)
- Have students exchange papers to check their work.
- Go over the answers with the class, emphasizing that no commas are needed between the clauses when this sentence structure is used.

4 MATCH the clauses to make sentences.

- Go over the directions and the example. Point out the two columns.
- Have students complete the exercise.
- Call on students to give the answers.

ANSWER KEY

1. d; **2.** f; **3.** e; **4.** a; **5.** c; **6.** b

5 WHAT ABOUT YOU? Complete the sentences about you. Then talk with a partner.

- Go over the directions.
- Have the students complete the sentences.
- Call on volunteers to tell the class one or two of the sentences they wrote.

EXPANSION ACTIVITY: Classmate conditionals

- On slips of paper, write several imaginative *if*-clauses with the subject omitted, such as *If _____ won the lottery, If _____ had a hot air balloon,* and so on. Make one slip of paper for each student in the class.
- Have the first student draw one of the slips from a bag. Tell him or her to read the clause, filling in the blank with the name of a classmate and completing the sentence.
- The student whose name was used in the previous sentence takes the next turn, continuing until everyone in class has participated.

ACADEMIC CONNECTION: Rhetoric

- Introduce the concept of rhetoric to students, explaining that writing and speaking for specific purposes often involves particular language.
- Point out that real conditionals are often used in persuasive speeches, such as in sermons, proverbs, or politics. Give quotes to illustrate this point, such as the Chinese proverb: "If you are patient in one moment of anger, you will escape a hundred days of sorrow."
- On the board, write Benjamin Franklin's quote: We must hang together, or surely we shall hang separately." Have students rewrite the quote using the real conditional.

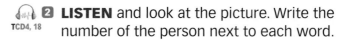

LESSON 2: Grammar Practice Plus

Talk about a job fair
Compare strengths and weaknesses

VOCABULARY

assertive	prepared
demanding	professional
impressed	sloppy

COMPETENCIES

Learn about a source of information for jobs
Talk about job-related personal strengths
  and weaknesses

WARM-UP ACTIVITY: First impressions

- On the board, write the saying: "You never get a second chance to make a first impression."

- Ask students what they think this quote means. Discuss ways in which people make good and bad first impressions.

1 TALK about the people at the job fair. What are they doing?

- Elicit ideas from the students. Help them identify cue words and other clues in the picture.

- Ask questions and encourage students to describe what they see.

TCD4, 18 **2 LISTEN** and look at the picture. Write the number of the person next to each word.

- Go over the directions and the words listed.

- Play the CD and have students write the correct number next to each word.

- Go over the answers with the class.

LISTENING SCRIPT
Lesson 2, Activity 2
TCD4, 18

1. Luis is very demanding of his employees. He expects a lot of them and gets upset if they make mistakes.

2. Jana is very professional. She does a good job with her work. She's punctual and has good training.

3. Allison works for the company. She is impressed by Kent.

4. Maria is prepared for her interview. She has her résumé, business card, and references.

5. Kirk is sloppy. He looks disorganized and his clothes don't look clean. He might have a hard time getting an interview.

6. Kent is assertive. He's not afraid to do new things or meet new people. He is confident about himself.

ANSWER KEY

6 assertive; **1** demanding; **3** impressed;
4 prepared; **2** professional; **5** sloppy

CULTURE NOTE

Talk to students about how assertiveness is viewed in the United States. In the business world, most people think of assertiveness as a positive quality—up to a certain point (after which assertiveness becomes pushiness or aggressiveness). Ask students how assertiveness is viewed in their home countries or cultures. Is it okay to be assertive with the boss? Can a woman be as assertive as a man? Is assertiveness a cultural taboo, and if so, what approach works best? Lead a discussion on these and other questions that arise.

3 WRITE the words from Activity 2 next to their meanings.

- Go over the directions and the example.
- Have students complete the exercise.
- Put students in pairs to compare their answers.
- Call on volunteers to read each word and its definition aloud.

ANSWER KEY

1. prepared; **2.** assertive; **3.** demanding;
4. sloppy; **5.** impressed; **6.** professional

BIG PICTURE LISTENING EXPANSION ACTIVITY: The Interview

- Photocopy and distribute Worksheet 31: *The Interview.*
- Project the transparency for Unit 11 or have students look at the Big Picture on page 168.
- Go over the directions and the questions on the worksheet. Preview any vocabulary or concepts that students may not know from the listening script, such as *computer programmer* or *internship*, or the idiom *chew out.*

- Read the script for the worksheet.
- Put students in pairs to write answers to the questions.
- Read the script again and have students listen to compare their answers.
- Go over the answers with the class.

LISTENING SCRIPT
Worksheet 31

Allison: So, Kent, I understand that you've just graduated from college, is that right?

Kent: Yes, it is. I just finished last month, and I'm definitely ready to take on my first job as a computer programmer.

Allison: Well, being a programmer may sound exciting, but it's not all that glamorous, actually. It's a very hard job to do, and our boss can be quite demanding.

Kent: I'm not worried about that. I know I'll love the job because I've already done an internship in a software company. The deadlines were crazy! You really have to be prepared.

Allison: True, very true. Well, I'm impressed! Tell me more about your internship.

Kent: Sure. You know, I have to admit that I didn't know what I was doing for the first few weeks. Some of my programming was sloppy, and the boss chewed me out once for not checking my work. I definitely learned a lot about what *not* to do, but I guess that's what internships are for, right?

Allison: (laughs) That's true. And the company can't complain much if you're working for free, either.

Kent: Something else I learned in the internship is how much I love working on a team. It's exciting to meet new people and try new things. One time, I had to conduct a meeting because the team leader got sick. I felt prepared, and it was a great experience for me.

Allison: That was very professional of you!

> *Kent:* I like to try new things like that, just for the experience. That's how you learn, by trying.
>
> *Allison:* That's fantastic, Kent. Thank you for coming to the job fair. We'll be in touch with you soon.
>
> *Kent:* You're welcome. Thanks for interviewing me.

WORKSHEET ANSWER KEY

1. Allison
2. computer programmer
3. He can be quite demanding.
4. He already had an internship in a software company.
5. His programming was sloppy and the boss chewed him out for not checking his work.
6. He loves it.
7. meet new people and try new things
8. his team leader got sick
9. Kent means that you learn by doing new things you've never done before.
10. Allison ends the interview by thanking Kent and telling him that she will be in touch.

4 COMPLETE the sentences with the vocabulary from Activity 2.

- Go over the directions and the example.
- Have students complete the sentences.
- Put students in pairs to compare answers.
- Go over the answers with the class.

ANSWER KEY

1. demanding; 2. prepared; 3. impressed;
4. assertive; 5. sloppy; 6. professional

EXPANSION ACTIVITY: Vocabulary practice

- Put students in six groups. Give each group one of the vocabulary words from this lesson.
- Have groups make a semantic map of their word, adding synonyms, related people and situations, associated feelings, and so on. Allow students to use a dictionary, thesaurus, or other resources as needed.
- Using their semantic maps, students should write five sentences with their vocabulary word that illustrate different uses or nuances of its meaning.

 5 LISTEN to information about Kent and Maria. List their strengths and weaknesses in the chart.

- Go over the directions and the example.
- Have students complete the chart as they listen. Repeat the listening if necessary.
- Go over the answers with the class.

 LISTENING SCRIPT
Lesson 2, Activity 5
TCD4, 19

1. Kent is assertive and very confident. He has taken the initiative and has been conducting a job search so he can make a career change in a new city. He has good communication skills, but he needs to build a stronger résumé. If the company wants him to have more work experience, he might ask to do an internship with the company.

2. Maria is very organized, so she's always prepared. She is a hard worker, but usually, she works too much. She often gets sick because she is so tired. Unfortunately, she's not very assertive, but when she goes to interviews, she is still given good feedback.

Kent–strengths: assertive, confident, takes initiative, good communication skills; weaknesses: needs a stronger résumé, needs more work experience
Maria–strengths: organized, prepared, hard worker, gets good feedback in interviews; weaknesses: works too much, gets sick, not very assertive

6 WRITE three sentences about Kent and three sentences about Maria. Use the real conditional.

- Go over the directions and the example.
- Have students write sentences, using information from the chart in Activity 5.
- Ask volunteers to read their sentences about Kent and Maria to the class.

7 WHAT ABOUT YOU? Think about your strengths and weaknesses. Then complete the sentences and talk with a partner.

- Go over the directions and the sentence starters.
- Have students complete the sentences with their own information.
- Put students in pairs to share their sentences verbally.
- Have partners present sentences about each other to the class.

EXPANSION ACTIVITY: Strengths and weaknesses of the rich and famous

- Have each student write a list of 2–3 famous people they like and 2–3 famous people they dislike.
- Have students make notes about each person's strengths or weaknesses, including either their personal qualities or actions that they have taken.
- Using their list and notes, have students write one sentence about each person, using real conditionals. For example, *If Angelina Jolie continues her charity work, she will become more popular than ever.*

COMMUNITY CONNECTION: Job preparation resources

- Have students research the kinds of job-training, networking, skills-training, and similar resources available in your community, such as career centers, government or community organizations, Toastmasters clubs, and so forth.
- Lead a class discussion about what resources students discovered. Have them tell what is offered by each club or organization.
- Compile a list of the locations and contact information for all organizations discussed and distribute it to the students.

LESSON 3: Listening and Conversation

OBJECTIVES

Rhythm of thought groups
Expressing agreement

PRONUNCIATION

Rhythm of thought groups

COMPETENCIES

Identify appropriate behavior for job
acquisition, retention, and advancement
Learn effective communication strategies

WARM-UP ACTIVITY: Work-life balance

• On the board, write the question: *Do you live
to work, or work to live?* Have students discuss
the question and what it means to them.

• Tell students that in the U.S., many people
are seen as "married to their jobs." They may
not spend much time doing anything except
working, going to the office early, coming home
late, and missing important events with their
families.

• Have students contrast the American style of
work-life balance with that of another country.
Encourage students to tell personal stories to
illustrate their points.

 1 **LISTEN** to the conversation. Then listen to
TCD4, a question. Fill in the circle for the correct
20–25 answer. Replay each item if necessary.

• Direct students' attention to the answer
bubbles.

• Play the CD and have students fill in the correct
circle for each item.

• Put students in pairs to compare answers.

• Go over the answers with the class.

 LISTENING SCRIPT
TCD4,20–25 **Lesson 3, Activities 1 and 2**

1. *A:* Let's talk about Jim first. What do you think
   is his greatest strength?
   B: Well, he's always ready and prepared. For
   example, if I ask him to give a presentation
   at a meeting, he comes with all of the
   information he needs.
   A: Yeah. That's true. And he's organized, too.
   B: Right. If I ask him for information about sales
   or whatever, he knows just where to find it.
   Which response is correct?
   A. Jim is assertive.
   B. Jim is prepared.
   C. Jim is demanding.

2. *A:* Okay, let's talk about Jan.
   B: She's had a good year.
   A: She sure has. The thing I like about Jan is
   that she's confident. She's not afraid to take
   initiative. If she hears about a project that
   she wants to work on, she'll come to me
   and tell me she wants to do it.
   B: That's great. If she continues to do well,
   she'll receive a promotion.
   Which is correct?
   A. Jan is impressed.
   B. Jan is sloppy.
   C. Jan is assertive.

3. *A:* All right, on to Sam.
   B: Oh yeah. Sam. Hmmm.
   A: What are we going to do about him? I like
   him. He's friendly, but he's always late. And
   when he does show up for meetings, he
   doesn't have the materials he needs.
   B: And his reports always have mistakes in
   them.
   A: If he wants to keep his job, he needs to take
   some steps to improve immediately.

Which is correct?

A. Sam is demanding and aggressive.

B. Sam is unprepared and sloppy.

C. Sam is punctual and helpful.

4. *A:* So what about Ann?

B: Well, she definitely has some strengths, but she has her weaknesses, too.

A: True. I mean she's very nice and everyone likes her.

B: Yes. And that's so important.

A: And she always offers to assist her coworkers.

B: But she needs to build her confidence. She's a little shy. She doesn't speak up enough.

Which is correct?

A. Ann is helpful but unassertive.

B. Ann is professional but sloppy.

C. Ann is organized but demanding.

5. *A:* Let's talk about Ed. How did he do this year?

B: Well, he does great work. He's had good training, and he's smart.

A: But . . .

B: But he makes his coworkers a little nervous. He expects a lot from everyone, sometimes too much.

A: I see. If that continues, we'll need to give him some feedback about that.

Which is correct?

A. Ed is sloppy but prepared.

B. Ed is assertive but unprepared.

C. Ed is professional but demanding.

6. *A:* Okay. The last person to talk about is Mary.

B: Mary took a professional development course this year, and it really helped her.

A: Really? How?

B: Well, she used to come to meetings without the information she needed. And she used to make a lot of mistakes in her work.

A: And now?

B: Well, now she's like a new person. She's always on time, and she always has the reports she needs. She's really improved.

Which is correct?

A. Mary used to be unprepared, but now she's prepared.

B. Mary used to be demanding, but now she's nice.

C. Mary used to be organized, but now she's sloppy.

ANSWER KEY

1. B; **2.** C; **3.** B; **4.** A; **5.** C; **6.** A

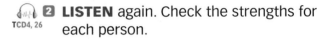 **2 LISTEN** again. Check the strengths for each person.

TCD4, 26

- Read the directions to the students. Point out the list of strengths and the columns for each person.
- Play the CD again and have students check the answers they hear.
- Put students in pairs to compare their answers.
- Go over the answers as a class.

ANSWER KEY

Jim:	prepared
Jan:	confident
Sam:	friendly
Ann:	helpful
Ed:	professional
Mary:	prepared

EXPANSION ACTIVITY: Formal vs. Informal English

- Show a transparency or make copies of the listening script from Activity 2.
- Elicit from students examples of informal language the speakers use that are generally not used in formal writing. Highlight the language on the transparency or have students underline it on their papers. Discuss grammar points as needed.

ANSWER KEY

Sample informal verbal language includes:
Well; Oh, yeah; Hmmm; All right; beginning
sentences with And *or* But*; etc.*

 3 LISTEN to the two managers continue their discussion about Mary. Then check True or False for each statement.

TCD4, 27

- Go over the directions and the statements listed.

- Play the CD or read the conversation and have students check the answers.

- Call on volunteers to give the answers, confirming each with the class.

 LISTENING SCRIPT
Lesson 3, Activity 3

TCD4, 27

A: Let's talk a little more about Mary.

B: Okay.

A: I know she took that professional development course this year, right?

B: Yes, and it's really helped her.

A: I agree. Do you think she's ready for a little more responsibility?

B: Do you want to give her a promotion?

A: No . . . not a promotion, at least not yet. I'd like for her to take over a major project in our department. Do you think she would be okay with more responsibility? If we give it to her, we will have to make sure it goes well.

B: Well, she really has improved. I'm not sure she has very much experience with leadership, though.

A: That's a good point. But I do think she has more confidence and better organization. If we ask her to do more, I think she will take the initiative to learn what she needs to know. She needs more experience.

B: If you think so . . . It can't hurt to see how it goes.

A: All right, then. I'll meet with her tomorrow.

ANSWER KEY

1. False; **2.** False; **3.** True

 PRONUNCIATION: Rhythm of
TCD4, 28 **Thought Groups**

- Play the CD or go over the information in the box.

 A. LISTEN. Mark these sentences to predict
TCD4, 29 the thought groups. Then listen and check.
SCD44

- Go over the directions.

- Play the CD and have students complete the exercise.

- Play the CD again for students to check their answers.

- Put students in pairs and have them read the sentences to each other, using the rhythm they believe is proper.

- Go over the correct pronunciation with the class.

ANSWER KEY

1. If I get up at five o'clock, I can go running.

2. If you work more,   you'll make more money.

3. Where will you go   if you get time off?

4. What'll Ed do   if he quits his job?

5. If she has a baby,   will she work?

6. My boss gets angry   if I am late.

B. LISTEN again and repeat.
TCD4, 30

- Play the CD again, pausing after each phrase or sentence for students to repeat chorally.

4 LISTEN and read.
TCD4, 31
SCD45

- Play the CD or read the conversation to the class.

- Answer any questions students may have about vocabulary from the conversation.

5 PRACTICE the conversation from Activity 4 with a partner. Use the conversation strategy.

- Go over the Conversation Strategy box.

- Put students in pairs to practice the example conversation.

- Have pairs use the expressions in the Conversation Strategy box to replace the underlined phrase as they practice.

6 WHAT ABOUT YOU? Circle a goal below, then write your own ideas about what to do and how to relax as you work toward your goal.

- Go over the directions and the goals listed.
- Have students circle one of the goals.
- Have students make notes about their goals and means of relaxation.
- Put students in pairs to share their thoughts.
- Have volunteers present their partner's ideas to the class.

EXPANSION ACTIVITY: Relaxation

- On the board, brainstorm a list of ways that people relax. Point out that many Americans today relax through yoga, meditation, breathing exercises, visualization, and other techniques. Add ideas like these to the list.
- Have each student choose two ideas from the list to write about: one method of relaxation that they already use and enjoy, and one method that they have never tried.
- Have students write a paragraph about each method or idea. In the first paragraph, they should explain why they enjoy the method they already use. In the second paragraph, they should explain why they would or would not like to try the new technique.
- Put students in pairs to share their paragraphs with each other.
- Have volunteers tell the class what their partner said, or call on students to read their paragraphs to the class.

---

7 ROLE-PLAY. Discuss your notes from Activity 6 with a partner. Then do a role-play, following the model in Activity 4. Talk about your goal and what you are doing. Your partner will give suggestions about how to relax.

- Go over the directions and the conversation model in Activity 4.
- Put students in pairs to discuss their notes from Activity 6.
- Then have them create role-plays.
- Have pairs present their role-plays to the class.

ACADEMIC CONNECTION: Educational goals

- Have students review their own educational goals at your school and write a paragraph about their progress. If students are pursuing a degree- or certificate-granting program, encourage them to visit their academic advisor to find out how many courses they still need to take to finish their studies. If students are not pursuing a degree or certificate, have them write a paragraph about how their current courses fulfill some of their own (or their employer's) educational goals.
- Call on volunteers to read their paragraphs about their educational goals. Are students on track with their programs? Are they pleased with the progress they are making?

LESSON 4: Grammar and Vocabulary

OBJECTIVES

Listen to descriptions about careers
Present unreal conditional

VOCABULARY

candidate	make a better
career change	impression
department	negotiate better
encourage teamwork	benefits
have good	networking
connections	people skills
interviewer	transfer

GRAMMAR

Present unreal conditional

COMPETENCIES

Set goals for job-related learning and
advancement
Transfer skills learned in one job to another

WARM-UP ACTIVITY: You've won!

- Write the names of valuable prizes and gag gifts on slips of paper and put them in a bag.

- Have each student draw a prize. Ask, "What will you do with your [name of prize]?" Have the student respond in the future tense. For example, *I'll have a party on my yacht!*

- Restate each student's plans to the class using present unreal conditionals: *If Lucho won a yacht, he would have a party on it.*

🎧 **1 GRAMMAR PICTURE DICTIONARY.**
TCD4, 32
SCD46   What would happen if these people made some changes at work? Listen and read.

- Have students look at the pictures. Ask: *Who are the people? What is each person doing?*

- Play the CD or read the sentences aloud as students follow along silently.

- Ask questions about the people in the picture and elicit answers: *How does Margo probably feel? Where is Isaac? Why won't Eliza transfer?*

2 READ the sentences in Activity 1 with a partner.

- Go over the directions.

- Put students in pairs to read the sentences.

- Call on students to read the sentences aloud to the class.

EXPANSION ACTIVITY: Networking party

- Have students do independent Internet research on what networking is and what people usually do when they network: introduce themselves, exchange business cards, give the fifteen-second "elevator speech" to promote themselves, and so on. Also tell students to research the types of places and events where people network.

- As a class, make a "Top Five" list of things to do when networking.

- Have students participate in a networking activity, as if meeting new business contacts at a job fair.

- After the activity has ended, lead a discussion about what was difficult or easy in such a networking situation.

BIG PICTURE READING EXPANSION ACTIVITY: An Unhappy Employee

- Photocopy and distribute Worksheet 32: *An Unhappy Employee.*

- Project the transparency for Unit 11 or have students look at the Big Picture on page 168.

- Go over the directions.

- Have students read the conversation and answer the questions.

- Put students in pairs to discuss their answers.

- Go over the answers with the class.

1. He's too demanding, he has a terrible temper, and he needs to work on his people skills.
2. He can't negotiate better benefits if he transfers within the company.
3. He's going to do some networking and maybe have an interview or two.
4. Ivan thinks George's idea is a bad one because Luis will be angry if George disappears for longer than 10 minutes.
5. Answers will vary.

❸ NOTICE THE GRAMMAR. Circle *if* and underline the clause that follows. In the *if*-clause of each sentence, what verb form is used?

- Have students circle each *if* and underline the following clause.
- Go over the answers with the class.

ANSWER KEY

1. (If) Maria completed her accounting program
2. (If) Margo had better people skills
3. (If) Isaac spent more time networking
4. (If) the manager encouraged teamwork
5. (if) she transferred to a different department
6. (If) Steven made a career change

Verb form: simple past

GRAMMAR CHART: Present Unreal Conditional

- Direct students' attention to the chart or project the transparency or CD.
- Go over the information in the chart, including the Grammar Professor note.
- Read the sample sentences in the chart and have students repeat.

EXPANSION ACTIVITY: Dictionary challenge

- Assign each student a letter of the alphabet. Have students select several nouns beginning with that letter.
- Challenge students to write present unreal conditional sentences for each noun.

❹ COMPLETE the present unreal conditional sentences with the correct form of the verbs in parentheses.

- Go over the directions and the example.
- Have students write sentences using the cues provided.
- Put students in pairs to compare sentences.
- Have volunteers read their completed sentences to the class.

ANSWER KEY

1. had, would update
2. became, would encourage
3. would/could negotiate, had
4. made, would be
5. would be, completed
6. would transfer, had

❺ WHAT ABOUT YOU? Complete the sentences about yourself.

- Go over the directions and the sentence frames.
- Have students complete the sentences.
- Put students in pairs to share their sentences orally.
- Call on volunteers to read what they wrote. Challenge partners to tell about their partners, changing the *I* in each sentence to *he* or *she*.

COMMUNITY CONNECTION: If it's broken, fix it!

- On the board, brainstorm important or high-profile people from your community. For example, the mayor, Board of Education members, police officers, owners of sports franchises, successful business owners, and so on.
- Put students in small groups. Have each group write about what they would do if they were the people listed on the board. For example, *If I owned the hockey team, I would trade some of our players.*
- Have groups share what they wrote with the class.

LESSON 5: Grammar Practice Plus

OBJECTIVES

Listen to communication about a job interview
Read a bar graph about job satisfaction

MATH

Bar graph and percentages

COMPETENCIES

Interpret a résumé and job evaluation form
Interpret a bar graph

WARM-UP ACTIVITY: Video humor

- Show students a humorous clip of a job interview, such as Monty Python's "Silly Job Interview" sketch. (Look on video-sharing websites such as YouTube.)
- Discuss the video with students. Elicit ideas from the students about why the video was (or wasn't) funny. For example, students might say that people don't really act that way in job interviews.

🎧 ❶ LISTEN to the conversation between two interviewers, and look at the résumé for Steven. Put a check by the sections that are strengths. Circle the sections that are weaknesses.

TCD4, 33

- Go over the directions.
- Play the CD and have students complete the exercise.
- Put students in pairs to compare their answers.
- Go over the answers with the class.

LISTENING SCRIPT
Lesson 5, Activities 1 and 2

TCD4, 33

A: So, Lilia, tell me about the interview.

B: Well, Marcos, the other interviewers and I met with Steven Hopkins today. He made a good impression.

A: Really?

B: Yes, I think he's a great candidate. I'm looking at his résumé right now. He's only had two jobs since he finished his degree, but I think he got a lot of great work experience at both places.

A: What about his education?

B: Well, unfortunately, that's not as good. He earned his certificate in management over ten years ago. If I were Steven, I would have completed some continuing education courses since then. He will need to do that soon.

A: Good point.

B: His skills and interests look good, though. He has good technical skills with computers. If we set up our new network next year, he could lead that project.

A: That's a good idea.

B: He's very easy to talk with, and I think he has good people skills. I'm not sure about his leadership skills, though. He's never really had to work with several people before. Teamwork might be new for him.

A: True, but if he has good people skills and good communication skills, I'm sure he'll encourage teamwork and make good connections.

B: I agree. Overall, I think he would make a great employee at our company. If we gave him the job, I think his coworkers would enjoy working with him. I would recommend him!

ANSWER KEY

Students should check: Work Experience, Skills
Students should circle: Education

2 LISTEN again. Complete the evaluation form by checking Steven's strengths and weaknesses. Then write a comment and a recommendation.

- Go over the directions and the form. Answer any questions that arise.
- Play the CD and have students check the strengths and weaknesses they hear.
- Have students write comments and recommendations.
- Go over the answers with the class. Call on volunteers to share the comments and recommendations they wrote.

ANSWER KEY

Strength: work experience, technical skills, people skills
Weakness: education and training, leadership skills, teamwork
Comments: answers will vary
Recommendation: answers will vary

EXPANSION ACTIVITY: Addressing mixed-ability classes

- Challenge advanced students to listen to the conversation from Activity 2 and write comprehension questions for their classmates.
- Have the question-writers ask the questions to the class, allowing volunteers to answer. Check answers by polling the class and/or listening to the CD again.

EXPANSION ACTIVITY: Employee evaluation forms

- Have students independently search the Internet for a sample employee evaluation form. Have them print the form and bring it to class.
- Put students in pairs and ask them to compare the forms they printed. What is similar or different?
- As a class, discuss what topics or information were common to all the forms and what topics or information were unusual or specific to a certain field of work.
- Have students tell what they liked or disliked about the forms, in general, and which kind of form they would prefer to use if given the choice.

3 WRITE. If you were Steven, what would you do to improve your weaknesses? Write at least three things.

- Go over the directions and the example.
- Put students in pairs to write their recommendations.
- Have two pairs exchange and read recommendations, then discuss whether both pairs made the same suggestions.
- Elicit from the class some of the recommendations made and write them on the board.

4 LISTEN to the interviews. Write one thing each person says he or she would do for the company. Use the ideas below.

TCD4, 34

- Go over the directions, the word bank, the example, and the sentence starters.
- Play the CD and have students complete the activity.
- Call on students to share their sentences with the class. Have peers correct information as needed, or have students listen to the interview again.

LISTENING SCRIPT
Lesson 5, Activity 4

TCD4, 34

1. *A:* Isabel, you have an excellent résumé. If you were hired at our company, what would you be able to contribute?

   B: Thank you. If I were hired at the company, I would be able to use my leadership experience in many ways. I would help my team find better ways of doing things. I would also make changes to the people who are on the team, maybe even firing one or two of them if necessary. Or transferring them to other departments. I think you have to have high standards to be a good leader.

   A: I see . . .

2. *A:* Nicholas, we are very impressed with your past work experience. Tell us—if you were hired at our company, what would you change or do differently?

   B: If I were hired, I would try to encourage everyone to be creative and think of new ideas. I think one of the most important things a team should do is always think of new ways of doing things. I know it sometimes takes longer and costs more money, but I think brainstorming and trying new things is very important.

   A: That's an interesting point . . .

3. *A:* Leyla, your résumé says you have skills in financial management. Tell us about that.

   B: Yes, I do! In my last job, I was responsible for the budget for our account. I am very careful with money, and I pay close attention to expenses. If I were hired at this company, I'd make sure we covered the costs of our projects with the budget we were given.

   A: Excellent.

4. *A:* Rob, your past work experience makes you seem like a very hard worker.

   B: Oh yes, I am! I never let anything stop me from finishing my work. If I were hired at this company, I'd meet every deadline and make sure all my coworkers did, too. At my last job, I worked 12 to 14 hours a day to get things done. I didn't always get to see my family, but my boss always knew a project would be finished on time.

   A: You sound like a very hard worker.

ANSWER KEY

1. If Isabel got the job, she would make changes to the team.

2. If Nicholas got the job, he would be creative.

3. If Leyla got the job, she would pay attention to the budget.

4. If Rob got the job, he would meet every deadline.

EXPANSION ACTIVITY: Intonation

- Point out to students that in each item from the listening in Activity 4, the interviewer expresses emotion through her intonation.

- One at a time, play each conversation from the listening. Have students tell how the interviewer probably feels, based on her intonation.

- Call on volunteers to role-play each conversation. Provide them with the script. Have the student who plays the interviewer change his or her intonation to reflect a new emotion. Ask the class to tell what emotion they think is being portrayed.

- If students have trouble expressing a particular emotion, model intonation for them.

5 WRITE answers to the questions. Then compare your answers with a partner's.

- Go over the directions and the example.
- Have students write their answers to the questions.
- Put students in pairs to compare their answers.
- Discuss each situation as a class, eliciting ideas from students.

BIG PICTURE GRAMMAR EXPANSION ACTIVITY: Unreal Conditionals

- Photocopy and distribute Worksheet 33: *Unreal Conditionals*.
- Project the transparency for Unit 11 or have students look at the Big Picture on page 168.
- Go over the directions.
- Have students write sentences using the cues.
- Put students in pairs to compare their answers.
- Go over the answers with the class.

---

1. If Luis caught George, he would fire him.
2. If Allison didn't like Kent, she wouldn't hire him.
3. If Kirk looked neater, interviewers would be more impressed.
4. If Marie wasn't prepared for her interview, Chris would be annoyed.
1. Luis would fire George if he caught him.
2. Allison wouldn't hire Kent if she didn't like him.
3. Interviewers would be more impressed if Kirk looked neater.
4. Chris would be annoyed if Marie wasn't prepared for her interview.

MATH: Bar Graph and Percentages

READ the information in the graph. Match the phrases with the correct information.

- Go over the directions and the graph with students. The graph provides possible answers from a survey of people in different jobs. Point out the three types of jobs listed in the graph: helping jobs, creative jobs, and manual jobs.
- Have students complete the exercise.
- Put students in pairs to compare their answers.
- Go over the answers with the class.

ANSWER KEY

1. c; 2. a; 3. e; 4. f; 5. d; 6. b

ACADEMIC CONNECTION: Creating bar graphs

- Review the basics of how to create a bar graph: labeling the x and y axes, choosing increments for the numbers, and making a key to explain any color coding or other features.
- Arrange a computer-lab tutorial or an in-class demonstration to train students how to create bar graphs on one or two typical software programs. Give students hands-on practice if possible, or use an LCD display so all students can easily view the tutorial.
- Have students create a sample graph on paper or by computer using data that you pre-select or data that they gather themselves from surveys, research, and so on.
- Display students' bar graphs in the classroom and have students circulate to look at them. As an added challenge, have each student add a question to his or her graph for classmates to answer.

LESSON 6: Reading

OBJECTIVES

Read tips on successful interviews
Make a T-chart to solve job problems

READING FOCUS

Identify issues and advice

VOCABULARY

get in your way
job interview
problem
put in a good word
put your best foot
  forward

sell yourself
solution
stand out from the
  crowd

COMPETENCIES

Understand the process of applying for a job
Recognize appropriate job interview strategies

WARM-UP ACTIVITY: Standing out from the crowd

- Ask students to think about a time when they noticed a person in a crowd. Why did they notice that person? Was he/she handsome or beautiful? Loud? Wearing strange clothes? Doing something unusual? List students' ideas on the board.

- Ask students whether they like to stand out from the crowd all of the time, most of the time, some of the time, rarely, or never. Have volunteers tell why they feel this way.

❶ THINK ABOUT IT. What should someone do to prepare for a job interview? List three things.

- Go over the directions.
- Have students think about the question silently and list three things.
- Elicit ideas from students, listing them on the board. Have the class vote to determine the three most important ideas.

❷ BEFORE YOU READ. Scan the article on the next page. Look at the headings. How many tips does the article give?

- Go over the directions and point out the Reading Strategy Summary box.
- Have students scan the article to count the number of tips.
- Call on students to answer and also tell what key information they found.

ANSWER KEY

The article gives six tips.

❸ READ the article. Circle each issue and underline the advice given.

- Direct students' attention to the Reading Focus box and go over the information in it.
- Go over the directions. Remind students that issues may be expressed as statements that imply a dilemma (e.g., "you will want to look your best" = "how can I look my best?") or as an outright question (e.g., "How can I stand out from the crowd?"). Tell students that there may be more than one way to address an issue, or that the advice may be expressed in more than one sentence.
- Have students read the article and identify each issue and the advice that is given.
- Have volunteers read each paragraph aloud. Ask the class to identify any issues and advice in the paragraph.

EXPANSION ACTIVITY: More do's and don'ts

- Put students in groups. Have groups discuss important do's or don'ts that were not included in the article.

- Have each group write one paragraph about a *do* and one paragraph about a *don't* to add to the article. Encourage them to follow the author's style: using imperatives, conditionals, and specific examples.
- Have groups present their paragraphs. As a class, vote on which paragraphs presented the most valuable advice.

4 AFTER YOU READ.

A. ANSWER the questions.

- Go over the directions.
- Have students write answers for the questions.
- Put students in pairs to compare answers.
- Go over the answers with the class.

1. The main idea is how to have a successful interview.
2. Press your clothes; wear simple, dark-colored clothes and little jewelry.
3. You should find out more about the company.
4. Talk about how your skills and experiences will fit with the new career.
5. If you know someone in the company, you may have a better chance of getting hired.
6. *Sell yourself* means to let others know about your good qualities.

B. COMPLETE a T-chart. Write issues and advice from the article.

- Go over the directions and the example in the chart.
- Put students in pairs to complete the chart.
- Go over the answers with the class. Encourage students to state their answers in their own words, paraphrasing from the article.
- Copy the chart on the board and write students' answers.

ANSWER KEY

Issues	Advice
You want to look your best.	Make sure your clothes are neatly pressed. Wear simple, dark-colored, clothing and not much jewelry.
You want to impress your interviewers.	Show them that this is more than just a job to you. Prepare for the interview by doing research about the company. Make a list of questions to ask about the company and the job.
You want to show that you have initiative.	Read the company's website to learn more about the company. Ask questions.
You want to change careers.	Be prepared to tell how your skills and experiences will fit with the new career.
You want to stand out from the crowd.	Take advantage of your networking connections. Ask your acquaintance to put in a good word for you.
You want to sell yourself.	Don't be shy. Brag about yourself. Tell the interviewer about your good qualities.

C. VOCABULARY. Use context clues to help understand meaning. Find each idiom below in the article. Reread the paragraph. Then match the idiom with its meaning.

- Go over the directions.
- Have students find each idiom in the article and complete the exercise.
- Put students in pairs to compare their answers.

- Go over the answers with the class. If necessary, describe other situations that help illustrate the meaning of the idioms.

ANSWER KEY

1. c, **2.** d, **3.** a, **4.** b

EXPANSION ACTIVITY: Idioms

- Divide the class into four groups. Assign each group one of the idioms.

- Have groups brainstorm at least three situations in which they would use their idiom. Have them write their ideas down. For example: *Ron wants a date with my friend Lisa, so I put in a good word for him.*

- Have groups share their ideas with the class.

EXPANSION ACTIVITY: I hate to brag, but . . .

- Share tall tales or exaggerations that are obvious examples of unrealistic bragging, such as the classic "fish story": *I hate to brag, but the fish I caught was so big, it was longer than our rowboat!*

- On slips of paper, have students write outrageous boasts about themselves, beginning with the phrase *I hate to brag, but . . .* Be sure to tell students that the sentences don't have to be true or realistic. Encourage them to be funny or ridiculous. Put the slips of paper in a bag.

- Draw out each slip of paper and read it. Have the class guess who wrote such an outrageous piece of fiction!

BIG PICTURE WRITING EXPANSION ACTIVITY: Creative Writing

- Project the transparency for Unit 11 or have students look at the Big Picture on page 168.

- Have students use the vocabulary and idioms from Lesson 6 and from previous lessons in Unit 11 to write descriptive or imaginative sentences about the people in the Big Picture. Encourage students to include details and to create a story or background for each person.

- Put students in pairs. Have students read their sentences to each other, replacing the subject's name with *he* or *she*. Partners should guess which character is being described or discussed. Remind students that they are allowed to ask questions if they don't have enough information to identify the subject of the sentence.

- Call on volunteers to read their descriptions aloud to the class.

COMMUNITY CONNECTION: Local businesses

- Have each student choose a local business or organization to research.

- Have students explore the organization's website, as suggested in the article from this lesson. Students should write down five reasons why the organization would be good (or not good) to work for, based on what they read on the website.

- Have students write three questions that they would ask if they were being interviewed by the company.

- Put students in small groups to discuss the organizations they researched.

- Call on volunteers to tell about businesses or organizations that they liked.

LESSON 7: Writing

WARM-UP ACTIVITY: I'm proud of that!

- Put students in pairs.

- Have partners tell each other something about their work, skills, or accomplishments that they are proud of. Model an example of your own before they begin, such as *All of my students passed the course with a B or above last semester. I feel like I really helped them learn the material.*

- Ask volunteers to tell what their partner shared. Encourage students to ask questions to find out more information about each person's accomplishment or skill.

1 THINK ABOUT IT. What jobs have you had in the past? What skills did you learn at each job? What were your achievements at each job? Tell a partner.

- Go over the questions for this activity. Answer any student questions that arise.

- Put students in pairs to discuss the questions.

- Have volunteers present one of their partner's skills or achievements to the class.

2 BEFORE YOU WRITE.

A. MAKE NOTES about your skills and achievements or awards at work, at school, or in other activities.

- Go over the directions.

- Have students complete the chart with the information they talked about in Activity 1.

EXPANSION ACTIVITY: Narrative writing

- Have students write a narrative paragraph about one of the skills or achievements they listed in Activity 2. Students should describe the situation, tell how their skill or achievement came into play, and tell what the consequences were. Encourage students to write about how they felt and how other people reacted.

- Have volunteers share their paragraphs with the class.

- Point out to students that writing paragraphs such as these can prepare them to answer questions in a job interview, since interviewers often ask candidates to describe a time when they accomplished something at work.

B. READ part of a résumé that a job-seeker wrote. What facts does she state? What details does she give to support the facts?

- Draw students' attention to the Writing Focus box on page 179 before students begin this activity. Read it aloud to the class.

- Go over the directions and the questions asked. Ask students for an example of a fact and an example of a detail from their own work experience. If students have difficulty doing this, provide your own examples.

- Put students in pairs to discuss the sample résumé and answer the questions.

- Go over the answers with the class.

ANSWER KEY

Fact	Specific Detail
assisted nurses with childcare tasks	read aloud, played games, transported children
helped hospital guests	directed visitors to rooms, checked identification
completed administrative work	filed paperwork, updated charts, stocked supplies

EXPANSION ACTIVITY: Editorials

- Gather several examples of editorials from newspapers or the Internet.
- Put students in groups and give each group one of the editorials.
- Have each group find facts and supporting details in the editorial. Tell them to mark each detail as *Fact* or *Opinion*.
- Have groups present their editorial to the class, telling whether on the whole its arguments were supported by facts or opinions.

❸ WRITE your résumé. Follow the steps and the example outline below.

- Direct students' attention to the Writing Focus box. Go over the information in it.
- Go over the directions, the steps, and the résumé template shown.
- Have students write their résumés.

EXPANSION ACTIVITY: Résumé fair

- Have students search the Internet for example résumés in their field of work.
- Ask students to print out one sample résumé.
- Display the résumés around the room and have students look at the various samples and get ideas for their own résumés.

❹ AFTER YOU WRITE.

A. EDIT your résumé. Ask yourself these questions.

- Go over the directions and the questions.
- Have students look at their résumés and address each question, making corrections and additions on the résumé as needed.

B. REWRITE your résumé. Make revisions and corrections.

- Go over the directions.
- Have students rewrite or type their résumés on a clean sheet of paper, including the corrections and additions they noted.

C. DISCUSS your résumé with a partner. Talk about how you can make the résumé stronger. Did you describe your duties clearly? Is there enough evidence to support your facts?

- Go over the directions and the questions.
- Put students in pairs to review each other's writing, answering the questions about their partner.
- Lead a class discussion. Which parts of résumé-writing did students have the most trouble with? What strategies can they use to overcome these problems?

ACADEMIC CONNECTION: Résumés

- Point out to students that on résumés, people do not usually list individual classes they have taken unless the classes are appropriate to a job. Individual grades are also not listed on résumés, though sometimes people include their overall GPA or special honors and awards.
- Some students may not have much work experience. Explain that it is acceptable to include participation in organizations or volunteer work, giving details of the skills they gained and their accomplishments.

Career Connection

OBJECTIVES

Listen to job interviews
Check your progress

COMPETENCIES

Identify and set career goals
Practice test-taking skills

WARM-UP ACTIVITY: Interviews

- Tell students about an interview that you had. Did it go well or poorly? Why?
- Have students share their own interview experiences. Encourage students to ask each other questions.

1 THINK ABOUT IT. Look at the picture. What do you think is happening? Do you think Sara knows the man who is interviewing her? Why or why not?

- Direct students' attention to the picture and ask questions such as: *Who do you see? What is she doing? Where are the people?*
- Have students tell what they think is happening and whether Sara knows the man.

2 LISTEN to the interview between Sara, a part-time restaurant employee, and her supervisor, Mr. Wilson. Does Sara sound confident when she discusses the following topics, or a little uncomfortable? Write **C** for *confident*, or **U** for *uncomfortable* for each.

TCD4, 35

- Go over the directions and the questions.
- Play the CD and have students complete the activity. Play the interview again if students need it.
- Go over the answers with the class.

LISTENING SCRIPT
Career Connection, Activity 2
TCD4, 35

Mr. Wilson: So, Sara, tell me . . . Why should we hire you for the assistant manager position?

Sara: Well, Mr. Wilson, I really want to pursue this opportunity because I think the job would be a great fit for me. Here's my updated résumé. If you read the first section, you'll see that I'm about to graduate with my degree in hotel and restaurant management.

Mr. Wilson: Wow, that's great!

Sara: And if you evaluate my credentials, you'll see that I'm in the top 5 percent of my class. Mr. Wilson, if you give me the chance, I guarantee that you would not be sorry! I'd be very dedicated and hard-working.

Mr. Wilson: I believe that, Sara. You've been one of our most reliable workers here for the last three years.

Sara: Mr. Wilson, there's something I should tell you. I've been doing some networking around town, and one of my connections has offered me a job as a front desk manager at a hotel. The job would pay about 10 percent more than you're offering for the assistant manager position.

Mr. Wilson: Oh, I see. So . . .

Sara: So, well, actually, if I had my choice, I'd rather stay here because I really want to concentrate on working in the restaurant business. But with student loans to pay off, I have to be practical, too. I guess what I'm saying is . . . if I were promoted here, I'd need a higher salary than the one advertised.

Mr. Wilson: I see . . . Well, I'll take that into consideration, Sara.

Sara: Thank you.

Mr. Wilson: Okay. As a full-time employee, you'll be eligible for a full benefits package: healthcare, dental, retirement . . . Do you have any questions about them?

Sara: Well, I know that there is a retirement plan here, but I don't know when an employee is vested. I was wondering if you could tell me more about that?

Mr. Wilson: Let's see . . . we pay 4 percent into the retirement plan, and you're fully vested in the plan after five years.

Sara: I see. OK. Um, I was also wondering about vacation and sick leave benefits.

Mr. Wilson: You get two weeks' vacation to start, and one sick day every three months. You will earn another week of vacation time after three years of employment.

Sara: All right. Let's see. . . . Uh, if I were hired as the assistant manager, I was hoping it would be possible to count my three years of part-time work here towards the extra week of vacation time.

Mr. Wilson: Oh, well, we might be able to do something about that. I'll discuss that with Human Resources.

Sara: Thank you.

Mr. Wilson: I appreciate your coming in today, Sara. We'll let you know our decision soon.

Sara: Thank you for your time, Mr. Wilson.

ANSWER KEY

1. C; 2. C; 3. U; 4. U; 5. U

3 DISCUSS. Look at the vocabulary below. How important are these benefits to you? Number them in order of importance (1–5). Compare your list with a partner's.

- Go over the directions and the vocabulary with students. Specify that 1 indicates the most important benefit and 5 indicates the least important benefit. Tell students to make notes about their reasons for each choice.

- Put students in pairs to talk about their choices.
- Lead a class discussion about which benefit is most desirable and why.

4 ROLE-PLAY. Look at these examples of language Sara used when she was talking with Mr. Wilson. With a partner, use the list you made in Activity 3 to practice negotiating a better benefits package.

- Go over the directions and the language in the box.
- Have students imagine that they are negotiating a job. You may wish to write a fictitious list of benefits on the board to give students a place to start their negotiations. For example, *Salary = $32,000 per year, 10 days of vacation,* and so on.
- Have a pair of advanced students model the activity for the class.
- Put students in pairs to practice interviewing and negotiating.
- Call on volunteers to perform their role-plays in front of the class. After each pair, ask the class questions about what happened in the conversation: *What did she say to his offer? How many sick days are allowed per year?*

EXPANSION ACTIVITY: Addressing mixed-ability classes

For students who need more structure with Activity 4:

- On the board, write a model conversation for students to follow, such as this:

Interviewer:
   We offer a salary of $32,000 per year.
Interviewee:
   Oh. I was hoping for more than that.

- Brainstorm with students other phrases that employers would use to make offers, such as: *we're prepared to (pay/offer), what would you think about, the best we can do is,* and so on. List the offer phrases on the board.

- Put students in pairs and have them outline the conversation before they role-play. Have pairs use the model conversation and the offer phrases to write new offers and counteroffers.
- Invite pairs to role-play before the class, using their notes if needed.

CULTURE NOTE

Students may not be accustomed to negotiating for salary or benefits in the workplace. Tell them that some businesses have set (published) salary scales, while others use negotiation to determine an employee's salary and benefits. Explain that salaries are usually considered highly confidential, so it can be difficult to know how much to ask for or expect. Tell students that most businesspeople research current salary levels for their profession and region before negotiating.

EXPANSION ACTIVITY: Idioms

- On slips of paper, write down idioms that may be used when discussing negotiations: *have (someone) over a barrel; drive a hard bargain; give and take; back down; close a deal; fall through;* etc.
- Have each student draw one of the idioms from a bag.
- Ask students to look up their idiom and find out what it means. Have them write a short conversation to illustrate its use.
- Have students present their idiom to the class, including its definition, whether it has a positive or negative connotation, and their example sentence or conversation.

5 WHAT ABOUT YOU? What kind of job would you like to have five years from now? Would this job be a promotion for you, a career change, or the same job you have now? What could you do in the next five years to get a promotion, or better benefits? Talk with a partner.

- Go over the directions.
- Put students in pairs.
- Call on volunteers to share what they discussed.

COMMUNITY CONNECTION: Human resources

- Arrange for a human resources professional to visit your class for a question-and-answer session.
- Before the visit, have students prepare questions that they want to ask, such as *What negotiating techniques work best? How many of your employees work on a flexible schedule?*
- You may wish to enact a role-play with your visitor in which you are an interviewee and he/she is negotiating benefits with you. Have students take notes about which phrases and tactics you each used during the conversation. If possible, videotape the role-play for the class to analyze later.

CHECK YOUR PROGRESS!

- Have students circle the answers.
- Have students check whether each answer is right or wrong.
- Have students total their correct answers and fill in the chart at the bottom of the page.
- Have students create a learning plan and/or set learning goals.

ANSWER KEY

1. get; 2. arrives; 3. turn; 4. leave; 5. had;
6. took; 7. Would; 8. would; 9. conduct;
10. take; 11. update; 12. give; 13. transfer;
14. interviewers; 15. make; 16. teamwork

UNIT 12 A Bright Future

Unit Overview

LESSON	OBJECTIVES	STUDENT BOOK	WORKBOOK
1 Grammar and Vocabulary 1	Discuss future career plans. Future continuous.	p. 182	p. 160
2 Grammar Practice Plus	Read a business email. Examine a community web page.	p. 184	p. 161
3 Listening and Conversation	Listen to a political campaign. Practice intonation and emotion.	p. 186	p. 162
4 Grammar and Vocabulary 2	Read about work improvement plans. Infinitives of purpose.	p. 188	p. 164
5 Grammar Practice Plus	Read pie charts. Infinitives that follow adjectives.	p. 190	p. 165
6 Reading	Read a personal goals statement. Compare goals.	p. 192	p. 166–167
7 Writing	Write about a life change. Plan goals for the future.	p. 194	p. 168–169
• Career Connection	Compare two jobs and make a choice.	p. 196	p. 170
• Check Your Progress	Monitor progress.	p. 197	p. 172–173

Reading/Writing Strategies

- Compare and contrast
- Organize ideas

Connection Activities

LESSON	TYPE	SKILL DEVELOPMENT
1	Academic	Predicting future educational needs
2	Community	Website analysis/writing an email
3	Academic	Researching/discussing educational policy
4	Community	Researching local companies
5	Academic	Completing course evaluations
6	Community	Interviewing
7	Academic	Giving effective oral presentations
Career Connection	Community	Calculating cost-of-living expenses

WORKSHEET #/FOCUS	TITLE	TEACHER'S EDITION
34. Reading	Pleasant City Editorial	p. 338
35. Grammar	Living in Pleasant City	p. 339
36. Listening	Plans for the City	p. 340

LESSON 1: Grammar and Vocabulary

OBJECTIVES

Discuss future career plans
Future continuous

VOCABULARY

accompanying	enjoying my
candidate	semester off
coordinating a	selecting classes
campaign	sightseeing
running finances	taking over

GRAMMAR

Future continuous

COMPETENCY

Communicate effectively by talking about
future plans

WARM-UP ACTIVITY: Unit opener

- Have students brainstorm topics that people usually think about when planning their future. List their ideas on the board.
- Have volunteers comment on the topics listed, telling why people are concerned with these things when they think of the future.

🎧 ❶ GRAMMAR PICTURE DICTIONARY.
TCD4, .36
SCD47
What are people's plans? Listen and read.

- Have students open their books and look at the pictures. Ask: *What do you see?* Write all the words the students say on the board.
- Say the sentences aloud or play the CD and have students repeat.
- Call on students and ask about the people in the pictures: *Where will the woman be next week? Who is Lina Hancock? What will Natalie be doing in the future?*

❷ PRACTICE the conversations from Activity 1 with a partner.

- Put students in pairs to read the sentences.
- Call on students to read the sentences to the class.

EXPANSION ACTIVITY: Crossword puzzle

- Divide the class into four groups and assign each group two vocabulary words from the Grammar Picture Dictionary. Have each group write clues for the words they are assigned.
- Using a free crossword puzzle maker on the Internet, have students create a puzzle by typing the words and clues into the puzzle maker.
- Print out the puzzle and have students complete it.
- Elicit answers from the class.

EXPANSION ACTIVITY: Next semester

- Have students look at Picture 4 in the Grammar Picture Dictionary. Call on volunteers to read the conversation aloud again.
- Put students in pairs to extend the conversation in writing. Have them write about what the man will be doing next semester, while the woman asks him questions.
- Have each pair read their conversation to the class. Have the class vote on which conversation was the most creative.

❸ NOTICE THE GRAMMAR. Underline *will be* and *be going to be* in the conversations above. Circle the verbs after *be* that end in *-ing*. Double underline the time phrases.

- Go over the directions, telling students to underline the subject that goes with each future verb as well. Remind students to only circle an -ing verb if it comes after the word *be*. Students should not circle *accompanying* or *working*, etc.

- Have students underline, circle, and double underline as directed.

- Put students in pairs to check their work with a partner.

- Go over the answers with the class.

ANSWER KEY

1. **A:** I'm going to be (attending) a business presentation next Wednesday. Do you want to come?

   B: Oh, sorry. Next week, I'll be (sightseeing) in California. I'm accompanying my aunt.

2. **A:** What are you working on?

   B: I'm going to be (coordinating) the campaign for Lina Hancock. She's a candidate for city mayor this year.

3. **A:** Why is Natalie taking so many business classes?

   B: In a few years, she's going to be (taking over) her parents' business. She'll be (running) the finances and marketing, so she has a lot to learn.

4. **A:** I'm selecting my classes for next semester. Can you help me? Which classes are you taking?

   B: Next semester? I won't be (taking) any classes! I'm going to be (enjoying) a semester off from school.

GRAMMAR CHART: Future Continuous

- Direct students' attention to the chart or project the transparency or CD.

- Go over the information on the chart and the usage notes, including the Grammar Professor note.

- Read the sentences, pausing to have students repeat.

- Point out or elicit that future continuous is sometimes called future progressive.

CHART EXPANSION ACTIVITY: Lifestyles of the rich and famous

- Have students imagine that they are part of the glamorous, international jet-set crowd. Elicit ideas about the kinds of things the rich and famous do.

- Put students in pairs and have them write two-line conversations using the future continuous. In the conversation, one character should issue an invitation or ask a question about the future. The other character should decline the invitation or answer in the negative. Prompt students to think of the most exotic or unbelievable excuses they can imagine. For example: A: *Are you going to be presenting at the Academy Awards again this year?* B: *Oh, no, darling. I'll be sunning myself on the yacht at Lake Como with George.*

- Have pairs present their conversation to the class. Encourage students to get into character and have fun with their roles.

4 COMPLETE the sentences with the future continuous using the words in parentheses.

- Go over the directions and the example.

- Have students complete the exercise.

- Put students in pairs to compare answers.

- Go over the answers with the class.

ANSWER KEY

1. will be enjoying; **2.** is going to be accompanying; **3.** will be taking over; is going to be coordinating; **4.** will be sightseeing; **5.** will be running; **6.** are going to be selecting

EXPANSION ACTIVITY: Tell me more

- Read each completed sentence from Activity 4 to the class.

- Have students tell more detail about each situation, using the future continuous to give ideas.

- Prompt students with questions as needed. For example, *What exactly will Chris be doing? Where are the students going to be shopping for the gift?* and so on.

5 WHAT ABOUT YOU? What will you be doing in the future? Write sentences about yourself. Use the future continuous. Then read your sentences to a classmate.

- Go over the directions and the sentence starters.

- Have the students write their sentences and share them with a partner.

- Call on volunteers to tell the class one or two of the sentences they wrote.

ACADEMIC CONNECTION: The educational future

- Lead a discussion about what the future holds in terms of education for your students. When they finish your course or their current program, will they be furthering their education? What is the likelihood that they will need more education to get ahead?

- You may wish to have students prepare for the conversation by doing research on the current job prospects and financial outlook for various professions.

- If students predict that they will be furthering their education, have them tell what they think they will be doing and when, using the future continuous.

LESSON 2: Grammar Practice Plus

OBJECTIVES

Read a business email
Examine a community web page

GRAMMAR

Future continuous

COMPETENCIES

Form opinions about political issues
Identify problems in a city and propose
  solutions for improvement

WARM-UP ACTIVITY: The city of the future

- Put students in groups.

- Have each group brainstorm what the ideal city of the future would be like. What would the buildings look like (or would there be buildings at all)? What special features would it have? How would it fit into the natural landscape?

- Have each group tell about their ideal city to the class. Discuss which ideas are most appealing and which ones may (or may not) come true some day.

❶ COMPLETE. Read this email to a Pleasant City administrator. Complete the email with the future continuous with *will*.

- Go over the directions and point out the glossary in the reading.

- Have students read the email and fill in the missing verbs using the words in parentheses.

- Have volunteers read the email aloud, supplying the missing answers as they read.

ANSWER KEY

1. will be taking over; 2. will be coordinating;
3. will be offering; 4. will be enjoying;
5. will be running

EXPANSION ACTIVITY: Vocabulary practice

- Put students in groups and have them write sentences using the words from the glossary in Activity 1. Tell them to leave a blank in each sentence where the vocabulary word should be.

- Have groups trade papers and complete each other's sentences.

- To check answers, have groups read their completed sentences aloud. Have peers confirm whether each sentence is correct and makes sense.

❷ WRITE. Brainstorm ideas for Pleasant City's plan for city improvement. Write an idea for each year.

- Go over the directions and the topics listed. Remind students to use future continuous to complete the chart.

- Have students fill in the chart using original ideas.

- Put students in pairs to compare ideas.

- Go over the answers with the class.

❸ TALK about the picture. What will life in Pleasant City be like in five years? What will people be doing?

- Go over the directions.

- Put students in pairs to talk about the picture.

- Elicit ideas from the class about what Pleasant City will be like. List their ideas on the board.

BIG PICTURE WRITING EXPANSION ACTIVITY: Pleasant City conversations

- Project the transparency for Unit 12 or have students look at the Big Picture on page 185.

- Put students in pairs.

- Have pairs imagine that they are two people in the picture. Have each pair write a conversation between the characters.
- Have each pair present their conversation to the class.

4 WRITE an article for the "Making Pleasant City Pleasant" website. Write more predictions about Pleasant City in five years. Use vocabulary from this unit and your own ideas.

- Go over the directions and the website.
- If desired, model the structure of an article on the board (headline, subtitle, body, captions, and so on).
- Have students write their articles, using as many steps in the writing process as needed (outlining, drafting, revising, and so on).
- Put students in groups to share their articles, and then choose one article to read to the class.

BIG PICTURE READING EXPANSION ACTIVITY: Pleasant City Editorial

- Photocopy and distribute Worksheet 34: *Pleasant City Editorial.*
- Project the transparency for Unit 12 or have students look at the Big Picture on page 185.
- Preview any difficult vocabulary words from the worksheet, such as *gas-guzzling* and *filtration*.
- Go over the directions. Have students read the editorial.
- Put students in pairs to ask and answer the questions, then review as a class.

ANSWER KEY

1. Pleasant City has come a long way, but there are still improvements that need to be made.
2. Five years ago, the traffic was really bad. Now, Personal Transport Vehicles, especially those operated by children, have become dangerous.
3. The writer thinks that laws should be made to ensure public safety.
4. It makes the city's air cleaner, but it's noisy and it uses a lot of electricity.
5. Answers will vary.

EXPANSION ACTIVITY: Grammar search/ language analysis

- Have students look at the worksheet they just completed (*Pleasant City Editorial*).
- Have students underline each use of future continuous in the editorial.
- Put students in pairs to compare what they underlined.
- Go over the answers with the class.
- Discuss the tone of the editorial. Ask students if they think it is formal or informal, and why? Point out features such as sentence fragments and punctuation that indicates dramatic pauses. What effect is the writer trying to achieve through each device?

5 WHAT ABOUT YOU? What are some problems in your community, your city, or your country? What will be different in the future? Talk with a partner about what you think citizens and leaders will be doing in the future.

- Go over the questions in the directions.
- Put students in pairs to discuss the questions, then review as a class.

COMMUNITY CONNECTION: Town website

- Have students search the internet for your town or city's official website.
- Discuss what type of information the website offers.
- Put students into groups to discuss ways they would improve the website.
- Have each group compose an "email" to send to the website's webmaster. In the email, have them tell what they like about the site, what could be improved, and any suggestions that they have.
- Have each group read their email aloud. As a class, work together to write one final email that incorporates the most important ideas. Then send the email to the webmaster and wait to see if you get a response!

LESSON 3: Listening and Conversation

Listen to a political campaign
Practice intonation and emotion

PRONUNCIATION

Intonation and emotion

COMPETENCIES

Analyze information about political candidates
Work as a team to find solutions to problems

WARM-UP ACTIVITY: Political slogans

- Ask students if they can think of any political slogans that are currently being used or that were popular in the past.
- Give a few examples of these slogans from American history, or challenge students to find examples through their own research.

TCD4, 37–42

1 **LISTEN** to the question. Then listen to the conversation with the candidate for mayor of Pleasant City. Listen to the question again. Fill in the correct answer. Replay each item if necessary.

- Direct students' attention to the answer sheet.
- Play the CD and have students fill in the correct circle.
- Put students in pairs to compare their answers.
- Go over the answers with the class.

TCD4, 37–42

LISTENING SCRIPT
Lesson 3, Activity 1

1. What will the candidate do about pollution?
    - *A:* We've seen a lot of positive changes to Pleasant City recently. But some problems remain. For example, pollution is getting worse. As mayor, what will you do about this?
    - *B:* Well, in the next few years, three more factories are going to be opening. So, as mayor, I will design a plan to help factories reduce pollution.

What will the candidate do about pollution?

- **A.** close the factories
- **B.** open new factories
- **C.** help factories reduce pollution

2. Why do the schools need help?
    - *A:* There are so many different ways to help improve the city. What do you think is the most important problem right now?
    - *B:* Well, I think our schools need a lot of help. In the next five years, hundreds of children are going to be entering our schools. We need more classrooms, more teachers, and more textbooks.

Why do the schools need help?

- **A.** In five years, they will need more classrooms, teachers and text books.
- **B.** In five years, hundreds of children will be leaving the schools.
- **C.** In five years, many of the schools will close.

3. Where is the candidate going to be speaking?
    - *A:* Your campaign is just beginning. A lot of people want to hear what you have to say. Where do you plan to speak?
    - *B:* Well, my campaign is all about improving public services. I'm going to be speaking at schools, firehouses, hospitals, and City Hall.

Where is the candidate going to be speaking?

- **A.** at shopping malls and on television
- **B.** in sports arenas and theaters
- **C.** in places where teachers, nurses, and firefighters work

4. How will the candidate help senior citizens?
    - *A:* Many people in Pleasant City are senior citizens. Do you think we will have enough public services for them?
    - *B:* No. Many older people in our city need better health care. If I am mayor, I will ask all health clinics to give all senior citizens a free health examination.

How will the candidate help senior citizens?

- **A.** She'll ask them to work at the hospitals.
- **B.** She'll ask the health clinics to offer free exams.
- **C.** She'll ask them to buy better health insurance.

5. Who can help reduce crime in Pleasant City?

   A: Crime is still a big problem in some parts of Pleasant City. What do you plan to do about it?

   B: Well, tomorrow I'm going to be speaking at the police station about this. Citizens need to help our local police officers. We all need to watch our neighborhoods carefully and call the police if we see or hear anything strange or suspicious. Neighbors can really help fight crime.

   Who can help reduce crime in Pleasant City?

   A. people who own shops in Pleasant City

   B. people who visit Pleasant City

   C. people who live in Pleasant City

6. How can the people of Pleasant City help the community?

   A: Do you think the people of Pleasant City can help the community?

   B: Absolutely. As mayor, I am going to be encouraging every person in Pleasant City to help the community.

   A: How so?

   B: Well, for instance, we can all help with donations. Anyone can donate food, clothes, and even money to community agencies. And people can volunteer to help in the schools and sports programs.

   How can the people of Pleasant City help the community?

   A. by encouraging the mayor to help

   B. by donating and by volunteering in the community

   C. by asking the police to volunteer

ANSWER KEY
TCD4, 43

1. C; 2. A; 3. C; 4. B; 5. C; 6. B

🎧 **2 LISTEN** to the candidate again. Put the correct number in the box on the campaign button.

- Go over the directions.
- Play the CD and have students complete the exercise.
- Call on volunteers to give the answers.

ANSWER KEY

1. Let's help keep the air clean!
2. Improve our schools today!
3. Our future is about public services!
4. Free health exams for the elderly!
5. Neighbors, keep our streets safe!
6. Help your neighbors. Give to the poor!

EXPANSION ACTIVITY: A good solution?

- Put students in six groups.
- Give each group the script to one of the listening items in Activity 1.
- Have groups discuss whether the solution proposed by the mayor is a sensible one, and whether she tells how she will implement the plan. Through what means could Pleasant City accomplish each goal? Or does the goal sound like an unworkable campaign promise?
- Have groups read their script aloud to the class and tell what they concluded. Allow the class to respond with counterpoints and questions.

🎧 **PRONUNCIATION: Intonation and**
TCD4, 44 **Emotion**

- Play the CD or go over the information about intonation and emotion.

🎧 **A. LISTEN** to the statements. Circle the
TCD4, 45
SCD48   emotion that is expressed.

- Go over the directions.
- Play the CD again and have students circle the answers.
- Go over the answers as a class.

ANSWER KEY

1. surprise; 2. disappointment; 3. excitement;
4. surprise

B. LISTEN again and repeat.

TCD4, 46

- Go over the directions.
- Play the CD and have students repeat.

EXPANSION ACTIVITY: Intonation practice

- Choose a play that students will enjoy reading and performing. If possible, choose a play for which you can obtain a copy of a video production.
- Make copies of a scene from the play and distribute them to the class. Explain briefly what has happened in the story up until the beginning of the scene.
- Divide the class into groups based on the number of characters in the scene. Have each group practice the scene using the intonation they believe is correct.
- Have each group present. Discuss what emotions they chose to portray.
- When all groups have presented, give your own interpretation of the emotions meant to be portrayed, or show a videotaped production of that scene in the play. Have students tell how their own interpretations differed from yours or from the video.

---

3 LISTEN to the conversation. Mr. Lewis is a candidate for mayor.

TCD4, 47
SCD49

- Direct students' attention to the picture. Ask question: *What is happening?*
- Play the CD or read the conversation as students follow along silently.
- Play the CD or read the conversation again and have students repeat.
- Ask: *What does Mr. Lewis say about schools? How many new schools does he want to build?*

BIG PICTURE CONVERSATION EXPANSION ACTIVITY: Pleasant City education

- Project the transparency for Unit 12 or have students look at the Big Picture on page 185.
- Put students in groups. Have each group imagine what the ideal educational system for Pleasant City would be. You may wish to brainstorm various factors in education on the board first (ages of students, subjects taught, faculty, facilities, and so on).
- Have groups describe their educational system to the class. After all groups have presented, lead a discussion about which ideas and aspects were the most inspiring and exciting.

CIVICS NOTE

Give students an overview of the ways that an average citizen can participate in politics, beyond voting. Discuss groups and organizations such as citizen action groups, government watchdog groups (for example, the ACLU or the National Organization for Women), and so on. You may wish to have students research ordinary citizens who have precipitated extraordinary changes in American law and politics.

---

4 PRACTICE the conversation in Activity 3 with a partner. Then make a new conversation. Write the problem and some solutions below each picture. Then use the information to practice the conversation.

- Go over the directions.
- Put students in pairs to practice the conversation in Activity 3.
- Then have each pair make notes about each picture, giving a problem and some solutions.

- Ask a pair of student volunteers to model a new conversation, using the information they wrote below one of the pictures.
- Have pairs practice their own new conversations, one for each picture.
- Walk around to monitor the activity and provide help as needed.

5 INTERVIEW three other classmates to find out their solutions to the problems in Activity 4.

- Go over the directions. Help students determine which three classmates they will interview.
- Have students take notes as they interview each other.
- Have volunteers report to the class the solutions they heard. Have the class vote to decide which solution is best for each picture.

6 WHAT ABOUT YOU? What will you be doing at different points in the future? Tell a partner.

- Go over the directions and the time frames given.
- Put students in pairs to discuss their responses to each time frame. Remind them to use the future continuous in their answers.
- Have pairs share information about their partners.

> **ACADEMIC CONNECTION: Educational policy**
>
> - Have students research current national, state, and local educational policies that affect education in your area. Encourage students to attend Board of Education meetings or to interview Board members.
> - Have students report what they found to the class.
> - Lead a discussion. Which policies make sense and which ones don't?

LESSON 4: Grammar and Vocabulary

OBJECTIVES

Read about work improvement plans
Infinitives of purpose

VOCABULARY

address the issue	expand efforts
avoid the problem	minimize stress
balance	promote
emphasize	quality of life

GRAMMAR

Infinitives of purpose

COMPETENCY

Recognize various ways of making positive
changes

WARM-UP ACTIVITY: That's crazy!

- Think of four absurd situations and write them on index cards. For example, *Renee dyed her hair purple and put on a chicken suit. Hank stood on one foot for 17 hours in a row.*

- Divide the students into four groups. Give each group one of the index cards.

- Have the group brainstorm as many logical reasons as possible that the person on the card might have taken such an action. Have them write sentences to tell each reason. For example, Renee dyed her hair purple and put on a chicken suit to make her sister laugh on her birthday. Hank stood on one foot for 17 hours in a row to break the world record.

- Have students read their absurd situation to the class, followed by their solution. If students write sentences using *because* instead of infinitives of purpose, try to rephrase their statements using infinitives of purpose.

1 GRAMMAR PICTURE DICTIONARY.
TCD4, 48 SCD50 Cutting Edge has many plans to improve employees' quality of life. Listen and read.

- Have students look at the pictures. Ask: *Who are the people? What is each person doing?*

- Play the CD or read the sentences aloud as students follow along silently.

2 READ the sentences in Activity 1 with a partner.

- Go over the directions.

- Put students in pairs to read the sentences.

- Call on students to read the sentences aloud.

3 NOTICE THE GRAMMAR. Underline the main verbs and circle the infinitives.

- Go over the directions and the example.

- Have students underline the main verbs (including auxiliary verbs) and circle infinitives.

- Go over the answers with the class.

ANSWER KEY

1. Cutting Edge, Inc. is changing its policies (to enhance) the quality of life for its employees.

2. The company is offering gym memberships (to promote) better health and (to minimize) stress for employees.

3. (To emphasize) the importance of a good balance between work and home, the company is giving workshops on time management.

4. Cutting Edge, Inc. is making changes (to expand) its efforts (to help) the environment.

5. (To address) the issue of paper waste, Cutting Edge is putting recycling bins in each office.

6. The company is also purchasing new, energy-saving equipment (to avoid) the problem of high electricity costs.

GRAMMAR CHART: Infinitives of Purpose

- Go over the information in the charts, including the usage and Grammar Professor notes.
- Read the sample sentences in the charts and have students repeat.

CHART EXPANSION ACTIVITY: Marooned!

- Have students imagine that they are stranded on a deserted island.
- Put students in groups. Have each group brainstorm what they would need to do to survive.
- Have groups write sentences about their ideas, using infinitives of purpose. For example, *To save water, we could collect rain in coconuts.*
- Have groups share their ideas with the class.

4 WRITE. Use infinitives of purpose to combine the sentences.

- Go over the directions and the example.
- Have students write the combined sentences in their notebooks.
- Put students in pairs to compare sentences.
- Have volunteers write the sentences on the board.

ANSWER KEY

1. Cutting Edge, Inc. is going to use email more often to reduce the amount of paper it uses.
2. Cutting Edge is allowing employees to work from home more often to minimize stress and help employees balance work and home.
3. The company is trying to enhance the quality of life for employees now to improve employee satisfaction.
4. Cutting Edge is using conference calls more often to avoid the high cost of travel.
5. Vending machines are being replaced with a café that serves fresh fruit and vegetables to promote better health for employees.
6. The managers are offering computer training classes to emphasize better use of technology.

5 COMPLETE the sentences with your own ideas. Then discuss with a partner.

- Go over the directions, the example, and the sentence starters.
- Have students write their sentences.
- Put students in pairs to share their sentences.
- Lead a class discussion about each sentence starter, eliciting sentences that students wrote and encouraging debate.

BIG PICTURE GRAMMAR EXPANSION ACTIVITY: Living in Pleasant City

- Photocopy and distribute Worksheet 35: *Living in Pleasant City.*
- Project the transparency for Unit 12 or have students look at the Big Picture on page 185.
- Have students complete the worksheet.
- Put students in pairs to compare their answers.
- Go over the answers with the class.

WORKSHEET ANSWER KEY

1. to save; 2. to help; 3. To emphasize; 4. to avoid; 5. To keep; 6. to enhance; 7. to promote; 8. to address; to improve

COMMUNITY CONNECTION: Local companies in the news

- Have students find articles about local businesses that are trying to improve their companies and their employees' quality of life. What are the companies doing?
- Have students report what they learned to the class and discuss each company. Are any of them doing the same things as the companies in this lesson?

LESSON 5: Grammar Practice Plus

Read pie charts
Infinitives that follow adjectives

MATH

Reading pie charts

COMPETENCIES

Interpret policies for employees
Interpret a circle graph

WARM-UP ACTIVITY: Guess that adjective

- On the board, write the list of adjectives from the "Infinitives That Follow Adjectives" box on page 191.

- Have a volunteer sit with his or her back to the board. Point to one of the adjectives for the class to see.

- Have students give one-word clues to describe the chosen adjective. The volunteer must guess which word it is.

- If one-word clues are not enough information, have students give sentences or describe situations that relate to the word.

 1 LISTEN to the radio report. Check the company that promises to make each change for its employees. Then listen again and write the reason the companies are making the changes.
TCD4, 49

- Go over the directions.

- Play the CD. Have students put check marks in the chart as they listen.

- Play the CD again and have students complete the last column of the chart with the reason.

- Put students in pairs to compare their answers.

- Go over the answers with the class.

LISTENING SCRIPT
Lesson 5, Activity 1
TCD4, 49

You're listening to KYOK radio, 99.1 FM. It's five o'clock and time for business news. A recent report in the *Business Journal* shows that several leading businesses are going to be making important changes this year to improve the quality of life for their workers.

Cutting Edge, Inc. is going to be allowing more flexibility in employees' work hours to encourage workers to spend more time at home, away from the office. That sounds like a great policy to me. They'll also be trying to improve relationships between managers and employees.

Software giant Macro Comp is going to be spending more money on employee training. To help its employees acquire more professional skills, the company will be sending them to professional workshops and paying for it.

Well-known auto manufacturer Go Auto is going to be offering employees free gym memberships. To encourage better health habits, the company is paying for its employees' exercise classes.

And finally, everyone's favorite travel agency, Zip Travel, is going to be decreasing employee travel. You heard that right. The travel agency is going to be buying a new conference calling system to reduce the amount of travel for employees.

We're going to be checking in with employees of these companies at the end of the year to see how their employers succeeded. Now, on to the stock market report for today . . .

ANSWER KEY

gym memberships: Go Auto (to promote better health)
flexible work hours: Cutting Edge (to spend more time at home)
manager-employee relations: Cutting Edge (to improve work relations)
conference calls: Zip Travel (to reduce travel)
training programs: Macro Comp (to help employees acquire skills)

❷ WRITE. Use the chart above. Write sentences about what each company in Activity 1 is doing and why.

- Go over the directions and the example.
- Have students write sentences about each company. Encourage them to use the future continuous in their sentences.
- Have volunteers share their sentences with the class.

MATH: Reading Pie Charts

READ. Pie charts show comparisons among items. The charts below show how employees felt about the changes their companies made. Match each company with a description. Write the correct letters on the lines.

- Go over the directions. Direct students' attention to the pie charts and the color coding. Make sure students understand that the charts are showing employees' opinions about how successful they felt their companies were in the changes they made (as outlined in Activity 1).
- Have students complete the exercise.
- Put students in pairs to compare their answers.
- Elicit answers from the class.

ANSWER KEY

1. D; 2. B and C; 3. A; 4. B

EXPANSION ACTIVITY: Fractions

- Use the pie charts in the Math activity to practice fractions.
- Have students find the fractions mentioned in the activity: *half* and *one quarter*. Ask students if they can think of another way to say *one quarter* (*one fourth*).

- Elicit the names of common fractions from 1 to 10: *one tenth, one fifth, one fourth, one third, one half*, and so on. Write them on the board along with their numerical equivalent and percentage. For example, *One tenth = 1/10 = 10%*
- Point out that fractions can usually be said with either *one* or *a*, as in *one quarter* or *a quarter.*

GRAMMAR CHART: Infinitives That Follow Adjectives

- Direct students' attention to the chart.
- Go over the information on the chart. Read the sentences and have students repeat.

CHART EXPANSION ACTIVITY: Feeling festive

- Elicit a list of holidays or festivals from the students and write them on the board.
- Have students write five sentences using adjective + infinitive to describe their personal experiences during holidays and festivals.
- Write a model example on the board, such as *Mom was pleased to receive so many roses on Mother's Day.*
- Put students in pairs to share their sentences.
- Call on students to read one or two of their sentences to the class.

❸ WRITE about the people below. How does the person feel about the company change in Activity 1? Are they happy or unhappy to support the changes at the company where they work? Why? Read your sentences to a partner.

- Go over the directions and the example.
- Put students in groups. Assign each group one of the pictures.

- Have groups write about the person in their picture, including details and reasons that each person supports or does not support their company's changes. Remind students to use infinitives that follow adjectives when they write. Have groups use the adjectives from the chart.

- Have groups read what they wrote to the class. Before each group reads, ask the class to predict what the group had to say. After the group reads, evaluate whether the class predictions were correct.

ANSWER KEY

Answers will vary. Possible answers include:

1. Sara works for Go Auto and is an avid runner. She is thrilled to hear that her company would begin offering gym memberships. She is going to be working out at the gym every day now!

2. Jimmy works for Cutting Edge. He has family and friends in a different country, and because of the time difference, it has always been difficult to stay in touch with them by phone. Jimmy is happy to learn that Cutting Edge will be creating more flexible schedules. Now he'll be able to call his family and friends more easily. However, he does not feel that he needs more time at home because there is no one to talk to there.

3. Mark is a father of three who works at Zip Travel. It hasn't been easy to take so many business trips. He always misses his kids when he travels. Mark is surprised to hear that Zip Travel will be cutting back on travel, but he is definitely pleased to know that he won't have to pack his bags quite so often.

EXPANSION ACTIVITY: Grammar scan

- Have groups exchange the sentences they wrote in Activity 3.

- Have each group look at the sentences they received and scan them for the adjective + infinitive combination. Have groups underline each occurrence.

- Have each group write one of the sentences on the board, underlining the adjective and infinitive. Challenge the class to replace the adjective with a synonym that doesn't change the meaning of the sentence.

- Ask students if any of the sentences used different adjectives from the ones listed in the chart on page 191. What adjectives were used?

4 ROLE-PLAY a conversation between a person in Activity 3 and a coworker. Use the example as a model.

- Go over the directions and the example conversation.

- Put students in pairs to practice their own role-plays.

- Have volunteers present their role-plays to the class.

- If desired, have several rounds of role-plays, assigning new partners and new pictures each time.

BIG PICTURE LISTENING EXPANSION ACTIVITY: Plans for the City

- Photocopy and distribute Worksheet 36: *Plans for the City.*

- Project the transparency for Unit 12 or have students look at the Big Picture on page 185.

- Go over the directions.

- Read aloud the script for the worksheet and have students complete the sentences. Read the listening script a second time if necessary.

- Put students in pairs to compare answers.

- Go over the answers with the class.

LISTENING SCRIPT
Worksheet 36

1. *Laura:* I heard the city is going to be closing the park at 9:00 P.M. every evening. I'm really not happy to hear that. I like to go to the park to look at the stars at night. Sometimes I'm there as late as midnight!

2. *Akeem:* I think it would be fun to paint a big mural on the City Hall building. It looks very plain right now. A mural would be colorful and attractive.

3. *Mayor Bynes:* I was discouraged to find out that our Board of Education decided not to fund the after-school children's program. We really need that program, but now I don't know where we'll find the money for it.

4. *Yolanda:* I'm thrilled to live in Pleasant City. It's so much nicer than the town where I used to live. I'm really glad I moved here.

5. *Giancarlo:* Pleasant City sure is different than it used to be. People are happier, the town is more beautiful, and life is just better. I'm pleased to see all the progress we've made.

6. *Mr. Han:* I was surprised to learn that a new supermarket will be opening in town. We don't really need one. The farmer's market has everything we need: fresh produce, meat, breads, and dairy products.

ANSWER KEY

1. Laura isn't happy to hear that the park will be closed at 9:00 P.M. because she likes to go there at night.

2. Akeem thinks it would be fun to paint a mural on City Hall to make it more colorful and attractive.

3. Mayor Bynes was discouraged to learn that the Board of Education did not fund the after-school children's program. He doesn't know how to pay for it now.

4. Yolanda is thrilled to live in Pleasant City because it's nicer than where she lived before.

5. Giancarlo is pleased to see the changes in Pleasant City. People are happier and life is better than it was before.

6. Mr. Han was surprised to learn about the new supermarket because he thinks Pleasant City doesn't need one.

ACADEMIC CONNECTION: Course evaluations

- Tell students that at the end of a course in adult education, students are often asked to complete a course evaluation.

- Point out that these evaluations often include space for writing comments. Have students imagine comments that they might make using infinitives following adjectives. For example, *It was difficult to complete so many assignments*.

- Put students in pairs.

- Have each pair write 2–3 fictional evaluation comments with infinitives.

- Have volunteers read their comments aloud. As a class, imagine that you are the professor receiving the comments. Respond to the comments by telling about your upcoming plans for improvement. Use the statements in the chart in Activity 1 as models.

LESSON 6: Reading

OBJECTIVES

Read a personal goals statement
Compare goals

READING FOCUS

Compare and contrast

VOCABULARY

compare
contrast

COMPETENCY

Compare and contrast others' goals

WARM-UP ACTIVITY: Get your priorities straight

- Ask students to think about different aspects of their lives, such as work, family, health, and leisure. List their ideas on chart paper, reaching agreement about main categories.
- Discuss with the class which aspects are probably more important at different stages in life. What takes priority during a person's twenties? During their forties? After retirement?
- Have a student scribe take notes on chart paper to summarize the discussion for later use.

1 THINK ABOUT IT. How often do you think about the future? Do you make plans about what to do with your life? How far in the future do you plan for—next month, next year, the next five years? Tell a partner.

- Go over the questions.
- Put students in pairs to discuss their answers.
- Call on students to share their ideas with the class.

2 BEFORE YOU READ. Scan the personal statements on the next page. Underline key information about these people's plans.

- Go over the directions.
- Have students scan the personal statements and underline the key information about Terry's and Perla's plans.
- Put students in pairs to compare what they underlined.
- Elicit ideas from the class, coming to agreement on what information is probably the most important.

ANSWER KEY

Students should underline the following:

Terry: My main goals are to address the issue of stress and to improve my home life; I am going to be spending more time at home to help manage the household; either I will be reducing my work hours to part-time, or I'll be telecommuting from home; I'm purchasing a treadmill so that I can get more exercise; I also will be spending more time relaxing; I'm going to take the kids sightseeing around the city; I am going to be donating some of my time to help out at the men's shelter.

Perla: I will be going back to school to get my degree; I will be selecting a college; I am going to attend a technology convention this spring; I will be volunteering for new duties.

3 READ the personal statements. Think about Terry and Perla. How are their goals and lives similar or different? Do they have similar or different goals and lives? Tell a partner.

- Direct students' attention to the Reading Focus box. Go over the information in it.
- Go over the directions and the question.
- Put students in pairs to discuss the personal statements.
- Elicit ideas from the class.

CULTURE NOTE

Tell students that telecommuting has become much more common in the United States in the last several years. Help students understand what telecommuting involves, such as working off-site (usually at home) but keeping up with office responsibilities such as attending meetings, and so on. Lead a discussion about the benefits and downsides of telecommuting. For students who wish to know more, have them research information on the Internet and report back to the class.

EXPANSION ACTIVITY: Vocabulary practice

- Have students read aloud the definitions for each word in the glossary, along with the sentence containing each word from the personal statements.
- Discuss the meaning of each word, giving further examples as needed.
- Have each student write sentences using the vocabulary words. Encourage them to use the words in contexts that are different from those used in the reading.
- Put students in pairs to share their sentences.
- Have volunteers read their sentences to the class.

CIVICS NOTE

Tell students that many people in America feel it is their civic duty to volunteer. Some people volunteer to help with elections, to provide services for community members, to keep national parks clean, and in many other ways. Show students some websites such as Volunteer.gov that tell of the many opportunities to volunteer around the United States.

❹ AFTER YOU READ.

A. TALK with a partner. Take turns asking and answering the questions.

- Go over the directions.
- Put students in pairs to ask and answer the questions. Ask students to switch roles after item 4 or to alternate roles with each question.
- Go over the answers with the class.

ANSWER KEY

1. Terry's two main goals are to reduce stress and improve his home life.
2. She will be running her own business soon.
3. He will spend more time at home and help manage the household.
4. He will buy a treadmill, relax more, and donate time to the men's shelter.
5. Perla has a daughter and an older sister.
6. Next month, Perla is going to choose a college.
7. At work this year, she will volunteer for new duties and attend a technology convention.
8. She is excited because she is looking forward to the future.

B. COMPARE. Complete the chart below using information from the personal statements. Then discuss your answers with a partner and compare and contrast Terry's and Perla's lives and goals. Use words and phrases such as *however, like, unlike, both, similar, different.*

- Go over the directions, the examples, and the questions.
- Have students complete the chart.
- Put students in pairs to compare and contrast the information from their charts.
- Go over the answers with the class.

ANSWER KEY

		Terry	Perla
1.	More or less time spent at work in the upcoming year?	less time	more time
2.	Like working for the company?	not sure	yes
3.	Number of children?	three	one
4.	Important to spend time with family?	yes	yes
5.	Married?	yes	no, single mom
6.	Main goals?	1. reduce stress 2. improve home life	1. go to college 2. accomplish more at work

COMMUNITY CONNECTION: Interviewing to gain perspective

- Post the lists and notes from the warm-up activity for this lesson. Review the information with the class, having students restate the main ideas.
- As a class, develop a set of 4–5 interview questions about priorities in life, such as *What was most important to you when you were in your twenties? What life events caused your perspective to change?*
- Have each student copy the questions.
- Put students into groups and assign each group a different age range. Have each group member find a person of that age range in the community to interview. Have students take notes on the interview.
- Have groups compare notes on what they learned from people in the age range they interviewed. Ask each group to summarize their findings to the class.
- Lead a class discussion about the overall results of the interviews. You may wish to have students create pie charts to show their data.

EXPANSION ACTIVITY: Personal statements

- Have students write their own personal statements, using the reading on page 193 as a model.
- Have students create a display poster featuring their personal statement, illustrations, quotes, and other creative ideas.
- Display the posters around the room and have students circulate to read and enjoy each other's hopes and goals.
- After students have viewed the posters, ask them if they found anything particularly inspirational from reading their classmates' statements. Encourage discussion.

LESSON 7: Writing

OBJECTIVES

Write about a life change
Plan goals for the future

WRITING FOCUS

Organize Ideas

COMPETENCIES

Brainstorm ideas
Write about personal goals

WARM-UP ACTIVITY: My style of organization

- Ask students how they usually organize large amounts of information. Do they make notes? Use index cards? Create a document or chart on the computer?
- Have students share their personal method of organization. Take a poll to determine which methods are most popular.

1 THINK ABOUT IT. Have you ever decided to change something in your life, like learn something new, or stop a bad habit? What did you do? Did the change improve your life? Why or why not? Tell a partner.

- Go over the questions. Give an example from your own experience to get students thinking.
- Put students in pairs to talk about the questions.
- Have volunteers tell stories from their own experience to the class. Encourage students to ask each other follow-up questions.

2 BEFORE YOU WRITE.

A. READ the brainstorming notes one student wrote about the topic *Things I Want to Learn*. Then look at how he organized his ideas. Finally, read his finished paragraphs. Which brainstorming ideas were not used in the paragraphs?

- Direct students' attention to the Writing Focus box. Go over the information in it.
- Go over the directions and the questions.
- Have students read the notes, chart, and paragraphs.
- Have students look for a change in one topic—from golf to waterskiing—in the written paragraph. Elicit ideas why the change may have occurred. *(Paolo got a summer job as a waterskiing instructor?)*
- Lead a class discussion to answer the questions.

ANSWER KEY

Ideas not used: learning to play golf this summer; learning Spanish within the next year

B. BRAINSTORM and organize your ideas about the topic *How I want to improve my life.*

- Go over the directions and steps for this activity.
- Have students choose three topics and complete the chart with their notes.
- Put students in pairs to share what they wrote.
- Call on students to tell the class about one of the topics they chose.

ACADEMIC NOTE

To help students brainstorm, introduce them to visual brainstorming tools such as VisualThesaurus.com or AquaBrowser Library (available on many public library websites). Point out that such tools are great for thinking of ideas for creative writing or academic projects.

EXPANSION ACTIVITY: Guest speaker

- Have your school's career counselor visit the classroom to speak about long-term planning and goal-setting. Before the visit, have students write down one question each that they would like to ask the visiting speaker about the topic.

- While the career counselor is speaking, encourage students to stop him or her to ask questions for clarification or further information.

- Have volunteers ask the questions they wrote if the career counselor did not answer them in the course of his or her informational talk. Encourage open discussion.

3 WRITE Choose one of the topics from your chart. Write 2–3 paragraphs that explain your goals for that topic over the next five years.

- Have students choose one of their three topics to write about.

- Direct students to write their paragraphs in their notebooks.

4 AFTER YOU WRITE.

A. EDIT your paragraphs.

- Go over the editing questions.

- Have students look at their paragraphs and make changes if necessary.

- Put students in pairs to review one another's writing, answering the questions about their partner's work.

B. REWRITE your paragraphs with corrections.

- Go over the directions.

- Have students rewrite their paragraphs, incorporating their partner's suggestions and any other corrections as needed.

- Have students present their paragraphs to the class.

- Lead a class discussion to compare and contrast students' goals.

EXPANSION ACTIVITY: Visualizing the future

- Have students imagine that it is five years from now and they have accomplished the goals they set for themselves in Activity 3. Have them visualize what their life is like.

- Have students write a paragraph that tells what their life is like and how they feel now.

- Have students share their paragraph with a partner or with the class if they wish.

ACADEMIC CONNECTION: Effective oral presentations

- Before students present their paragraphs to the class, brainstorm with them the characteristics of effective oral presentations in the classroom. Consider questions such as where to stand, where to look, whether/how to use gestures or facial expressions, and characteristics of speech (clarity, loudness, pauses, etc.).

- Create a rubric as a class for rating oral presentations, e.g., *excellent – good – needs improvement*. Leave room after each category for students to make brief notes explaining their rating.

- Have students use the rubric to evaluate their peers' presentations. Students may either give their rubrics directly to the speaker or may use them as a memory aid for giving feedback.

Career Connection

Compare two jobs and make a choice

COMPETENCIES

Evaluate two job offers
Practice test-taking skills

WARM-UP ACTIVITY: Gut instincts

- On the board, write the phrase *go with your gut.* Ask students to guess what it means. If students can't guess, write short clues to help them, such as *instinct, hunch, feeling*, and so on.
- Tell a story about a time you followed your instincts when making a decision. Did the situation turn out well or badly?
- Encourage students to tell stories about times that they followed their intuition when making a decision.

1 THINK ABOUT IT. How do you make important decisions in your life? Do you make lists, think things over by yourself, or talk with your family? Discuss in a group or with a partner.

- Go over the directions and the questions.
- Put students in pairs or groups to talk about the questions.
- Elicit ideas from the class about making decisions. What do the majority of the students do when they make decisions?

2 READ about Jonathan, an employee in the field of Information Technology. Now read the notes Jonathan wrote about the two jobs. As you read, circle the positive things about each company (pros) and underline the negative aspects (cons).

- Direct students' attention to the photo and ask questions: *Who do you see? What do you think he is doing? How does he probably feel?*

- Go over the directions. Point out the glossary below the chart and have students preview the words.
- Have students read about Jonathan and then read his notes about the jobs. Have them circle and underline the pros and cons as they read.
- Put students in pairs to compare what they underlined and circled.

ANSWER KEY

A–Z Internet

- Pros: will probably be doubling in size; will have more responsibilities; is going to be offering promotions; is going to be investing in state-of-the-art technology; management emphasizes how to avoid major problems; will be learning new skills
- Cons: Will have to move; $62,000 per year; 10 days vacation; retirement package and health insurance are not great—the family plan is very expensive

IT-2000

- Pros: Don't have to move; $70,500 per year, plus $2,000 raise; 15 days vacation; excellent retirement package and health insurance; paid for my M.Sc. degree
- Cons: will not be growing in the future; will not be receiving a promotion; no plans to expand the computer programming department, or to improve our current technology; will not be addressing the issue of our outdated computers; doesn't provide the opportunity to learn new skills or take on new challenges

EXPANSION ACTIVITY: Responsibility

- Review Jonathan's notes from the chart in Activity 2. What does he say about taking on responsibilities? Is that something he wants to do?
- Divide the class into groups.
- Have each group discuss how much responsibility at work is too much, and how much is just right. Do some students want to be the boss eventually? Do others prefer to have a low level of responsibility so they can maintain regular, reasonable hours?
- Have groups report their opinions. Discuss as a class.

3 TALK with a partner about the pros and cons of the two positions above. What will happen if Jonathan takes the job at A-Z Internet? What will happen if he stays at IT-2000?

- Go over the directions.
- Put students in pairs to talk about the questions.
- Lead a class discussion, eliciting ideas from students. Be sure to point out factors such as moving and cost-of-living expenses.

EXPANSION ACTIVITY: Cost-of-living investigation

- Find a cost-of-living calculator on the Internet.
- Have students enter the information from the chart in Activity 2 into the cost-of-living calculator and view the results.
- Discuss the results. Financially, would Jonathan benefit from moving or staying where he is?

4 WHAT ABOUT YOU? Which is more important to you: growth potential, or benefits and salary? What issues would influence your decision to accept or turn down a job? Talk with a partner.

- Go over the directions and the questions.
- Put students in pairs to discuss and give their opinions.
- Call on students to give their opinions.

COMMUNITY CONNECTION: Local cost of living

- After completing the cost-of-living investigation in Activity 3, have students examine the cost of living in your own community.
- Ask students if they have considered moving to a different state or city. Have them compare the cost of living in your current town with the new state or city. Using the tools on the cost-of-living calculator on the Internet, have each student calculate how much money they would save or lose by moving to the new location.
- Have students report their findings to the class if they wish to do so, as well as whether completing the activity made them reconsider what to do in the future.

CHECK YOUR PROGRESS!

- Have students circle the answers.
- Have students check whether each answer is right or wrong.
- Have students total their correct answers and fill in the chart at the bottom of the page.
- Have students create a learning plan and/or set learning goals.

ANSWER KEY

1. running; 2. be finishing; 3. going to be;
4. giving; 5. to; 6. To promote; 7. minimize;
8. to save; 9. accompanying; 10. select;
11. taking over; 12. enjoying; 13. efforts;
14. minimize; 15. of; 16. promote

Name: _____   Date: _____

Verb Review: Simple Present and Present Continuous

🎧 **A** **DIRECTIONS:** Look at the Big Picture on page 8 and listen to the CD. Complete each sentence
TCD1, 8   by filling in the missing verbs you hear. NOTE: Some verbs may be contractions.

1. Carlos _____ in the business program at the community college. He _____ accounting and business management.

2. Rebecca, his wife, also _____ the community college. She _____ in the nursing program. This semester, she _____ Medical Assisting Skills, and she _____ also _____ Introduction to Health Care online.

3. Ana _____ a high school student, but she _____ already _____ about college. She _____ into early childhood education, restaurant management, and hotel and hospitality.

4. Luis _____ in middle school, but he _____ to fix things. He _____ through two books—one about electrical work and one about air conditioning science.

5. Paulo _____ in elementary school, but he really _____ cars and computers. He _____ at the pictures in a book about auto body repair. He also _____ a book about computer programming.

B **DIRECTIONS:** Write questions to ask a partner. Use the simple present and present continuous tenses. Record your partner's answers below each question.

Example: Q: Are you taking a vacation this year?
            A: Yes, my family is going to Puerto Rico to visit relatives.

Q: _____

A: _____

Q: _____

A: _____

Q: _____

A: _____

Name: _____   Date: _____

Vocabulary Review

DIRECTIONS: Read the words in the box. Then fill in the blanks in the sentences below.

earn	credit	contact	make improvements	prioritize
tasks	organize	meet with	personality test	research

1. Next week, I'm going to _____ my financial advisor to plan for my retirement. I have an appointment at her office on Tuesday.

2. Juanita thinks she should _____ more money at her job, so she's going to ask her boss for a raise.

3. Ahmed has many _____ to complete tomorrow. He has to finish his homework, go to the bank, help his family paint the house, and pay his bills for the month.

4. Lana took a _____ last week. It said that she was outgoing, friendly, and optimistic.

5. If Serena doesn't _____ on her test scores, she will not pass her classes this semester.

6. Although the Physical Education class was only worth one _____ , Dean decided to take it because he wanted to learn how to play different sports.

7. Alexis is a talented painter. I think she should _____ taking classes at the Academy of Art downtown.

8. When you have many things to do, it can be difficult to _____ them so that you do the most important tasks first.

9. Be sure to _____ your professor if you have any questions about the upcoming examination.

10. Jacob is going to _____ the food drive for the local women's shelter next month.

Name: _____

Date: _____

Name That Person

DIRECTIONS: Look at the Big Picture on page 8. Then answer the questions below.

1. This man is browsing for books in the business section of the library. He is wearing glasses, a long-sleeved shirt, and pants. He's carrying an armful of books.

   Who is this student? _____

   What is he looking for? _____

2. This girl is walking out of the book aisles with a stack of several books. She has short black hair and is wearing a short-sleeved shirt.

   What color is her shirt? _____

   What is she carrying? _____

3. This woman is sitting next to a small table. She has a book open in her hands and another book next to her on the table. She is looking at the girl with black hair who is carrying the stack of books.

   Who is this student? _____

   What is she reading? _____

4. This boy is pulling two books off the shelves in the vocational aisle. He is next to the man in glasses.

   Who is this student? _____

   Who is he looking at? _____

5. In one of the aisles, a young boy is pulling all of the books off the shelves. The books are lying in a pile around him, and he is reaching up to a shelf to grab another book. A man has just discovered this mess and looks upset.

   On which aisle is this happening? _____

   _____

Name: _____   Date: _____

Today's Meeting

DIRECTIONS: Look at the Big Picture and your answers to Activity 2 on page 24. Read the emails. Write the name of the character on the line.

1.

Hi Lorenzo,

I'm sorry I was a little distracted at today's meeting. Before the meeting, I told Thomas I would help him pull together some materials. He needed a lot more help than I thought. Then during the meeting, Donna spilled my water, and I had to clean it up. After the meeting, I had an important doctor's appointment. Luckily, Silvia covered for me. Next time, I'll be able to contribute more to the meeting.

Welcome to the company!

_____

2.

Lorenzo,

I was very unhappy about our meeting today. Before the meeting, I had to pull some materials together. That took a lot of time Then the meeting started 15 minutes late. During the meeting, I was supposed to make a presentation, but we ran out of time. Now I have to follow up with each person to make sure he or she knows what to do. I'm a very busy person and don't have time for this.

In the future, please start the meetings on time.

Thanks, _____

3.

Hi Lorenzo,

Welcome to the prison. Oops! I mean, welcome to the company. It was nice to meet you at the meeting. I'm sorry that I feel asleep during the meeting. Before the meeting, I wanted to get some coffee to help me wake up, but Jenny and I were working on a project. I hope that we don't have meetings too often. We have enough work to do here without having to talk to each other every day.

_____

Name: _____   **Date:** _____

What were they doing?

DIRECTIONS: Look at the Big Picture on page 24. Write sentences about what you imagine each person was doing on the day of the meeting. Use *as soon as, after*, and *until*.

Example: *After the meeting, Jenny will join a conference call.*

1. Luke

   (as soon as) _____

   _____

   (after) _____

   _____

   (until) _____

   _____

2. Donna

   (as soon as) _____

   _____

   (after) _____

   _____

   (until) _____

   _____

Name: _____   Date: _____

Simple Past or Present Perfect

DIRECTIONS: Look at the Big Picture on page 24. Lorenzo is writing to his supervisor about his team. (Circle) the correct form of the verb.

1. Jenny **got / has gotten** along well with her coworkers except for a couple of weeks last year when she **showed / had shown** a bad attitude.

2. Luke **pulled together / has pulled together** all the materials on the Thompson project last week. He **met / has met** every deadline so far.

3. For the past six months, Thomas **left / has left** many voicemails complaining about his job. He **already asked / has already asked** Donna to cover for him twice this month and it's only the first week.

4. Six months ago Donna **thought / has thought** of the great idea of a monthly newsletter, but she **did not complete / has not completed** a newsletter yet.

5. Silvia **attended / has attended** many workshops and **showed / has shown** great leadership skills.

DIRECTIONS: Write two sentences about Lorenzo's job performance. Use the simple past and the present perfect.

_____

_____

_____

_____

Name: _____   Date: _____

Participle Review

A **DIRECTIONS:** Write the correct participles on the lines.

1. make _____
2. leave _____
3. like _____
4. drive _____
5. eat _____

6. do _____
7. learn _____
8. tell _____
9. drink _____
10. give _____

11. come _____
12. forget _____
13. buy _____
14. write _____
15. walk _____

B **DIRECTIONS:** Write five sentences with the past perfect and the simple past.

Example: *Mary had done her homework by the time Jim came over.*

1. _____

   _____

2. _____

   _____

3. _____

   _____

4. _____

   _____

5. _____

   _____

Name: _____   Date: _____

What did they do before?

A **DIRECTIONS:** Look at the Big Picture on page 40. What did the people do before the things you see in the picture? Complete the sentences using the past perfect and the verbs in parentheses.

1. Tony _____ (got) to work at 1:00.

2. Mark and Jill _____ (take) the bus to the theater.

3. Joey _____ (go) on the merry-go-round.

4. Jane _____ (eat) lunch.

5. Tom and Tammy _____ (ask) their mother to take them to the museum.

B **DIRECTIONS:** Complete the sentences using the past perfect.

1. Andy and Amy _____

_____.

2. The server _____

_____.

3. Uma and Rajiv _____

_____.

4. Tom and Tammy's mother _____

_____.

5. Joey's father _____

_____.

Name: _____   **Date:** _____

What a terrible day!

A **DIRECTIONS:** Look at the Big Picture on page 40. Read Dan's story.

I had a really terrible day yesterday. I had been looking forward to spending the day downtown with my wife, Sue. We had planned on meeting at the café next to the Natural History Museum at 1:00 and then going to see *Macbeth* at 2:00. By the time Sue showed up, I had been waiting for 45 minutes! Sue said she was sorry. She had been looking for her car keys. We decided to skip lunch and go see the play.

When we got to the theater, the play had already sold out. We decided to go the amusement park because we could eat and ride the roller coaster. After we ate lunch, we got on the roller coaster. Once we got to the top, the ride stopped. There was a problem, and we had to wait at the top of the ride. We had been sitting on the roller coaster for 20 minutes when it started to rain! Finally, the ride started and we could get off.

After that, we were wet and cold. Sue suggested we go to the symphony. A nice usher showed us to our seats just as the musicians came on stage. The musicians had only been playing for a few minutes when the electricity went out. The concert hall workers gave us our money back and said the theater was closing for the day.

Sue and I decided we had had enough bad luck! After Sue found her car keys, we drove home. All in all, it was a terrible day.

B **DIRECTIONS:** Check *True* or *False*.

1. Sue was late because she had been looking for her keys.   ❑ True   ❑ False

2. Dan and Sue had already bought tickets to *Macbeth*.   ❑ True   ❑ False

3. Dan and Sue enjoyed their ride on the roller coaster.   ❑ True   ❑ False

4. The electricity went out at the beginning of the concert.   ❑ True   ❑ False

5. They had a nice time at the Natural History Museum.   ❑ True   ❑ False

Name: _____   **Date:** _____

I love my job!

DIRECTIONS: Look at the Big Picture on page 56. Read the personal statements below from the people who work at the bank. Then answer the questions.

Security Guard: I love my job! I think it is important to keep people safe, and every day I feel grateful that I can help others. Last month, I stopped an armed robbery! That was exciting, but the best part was how proud my family was of me.

What are three reasons that the man loves his job?

1. _____

   _____

2. _____

   _____

3. _____

   _____

Teller: Hm, I can't say I'm crazy about my job as a teller. To be honest, people can be pretty rude when they come in here. Lunchtime is especially bad. Sometimes twenty people come in at the same time, and they all want to be helped right away. They glare at me while they're standing in line. Well, it's not *my* fault they came at a busy time!

4. Does the teller like or dislike her job? How do you know? _____

   _____

5. What time of day is the worst for the teller? _____

   _____

6. What happens at that time? _____

   _____

Mortgage Loan Officer: I really enjoy my job. I love talking to people, and that's what I get to do most of the day. It is really satisfying to help people, too, especially if they are making their dreams come true. I love helping first-time home buyers and people who are starting their own business. It's very interesting to hear their stories and to talk about their hopes and plans for the future. I'm also pretty good at explaining complicated rules and processes, so it is easy for me to teach people about loans and how they work.

7. Who does the mortgage loan officer most enjoy helping? _____

   _____

8. What interests the mortgage loan officer about people?_____

   _____

Name: _____   Date: _____

What did she say?

DIRECTIONS: Look at the Big Picture on page 56. Listen to your teacher read each conversation below. Fill in the words that are missing.

Millie: Hi there. I'd like to _____ a personal _____.

Teller: Great. I'll _____ the check and _____ ID.

Millie: Just a _____. I'm sure it's here _____. Oh dear, I must have _____ it in the car.

Teller: If _____ like to go get it and come back, I can _____you then. Just come back to my _____. You don't have to stand in line _____.

Millie: Thanks. _____ be right back.

_____

Loan Officer: Hello. _____ may I help you today?

Rosa: We're not _____ sure. We are thinking of _____ a house but we don't know _____ to start.

Juan: Our real estate _____ said that if we get prequalified for a _____, it will be _____ to buy a house.

Rosa: That's right. We wanted to _____ about getting a mortgage loan here. We saw your _____ in the paper and your _____ rates look very competitive.

Loan Officer: We do have great _____ right now—it's a good time to buy a home! The __ step you'll need to take is to request your _____ report.

Juan: Oh, we _____ got a credit report last year when we financed _____ new car. We can use that one, can't we?

Loan Officer: I'm _____ not. You need a current credit report in order to _____ for a mortgage here. But don't worry, it's free and it only takes a _____ days to get the information back.

Rosa: Well, that _____ all right. Let's get started on the paperwork.

Name: _____   Date: _____

Roll-a-Sentence Tag Questions

DIRECTIONS: Look at the Big Picture on page 56 and review the people in the picture. Roll two dice. Find the box below that has the number you rolled to find your subject. Roll the dice a second time to find your verb. Make a question using the subject and the verb by forming a tag question. Write five questions on the lines below.

Example: First roll for subject = 8 = Juan and I
Second roll for verb = 10 = need

Sentence: *Juan and I need a credit report, don't we?*

Note: If your subject is *it*, you may choose your own verb. You may also change the word *it* to any object in the Big Picture.

Roll-a-Sentence	2 Rosa be	3 You have
4 Tamir wear	5 The guard and the man do	6 I stand
7 You and Millie try	8 Juan and I want	9 The tellers ask
10 It need	11 Sarah look	12 Paolo and Bart wait

1. _____

_____

2. _____

_____

3. _____

_____

4. _____

_____

5. _____

_____

Name: _____ **Date:** _____

Where's the focus?

A **DIRECTIONS:** Read the sentences. Put a check (✓) next to the sentence you think has the correct focus. Be prepared to explain your answer.

1. _____ Someone in China made my sweater.

   _____ My sweater was made in China.

2. _____ Mary gave a speech.

   _____ Some people were given a speech by Mary.

3. _____ Someone told me to be here at 10:00.

   _____ I was told to be here at 10:00.

4. _____ Peter stole a car.

   _____ A car was stolen by Peter.

5. _____ The orchestra performs Mozart's *Requiem* on Tuesday night.

   _____ Mozart's *Requiem* is performed on Tuesday night.

6. _____ Someone hired Kelly to teach singing lessons.

   _____ Kelly was hired to teach singing lessons.

7. _____ Bill Gates and Paul Allen created Microsoft.

   _____ Microsoft was created by Bill Gates and Paul Allen.

8. _____ Mr. Clark prepared our tax return.

   _____ Our tax return was prepared by Mr. Clark.

B **DIRECTIONS:** In groups, compare your answers. Explain why you chose each sentence.

Name: _____   Date: _____

Can you help me?

A **DIRECTIONS:** Put the conversations in the correct order.

Conversation 1

_____ How about Wednesday at 4:00?

___1___ Free Clinic. How may I help you?

_____ My son has a terrible cough and a fever.

_____ Okay. Would you like to set up an appointment to see a doctor?

_____ We will be there. Thank you.

_____ Yes, please.

Conversation 2

_____ He is a golden retriever with white around the eyes and mouth.

_____ I live at 933 Scott Street. Thank you so much for your help.

_____ Good afternoon. Animal Control. What can we do for you?

_____ Hi. I just came home from work and my dog isn't in the backyard.

_____ Okay, I'll have my people look for him. Where do you live?

_____ What kind of dog do you have?

B **DIRECTIONS:** Write a telephone conversation using one of the public services in the Big Picture on page 70.

_____

_____

_____

_____

C **DIRECTIONS:** Practice the three conversations with your partner.

Name: _____ **Date:** _____

Tax Form

DIRECTIONS: Fill in the tax form with information your teacher gives you.

Form **1040** Department of the Treasury—Internal Revenue Service
U.S. Individual Income Tax Return 2007   IRS Use Only—Do not write or staple in this space.

For the year Jan. 1–Dec. 31, 2007, or other tax year beginning ____ , 2007, ending ____ , 20 ____   OMB No. 1545-0074

Label (See instructions on page 12.)
Use the IRS label. Otherwise, please print or type.

L A B E L   H E R E

Your first name and initial	Last name		Your social security number
If a joint return, spouse's first name and initial	Last name		Spouse's social security number
Home address (number and street). If you have a P.O. box, see page 12.		Apt. no.	▲ You **must** enter your SSN(s) above. ▲
City, town or post office, state, and ZIP code. If you have a foreign address, see page 12.			Checking a box below will not change your tax or refund.

Presidential Election Campaign ▶ Check here if you, or your spouse if filing jointly, want $3 to go to this fund (see page 12) ▶   ☐ You ☐ Spouse

Filing Status
Check only one box.

1 ☐ Single
2 ☐ Married filing jointly (even if only one had income)
3 ☐ Married filing separately. Enter spouse's SSN above and full name here. ▶
4 ☐ Head of household (with qualifying person). (See page 13.) If the qualifying person is a child but not your dependent, enter this child's name here. ▶
5 ☐ Qualifying widow(er) with dependent child (see page 14)

Exemptions

6a ☐ **Yourself.** If someone can claim you as a dependent, **do not** check box 6a . . . .
b ☐ **Spouse** . . . .

Boxes checked on 6a and 6b ____
No. of children on 6c who:
• lived with you ____
• did not live with you due to divorce or separation (see page 16) ____

c **Dependents:**

(1) First name Last name	(2) Dependent's social security number	(3) Dependent's relationship to you	(4) ✓ if qualifying child for child tax credit (see page 15)
			☐
			☐
			☐
			☐

If more than four dependents, see page 15.

Dependents on 6c not entered above ____
Add numbers on lines above ▶ ☐

d Total number of exemptions claimed . . . .

Income

Attach Form(s) W-2 here. Also attach Forms W-2G and 1099-R if tax was withheld.

If you did not get a W-2, see page 19.

Enclose, but do not attach, any payment. Also, please use **Form 1040-V.**

7	Wages, salaries, tips, etc. Attach Form(s) W-2		7	
8a	**Taxable** interest. Attach Schedule B if required		8a	
b	**Tax-exempt** interest. **Do not** include on line 8a	8b		
9a	Ordinary dividends. Attach Schedule B if required		9a	
b	Qualified dividends (see page 19)	9b		
10	Taxable refunds, credits, or offsets of state and local income taxes (see page 20)		10	
11	Alimony received		11	
12	Business income or (loss). Attach Schedule C or C-EZ		12	
13	Capital gain or (loss). Attach Schedule D if required. If not required, check here ▶ ☐		13	
14	Other gains or (losses). Attach Form 4797		14	
15a	IRA distributions	15a	b Taxable amount (see page 21)	15b	
16a	Pensions and annuities	16a	b Taxable amount (see page 22)	16b	
17	Rental real estate, royalties, partnerships, S corporations, trusts, etc. Attach Schedule E		17	
18	Farm income or (loss). Attach Schedule F		18	
19	Unemployment compensation		19	
20a	Social security benefits	20a	b Taxable amount (see page 24)	20b	
21	Other income. List type and amount (see page 24) ____		21	
22	Add the amounts in the far right column for lines 7 through 21. This is your **total income** ▶		22	

Adjusted Gross Income

23	Educator expenses (see page 26)	23		
24	Certain business expenses of reservists, performing artists, and fee-basis government officials. Attach Form 2106 or 2106-EZ	24		
25	Health savings account deduction. Attach Form 8889	25		
26	Moving expenses. Attach Form 3903	26		
27	One-half of self-employment tax. Attach Schedule SE	27		
28	Self-employed SEP, SIMPLE, and qualified plans	28		
29	Self-employed health insurance deduction (see page 26)	29		
30	Penalty on early withdrawal of savings	30		
31a	Alimony paid b Recipient's SSN ▶ ____	31a		
32	IRA deduction (see page 27)	32		
33	Student loan interest deduction (see page 30)	33		
34	Tuition and fees deduction. Attach Form 8917	34		
35	Domestic production activities deduction. Attach Form 8903	35		
36	Add lines 23 through 31a and 32 through 35		36	

Name: _____   **Date:** _____

Definite and Indefinite Articles

DIRECTIONS: Fill in the blanks with *a*, *an*, *some*, or *the*.

1. _____ new student joined our class today. _____ new student is from Mexico.

2. _____ phone company is sending someone over to fix our phone this afternoon.

3. We have _____ problem with our stove. I don't think _____ problem is serious.

4. _____ cat can be a wonderful pet!

5. I think that the bank made _____ error on my bill.

6. We are having _____ problems with our Internet connection.

7. _____ refrigerator in my apartment is broken.

8. If you eat _____ apple every day, you will be very healthy.

9. Harry needs _____ new car.

10. Russia is _____ biggest country in the world.

11. Do you have _____ good signal on your cell phone?

12. We saw _____ electric car yesterday. _____ car was going really fast.

13. Someone from _____ gas company called. They want to check our pipes.

14. I have to go to the bank to get _____ money.

15. _____ man over there is my English teacher.

Name: _____   **Date:** _____

Embedded Questions

A **DIRECTIONS:** (Circle) the correct word in parentheses.

Dear Mom and Dad,

I'm not doing so well here in San Francisco. I got here last week and rented an apartment. It has a lot of problems, and I wonder (**1.** if / where) I made a mistake renting this one. The rent is expensive. I pay $1,500 per month for a two-bedroom apartment. I need someone to share the rent, but I don't know (**2.** why / where) to find a roommate. The landlord isn't a very nice person. She won't fix some leaking pipes, and the carpet is dirty and stained. I'm not sure (**3.** how / if) to file a complaint. Do you know (**4.** if / why) Uncle Harry can help? I remember that he's a lawyer here in San Francisco. I'd like to know (**5.** who / whether) he knows about rental law. Can you send his phone number? I might call him tomorrow.

Love,

Kim

B **DIRECTIONS:** Rewrite each question as a sentence (ending with a period) containing an embedded question.

1. Is she coming to the party tonight?

_____

2. What is her name?

_____

3. Did the landlord fix the problem?

_____

4. Why did he come home so late?

_____

5. Should I ask the teacher for help?

_____

Name: _____   **Date:** _____

Advice Column

A **DIRECTIONS:** Read the advice column on page 94 again. (Circle) the correct answer for each question.

1. How does Jean tell "Anxious to Move" to find information about moving out?
   a. She says to look in a newspaper.
   b. She suggests checking the lease.
   c. She says to call the landlord.
   d. She suggests not moving out.

2. What does the lease of "Evicted in Evanston" say about subletting?
   a. It says nothing about subletting.
   b. It says that "Evicted in Evanston" cannot sublet.
   c. The lease says that subletting is acceptable.
   d. It says that subletting is sometimes okay.

3. What advice does Jean give "Evicted in Evanston"?
   a. Talk to the landlord.
   b. Read the lease.
   c. Move out quickly.
   d. Get legal help.

4. How long was "Evicted in Evanston" out of town?
   a. two months
   b. three months
   c. four months
   d. five months

5. How does the new apartment of "Anxious to Move" compare to the old apartment?
   a. It's more expensive, but it's bigger.
   b. It's cheaper and a little smaller.
   c. It's larger and is the same price.
   d. It's larger and is less expensive.

6. How much notice do renters usually have to give landlords before moving out?
   a. 15 days
   b. three weeks
   c. 30 days
   d. two months

Name: _____ **Date:** _____

Vocabulary Poll

DIRECTIONS: Talk to people in your community. Have them describe the Big Picture on page 105. Write down new vocabulary words that you hear and a definition or translation for each one. Be sure to ask for correct spelling if needed.

VOCABULARY WORD	DEFINITION

Name: _____   Date: _____

A Funny Thing Happened . . .

DIRECTIONS: Look at the Big Picture on page 105. Read this email that Officer King wrote about the incident. Then answer the questions.

Date: March 21

Subject: A Funny Thing Happened . . .

Dear Sis,

You'll never believe the latest story from work. Officer Dill and I were called to Lee's Butcher Shop to investigate a robbery. Mr. Lee was really upset because the steaks that were stolen were very expensive. Nobody who was in the shop had seen the thief. The woman on the street that said she'd seen the thief couldn't describe him, either. I called the officer who was on duty, and he told us to take a look around the neighborhood. Then we saw some muddy paw prints that led toward the park. There was a girl there who was laughing and pointing at something. When we arrived there, we saw two dogs that were really enjoying a couple of juicy steaks! Mr. Lee and I both had a good laugh at the dogs that got away with it!

---

1. Why was Mr. Lee upset? _____

_____

2. Who did Officer King call? _____

_____

3. What did he advise the police officer to do? _____

_____

4. What was the girl at the park doing? _____

_____

5. What does the phrase "got away with it" mean? _____

_____

Name: _____   Date: _____

Mr. Lee's Dilemma

DIRECTIONS: Mr. Lee is tired of owning a business downtown. He is thinking of moving his business to Glendale, the suburb where he lives. Listen to the conversation between Mr. Lee and his wife. Fill in the missing information below.

Mr. Lee: I'm so tired of all the _____ downtown. My butcher shop has been broken into _____ times this year!

Mrs. Lee: That's true, but crime isn't much better here in _____. And besides, the police downtown have always been so _____ when you needed them. Officer King always does a great job, and Officer Dill is so nice.

Mr. Lee: I know, I can't complain about the police. But what bothers me is that I've had to pay to replace nearly _____ worth of food that was stolen.

Mrs. Lee: Hmm, that is a lot of money. On the other hand, the _____ on a shop here would be much _____ than it is downtown. You might end up losing money if you move the business here.

Mr. Lee: What about the money I'd save on commuting? If I worked here in Glendale, I could _____ instead of driving.

Mrs. Lee: Well, you may have a point. But wouldn't you miss all the friends you've made over the years? People come into the shop every day just to _____ with you. If you move, you probably won't see them anymore. You might get _____ in a new shop.

Mr. Lee: I don't think so. So many of my old _____ have moved to the suburbs, anyway. Nobody wants to shop downtown anymore. Everyone wants to go to the _____ in the suburbs.

Mrs. Lee: If that's the case, how do you think you can _____ against the superstores here in Glendale?

Mr. Lee: I'm not sure, to be honest. I guess I need to _____ the market more before I make such a big decision.

Mrs. Lee: That sounds like a good idea.

Name: _____   Date: _____

Gerunds as Objects of Prepositions

A **DIRECTIONS:** (Circle) the correct word in parentheses.

1. My 90-year-old mother isn't nervous (at / about) living alone.

2. The weather bureau is (serious / excited) about taking precautions.

3. He's nervous about (driving / to drive) to Chicago in the winter.

4. I'm happy (because / about) staying home during the rain storm.

5. They are worried about (keeping / to keep) their food cold.

6. The children were (exciting / excited) about playing soccer in the rain.

7. We're (worried / happy) about having a smog advisory today.

8. The government is serious about (to warn / warning) the public about the storm.

B **DIRECTIONS:** Put the sentences in the correct order. Capitalize the first word of each sentence.

1. worried / outdoors / I'm / about / exercising / today

   _____

2. visiting / they / their / parents / were / about / excited

   _____

3. taking / she / serious / shelter / during the storm / was / about

   _____

4. are / driving / we / about / in this torrential rain / concerned

   _____

5. a power outage / Martin / nervous / having / was / about

   _____

Name: _____

Date: _____

Gerunds as Objects of a Verb + Preposition

A **DIRECTIONS:** Fill in the blanks in the sentences with words from the word box.

in	help	focuses	care	volunteering	on

1. The Sierra Club is a wonderful nonprofit organization. It _____ on protecting our natural environment.

2. The Sierra Club believes _____ educating the public about nature and environmental issues.

3. Members of the Sierra Club _____ about protecting national forests.

4. Friends of the Urban Forest is another interesting organization. It works _____ planting trees in cities.

5. I plan on _____ with them this month.

6. All of my friends _____ with planting the trees.

B **DIRECTIONS:** Circle the correct word in parentheses.

1. The Environmental Protection Agency works on (to remove / removing) toxic waste.

2. Many organizations believe (in / on) helping people after disasters.

3. The Natural Resources Defense Council plans on (focusing / focus) on global warming.

4. The Red Cross helps (with / about) evacuating victims.

5. The Federal Emergency Management Agency (works / cares) on helping people in crises.

6. Habitat for Humanity is an organization that cares (in / about) building houses for people.

Name: _____   **Date:** _____

Four Problems

DIRECTIONS: Listen to the TV talk show again. (Circle) the correct answer to each question.

TCD3, 33

1. Who is Ms. Eva Erickson?

   a. the host of a TV program called "The Solutions Hour"

   b. head of the U.S. Department of Agriculture

   c. an expert on preparing for natural disasters

   d. head of the National Resources Defense Council

2. How many tornadoes did Wisconsin have one year?

   a. more than 16

   b. more than 60

   c. more than 160

   d. more than 6

3. In what year was there a power outage in New York?

   a. 2005

   b. 2004

   c. 2000

   d. 2003

4. After Hurricane Katrina, what was a problem where children were playing?

   a. bad food

   b. toxic waste

   c. wildfires

   d. flooding

5. When does the USDA take extra precautions against wildfires?

   a. during tornadoes

   b. during the winter

   c. during droughts

   d. during extreme cold

6. What was in danger during the power outages in New York?

   a. the food supply

   b. air conditioning

   c. the subways

   d. the government

Name: _____   Date: _____

What were they thinking?

DIRECTIONS: Look at the Big Picture on page 136 and listen to your teacher read what some of the people in the picture are thinking. Fill in the blanks to complete the thoughts below. Then tell who is thinking each thought.

1. "Boy, I'll be glad when this _____ is finished. I'm never going to

   _____ to _____ on time!"

   Who's thinking it? _____

2. "I really _____ I _____ my _____ test this time!"

   Who's thinking it? _____

3. "Oh, dear, I hope _____ will let me _____ without _____

   me a ticket! I was only out of the car for a few minutes."

   Who's thinking it? _____

4. "I hope he's okay _____ by _____."

   Who's thinking it? _____

5. " Great! I _____ found a _____ to _____!"

   Who's thinking it? _____

6. "Hm—that _____ looks awfully _____. I don't know if we really can

   park there."

   Who's thinking it? _____

Name: _____   **Date:** _____

Try and *Regret*

DIRECTIONS: Complete the sentences using a gerund or an infinitive from the word in parentheses.

1. I regret (lend) _____ Tom that $85. He hasn't paid me back yet.

2. Did you try (do) _____ the homework yet? It's really hard.

3. I regret (tell) _____ you that you did not get the job.

4. I regret (tell) _____ her about my idea. She's trying (make) _____ the boss think it was *her* idea!

5. When you are trying (learn) _____ something new, you should accept that you're going to make mistakes.

6. I tried (fix) _____ my car myself, and then I tried (take) _____ it to a mechanic, but it still keeps making that noise. I regret ever (buy) _____ that car!

7. The airline regretted (inform) _____ the passengers that there would be another two-hour delay in their departure time.

Name: _____   **Date:** _____

A Fender Bender

DIRECTIONS: Read the transcript from a TV report below. Answer the questions that follow.

Marty: And now we go to Sasha Roon, reporting live from an accident on Third Street downtown.

Sasha: Thank you, Marty. I'm here at the scene of an accident at the intersection of Third Street and Rodney Boulevard. Although the cause of the accident is still unclear, it appears that the driver of the blue car stopped suddenly and was then hit on the back left bumper by the red car. Eyewitnesses report that both drivers were using cell phones at the time of the accident, and one of them was also eating. Luckily, this was just a fender bender and neither of the drivers was seriously hurt, although both were taken to Patton Hospital immediately following the accident to check for spinal injuries. They have since been released. This is Sasha Roon reporting live from downtown.

1. Where did the accident take place? _____

_____

_____

_____

2. What vehicles were involved? _____

_____

_____

_____

3. What caused the accident? _____

_____

_____

_____

4. Is a fender bender a serious accident? How do you know? _____

_____

_____

_____

5. What happened to the drivers? _____

_____

_____

_____

Name: _____   **Date:** _____

At the Community Center

DIRECTIONS: Look at the Big Picture on page 152. Then read the conversation below and answer the questions.

Doris: You should really sign up for the Home Safety course on Saturday at the community center.

Rick: Oh, I'm sure my home is safe enough.

Doris: That's what I thought, but I found out about a lot of hazards that were putting my kids in danger. The course has really paid off. My home is much safer now than it was before.

Rick: Really? Well, maybe it would be a good idea. I'll think it over.

Doris: Great. I'll look up the number of the community center for you.

Rick: All right. I don't know if I'll follow through with it or not, though. I hate to give up a Saturday when I need the time to relax.

Doris: Trust me, you'll feel much better knowing your kids are safe.

Rick: Okay, you talked me into it! How do I register for the course?

Doris: Just show up on Saturday and you can sign up on the spot. You can even bring your kids so they can swim at the pool while you're taking the class.

Rick: That's a great idea. I think I will. The kids will have a ball!

1. What course is on Saturday? _____

   _____

2. Why doesn't Rick want to sign up? Give two reasons. _____

   _____

3. What does *on the spot* probably mean? _____

   _____

4. What does Doris suggest Rick do with his kids on Saturday? _____

   _____

Name: _____ **Date:** _____

Vocabulary Practice

DIRECTIONS: Look at the Big Picture on page 152. Complete the sentences with the words from the box below.

lifestyle	dozen	advice	dizziness	rash	swelling

1. There are always a _____ things going on at Doris's house at any time. Her family is very busy.

2. Johnny is only three years old, so he didn't know to stay away from the toxic cleansers. He got an itchy _____ on his hands when he tried to open a leaky bottle.

3. Mr. Morris fell on a toy on the steps and hit his head. He had to sit down until the _____ went away because his head was spinning.

4. Mia accidentally put her hand on the hot frying pan and got a bad burn. It was red and painful, but the _____ went away when she put some ice on the burn.

5. Mia followed Doris's _____ and put up the child safety gates so the kids wouldn't fall on the stairs.

6. If you want to lead a safer _____ , you should check your home for common hazards.

Name: _____   Date: _____

Winter Safety

DIRECTIONS: Listen to a nurse as she speaks to parents about child safety. Fill out the graphic organizer with the information you hear.

Safety hazard	Problems it can cause	How to prevent problems
Food	*Nausea.*	

Name: _____   **Date:** _____

The Interview

DIRECTIONS: Look at the Big Picture on page 168. Listen to the conversation between Kent and Allison, who are having an interview at the job fair. Then answer the questions.

1. Who is the interviewer? _____
_____

2. What job is Kent applying for? _____
_____

3. What does Allison say about the boss? _____
_____

4. Why is Kent confident he will love the job? _____
_____

5. Give two details about Kent's first few weeks at the internship. _____
_____

6. How does Kent feel about working on a team? _____
_____

7. Kent finds it exciting to _____
_____

8. Kent conducted a meeting because _____
_____

9. What does Kent mean when he says, "That's how you learn, by trying"? _____
_____

10. How does Allison end the interview? _____
_____

Name: _____   **Date:** _____

An Unhappy Employee

DIRECTIONS: Look at the Big Picture on page 168. Read this conversation between two workers at New Tech, Inc., a company at the job fair. Then answer the questions.

George: I just can't work for Luis anymore. He's too demanding, and he's got a terrible temper. He needs some serious work on his people skills.

Ivan: What about transferring to another department?

George: I've thought about it, but I wouldn't get a raise if I did that. Because of company policy, I can't negotiate better benefits if I transfer to a new department.

Ivan: Well, what are you going to do, then?

George: I think it's time for me to make a career change. This job fair is the perfect opportunity for me to do some networking. I'd love to make some new connections and maybe have an interview for a job or two. I always make a good impression with interviewers.

Ivan: How are you going to do all that? Aren't you supposed to stay here and help us pass out our promotional materials? Luis will have a fit if you disappear for longer than ten minutes.

George: I really don't care anymore. Anyway, he's going to lunch and he won't be back for two hours—you know how long his lunches always are. Must be nice to be the manager!

Ivan: Well, I won't lie to cover for you, so don't blame me if you get caught and Luis fires you.

1. Why doesn't George like Luis? Give three reasons. _____
_____

2. Why doesn't George want a transfer within the company? _____
_____

3. What will George do at the job fair? _____
_____

4. What does Ivan think of George's idea? Why? _____
_____

5. What do you think of George's idea? Why? _____
_____

Name: _____   **Date:** _____

Unreal Conditionals

A **DIRECTIONS:** Look at the Big Picture on page 168. Write sentences with unreal conditionals using the cues below.

1. If Luis / catch / George / fire / him _____

   _____

2. If Allison / not like / Kent / not hire / him _____

   _____

3. If Kirk / look / neater / interviewers / be / more impressed _____

   _____

4. If Marie / not prepared for / her interview / Chris / be / annoyed_____

   _____

B **DIRECTIONS:** Now rewrite each sentence above with the main clause first and the *if*-clause second.

1. _____

   _____

2. _____

   _____

3. _____

   _____

4. _____

   _____

Pleasant City Editorial

DIRECTIONS: Read part of an editorial from the *Pleasant City Tribune*—published five years from now! Then answer the questions with a partner.

Dear Editor,

Pleasant City may have come a long way in the last five years, but we still have a long way to go. There are many issues that people in this town don't want to talk about. But if people don't get involved now and learn to cooperate, these problems will never change.

First of all—traffic. Sure, we got rid of all those gas-guzzling automobiles, but now we have a problem just as big: Personal Transport Vehicles. Kids are running all over the city on them. Soon, they will be driving right into the buildings! I'm afraid I'll look up and some 10-year-old is going to be heading straight for me. I could easily get run over! We need to be working on laws to ensure public safety from out-of-control PTV drivers . . . especially kids.

The next issue is pollution. Five years ago, we had a lot more pollution than we do today. Don't get me wrong—I love breathing clean air. The problem is that our city's new air filtration system is not only noisy, but it also uses a lot of electricity. I heard at the last City Council meeting that Pleasant City's electricity bill will be going up by 20 percent every year for the next 10 years—that's outrageous! And the noise is unbearable. That low hum never stops. I sure miss the days of peace and quiet, when I could hear the birds chirp and the wind blow through the trees. Can you imagine: someday you'll be taking your kids for a walk in the park, and in the background will be the lovely sound of . . . machinery? No, thank you! We've got to fix this problem now.

1. What is the main idea of the first paragraph? _____
   _____

2. What was wrong with transportation five years ago? What is wrong with it today? _____
   _____

3. What solution does the writer propose to fix the problem with PTVs? _____
   _____

4. What is one positive aspect about the city's air filtration system? What negative effects does it have?
   _____

5. Do you think it is possible that someday society will be "perfect"? _____
   _____

Name: _____   **Date:** _____

Living in Pleasant City

DIRECTIONS: Look at the Big Picture on page 185. Complete the sentences with the correct infinitive of purpose from the box.

to help	to avoid	to address	to enhance	to emphasize
to promote	to save	to keep	to improve	

1. People in Pleasant City use Personal Transport Vehicles or walk almost everywhere _____ gasoline.

2. The mounted police officer rides his horse around town _____ anyone who is having a problem.

3. _____ taking care of the environment, the city has posted signs about conserving energy and water.

4. Pleasant City banned all cars _____ creating smog that is dangerous for people to breathe.

5. _____ the park clean, a group of volunteers collects trash every morning, cuts the grass once a week, and plants flowers every season.

6. Local artists have created large outdoor sculptures _____ the beauty of the town.

7. City Council started a new Walk and Talk social club for seniors _____ physical fitness and friendship in the community.

8. Pleasant City still needs _____ the problem of education. The school system needs more money _____ its programs and facilities.

Name: _____   **Date:** _____

Plans for the City

DIRECTIONS: Look at the Big Picture on page 185. Listen to each person from Pleasant City give an opinion. Then complete the sentences below. Be sure to tell each person's reason for his or her opinion.

7. Laura isn't happy to hear that _____
_____
_____

8. Akeem thinks it would be fun to _____
_____
_____

9. Mayor Bynes was discouraged to learn that _____
_____
_____

10. Yolanda is thrilled to live _____
_____
_____

11. Giancarlo is pleased to see _____
_____
_____

12. Mr. Han was surprised to learn _____
_____
_____

Pre-Unit

Page 2

1
1. third, to go to community college
2. second, for his job
3. first, to take an exam

2
1. Sun-Hi
2. first time here
3. third
4. studying English
5. study at the community college
6. How about you
7. English for my job
8. Great

Page 3

5
1. d   5. e
2. a   6. g
3. b   7. c
4. h   8. f

6
1. understand that
2. Write in our notebooks
3. spell that
4. say that again, please

Page 4

1
1. does Jim go
2. are you studying
3. are you going to take
4. did she take
5. were you doing
6. Has he ever been
7. have you been in this class
8. will she do

2
1. My
2. I've
3. take
4. friendly
5. I'm
    a. 4
    b. 5
    c. 2
    d. 3
    e. 1

Page 5

1
1. 2:00 p.m. to 6:00 p.m.
2. 9:00 a.m. to 12:00 p.m.
3. She's going to the ATM, she's going to the dentist, and she's going to have lunch with Marco.
4. circle: textbooks, insurance card, ATM card, and DVD
5. She can go to a movie in the evening, after 6:00 p.m.

2 Possible answer:
Lina is very busy today. First, she has to go to the ATM at 8:00 a.m. Then she goes to English class from 9:00 a.m. to 12:00 noon. She is going to have lunch with Marco at 12:00 noon, and she's going to give him a DVD. After lunch, she has a dentist appointment at 1:00 p.m. Then she goes to work from 2:00 p.m. to 6:00 p.m.

Unit 1

Page 6

1
1. c   5. h
2. e   6. b
3. g   7. f
4. a   8. d

2
1. am looking
2. am applying
3. meets
4. starts
5. closes
6. is researching
7. is getting
8. enroll

3 Answers will vary.

Page 7

1
1. health care
2. early childhood education
3. electrical work
4. restaurant management
5. accounting
6. computer programming

2
1. both Business Management and Accounting
2. neither health care nor business management
3. either Hotel and Hospitality or Business
4. both nursing and health care
5. either electrical work or auto body repair
6. neither business nor accounting

3
1. Auto Body Repair—Ben
2. Business Management— Isabel
3. Nursing—Alex
4. Computer Programming: Kara
5. Accounting—Mark
6. Restaurant Management—Claire

Page 8

1
1. a
2. c
3. b

2
1. b
2. c
3. a

3 6, 2, 8, 3, 5, 1, 4, 7

5 Circle: aren't, weren't, wasn't, can't

Page 9

2
1. d
2. e
3. b
4. a
5. c

3
1. She doesn't like Principles of Management.
2. She's going to drop it.
3. She's interested in computers.
4. She can go to the school website for the procedures.

Page 10

1
1. organize
2. credits
3. meet with
4. prioritize tasks
5. on track
6. make improvements
7. school administrator
8. earn

2
1. Ana is going to meet with her advisor after class.
2. Ana is going to do an internship at the clinic.
3. Next week, she is going to take a personality test.
4. After graduation, she will look for a new job.
5. Balbir will help Nate study for his test.
6. They are going to review the notes for the history class.
7. Nate is making improvements in his grades.
8. He's going to be on track for graduation next year.

3 Answers will vary.

Page 11

1
1. is going to
2. is going to
3. will
4. is going to
5. is going to
6. will

2
1. No
2. Yes
3. No
4. Yes
5. No
6. Yes

3

SUBJECT	Units		GRADE	Grade Point Value	Grade Points
English 205	4	x	B	3	12
History 310	4	x	D	1	4
Math 108	4	x	A	4	16
Science 211	4	x	B	3	12
P.E. 120	2	x	B	3	6
Totals	18				50
GPA					2.78

Page 12

2
1. financial aid
2. FAFSA
3. grants
4. scholarships
5. loans
6. tuition

Page 13

3
1. T
2. F
3. F
4. F
5. T
6. F

4 Sample answers.
1. Victor needs help to pay for the courses.
2. There are several types of financial aid.
3. To apply, Victor needs to fill out a long form.
4. Loans do need to be paid back.

Page 15

2
1. Apprenticeship program
2. Community college
3. Community adult education program
4. Technical education

3
1. d
2. h
3. i
4. a
5. g
6. b
7. e
8. c
9. f

4 Answers will vary. Possible answers:
1. sponsorship
2. certification
3. technical
4. refreshing, refreshment
5. explorer, exploration

Page 16

2
1. hard skill
2. soft skill
3. soft skill

3 Beatriz is in school to become a medical assistant. She **is** preparing a resume because she is going to apply for jobs when she finish**es** school. She is learning many new skills that she is go**ing** to put on her resume. She knows how to take a patient's blood pressure and pulse. She also **is** speaks Spanish and English, so she can ask people questions about their health in either language. In addition, Beatriz is organized and good at working with people. She hope**s** that the skills she has will **to** help her get a job when she finishes school

Page 17

Technology Connection
A. 1. b
2. d
3. e
4. a
5. c

Page 18

1. a	11. c
2. c	12. b
3. c	13. c
4. b	14. a
5. b	15. c
6. c	16. a
7. b	17. d
8. c	18. c
9. a	19. a
10. b	20. c

Unit 2

Page 20

1
1. scheduled
2. covered for
3. pulled together the materials
4. met the deadline
5. made the presentation
6. follow up
7. joined the conference call
8. accepted

2 Answers may vary.
1. *as soon as* she arrived at her job
2. *after* she began work
3. *before* she pulled together her materials
4. *until* it was time for lunch
5. *After* she ate lunch,
6. *as soon as* everyone's arrival at 3:00 p.m.
7. *until* she had a conference call with Andy.
8. *After/when* Sara finished her sales assignment,

3 Answers will vary.

Page 21

1
1. organized
2. overwhelmed
3. creative
4. punctual
5. helpful

2 Answers will vary.

3
1. Jill showed her poster . . . At the meeting . . . She is creative.
2. Ben had papers all over his desk . . . Before the meeting . . . He is overwhelmed.
3. Ariel cleaned the meeting room . . . After the meeting . . . She is helpful.
4. Answers will vary.

Page 22

1
1. C
2. A
3. B

2
1. True
2. True
3. False
4. True
5. False

3 3, 2, 6, 4, 1, 5

5
1. d	6. Id
2. Id	7. d
3. d	8. t
4. t	9. Id
5. t	10. d

Page 23

1
1. offering help
2. responding to an offer
3. offering help
4. offering help
5. responding to an offer
6. offering help
7. offering help
8. responding to an offer
9. responding to an offer
10. responding to an offer

2
1. e	4. c
2. f	5. a
3. b	6. d

3 Answers will vary.

Page 24

1
1. e
2. g
3. a
4. c
5. i
6. b
7. d
8. f
9. h

2
1. since 2007; has received
2. two weeks ago; received
3. so far this month; have prepared
4. last year; attended
5. last summer; Did, obtain
6. ever; Have, talked
7. Yesterday; didn't manage
8. never; have, missed

3 Answers will vary.

Page 25

1 Answers may vary. Possible answers include:
1. neither is Marek *or* Marek isn't either.
2. so is Olga *or* and Olga is, too.
3. Eric does, too *or* and so does Eric.
4. neither does Marek *or* Marek doesn't either.
5. so does Olga *or* Olga does, too.
6. Marek doesn't either *or* neither does Marek.
7. Answer will vary.
8. Answer will vary.

2
1. c	4. f
2. e	5. a
3. b	6. d

3
1. $18,020
2. $23,100
3. $22,470
4. $24,960
5. $20,600
6. $22,260

Page 26

2
1. C Benefits
2. B Wages
3. E Retirement Plans
4. D Health Insurance
5. A Contract

Page 27

3
1. F	4. T
2. F	5. T
3. T	6. F

4
1. New employees can decide to join the union.
2. The union helps with contracts every 3 years.
3. Retirement plans help workers save for the future/save for when they finish working.

5 Answers may vary.
1. Health Insurance or Benefits
2. Retirement Plans
3. Wages
4. Benefits

Page 28

2
1. c
2. e
3. a
4. d
5. b

3
1. Best Gym
2. Best Hair Salon
3. Best Mechanic

Page 30

2
1. bookkeeper
2. Green Valley Health Center
3. $41,000
4. July 1, 2009
5. Yes, Green Valley Employee Union
6. President of Green Valley Health Center

3
1. agreement: contract
2. triplicate: three copies
3. annual: every year
4. regulations: laws, rules
5. corporation: a large company

Page 31

5 Dear Eva,

We ~~didn't meet~~ **haven't met** so far, but I am the director of Green Valley Health Center. I always ~~liked~~ to welcome new staff members so please ~~calling~~ my secretary to make an appointment to ~~saw~~ **see** me on your first day of work. I ~~was~~ **have been** the director here for five years. I hope you ~~have~~ enjoyed working at Green Valley Health Center as much as I do.

Good luck,
Sylvia Gomez
Director

Technology Connection
A.
1. d
2. a
3. d
4. b
5. c
B.
1. Check website for current wage.
2. The Labor-Management Reporting & Disclosure Act of 1959
3. Occupational Safety and Health Agency; it makes sure workplaces are safe.

Page 33

1. b	11. b
2. a	12. c
3. c	13. d
4. b	14. a
5. b	15. d
6. a	16. b
7. d	17. d
8. c	18. a
9. d	19. c
10. a	20. d

Unit 3

Page 34

1.
1. e
2. g
3. h
4. b
5. a
6. c
7. d
8. i
9. j
10. f

2.
1. had made
2. had finished
3. had bought
4. had organized
5. had already gone
6. had given
7. hadn't found
8. had already started
9. hadn't been
10. had already seen

3. Answers will vary.

Page 35

1.
1. theater
2. natural history museum
3. sidewalk café
4. dinosaur exhibit
5. modern art museum
6. box office

2.
1. Before I saw the film, I had never heard of Bruce Willis.
2. Before my brother went to Florida, he had never been in an airplane.
3. Before Ann moved to San Francisco, she had never used the subway.
4. Before we went to the museum, we had never seen a dinosaur exhibit.
5. Before my cousins visited, I had never gone to the museum.
6. Before you invited me, I had never been to an amusement park.

3. Answers will vary.

Page 36

1.
1. A
2. C
3. A

2.
1. F
2. F
3. T
4. T
5. T

3. 6, 3, 2, 5, 1, 4, 7

5.
1. TV
2. green
3. cooking
4. house
5. movie

6. street
7. White
8. house
9. playing
10. concert

Page 37

1.
1. refuse
2. accept
3. refuse
4. refuse
5. refuse
6. accept
7. accept
8. refuse

2.
1. d
2. e
3. b
4. f
5. c
6. a

3. Answers will vary.

Page 38

1.
1. stadium, soccer game
2. street fair, sidewalk café
3. Ferris wheel, amusement park
4. tennis match

2.
1. had been watching, started
2. had been riding, stopped
3. had been talking, saw
4. had been listening, rang
5. had been explaining, ran
6. had been studying, asked
7. had been talking, entered
8. had been shopping, met

Page 39

1.
1. frustrated, goal
2. ex-boyfriend, upset
3. cotton candy, sick
4. power, roller coaster
5. racket, disappointed

2. Answers will vary.

3.
1. $9.00; $.63; $9.63
2. $17.00; $1.19; $18.19
3. $26.00; $1.82; $27.82

Page 40

2.
1. 6:00-7:30 p.m.
2. Mondays and Wednesdays
3. Tuesdays–Sundays
4. $14.00
5. Thursdays
6. 9:00 p.m.

Page 41

3.
1. Junior Clinics
2. Adult League Basketball
3. Adult Tournaments
4. Yoga classes

5. Family Recreational Swim
6. Junior Clinics

4 MAIN STREET FITNESS CENTER ANNOUNCES ITS GRAND OPENING

Two floors of the latest fitness equipment. Air-conditioned weight room. Olympic indoor swimming pool. Aerobics and yoga classes. Therapeutic massages available by appointment.

Sign up for a membership now! Three-month, six-month, or one-year options. Stop by today and see the beautiful facilities.

Page 42

2
1. Appetizers
2. Salads
3. Pasta Dishes
4. Main Dishes
5. Desserts

Page 43

3
1. Green beans and baked potato.
2. Salmon
3. $12.50
4. 6
5. The house salad
6. Brownie à la mode

4
1. sushi: a Japanese dish; cold rice mixed with bits of seafood or vegetables
2. mesclun: a salad of leafy greens and herbs
3. tempura: seafood or vegetables dipped in batter and fried in deep fat
4. poached: cooked in simmering liquid
5. asparagus: a stalk-like vegetable

5 Answers will vary.

Page 44

1 Answers will vary.

2
1. signed up
2. to play
3. fun
4. to meet
5. regular schedule
6. champions
7. haven't played
8. sign up

3 Answers will vary.

Page 45

Technology Connection
A. 1. Insert
2. PIN
3. tickets
4. how many
5. price
6. card
7. good time
B. Answers will vary.

Page 46

1. a	11. a
2. b	12. b
3. b	13. d
4. b	14. d
5. c	15. c
6. c	16. d
7. a	17. a
8. b	18. b
9. c	19. c
10. b	20. c

Unit 4

Page 48

1
1. f
2. g
3. d
4. e
5. h
6. a
7. i
8. b
9. c

2
1. should have
2. should have
3. must have
4. should have
5. should have
6. must have
7. must have
8. must have

3 Answers will vary.

Page 49

1
1. deposit slip
2. withdrawal
3. insufficient funds
4. mortgage loan
5. credit report
6. teller
7. credit card fraud

2 Answers will vary.

3 Answers will vary.

Page 50

1
1. A
2. B
3. B

2
√ Make all payments on time.
√ Use $2000 from a certificate of deposit to pay credit card debt.
___ Balance checkbooks every week.
√ Stop using the credit card to buy things.
___ Protect your credit cards from thieves.
√ Find a credit card with a lower interest rate.

___ Move to a cheaper house.
___ Borrow more money on the house.

3 7, 4, 6, 9, 3, 8, 10, 2, 1, 5

4
1. $60
2. $100
3. $120
4. $240

Page 51

1
1. requesting
2. requesting
3. giving
4. giving
5. requesting
6. requesting
7. requesting
8. giving

2 Sample answers.
1. Could you explain this fee, please?
2. Would you tell me why there's a penalty?
3. Could you show me the reason?
4. Please, could you help me with this?
5. Could you answer my question, please?
6. Would you show me the account policy, please?

3 4, 1, 7, 6, 3, 2, 5

Page 52

1
1. shred
2. credit card offers
3. mortgage payment
4. automated payment
5. credit report, credit score
6. monthly budget
7. spending allowance

2
1. didn't you; I did
2. has she; she hasn't
3. aren't you, I am
4. won't you, I will
5. doesn't she, she doesn't
6. weren't you, I was

Page 53

1
1. Sure
2. Not Sure
3. Not Sure
4. Sure
5. Sure
6. Not Sure

2
A. isn't it
B. haven't you
C. won't you
D. hasn't it
E. don't we
H. didn't you
I. can't we

3
1. E   6. H
2. I   7. D
3. B   8. G
4. J   9. C
5. A   10. F

Page 54

2
1. d
2. c
3. e
4. b
5. a

3 Answers will vary. Possible answers:
1. consumer: consumerism
2. guilty: guilt
3. control: controlling
4. debt: debtor
5. shred: shredder

Page 55

4
1. T   5. T
2. F   6. F
3. F   7. T
4. T   8. F

5
1. c   4. f
2. e   5. a
3. b   6. d

6 Answers will vary.

Page 56

3
1. 0 – no annual fee
2. $15
3. 0 – no fee
4. $1.50
5. $25
6. $60

Page 57

4
1. fees
2. services
3. unlimited
4. transaction
5. overdraw

5 Possible answers
1. He should have used his card at his own bank.
2. He must not have looked into his bank's services and fees.
3. He should be careful not to overdraw his account.
4. He should use his ATM card less often.
5. He shouldn't have taken money out without checking the balance.

Page 58

2 T, F, F, T, T, F

3 1. e
2. a
3. d
4. c
5. b

Page 59

4 Paul has ~~have~~ **had** a lot of problems with managing his money lately. Last month he bounced a check because he had insufficient fund**s** in his bank account. He gets a paycheck every two weeks, so at first he was ~~have~~ surprised, but then he realized that he must ~~had~~ **have** forgotten to deposit his paycheck in his bank account. His friends and family said he should have sign**ed** up for Direct Deposit at work. Paul decided they were right. He is plann**ing** to go to the Human Resources Office next week to fill out a request form.

Technology Connection
  A. 5, 6, 7, 3, 1, 4, 2, 8

Pages 60–61

1. c	**11.** c
2. b	**12.** d
3. c	**13.** b
4. b	**14.** d
5. a	**15.** a
6. b	**16.** c
7. a	**17.** c
8. a	**18.** b
9. a	**19.** a
10. d	**20.** b

Unit 5

Page 62

1
1. f	**6.** i
2. h	**7.** d
3. b	**8.** a
4. c	**9.** j
5. g	**10.** e

2 1. All the laws are read by the president.
2. The laws are explained by the court.
3. State problems are discussed by the governors.
4. Questions were asked about the new law by some citizens.
5. The questions were answered by the governor.
6. Pictures were taken of the governor by the photographers.
7. The budget wasn't approved by the senators.
8. The mayor wasn't re-elected by the citizens.

3 Sample answers.
1. The homework was done.
2. Dinner wasn't prepared.
3. The kitchen was cleaned.
4. The dishes were washed.
5. The laundry was folded.
6. The mail wasn't opened.
7. A letter was emailed to my senator.

Page 63

1 1. knock over
2. provide
3. collect
4. give his speech
5. sponsor
6. hand (them) out

2 1. was interviewed
2. was provided
3. was given
4. were put out
5. were saved
6. was advertised
7. were served
8. were organized
9. was raised

Page 64

1 1. A
2. C
3. B

2 Possible answers:

Person's name	Problem
Maria	Has to work overtime but is not paid for it. Terrible smell in factory makes her sick.
Ivan	Landlord comes into his apartment when he is not at home. Landlord will not install new locks.

3 1. d
2. a
3. b
4. c

4 1. This is an <u>employment rights issue</u>.
2. My <u>working conditions</u> are <u>not safe</u>.
3. The <u>employer</u> <u>doesn't do</u> <u>anything</u> about them.
4. I <u>have</u> a <u>problem</u> with my <u>job</u>.
5. Would you <u>like</u> to <u>set up</u> an <u>appointment</u>?
6. I <u>have</u> a <u>problem</u> with my <u>job</u>.
7. There's an <u>opening</u> on <u>Thursday</u> at <u>10:00</u>.

Page 65

1
1. Senior Center
2. phone call
3. Transportation Program
4. doctor's appointment
5. name and address
6. phone number
7. Health Clinic
8. van

2
1. e   4. c
2. f   5. d
3. a   6. b

Page 66

1
1. guilty
2. innocent
3. arrested
4. trial
5. attorney
6. defendant
7. serve on the jury
8. accused

2
1. What is the boy accused of doing?
2. Where was he arrested?
3. Is the boy allowed to make a phone call?
4. Where was the trial held?
5. Was he found guilty by the jury?

3 Possible answers
1. guilty: innocent
2. defendant: plaintiff/accuser
3. taken: given
4. allowed: forbidden/disallowed
5. catch: release

Page 67

1
1. withhold
2. tax return
3. W-2 form
4. federal tax
5. state tax
6. file
7. wages
8. income tax

2
1. Refund $220.00
2. Amount owed $213.00
3. Refund $195.00
4. Refund $455.00
5. Amount owed $118.00

Page 68

1
1. leave
2. Family
3. stroke
4. weeks
5. allowed
6. posted

Page 69

3
1. An employee can have 12 weeks of family and medical leave in a year.
2. It is unpaid leave.
3. Beatriz can't take family or medical leave for her sister who is sick.
4. Hector can take medical leave to be with his wife.
5. Nadia can take a medical leave to take care of her son.
6. Tomas can take medical leave for three weeks while he receives treatments.
7. Victor can't take a paid leave to help care for his new baby at home.
8. Yes, Mr. or Mrs. Johnson can take a medical leave to care for the adopted baby.

4 Answers will vary.

Page 70

2
1. b
2. d
3. e
4. c
5. a

Page 71

3
1. T
2. F
3. T
4. T
5. T
6. F
7. F

4
1. √
2. –
3. √
4. √
5. –

5 Legal aid is a system of non-profit groups and organizations that provide legal help to people who cannot afford to pay an attorney. The first legal aid agency was founded in New York City in 1876. There are more than 1600 legal aid agencies across the United States.

Page 72

2
1. d
2. b
3. e
4. c
5. a

Page 73

4
1. Mandatory deductions: Federal Income Tax, Social Security Tax, Medicare Tax, CA State Income Tax. Social Security Tax and Medicare tax cannot be changed.
2. Carlos has 4 exemptions.

3. Carlos has money withheld for medical insurance.
4. Carlos's gross pay is $498.75.
5. Carlos's take-home pay is $318.77

Technology Connection
A. 1. a
   2. c
   3. d
   4. b
   5. e
B. Answers will vary.

Page 74

1. c	11. d
2. a	12. a
3. c	13. c
4. c	14. b
5. b	15. a
6. c	16. c
7. a	17. d
8. b	18. a
9. b	19. a
10. d	20. d

Unit 6

Page 76

1
1. an error
2. dead
3. a gas leak
4. losing my Internet connection
5. signal
6. weak
7. is out
8. a power outage

2
1. a
2. the
3. a
4. the
5. a
6. the

3
1. e	4. c
2. b	5. e
3. e	6. a

Page 77

1
1. peeling
2. broken
3. stained
4. cracked
5. dripping

2
1. a
2. the
3. some
4. a
5. the
6. some

7. the
8. a
9. the
10. an
11. the
12. a

3 rate: $275 × days: 3 = $825
wood: $108 + nails $18 + paint: $35 = $161
ESTIMATE: $986

Page 78

1
1. C
2. B
3. C

2
1. True
2. False
3. False
4. False
5. True

3
1. How can I help you?
2. are the problems with your bill
3. didn't call Boston
4. what is the second error
5. paid my bill on time last month
6. Thank you for your help.

Page 79

1
1. Impolite
2. Impolite
3. Polite
4. Polite
5. Impolite
6. Polite
7. Impolite
8. Polite

2 Underline: I'm sorry, I didn't understand that. Would you mind repeating that, please?

3 Answers will vary.

Page 80

1
1. f	4. b
2. e	5. d
3. a	6. c

1. condition
2. discriminate against
3. file a complaint
4. break my lease
5. policy
6. consent

2 Answers will vary. Possible answers:
1. I don't know if they discriminated against you.
2. I'm not sure what the pet policy is.
3. I wonder where the legal aid office is.
4. I'm not sure who the landlord is.
5. I wonder whether we should file a complaint.
6. I don't know how long he has lived here.

3 1. com - di - tion; circle *di*
2. con - sent; circle *sent*
3. dis - cri - mi - nate; circle *cri*
4. com - plaint; circle *plaint*
5. a - part - ment; circle *part*
6. po - li - cy; circle *po*

Page 81

1 Answers will vary. Possible answers:
1. A: Can you tell me what I should do about noisy neighbors? B: Talk to your neighbors first. If that doesn't work, talk to your landlord.
2. A: Do you know when I have to tell my landlord? B: You usually have to give your landlord 30 days notice before you move out.
3. A: Do you know what I should do if a landlord has discriminated against me? B: You should call a legal aid office for advice.
4. A: Can you tell me what I should do about bugs in my apartment? B: This is a health issue, so your landlord should take care of it right away.
5. A: Can you tell me what I should do if my landlord comes into my apartment without my consent? B: This is against the law. You should contact a legal aid office for advice.

2

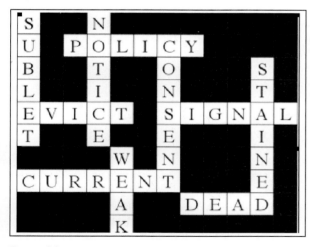

Page 82

1 Answers will vary.

3 1. b
2. a
3. b
4. c

Page 83

4 1. $1,670; $2,830
2. $1,475; $2,225
3. $2,390; $4,110

Page 84

2 1. tenant-landlord problems such as discrimination, eviction, and rent increases
2. electrical, plumbing problems, or heating
3. No; volunteers often work at tenant's rights organizations.
4. Check your telephone book or do an Internet search.

3 1. c
2. d
3. b
4. a

Page 85

4 Answers will vary. Possible answers:
1. I wonder what kind of problems tenants' rights organizations help people with.
2. Do you know what some examples of building safety issues are?
3. Can you tell me if you usually have to pay for help at a tenants' rights organization?
4. Do you know how you can find a tenants' rights organization in your community?

5 Check all boxes.

Page 86

2 1. b
2. a

3 1. Email mistakes
2. Misunderstandings can cost the company money.
3. Spell-check and proofread emails before you send them.
4. Jack will send an email to his team.

Page 87

Technology Connection

A Mistakes:
1. the subject is unclear
2. the writer uses capital letters
3. the writer didn't proofread; there's a spelling mistake in the second paragraph (*emale* should be *email*)
4. the writer changes the topic in the third paragraph
5. the writer makes a comment in the third paragraph that should not be there

B Answers will vary.

Page 88

1. b	11. d
2. c	12. a
3. b	13. b
4. c	14. d
5. a	15. b
6. c	16. b
7. d	17. c
8. c	18. b
9. a	19. a
10. b	20. a

Unit 7

Page 90

1
1. e	5. d
2. f	6. b
3. h	7. a
4. g	8. c

2
1. The woman who is running for mayor spoke at our school.
2. The building that is next to my apartment is for sale.
3. The police stopped the boys who broke the window.
4. The doctors are concerned about the epidemic that began last month.
5. The demonstration that was held today didn't end until 8:00.
6. I talked to the police officer who investigated the crime.

3 Answers will vary.

Page 91

1
1. committed
2. suspects
3. identify
4. evidence
5. theory
6. investigation

2
1. I reported the crime that happened on Main Street.
2. The witnesses who saw the robbers were in the bank. *or* The witnesses who were in the bank saw the robbers.
3. The robbers wore masks that were green.
4. The police who were looking for the robbers found the money.
5. The bank that was robbed yesterday is closed today. *or* The bank that is closed today was robbed yesterday.
6. The bank is hiring a new security guard who will watch the bank all day.

Page 92

1
1. A
2. C
3. B

2
1. dropped his wallet.
2. was burned a little but is going to be OK.
3. was completely peaceful.
4. has been found.

3 7, 4, 2, 5, 1, 3, 6

5
1. the student that arrived late for his test
2. the announcement that is very exciting
3. the firefighters that are injured
4. the crimes that are committed
5. the driver that offered to help

Page 93

1
1. d
2. e
3. b
4. c
5. a

3 Answers will vary.

Page 94

1
1. g
2. d
3. i
4. k
5. a
6. c
7. b
8. j
9. e
10. f
11. h

2 Sample answers.
1. The story that I told you about was in the local news.
2. Irina Charles who/whom you met yesterday is a columnist for the newspaper.
3. The blog that I found on the Internet has some good ideas.
4. The news program that you like is not on any more.
5. There was an interesting story in the newspaper that I lost.
6. I read the blog that you wrote.
7. The photo that Tran took was on the front page.

Page 95

1
1. that
2. that
3. that
4. who/that
5. that
6. that

2
1. soda
2. water
3. fruit juice
4. The percentage went down.
5. The percentage went up.

Page 96

1
1. outreach
2. referral
3. hotline
4. donation
5. shelter
6. support

2

Local Company Supports Greenville Families

Thanks to a $30,000 (donation) from the Pratt Company, the city of Greenville can offer help to more families in need. At today's opening of the new Greenville Family Services Center, Mayor Billings thanked the Pratt Company for its generous contribution.

"The families of Greenville are important to the success of our company and our community," explained Maria Ortiz, spokesperson for the Pratt Company. "We believe we should (support) them."

The $30,000 gift from the Pratt Company has helped set up a (hotline) in the Family Services Center. The (hotline) is a 24-hour-a-day service that people can call for emergency help. "We provide emergency housing, counseling, and (referrals) for a variety of situations," said Mai-Li Chen, director of the center. "Our goal is to help families in need."

We've expanded Safe Haven, a (shelter) that can house up to 50 people. There are suites for families, and rooms for individuals who need temporary (shelter).

In addition, the center is starting an (outreach) program to inform the community about services. "There are many people who are victims of unfortunate circumstances. They need help but don't realize that we are here for them. We need to reach out to them," added Mai-Li Chen.

The Greenville Family Services Center also operates the food bank on Center Street. Volunteers and (donations) are always welcome.

Send (donations) to: Greenville Family Services Center, 1240 Western Avenue, Greenville. For volunteer opportunities, check: www.greenvillefamilyservices.com.

Page 97

3
1. The Pratt company made a $30,00 donation to the city.
2. People can call the hotline 24 hours a day.
3. The Family Services Center provides emergency housing, counseling, and referrals for a variety of situations.
4. The victims of unfortunate circumstances.
5. People can volunteer or make donations to the Family Services Center.

4
Answers will vary.

Page 98

3
1. Call the police.
2. In the vehicle.
3. A police officer/law enforcement officer.
4. She should call 888-555-3341.
5. Driver's name, address, and telephone number, and the insurance company and policy number for any other car involved in the accident.
6. Yes, she does.
7. No, she doesn't.
8. 888-555-8800

Page 99

4
1. policy number
2. vehicles
3. notify
4. driver
5. passengers
6. witness

5 Answers will vary.

Page 100

1
1. d
2. b
3. c
4. a
5. b
6. d
7. a

2
1. b
2. c
3. d
4. a

3
1. accident
2. happened
3. electric
4. shock
5. alright
6. happen

Page 101

4 Firefighters **were** called to the warehouse of the Hudson Company at 3 p.m. yesterday to fight a fire that **started** in a second floor bathroom. The fire was extinguished quickly and, fortunately, no one **was** injured. The fire chief **said** later that the fire **was** started by a cigarette. No one has taken responsibility for causing the fire so the chief will continue his investigation until the guilty person is **found**.

B. 1. √
2. √
3. −
4. −
5. −
6. −
7. √
8. −

Pages 102–103

1. a		11. c
2. c		12. b
3. c		13. a
4. b		14. d
5. a		15. b
6. c		16. d
7. a		17. c
8. d		18. a
9. c		19. b
10. b		20. b

Unit 8

Page 104

1
1. c
2. d
3. a
4. b

2
1. was concerned about driving
2. was worried about being
3. weren't concerned about running
4. is serious about taking
5. weren't worried about walking
6. I'm/am concerned about exercising

Page 105

1 Possible answers:
1. People in Boston are concerned about driving in heavy snowstorms.
2. Residents should be cautious about returning to their homes after the fire.
3. The local government is serious about conserving water during the drought.
4. San Francisco residents are nervous about being outdoors after the earthquake.
5. Parents in Mississippi are unsure about taking their children to school today.
6. Many people were worried about staying in their homes during the tornado.

2

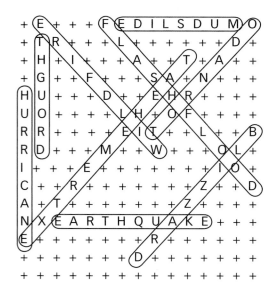

Page 106

1
1. A
2. B
3. B

2 C

3
1. freezing, –7
2. warm, 21
3. cold, 7
4. cool, 11
5. hot, 32

Page 107

2 Answers will vary.

Page 108

1
1. f   6. b
2. i   7. d
3. h   8. c
4. g   9. a
5. j   10. e

2
1. with
2. work
3. focuses
4. about
5. plans
6. in

3
1. focuses on protecting
2. focuses on saving
3. cares about solving
4. works on reducing
5. focuses on working
6. believes in improving

Page 109

1
1. be - lieve
2. con - trol
3. dis - as - ter
4. e - va - cu - ate
5. fo - cus
6. re - lief

2
1. on
2. on
3. about
4. in
5. on
6. about
7. about

3 They work on protecting wildlife.
She focuses on building homes.
He believes in helping victims.
I care about the environment.
Bob believes in helping others.
We count on your help.

Page 110

1
1. occurs
2. kit
3. Assembling
4. essential
5. container
6. nonperishable
7. at a moment's notice

2 Circle: occurs, assembling, kit, kit, essential, kit, at a moment's notice, container, kit, nonperishable, containers

Page 111

1
1. When a natural disaster occurs, people often do not have access to food, water, or electricity for several days.
2. A disaster supplies kit is a collection of essential items that your family will need to stay safe and healthy during a crisis.
3. A container that is easy to carry makes a good disaster supplies kit.
4. Keep it by the door in case you have to leave at a moment's notice.
5. You should have a three-day supply of food for each person.
6. Food in your kit should be nonperishable.
7. You should have about one gallon of water per person for three days.

4
1. 15 gallons
2. 36 cans
3. baby items such as baby food, formula, and diapers

Page 112

3
1. d
2. c
3. e
4. a
5. b

Page 113

4
1. California Coastal Cleanup Day is a volunteer event for people who are concerned about keeping the shoreline and coasts clean.
2. People have removed more than 12 million pounds of garbage from local beaches.
3. Families, neighbors, and volunteer groups participate in Coastal Cleanup Day.
4. Coastal Cleanup Day is important because of the growing amount of plastic in oceans around the world.
5. Sailors have found large masses of plastic material in oceans around the world.
6. Toxins in plastic are harmful to ocean plants and animals and to humans.

5 Dear Congressman Silver:
I am writing this letter because I am concerned **about** polar bears and other endangered wildlife. I urge you to **protect** our polar bears as **required** by the Endangered Species Act to ensure these struggling animals **survive**. As you know, the threat to polar bears, due to **global** warming, is very real. Please help **with** this important issue.

Sincerely,
Diana Dominguez

Page 114

1
1. b
2. c
3. a

2
1. C
2. H
3. B
4. A
5. F
6. E
7. G
8. D
9. X

3
1. Go to Exit 1 or 2. Do not take the elevator.
2. Exit 2
3. Exit 3

Page 115

1 Circle "Boston," "3/5/2009," and "57°."

2
1. Click "Switch to Celsius"
2. cooler
3. Thursday and Sunday
4. wind
5. Click "Severe Weather Alerts"

Pages 116–117

1. B	11. A
2. C	12. B
3. C	13. D
4. B	14. C
5. B	15. D
6. D	16. A
7. A	17. C
8. C	18. B
9. A	19. D
10. D	20. C

Unit 9

Page 118

1
1. crossing guard
2. driver education
3. guide dog
4. handicapped passenger
5. pedestrians
6. school zone

2
1. requires, to wear
2. let, walk
3. allows, to enter
4. let, cross
5. made, stay
6. had, stop

Page 119

1
1. Sam had/got his hair cut on Monday.
2. Sam had/got his car repaired on Tuesday.

3. Sam had/got his refrigerator repaired on Wednesday.
4. Sam had/got his computer fixed on Thursday.
5. Sam had/got his house painted on Friday.

2
1. fire hydrant
2. parking meter
3. road construction
4. tow-away zone
5. wheelchair access ramp

3
1. You're not/You aren't allowed
2. Drivers are not/aren't allowed
3. He's not/He isn't allowed
4. I'm/ I am allowed
5. You're/you are allowed

Page 120

1
1. B
2. C
3. C

2

Person's name	Problem	Solution
Katia	Her car broke down and she was late for work.	A mechanic fixed the car.
Carlos	His driver's license expired.	He renewed his license the next day.

3
1. to take care of a problem
2. car broke down yesterday
3. my friend pick me up
4. my car taken to a gas station.
5. got it fixed

4
1. two
2. to
3. too
4. to, to
5. to.

Page 121

1 Answers will vary.

2
1. Underline *Oh, I'm terribly sorry.*
2. Underline *I'm really sorry. I should've called you.*
3. Underline *I'm sorry, Ms. Green. I'll turn it off.*

3 Answers will vary.

Page 122

1
1. change of address
2. proof of insurance
3. Visitor Information Center
4. tow truck
5. engine trouble
6. convenience store
7. road test
8. Town Hall

2
1. to fill out
2. seeing
3. taking
4. to let
5. to bring
6. putting

Page 123

1 I need to get my car fixed, so I have to remember **to make** an appointment with the mechanic. I forgot **to** make an appointment last time. I remember **going** to the auto shop and Tony wouldn't see me. He's always so busy! Sometimes he doesn't even answer the phone! I'll try **calling** him first thing tomorrow. Or maybe I'll stop **to see** him on my way home from work tomorrow and make the appointment in person. But if he's too busy, I might stop **going** to him and find another mechanic.

2
1. nouns
2. nouns
3. Possible answers: driver's license, car mechanic, wheelchair access

3
1. 4
2. 381,024
3. 275,184

Page 124

2 Circle: hood, battery engine, oil dipstick, coolant, windshield, tires, spare tire, jack, trunk, back-up lights, windshield, first-aid kit.

Additional car vocabulary students may circle: wiper fluid, tread, brake lights.

Page 125

3 Answers may vary.
1. to save money
2. all drivers
3. the battery, the engine, the oil dipstick, where the coolant goes, wiper fluid
4. filled with air, enough tread
5. It lifts the car when you have to change a tire.
6. once a month

4
1. b   4. a
2. d   5. f
3. c   6. e

Page 126

2
1. c   4. a
2. e   5. d
3. b   6. f

Page 127

3
1. no
2. $1.00
3. $2.70
4. no
5. $3.70
6. Lane Construction

Page 128

1 1. d 4. a
  2. f 5. e
  3. c 6. b

2 1. Employees are not allowed to smoke in the warehouse.
  2. I'm not allowed to bring food into the warehouse.
  3. We're not allowed to put food wrapped in foil into the microwave.
  4. You're not allowed to block the entrance to the warehouse.
  5. Some employees are not allowed to enter a dangerous area in the warehouse.
  6. I'm not allowed to park in the "Employee of the Month" parking space.

Page 129

B 1. E 4. C
  2. A 5. F
  3. B 6. D

Page 130

  1. B 11. B
  2. B 12. C
  3. B 13. A
  4. A 14. D
  5. B 15. C
  6. D 16. B
  7. B 17. A
  8. A 18. D
  9. D 19. D
  10. C 20. B

Unit 10

Page 132

1 1. smoke detector
  2. handrails
  3. outlet covers, child-safety locks
  4. safety devices

2 1. Sue said (that) she had put outlet covers on all the outlets last week.
  2. Jane said (that) they were going to have a fire drill next week.
  3. Jake said (that) they had smoke detectors in all the bedrooms.
  4. Ana said (that) Dan hadn't bought child-safety locks yet.
  5. John said (that) he was installing handrails at his house today.
  6. Rob said (that) I didn't have enough safety devices in my house.

Page 133

1 1. *d.* Jane told Rob (that) he needed a safety gate.
  2. *a.* Jane said (that) the smoke detector needed a new battery.

  3. *e.* Jane said (that) the children could reach the toxic cleansers.
  4. *b.* Jane told Rob (that) the electric outlets were dangerous.
  5. *c.* Jane told Rob (that) there were too many electrical cords.
  6. *f.* Jane said (that) these small toys could be a choking hazard.

2 1. 1.15
  2. 65
  3. 2.23
  4. 4.4
  5. 1.97

Page 134

1 1. B
  2. A
  3. C

2 ___ Smoke detectors in every room
  √ Outlet covers
  √ Child-safety locks
  ___ Handrails on stairways
  ___ A fire drill
  ___ Checking electrical cords
  √ A safety gate

3 1. (that) he had taken a child-safety class last weekend
  2. (that) he (had) wanted to make their home safe for the new baby
  3. (that) he had learned about child-safety locks and child-safety gates
  4. (that) they had also learned about outlet covers
  5. (that) the baby was due in two months

Page 135

1 Answers will vary.

2 1. Underline *I'm sorry to hear that.*
  2. Underline *I'm sorry to hear that you aren't feeling well. I hope you feel better soon.*
  3. Underline *How scary! Is there anything I can do to help?*

3 Answers will vary.

Page 136

1 1. thought it over
  2. found out about
  3. signed up
  4. give up
  5. followed through with
  6. paid off

2 1. show up
  2. count on
  3. look up
  4. fall for
  5. use up
  6. talk into
  7. think over
  8. pay off

3
1. I didn't fall for her excuse.
2. Sue found out about a new running group.
3. Peter talked me into losing weight.
4. I looked the number up online./I looked up the number online.
5. Jack counts on me for everything.

4 Possible answers:
call **on**: ask someone to speak in class; transitive inseparable
get along **with**: have a good relationship with; transitive inseparable
put **off**: postpone; transitive separable
wind **up**: end; transitive separable

Page 137

1
1. I used to eat a lot of unhealthy food, but now I eat well.
2. Ana didn't use to exercise, but now she exercises every day.
3. It was hard to start an exercise program, but now I'm used to it.
4. They aren't used to eating healthy food. They usually eat at fast-food restaurants.
5. Bob used to smoke, but he stopped smoking about a year ago.
6. Sue didn't used to eat fresh fruits and vegetables, but now she loves them.

2
When I was in college, I was in really bad shape. I wasn't **used to** taking care of myself. I wasn't **used to** shopping or cooking for myself. I **used to** eat at fast-food restaurants every day. I never went to the gym, and I never **signed up** for a P.E. class. I was about 25 pounds overweight. I went on diets, but I never used to **follow through**. Now I'm in great shape. I exercise every day. I eat healthy food. It was hard at first, but now I'm **used to** it. Now, I'm **looking forward to** living a healthy life!

3 Answers will vary.

Page 138

1
1. c
2. e
3. a
4. f
5. g
6. d
7. b

2
1. c   4. e
2. a   5. f
3. d   6. b

Page 139

4
1. no
2. no
3. a fever of 103 degrees or higher, a fever that lasts more than three days, a high fever

combined with a sore throat, an earache, or trouble breathing
4. a sore throat and a fever
5. Yes, because the child has a combination of a sore throat and a fever.

5
1. Sam said (that) he had a sore throat and (that) he felt hot.
2. Mary said (that) she had had a headache and a stomachache last night.
3. My daughter said (that) she had an earache and (that) she couldn't breathe through her nose. *or* My daughter said (that) she has an earache and (that) she can't breathe through her nose.
4. My son said (that) he had fallen off his bike yesterday and had hurt his arm
5. Sue told Dan (that) she couldn't come to work today because she had a fever of 101 degrees.
6. My mother told me (that) she had a fever of 103 degrees for three days, so she was going to call the doctor.

Page 140

1
1. efficient
2. sliding scale
3. health insurance
4. annual
5. immunizations

2 Circle: health insurance, sliding scale, annual, immunizations, efficient

Page 141

3
1. F   4. T
2. T   5. F
3. F   6. T
1. HSRSA health clinics do not require patients to have health insurance.
2. HRSA health centers provide services for anyone.
3. HRSA health centers make the emergency rooms of local hospitals more efficient and less crowded.

4
1. find out about
2. looked up
3. found out about
4. thought . . . over
5. count on
6. look forward to

Page 142

1 Possible answers:
hospitals: accidents from chemicals
restaurants: burns, falls, accidents from dangerous kitchen machines such as slicers
warehouses: accidents from carrying things or slipping
factories: accidents from dangerous manufacturing machines; injuries from doing the same thing everyday

offices: illness from stress or bad air quality; injuries from sitting in uncomfortable chairs and/or doing the same thing every day.

3 1. Lane Industries
2. in the warehouse
3. putting boxes onto shelves
4. his chest
5. yes
6. the manager's assistant

Page 143

B Answers will vary.

Pages 144–145 Unit 10 Test

1. C   11. B
2. B   12. A
3. B   13. D
4. C   14. D
5. A   15. C
6. C   16. D
7. C   17. C
8. A   18. A
9. B   19. A
10. A   20. C

Unit 11

Page 146

1 1. evaluate your credentials
2. conduct a job search
3. update
4. initiative
5. opportunities to pursue
6. professional development
7. take steps
8. build a stronger résumé
9. strengths and weaknesses
10. cover the costs

2 1. e   4. f
2. a   5. c
3. d   6. b

Page 147

1 Possible answers:
1. assertive
2. demanding
3. impressed
4. prepared
5. professional
6. sloppy

2 Answers will vary.
3 Answers will vary.

Page 148

1 1. A
2. C
3. C

2 **c** Kaoru's boss will notice her more
d Kaoru might get a promotion
e Kaoru can impress her boss with her new knowledge
a People sometimes think you don't know anything
b Kaoru thinks she will get a raise

3 1. get a promotion
2. taking a professional development course
3. take the initiative
4. want to reach my goals
5. you work this hard
6. Good point

4 1. first thought group: If you move to New York; second thought group: where will you live?
2. first thought group: What'll the boss say; second thought group: if you come in late?
3. first thought group: If he gets a raise; second thought group: he'll buy a car.
4. first thought group: If I'm assertive; second thought group: I may get a promotion.
5. first thought group: Sue will keep her job; second thought group: if she has a baby.
6. first thought group: Where will you work; second thought group: if you quit your job?

Page 149

1 Underline: Yes, I have. In fact, I have a degree in computer programming; No, I haven't, but I've supervised employees. I've also taken a couple of management courses. Yes, I can. One of my greatest strengths is organization. I'm always very well prepared.

2 Answers will vary.

Page 150

1. 1. teamwork
   2. a better impression
   3. networking
   4. negotiate better benefits
   5. people skills
   6. a career change
   7. department
   8. transferred

2. 1. had, would make
   2. would get, completed
   3. would be, encouraged
   4. wanted, would transfer
   5. made, would get
   6. would be, did

Page 151

1. Answers will vary.

2. If I **were** hired, I would **encourage** teamwork. If I had an employee who **didn't** work well on the team, I **would** have him or her transferred to another department. If I **got** this job, I would also **pay** attention to the budget and meet every deadline. If I **had** to get a project finished on time, I would work late at night and on weekends.

3. 1. e
   2. d
   3. c
   4. a
   5. b

Page 152

1. 1. f
   2. d
   3. a
   4. e
   5. g
   6. c
   7. b

Page 153

3. 1. T   5. T
   2. T   6. F
   3. F   7. F
   4. F   8. T

4. Answers may vary.
   1. If Kyle took zero deductions, he would get a smaller paycheck now.
   2. If Kyle took zero deductions, he would probably get money back at tax time.
   3. If she wants more money in her paycheck now, she should add deductions for her husband and for childcare.

Page 154

2. 1. for job or career experience, for job or career advancement; for applying to college, to meet people, to "give back"
   2. Mary S.
   3. Amy C.
   4. Ricky T. and Amy C.
   5. José M.

Page 155

4. Possible answers:
   1. Sara could work at the Greenville Health Center because she speaks Spanish and she can get experience in a career that she's interested in.
   2. Maya could work for the Greenville Computer Recycling Center because it will give her some job experience that she can put on her résumé.
   3. Joy could work for the Greenville Parks and Recreation Department because it would be a good way for her to find out if she likes that kind of work.
   4. Ian could work at the Greenville Community Center. It would give him some experience as a theater director, and also some experience with working with teenagers.
   5. Lisa could work at the Greenville Newcomers Organization to get some experience working with elementary school-aged children.

Page 156

2. 1. letter of recommendation
   2. reference
   3. letters of recommendation
   4. happy
   5. week
   6. is
   7. is not
   8. should not

Page 157

B Circle: 123-45-6789, 16, music teacher

Pages 158–159

1. B   11. D
2. A   12. A
3. A   13. C
4. C   14. B
5. A   15. D
6. B   16. B
7. A   17. B
8. D   18. C
9. B   19. D
10. C   20. D

Unit 12

Page 160

1
1. b
2. d
3. e
4. a
5. c

2
1. will be running
2. is going to be taking
3. will be coordinating
4. will be accompanying
5. is going to be sightseeing
6. will be selecting

Page 161

1
1. will be improving
2. will be hiring
3. will be adding
4. will be coordinating
5. will be offering
6. will be enjoying

2 Answers will vary.

3 I will be **coordinating** a family vacation next year. We are going to **be** traveling around California. My mother, aunt, and one cousin **will** be accompanying my husband and me. We're going to go to San Francisco first. We'll be **sightseeing** around the city for a few days. Then we'll **be** driving down the Pacific Coast to Los Angeles. We're going to be **stopping** at interesting places along the coast. We'll be **spending** a few days in Los Angeles before we go home.

Page 162

1
1. B
2. A
3. A

2
___ Pay for a new waste-disposal plant
√ Build a new train system
√ Construct a new public university
___ Improve all of the city's parks
√ Start a new vocational-training center
___ Construct a new highway through the city
√ Offer free day care to poor people

3
1. improving our schools
2. too crowded
3. to do about it
4. be coordinating our efforts
5. hiring many new teachers
6. providing more supplies

5
1. excitement
2. disappointment
3. excitement
4. surprise

Page 163

1 Formal: 2, 3, 5, 8; Informal: 1, 4, 6, 7

2
1. Underline: I completely agree. In my opinion; I'm sorry, but I disagree with you. I feel that
2. Underline: I couldn't agree more. I think that; I completely disagree. I feel that

3 Answers will vary.

Page 164

1
1. c
2. e
3. f
4. a
5. g
6. d
7. b

2
1. Sophia goes to the company gym every day to lose weight.
2. Chris is starting a recycling program at work to address the issue of paper waste.
3. Zee Company is offering gym memberships to promote better health for employees.
4. Ashley is taking the bus to work to save money and (to) reduce air pollution.
5. The Smith Company is offering stress management classes to enhance the quality of life for all employees.
6. Alvin is taking a computer training class to improve his knowledge of technology.

3 *Address* has the same noun and verb forms. The first syllable of the noun form is stressed; the last syllable of the verb form is stressed.
1. avoidance
2. address
3. emphasis
4. enhancement
5. expansion
6. promotion

Page 165

1
1. b
2. a
3. c
4. e
5. d

2
1. to be
2. to learn about
3. to find out
4. to go
5. to make
6. to meet
7. to learn

3
1. B
2. A
3. C
4. D

Page 166

1 Answers will vary.

3
1. d
2. c
3. a
4. b

Page 167

```
Greenville Bank Savings Account Application
Please have the following information ready:
1. Your Social Security or Tax ID Number
2. Your driver's license or ID card issued by a state Department of Motor Vehicles

Account selection                          Type of application
Please select the accounts you would like to open.   ☐ Individual
☒ Savings                                  ☒ Joint
☐ Checking
Amount of deposit $  $25.00

Your personal information                  Joint account holder's name:
First Name     Last Name                   First Name      Last Name
William        Graves                      Lucy            Graves
Social Security Number: 123-45-6578
Date of birth (MM/DD/YYYY):  02/11/1985
Home telephone: 213-555-7980  Email address: graveswl@mymail.com
Services required
☐ checks  ☐ ATM card
```

5 Answers will vary.

Page 168

1
1. the election
2. people will be voting for mayor and for two bond measures
3. 2
4. 2; to improve the schools and to help solve traffic problems
5. no; "Yes, these bond measures will cause an increase in taxes" and "Are these bond measures the best way to solve these problems? You decide!"
6. It's important to vote; "However, everyone must vote in this election" and "Don't stay home next Tuesday! Go out and vote!"

Page 169

3
1. a
2. a
3. b

4 Voter 1 will probably vote for David Green for mayor, vote "no" on Bond Measure A, and vote "yes" on Bond Measure B. Voter 2 will probably vote for Alicia Brown for mayor, and vote "yes" on both bond measures.

Page 170

2 Possible answers.
1. To get more responsibility at work, Lucy will volunteer to manage different projects.
2. To become a better speaker, Lucy will read articles on how to give good presentations.
3. To improve her management skills, Lucy will take a management class at the community college.
4. To improve her business writing skills, Lucy will take business writing class at adult school.
5. To get more attention at work, Lucy will write articles for the company website.

Page 171

3 Answers will vary.

B Answers will vary.

Pages 172–173

1. C	11. C
2. A	12. A
3. C	13. C
4. B	14. D
5. A	15. B
6. C	16. C
7. A	17. A
8. C	18. D
9. B	19. A
10. D	20. B

Pre-Unit

LISTEN. Complete the sentences. Use the words and phrases in the box.

Ana: Hi. My name's Ana.

Sam: Hi Ana. My name is Sam.

Ana: Nice to meet you, Sam. Is this your first time here?

Sam: This is my second class. I started last semester. How about you?

Ana: I've been studying here for two semesters already. This is my third time.

Sam: Oh. Why are you studying English?

Ana: I want to study at the community college next year. How about you?

Sam: I need English for my job.

Lin: Hi, Ana!

Ana: Oh, hi, Lin! Sam, this is Lin. This is Lin's first time here.

Sam: Nice to meet you, Lin.

Lin: Nice to meet you, Sam.

Sam: So why are *you* studying English, Lin?

Lin: I need to take a big exam.

Sam: Well, you're going to like this class. This teacher is great.

LISTEN. Then listen again and write the missing words or phrases.

Sun-hi: Hi. I'm Sun-hi.

Raul: Hi, Sun-hi. My name is Raul.

Sun-hi: Nice to meet you, Raul. Is this your first time here, too?

Raul: No, this is my third class.

Sun-hi: Oh, why are you studying English?

Raul: I want to study at the community college next semester. How about you?

Sun-hi: I need English for my job.

Raul: Great. You're going to like it here. The teacher is very nice.

LISTEN. Complete the conversations. Use the words and expressions in the box.

1. *A:* I want you to work with Sam.

 B: I'm sorry. I didn't understand that.

 A: Oh. I'd like you to work with another student— with Sam.

2. *A:* Please write your answers in your notebooks.

 B: Write in your notebooks.

 A: Yes.

3. *A:* Could you spell that, please?

 B: Sure. It's R-A-M-I-R-E-Z.

4. *A:* Please open your books.

 B: Excuse me. Could you say that again, please?

 A: I said open your books.

Unit 1

LISTEN to the question. Then listen to the conversation. Fill in the circle for the correct answer.

1. Why does Rick want to talk to his mom?

 Rick: Hey, Mom.

 Mom: Hi, Rick. How are things going?

 Rick: Okay. Do you have a minute?

 Mom: Sure. What do you want to talk about?

 Rick: Well, you know I'm registering for classes next week.

 Mom: Yes . . .

 Rick: And I want to check with you about schedules.

 Mom: Okay.

 Why does Rick want to talk to his mom?

 A. He wants to discuss schedules.

 B. She doesn't want to register for classes.

 C. He wants to take accounting.

2. Who could study at the library in the afternoon?

 Rick: I'm looking into a computer course on Tuesday and Thursday afternoons.

 Mom: But what about your sister when she comes home from school?

 Rick: Oh. I didn't think about that.

 Mom: Well, maybe Kathy can study at the library those afternoons. I can pick her up on those days.

 Who could study at the library in the afternoon?

 A. Rick

 B. His mom

 C. Kathy

3. Who is taking accounting?

   Rick: Does your accounting class still meet on Monday and Wednesday nights?

   Mom: Yes, so . . . you can stay with Kathy those evenings, right?

   Rick: Of course.

   Who is taking accounting?

   A. Rick

   B. His mom

   C. Kathy

LISTEN. Match the day and time with the activity.

   Rick: I'm also looking into an English course. I need one more to satisfy the English requirement for my program. There's one Monday afternoon . . .

   Mom: But what about your work schedule? Can you change it?

   Rick: That's the problem. I don't have a lot of flexibility there . . .

   Mom: I see. Maybe you can check the online courses.

   Rick: That's a good idea, Mom. . . . So when does your accounting class start?

   Mom: Next Monday night.

   Rick: Then I'm going to register for that computer course on Tuesday and Thursday afternoons.

Practice Test

LISTEN to the question. Listen to the conversation. Listen to the question again. Choose the correct answer.

1. Why is Jose going to take a class in world history?

   A: José, why are you taking a world history class? Your major is economics, isn't it?

   B: Yes, that's right, but world history is a requirement for my major.

   A: That's great! It's a really interesting class! I took it last semester.

   Why is José going to take a class in world history?

   A. Because it's a requirement for his major.

   B. Because he is majoring in world history.

   C. Because he really enjoys world history.

2. What is Lee doing?

   A: Hey, Kim. I'm looking for Lee. Is he here?

   B: No, he's not here right now. He's at school taking a placement test. He wants to test out of some beginning classes.

   A: That's a great idea! I'll do that, too.

What is Lee doing?

   A. He's at school studying for a big test.

   B. He's in a beginning class right now.

   C. He's trying to test out of some classes.

LISTENING: Listen to the conversation. Then choose the correct answer.

   Marta: Jim, how are you doing?

   Jim: Marta, it's good to see you. I'm fine, but very busy.

   Marta: Why are you so busy?

   Jim: Well, I'm working at the factory during the day. And I'm taking two continuing education classes at the community college. They're in the evening, so my days are pretty long.

   Marta: I'm so happy for you! What are you studying?

   Jim: I'm taking classes in elementary education. I'm going to be a teacher.

   Marta: That's fantastic! I'm going to take a class also.

   Jim: Really? What are you going to study?

   Marta: I'm going to take an online class in business. I want to work for a big company.

   Jim: That's terrific!

Unit 2

LISTEN to the question. Then listen to the conversation. Listen to the question again. Fill in the circle for the correct answer.

1. Why is the boss happy with Susan and Mark?

   Boss: Susan, you and Mark did a great job on that software project. You met the deadline and made a clear presentation for the whole team.

   Susan: Thanks! I'm really glad you liked it.

   Boss: You two worked really hard. After we meet this morning, you should both take the rest of the day off.

   Susan: That sounds great!

   Why is the boss happy with Susan and Mark?

   A. Because they made a presentation about finance.

   B. Because they were on time for a presentation.

   C. Because they did a good job on a software project.

2. What did Kim have to do when he got to work?

A: Hey, Kim. How was your day?

B: Very difficult. As soon as I got to work, the boss told me to give a presentation on my budget ideas.

A: I'm sorry to hear that. How did it go?

B: Not bad. I think that it was fairly clear.

What did Kim have to do when he got to work?

A. Present his ideas about the budget.

B. Go to a long meeting with his boss.

C. Talk to his boss about his product ideas.

3. Why did Joe have a difficult day?

Boss: Hey, Joe. I'm really sorry about today. Thanks for covering for Rachel.

Joe: I understand. After she got sick and went home, someone had to do her work. I'm just having a little trouble getting my own work done.

Boss: Well, I asked you to do it because you're very organized. When she comes back, please take a day off.

Joe: Thanks!

Why did Joe have a difficult day?

A. He's not a very organized person.

B. He was covering for a sick co-worker.

C. He was sick and felt really bad.

LISTEN to the conversation. Circle *True* or *False*.

Dan: Hi, Jamie. How's your work coming?

Jamie: Just fine, Dan. I've been really busy, but I'm trying to get everything done.

Dan: Did you start on that new assignment?

Jamie: Yes. I started it as soon as I met with my supervisor.

Dan: That's great! And did you pull together the materials you need?

Jamie: No, I didn't. I didn't have time before I left work yesterday. I'll get started on that as soon as I finish these files.

Dan: Are we still going out for lunch today?

Jamie: I don't think I can. I'm covering the front desk for a co-worker.

Practice Test

LISTEN to the question. Then listen to the conversation. Listen to the question again. Choose the correct answer.

1. What did Kristen do after she talked to her team?

A: Kristen, did you schedule the budget meeting for tomorrow?

B: Yes, but before I scheduled the meeting, I talked to the team to get a good time. Tomorrow, I'll write up a summary after the meeting and send it in an email.

A: You're so organized! Thanks.

What did Kristen do after she talked to her team?

A. She wrote up a summary.

B. She scheduled a meeting.

C. She sent out many emails.

2. What does Lee have to do before he goes home tonight?

A: Hey, Lee. Aren't you going home now?

B: No. After I finish my report on staffing, I'll go home.

A: Well, good luck with it.

B: Thanks!

What does Lee have to do before he goes home tonight?

A. He has to write a report on staffing.

B. He has to write some emails to the staff.

C. He has to return some phone calls.

LISTEN to the conversation. Then choose the correct answer.

A: Linda, did you follow up with Ms. Jones about the schedule?

B: Oh, no. I forgot.

A: You need to ask her about the time for the meeting.

B: Okay. I'll ask her about that before I go to lunch. Sorry. I'm just overwhelmed.

A: Can I help you at all?

B: Maybe. I haven't pulled together the materials for the presentation yet.

A: No problem. I'll help you get them as soon as I come back from lunch.

B: Oh, thanks.

A: Don't mention it.

Unit 3

LISTEN to the beginning of a conversation. Then listen for the next best sentence. Fill in the circle for the correct answer.

1. *A:* Hey, Nate. Did you and Michelle see the dance performance on Saturday?

   B: No. By the time we got there, it had already sold out.

   Which is the next best sentence?

   A. Oh, that's too bad.

   B. Well, that's good news.

   C. Did you buy the tickets?

2. *A:* So, then what did you do?

   B: We went to get a movie at the new video store.

   Which is the next best sentence?

   A. Sorry to hear that.

   B. Oh, that's a shame.

   C. Oh, really?

3. *A:* So, what's the new video store like?

   B: Well, I'd never seen such a wide selection of videos before.

   Which is the next best sentence?

   A. Great. I'll have to go there sometime.

   B. I see. Maybe next time.

   C. That's a good idea.

LISTEN to the conversation between Judy and Henry. Read the sentences below. Circle *True* or *False*.

Henry: Judy, how was your day off?

Judy: Well, it ended up okay, Henry. I wanted to see the Picasso exhibit at the museum, but by the time I arrived, it had sold out.

Henry: Oh, that's a shame!

Judy: Yeah, but there was a film festival at the Claremont Theater, so I saw a great film.

Henry: Wow! You did? What was the film?

Judy: It was *Wings of Aid.* It was an excellent film about doctors who fly around helping sick people.

Henry: That's amazing! I was there too, but I didn't see you.

Judy: How did you like the film?

Henry: I liked it a lot, but I thought it was too long.

Practice Test

LISTEN to the beginning of a conversation. Then listen for the next best sentence. Choose the correct answer.

1. *A:* What did you think of the concert last night?

B: We didn't get to see it. By the time we arrived at the box office, the tickets had sold out.

Which is the next best sentence?

A. Oh, that's too bad.

B. That's great news.

C. Did you sell the tickets?

2. *A:* I took my kids to the amusement park last weekend.

   B: That sounds like fun. What did you do?

   Which is the next best sentence?

   A. We saw a lot of interesting modern art.

   B. We rode the Ferris wheel and some other rides.

   C. We heard a very nice symphony orchestra.

LISTENING. Listen to the conversation. Then choose the correct answer.

A: Carol, would you like to go to the new Japanese restaurant for dinner tonight?

B: I don't know, Mark. I had planned to go to the movies with Jane this evening.

A: I see . . . Well, what time does the film start?

B: 6:45.

A: Maybe we could go out to eat after the movie?

B: Well, we had been planning to have some coffee after the film . . . Let me check with Jane.

Unit 4

LISTEN to the beginning of a conversation. Then listen for the next best sentence. Fill in the circle for the correct answer.

1. *A:* Good afternoon. Northwood Bank. This is Sharon speaking. How can I help you?

   B: Hi, I'm calling about my checking account statement.

   Which is the next best sentence?

   A. All right. May I have your name and account number?

   B. Do you want to open an account?

   C. Thank you for your help.

2. *A:* My name is Mai Li. My account number is 5432-1789.

   B: And what can I do for you, Ms. Li?

   A: Why is there a $35 charge for insufficient funds on my statement?

Which is the next best sentence?

A. You should transfer some money.

B. Just a minute. Let me check that.

C. I'll do that.

3. *A:* Okay. I see that charge on your account. It looks like you should have made a deposit or a transfer.

B: Oh, I must have forgotten to check that. What should I do now?

Which is the next best sentence?

A. You're welcome.

B. You should make a transfer today.

C. No problem.

LISTEN to the conversation between Harry and his financial advisor. Check the financial advice that you hear.

A: Well, Harry, you have some problems, but generally, you're in good shape.

B: I'm glad to hear it.

A: Of course, you shouldn't have bought so much on credit. You must stop using your credit card for a while.

B: I'll do that, thanks.

A: And you need to change credit cards. Find one with a lower interest rate.

B: I never thought of that.

A: And Harry, you have to make your payments on time. Last year, you lost a lot of money in penalties for late payments.

B: That's certainly true.

A: Also, you have a certificate of deposit for $4000, don't you?

B: Yes, I do.

A: Well, you should keep only $2000 of it. Use the other $2000 to pay off some of your credit card debt.

B: That's an excellent suggestion! Thanks for all of your help!

LISTEN to the audio with the student.

Practice Test

LISTENING: Listen to the beginning of a conversation. Then listen for the next best sentence. Choose the correct answer.

1. *A:* Good afternoon. Southside Bank. How can I help you?

B: I'd like to find out about your certificates of deposit. How much is the interest rate?

Which is the next best sentence?

A. It's two months.

B. It's thirty-five dollars.

C. It's four percent.

2. *A:* Did you see the account statement?

B: No. Why?

A: Well, there's a fee there and I don't understand it.

Which is the next best sentence?

A. It's the balance of the account.

B. It's a penalty for overdrawing the account.

C. It's the account number.

LISTEN to the conversation. Then choose the correct answer.

A: Next please . . . How can I help you?

B: Yes, please. I have a question about my checking account.

A: Let me check your account. Your name and account number, please?

B: Yes, Nathalie Peters. Here's my account number.

A: Okay. Let's see. It looks like you have insufficient funds in your account.

B: Hmmm. I used my debit card. Maybe I forgot to write it down.

A: Can you make a deposit today? That would help.

B: Sure. I can transfer some money from my savings account, can't I?

A: That'll be fine.

Unit 5

LISTEN to the conversation. Then listen to the question. Fill in the circle for the correct answer.

1. *A:* Good morning. Northville Medical Clinic. How can I help you?

B: Hello. My name's John Dana. My grandfather has a doctor's appointment this Friday at 3:00, and I'd like to schedule a ride for him.

Which is correct?

A. John Dana is calling to schedule a ride for his grandfather.

B. A ride was scheduled by John's doctor last week.

C. John's grandfather scheduled a ride for him last week.

2. *A:* Jefferson Community Center. What can I do for you?

B: Hi. I just signed up for one of your computer courses. Do I need to bring my own laptop computer?

A: No, the computers are provided for you to use here.

Which is correct?

A. People need to bring their own computers.

B. Computers are not provided.

C. Computers are provided by the community center.

3. *A:* Good afternoon. Animal Control. What can I do for you?

B: Hello. My garbage cans were knocked over last night and some of my neighbors have had the same problem. I think there is a wild animal running around.

A: We'll send someone over. Can I have your address, please?

Which is correct?

A. There is an animal in the caller's garbage can.

B. The caller wants Animal Control to help him find an animal.

C. The neighbors knocked over the garbage cans.

LISTEN to the conversation. Fill in the chart with information about problems that Maria and Ivan are having.

Ivan: Hi, Maria, what are you doing here? This is the Legal Aid Society.

Maria: Oh, Ivan. I'm having trouble at work. My boss makes me work 10 hours every day, but I wasn't paid for overtime.

Ivan: That's terrible!

Maria: Yes, and there's a terrible smell in the factory. It makes me sick!

Ivan: Well, you're in the right place. I'm here because I'm having problems with my landlord.

Maria: Really?

Ivan: Yes, he thinks that there are a lot of people living with me. He comes into the apartment when I'm not at home.

Maria: That's awful!

Ivan: Yes, and my neighborhood is dangerous. My apartment was broken into and he won't install a stronger door and locks.

Maria: Well, we're both in the right place!

Practice Test

LISTENING: Listen to the conversations. Then choose the correct answer.

1. *A:* Riverside Medical Clinic. How may I help you?

B: Hello. My name's Chu Peng. My appointment was scheduled for 3:00, but I can't come in today.

A: We have an opening tomorrow morning. Is that okay?

Which is correct?

A. Chu Peng is going to an appointment today at 3:00.

B. Chu Peng is setting up an appointment for 3:00.

C. Chu Peng is calling to change his appointment.

2. *A:* I haven't seen Stan at work this week? Where is he?

B: He was called to serve on a jury.

Which is correct?

A. Stan reported for jury duty.

B. Stan is calling people.

C. Stan is working this week.

LISTENING. Listen to the conversation. Then choose the correct answer.

A: Legal Aid Services. How may I help you?

B: Hello. I'm having a problem with my work visa.

A: I see. This is an immigration issue. Would you like to set up an appointment?

B: That would be great.

A: How about Thursday at 4:00 P.M.?

B: That's fine. Thank you.

Unit 6

LISTEN to the question. Then listen to the conversation. Fill in the circle for the correct answer.

1. *A:* InterCast Cable TV. May I have your name and phone number, please?

B: My name is Mary Jones. My phone number is 213-555-4675.

A: How may I help you?

B: I'm calling because there are some errors on my bill.

Which is correct?

A. Mary is calling the phone company.

B. Mary is calling her landlord.

C. Mary is calling the cable TV company.

2. *A:* I'm sorry. O.K. I'm looking at your bill. What are the problems?

B: First, there's a charge for a movie on January 12th. I wasn't home on January 12th.

A: Is it possible that someone else in your home ordered the movie?

B: No, I live alone.

Which is correct?

A. Mary has roommates.

B. Mary didn't order a movie.

C. Mary was home on January 12th.

3. *A:* O.K. I fixed that part of your bill. Is there anything else?

B: Yes. There's a late charge. I paid my bill on time.

A: O.K. Please hold. O.K., I have corrected the errors. We'll send an updated bill this week. Is there anything else?

B: No. Thank you for your help.

Which is correct?

A. Mary has to pay a late charge.

B. Mary didn't pay her bill on time.

C. The cable company will send a correct bill.

LISTEN to the conversation between Jenny and her father. Circle *True* or *False*.

Father: Hello?

Jenny: Hi, Dad. It's Jenny.

Father: Jenny, it's good to hear from you. How are you doing?

Jenny: Not so good, actually. I'm calling because I'm having some problems out here.

Father: Well, that's natural. You're living alone for the first time.

Jenny: Yeah, my little apartment is really different from the apartment that I shared with my friends.

Father: So, what's your problem?

Jenny: Well, I have a couple of problems. First, the sink in the bathroom is leaking. Water is dripping onto the floor.

Father: Well, you have to tell the landlord quickly. Tell him that the water is damaging the floor.

It's going to start leaking into the apartment below you. Then that tenant will start complaining too!

Jenny: Okay, I will. Also, I'm paying for a high-speed Internet connection, but it's really slow and I completely lose the connection.

Father: Jenny, tell your Internet service provider that they have to fix the problem. You can always change companies.

Jenny: I know that you're right, Dad. I'll do that today. Thanks for listening to my problems.

Father: It's no problem.

Jenny: Bye!

Practice Test

LISTENING: Listen to the conversation. Then choose the correct answer.

1. *A:* Union Gas and Electric. How may I help you?

B: I'm calling because there are some errors on my bill.

Which is correct?

A. The woman is calling the phone company.

B. The woman is calling the utility company.

C. The woman is calling the cable company.

2. *A:* I'm sorry about that. May I have your name and account number please?

B: My name is Sara Jones. My account number is 4535674987.

Which is correct?

A. Sara's phone number is 4535674987.

B. Sara is calling 4535674987.

C. Sara's account number is 4535674987.

LISTENING. Listen to the conversation. Then choose the correct answer.

A: Good morning. General Telephone. How can I help you?

B: I'm calling because there's an error on my bill. My name is Mary Wong. My phone number is 213-555-4948.

A: I'm sorry about that, Ms. Wong. Can you tell me what the errors are?

B: Yes. First, you charged me for a call to Chicago on June 3rd. I didn't call Chicago on June 3rd. I was out of town on that day.

A: O.K. I've taken the extra charge off your bill. You will receive an updated bill in about a week.

Unit 7

LISTEN to the conversation. Then listen to the question. Fill in the circle for the correct answer.

1. *A:* Did you hear about the accident at the factory?

 B: No. What happened?

 A: A truck hit the back of the building and broke through the wall. Some people inside the factory were hurt.

 B: Oh, that's terrible!

 Which is correct?

 A. A truck hit a wall at the factory.

 B. The driver of the truck was hurt.

 C. A truck hit a car behind the factory.

2. *A:* Did you hear about the students who are demonstrating?

 B: Yes, I have. They've been demonstrating for two days in front of the school. They're asking for lower tuition.

 Which is correct?

 A. Students want more tuition.

 B. The students have been demonstrating for two weeks.

 C. The students started their demonstration two days ago.

3. *A:* Did you know that Toni Ronaldo donated ten thousand dollars to the city parks?

 B: You mean the soccer star? Wow! That's great. He's a great role model for children and young people.

 Which is correct?

 A: Toni Ronaldo is building a soccer park.

 B: Toni Ronaldo gave money to the city parks.

 C: Toni Ronaldo is a movie star.

LISTEN to the conversation between Kathy and Bob. Then complete the sentences.

Kathy: Bob, there was a lot of interesting news today. Did you hear about the stupid bank robber?

 Bob: No, I didn't.

Kathy: He dropped his wallet during the bank robbery. The police immediately went to his house and arrested him.

 Bob: No way! That's incredible. Well, did you hear about the fire two blocks from here?

Kathy: No, what happened?

 Bob: A firefighter rushed into a burning house and rescued an old man. The firefighter was burned a little bit, but he's going to be OK.

Kathy: I'm glad to hear it. And that demonstration at City Hall was completely peaceful.

 Bob: That's good. And they found the child who was lost in the woods.

Kathy: Really! That's wonderful.

Practice Test

LISTENING. Listen to the conversation. Then listen to the question. Choose the correct answer.

1. *A:* Did you read about the public service workers who are demonstrating?

 B: Yes, I did. They've been demonstrating for three weeks. They're asking for higher pay and better health care.

 Which is correct?

 A. Public service workers want higher salaries and better health insurance.

 B. Health service workers want higher salaries and better health insurance.

 C. Public service workers are going to demonstrate for three weeks.

2. *A:* Did you hear about the fire at the school that happened this morning?

 B: No, I didn't. What happened?

 A: They don't know, but two classrooms were burned. The others are all right.

 B: Oh, that's awful!

 Which is correct?

 A. All the classrooms were burned in a fire.

 B. Only two classrooms are all right.

 C. The fire burned two classrooms.

LISTENING. Listen to the conversation. Then choose the correct answer.

A: Did you read the article about the robbery at the shopping mall?

B: No, I didn't. What happened?

A: Well, about twelve o'clock today, four women walked into the mall with masks and bags. They went to the main store and took over two thousand dollars. They weren't caught!

B: That happened in the middle of the day?

A: Yes, it's true!

B: Really? Do the police have any clues?

A: Yeah. They have a picture of the robbers' car, so they think that they'll find them!

Unit 8

LISTEN to the beginning of a conversation. Then listen for the next best sentence. Fill in the circle for the correct answer.

1. *A:* What are you doing today?
   B: Well, I'm going running in the park.
   A: Aren't you worried about exercising during a smog alert?

   What does the woman say next?

   A. Yes, maybe I should exercise at the gym, instead.
   B. Yes, maybe I should find shelter right away.
   C. Yes, maybe you should take the train today.

2. *A:* What's the weather forecast for today?
   B: The National Weather Service issued a tornado warning.
   A: Wow! That was a strong gust of wind!

   What does the woman say next?

   A. Maybe we should use less electricity today.
   B. Maybe we should try to find shelter immediately.
   C. Maybe we should run in the park today.

3. *A:* How was your trip to Chicago?
   B: There was an extreme heat alert when I was there.
   A: Were people worried about having a power outage?

   What does the woman say next?

   A. No. People were cautious about going outside.
   B. No. People were cautious about using energy.
   C. No. People were cautious about driving in the snow.

LISTEN to the news story. Circle the letter of the best summary of the story.

Welcome to the six o'clock news. Our first story this evening is about the spreading wildfires in California. The governor of California said today that there are over 1000 wildfires currently in California. Firefighters are doing their best to contain the fires, but extreme heat, high winds, and the long drought have created perfect conditions for wildfires. The state government has declared an emergency in the Big Sur region in Central California. Firefighters are worried about the speed of the fire. They are concerned about people

who do not want to leave their homes. The weather forecast is for cooler weather tomorrow across the state, which should help firefighters a great deal.

Practice Test

LISTEN to the beginning of a conversation. Then listen for the next best sentence. Choose the correct answer

1. *A:* What's the weather forecast for today?

   What does the woman say next?

   A. There's a wildfire.
   B. There's a severe thunderstorm warning today.
   C. There's a drought.

2. *A:* Uh-oh! We just had another power outage!

   What does the woman say next?

   A. Yes, I'm concerned about exercising outside.
   B. Yes, we need to find shelter right away!
   C. Yes, the power went out because of the extreme heat.

LISTEN to the conversation. Then choose the correct answer

A: Did you feel that?
B: Yes, I think we just had an earthquake.
A: What should we do?
B: We should evacuate immediately.
A: No, no! It's dangerous to go outside.
B: Then we should get underneath the table.
B: Yes, you're right.

Unit 9

LISTEN to the question. Then listen to the conversation. Listen to the question again. Fill in the circle for the correct answer.

1. Why can't the man park there?
   A: You're not allowed to park here.
   B: Why not?
   A: There's a fire hydrant right there.
   B: Oh, I didn't see it.
   Why can't the man park there?

   A. He's visually impaired.
   B. There's a fire hydrant.
   C. There's a fire engine.

2. What did the man do?

   A: Where have you been?

   B: My car broke down, so I had the mechanic fix it.

   A: You should have called me on your cell phone!

   B: I know. I'm sorry.

   What did the man do?

   A. He fixed his own car.

   B. He had his cell phone fixed.

   C. He had his car fixed.

3. What is the woman's new job?

   A: How's the new job?

   B: Great! I like helping people.

   A: What kinds of things do you do?

   B: Well, yesterday, I helped a student practice parking on the street.

   What is the woman's new job?

   A. She's a bus driver.

   B. She's a crossing guard.

   C. She's a driver education teacher.

LISTEN to the conversation. Complete the chart.

Carlos: Katia, how are you doing? I haven't seen you for a long time.

Katia: Oh hi, Carlos! It's good to see you. Actually, I'm doing okay now, but I had a big problem last week.

Carlos: What happened?

Katia: My car broke down. It wouldn't start, so I was late to work.

Carlos: What did you do?

Katia: I had a mechanic fix it. It cost $600!

Carlos: I'm really sorry to hear that. I had a problem last week too, but it wasn't as serious as yours.

Katia: What was it?

Carlos: I didn't realize that my driver's license had expired. A police officer stopped me, but she didn't give me a ticket. She allowed me to get it renewed the next day.

Katia: You were lucky!

Carlos: I know!

Practice Test

LISTEN to the question. Then listen to the conversation. Listen to the question again. Choose the correct answer.

1. What did the man tell the woman?

   A: What's going on?

   B: My truck wouldn't start this morning.

   A: How did you get to work?

   B: I had my friend pick me up.

   What did the man tell the woman?

   A. He took his friend to work today.

   B. His friend took him to work today.

   C. His friend's truck wouldn't start.

2. What did the woman tell the man?

   A: Excuse me. You're not allowed to smoke here.

   B: Oh really?

   A. It says so right there.

   B. Oh, I'm sorry. I didn't see the sign.

   What did the woman tell the man?

   A. The man is allowed to smoke there.

   B. The man is not allowed to smoke there.

   C. The man didn't see the sign.

LISTEN to the conversation. Then choose the correct answer.

A: You were late yesterday, weren't you?

B: Yes. I had to take care of a problem.

A: Oh. What happened?

B: My car broke down. I had to get it repaired.

A: So, did you take the bus?

B: No, I rode my bicycle.

A: Why don't you ride your bicycle every day?

B: I might do that.

Unit 10

LISTEN to the conversation. Then listen to the question. Fill in the correct answer.

1. *A:* Do you have a smoke detector?

   B: No, but we have a carbon monoxide detector.

   A: You need a smoke detector, too.

   Which is correct?

   A. She told him he needed a carbon monoxide detector.

   B. She told him he needed a smoke detector.

   C. He said he didn't need a smoke detector.

2. *A:* Okay, we need to buy outlet covers . . .

   B: We also need some child-safety locks.

A: No, we don't. I bought them yesterday.

B: Oh, okay.

Which is correct?

A. She said that she had bought child-safety locks yesterday.

B. She said that she had bought outlet covers yesterday.

C. He told her that they needed outlet covers.

3. *A:* Why is there a cabinet lock on the cabinet under the sink?

B: Because there are toxic cleansers in that cabinet.

A: I think we should move the toxic cleansers to a higher cabinet.

B: I agree. That's a good idea.

Which is correct?

A. He told her that the cleansers were in a higher cabinet.

B. She told him that there should be a lock on the cabinet under the sink.

C. She told him that the cleansers should be in a higher cabinet.

LISTEN to the conversation between Martin and Sally. Check the safety precautions that you hear mentioned.

Martin: Sally, the child-safety class was great!

Sally: What did you learn?

Martin: Well, the instructor said that we had to install outlet covers on all the electrical outlets. A lot of babies get electrical shocks.

Sally: That's great advice. I'll buy some.

Martin: And she said that we had to buy a safety gate for the head of the stairs. Some babies fall down stairs.

Sally: That sounds awful! I'll get one of those also.

Martin: And finally, she said that we need to get child-safety locks on our cabinets. Some of our household chemicals are really dangerous.

Sally: That's all great advice!

Practice Test

LISTEN to the conversation. Then listen to the question. Choose the correct answer.

1. *A:* Did you know that you need a smoke detector in this room?

B: But we have them in the living room and the hall.

A: You need one in the kitchen, too.

Which is correct?

A. She told him he needed smoke detectors in every room.

B. She told him he needed a smoke detector in the living room.

C. She told him he needed smoke detectors in the kitchen.

2. *A:* This handrail is broken.

B: Oh. I'll fix it tomorrow.

A: Can't you fix it now?

B: I don't have the tools.

Which is correct?

A. He told her she needed to fix the handrail tomorrow.

B. He told her he'd fix the handrail tomorrow.

C. She told him she'd fix the handrail tomorrow.

LISTEN to the conversation. Then choose the correct answer.

A: I saw Sue yesterday at the store.

B: Oh, really? What was she doing?

A: She was buying safety devices. She said that she and Dan were going to have a baby.

B: Wow, that's great! Did she buy child safety locks? They're really important.

A: No, she said they already had safety locks. She said they needed outlet covers and a safety gate.

Unit 11

LISTEN to the conversation. Then listen to the question. Fill in the correct answer.

1. *A:* So, what are Ana's strengths?

B: Ana always takes the initiative. If she sees that something needs to be done, she'll do it. She doesn't wait until someone tells her to do it.

A: Yes, she's very confident.

Which is correct?

A. Ana is assertive.

B. Ana is aggressive.

C. Ana is demanding.

2. *A:* So, what do you think is Sue's greatest strength?

B: She's always prepared. For example, if I ask her to give a presentation, she always has the materials she needs.

A: Yes. She's always on time, too. She never misses a meeting.

Which is correct?

A. Sue is demanding and aggressive.

B. Sue is sloppy and unprepared.

C. Sue is prepared and punctual.

3. *A:* So, let's talk about Rob.

B: Yes, Rob is a very nice guy. Everyone likes him.

A: And his work is neat. He isn't sloppy.

B: Yes, but I think he needs to become more confident. He's a bit too unassertive.

Which is correct?

A. Rob is nice but sloppy.

B. Rob is assertive but sloppy.

C. Rob is nice but unassertive.

LISTEN to the conversation between Kaoru and her career counselor. Then match the two parts of the sentences.

Career Counselor: Well, Kaoru, I have some advice for you in your job.

Kaoru: I'm happy to hear it. I'd really like to get a promotion.

Career Counselor: It's definitely possible, if you're willing to make some changes. You're very well educated, hard-working, and professional. However, you're rather shy. If you're shy in business, people sometimes think that you don't know anything.

Kaoru: I hadn't thought of that. I always think, "If I work hard, my boss will give me a promotion."

Career Counselor: You need to be more assertive in telling your boss what you do.

Kaoru: I see what you mean.

Career Counselor: Finally, you need to do some professional development. You're a computer programmer, but programming is always changing. If you take some advanced classes, you'll be able to impress your boss with your new knowledge.

Kaoru: That's a good point. Thanks so much for giving me this advice.

Career Counselor: It's my pleasure. If you need any more help, just make another appointment.

Practice Test

LISTENING. Listen to the conversation. Then listen to the question. Choose the correct answer.

1. *A:* Okay, let's talk about Sara.

B: Sara always arrives at meetings on time. And her reports never have any mistakes.

A: Yes, she's very professional.

Which is correct?

A. Sara is unprofessional.

B. Sara is punctual.

C. Sara is sloppy.

2. *A:* So what about Dan?

B: Dan is friendly, His team members like him . . .

A: Yes, but he needs to be more confident. He's very shy.

Which is correct?

A. Dan is unassertive.

B. Dan is unfriendly.

C. Dan is unprepared.

LISTEN to the conversation. Then choose the correct answer.

A: Do you think we should give Sue a promotion?

B: Well, Sue often comes to meetings unprepared.

A: Yes, I've noticed that. And she makes a lot of mistakes in her work.

B: If she takes a professional development course this year, maybe she'll improve.

A: Yes. That might help. For now though, she doesn't seem to be ready to advance in the organization.

B: I agree.

Unit 12

LISTEN to the question. Then listen to the conversation. Listen to the question again. Fill in the circle for the correct answer.

1. What is the most important problem in Greenville?

A: We have many problems here in Greenville. What do you think is the most important problem right now?

B: Well, I think that pollution is getting worse. In the next five years, two more factories are going to be opening. This will be bringing more jobs to our city, but it will also be increasing our air and water pollution.

What is the most important problem in Greenville?

A. There aren't enough jobs.

B. Pollution is increasing.

C. Factories are closing.

2. What will the candidate be speaking about?

A: How can we help our schools?

B: Well, tomorrow night, I'm going to be speaking about that at the high school. And on Wednesday, I'll be covering the same topic at City Hall.

What will the candidate be speaking about?

A. improving schools

B. City Hall

C. the high school

3. What does the candidate say about homeless families?

A: We have many homeless families in Greenville. What can we do to help them?

B: Well, we need to work harder on this problem. We aren't doing enough. First of all, I'm going to be encouraging all citizens to donate food and clothing to the Greenville Homeless Shelter.

What does the candidate say about homeless families?

A. We aren't doing enough.

B. We are working hard enough.

C. We need to build a homeless shelter.

LISTEN to the conversation between Martina and Ivan. Check the urban improvements that the city wants to make.

Martina: Ivan, the city council meeting was fantastic.

Ivan: Really? What did they talk about?

Martina: They talked about all of the improvements the city is going to be making in the next few years.

Ivan: What are they planning to do?

Martina: Well, the city is going to be building a new light rail system. We'll be going to work in trains instead of in cars.

Ivan: That's fantastic. So we'll be breathing cleaner air?

Martina: Yeah. And they're going to be building a new public university just outside town.

Ivan: Really? That's fantastic! Maybe in a few years my little brother will be going there!

Martina: And the city will be starting a new anti-poverty program. A new job-training center will be going up and the city will be offering free day care to low-income families.

Ivan: That's wonderful! Poor people really need some relief.

Martina: The future in this city sounds exciting, doesn't it?

Ivan: Yeah. It sure does!

Practice Test

LISTEN to the question. Then listen to the conversation. Listen to the question again. Choose the correct answer.

1. What will the candidate do about crime?

A: Crime is getting worse in our city. As mayor, what will you do about this?

B: I'm going to be asking all citizens to help our local police officers with this. We all need to watch our neighborhoods carefully and call the police if we see anything strange or suspicious.

What will the candidate do about crime?

A. ask police officers to call if they see anything strange

B. ask police officers to watch the neighborhoods more carefully

C. ask citizens to help by watching the neighborhoods carefully

2. Where will the candidate be speaking tomorrow?

A: What are you going to be doing about improving public services?

B: Well, our seniors need better healthcare. Tomorrow, I'm going to be speaking about this at the senior center. And this evening, I'll be speaking at the hospital.

Where will the candidate be speaking tomorrow?

A. at the senior center

B. at the health clinic

C. at the hospital

LISTEN to the conversation. Then choose the correct answer.

A: Could you please explain your plans for improving traffic problems?

B: Yes, of course. Our roads right now are too crowded.

A: What do you plan to do about it?

B: If I am elected mayor, I will build new roads. We will also improve the roads that we have.

A: What about the cost?

B: We are going to study the budget very carefully. We already have the money for this. Citizens are not going to be paying for this.

Name: _____   **Date:** _____

🎧 **LISTENING:** Listen to the question. Listen to the conversation. Listen to the question again.
TCD5, 2   Fill in the circle for the correct answer.

1. Ⓐ   Ⓑ   Ⓒ

2. Ⓐ   Ⓑ   Ⓒ

3. Ⓐ   Ⓑ   Ⓒ

🎧 **LISTENING:** Listen to the conversation. Choose the best response.
TCD5, 2

4. Ⓐ   Ⓑ   Ⓒ

5. Ⓐ   Ⓑ   Ⓒ

GRAMMAR: Choose the correct answer to complete each sentence.

6. What _____ for lunch today?

   A. are you doing   **C.** have you done

   B. do you do   **D.** did you do

7. Every Sunday, I _____ my study group for coffee.

   A. am meeting   **C.** meet

   B. will meeting   **D.** am going to meet

8. My current professor _____ us to work very hard.

   A. is expecting   **C.** expected

   B. expect   **D.** expects

9. Rania has studied _____ geometry _____ calculus for her math major.

   A. both, and   **C.** both, or

   B. neither, and   **D.** either, nor

10. _____ I pass this course _____ I don't graduate!

    A. Either, and   **C.** Neither, and

    B. Either, or   **D.** Either, but

11. Eric has _____ registered for classes _____ paid his fees.

    A. both, nor   **C.** both, or

    B. neither, and   **D.** neither, nor

12. _____ that door for me?

    A. Are you opening   **C.** Will you open

    B. Do you open   **D.** Will you opening

13. Tonight, Seth _____ for his biology test.

    A. is going to study   **C.** will do studying

    B. studies   **D.** is doing studying

14. When George finishes college, he _____ a bachelor's degree.

    A. earns   **C.** is earning

    B. will earn   **D.** will be earning

15. Sure, _____ English with you. Let's start!

    A. I am practicing   **C.** I practiced

    B. I practice   **D.** I'll practice

Name: _____   **Date:** _____

READING: Read the paragraph about Marcus. Choose the best answer.

> I decided to take an online class in digital photography because I want to open my own business. I already shoot photos for weddings part-time, but I use a regular film camera. I'd like to learn how to use the latest digital cameras and equipment so that I can decide what to buy. I also want to be able to put my customers' photos online right away so that they can choose and click on the ones they want to buy. My class is teaching me all about digital cameras, digital editing software, how to set up photo websites, and more. I'm very satisfied with the course so far. Later, I hope to expand my business to sell family portraits, senior pictures, and artistic photos of nature.

16. What class is Marcus taking?
    A. film photography   C. digital editing software
    B. digital photography D. camera equipment

17. What does Marcus take photos of now?
    A. weddings   C. nature
    B. families   D. seniors

18. Why does Marcus want to learn about the latest equipment?
    A. He likes to use a regular film camera.
    B. He enjoys new technology.
    C. He doesn't know what to buy yet.
    D. He wants to sell camera equipment.

19. Why does Marcus want to put his photos online?
    A. so his family can look at them
    B. so his customers can buy them easily
    C. because he doesn't like printing out photos
    D. because it costs less to put photos online

20. What will Marcus not learn in his class?
    A. how to sell more photos
    B. types of digital cameras
    C. how to make photo websites
    D. digital editing software

VOCABULARY: Choose the best word to complete the sentence.

21. Zack is _____ a course on repairing cars.
    A. testing out of   C. earning
    B. contacting   D. looking into

22. I'm going to _____ my academic counselor after class.
    A. attend   C. apply for
    B. meet with   D. look into

23. Selena has five _____ to finish today.
    A. credits   C. tasks
    B. personality tests D. improvements

24. You should _____ the financial aid office for help.
    A. submit to   C. cover
    B. satisfy   D. contact

25. The group is _____ to finish their project on time.
    A. on track   C. applying
    B. registering   D. earning credits

Name: _____   Date: _____

🎧 **LISTENING:** Listen to the question. Listen to the conversation. Listen to the question again.
TCD5, 3   Fill in the circle for the correct answer.

1. Ⓐ   Ⓑ   Ⓒ

2. Ⓐ   Ⓑ   Ⓒ

3. Ⓐ   Ⓑ   Ⓒ

🎧 **LISTENING:** Listen to the conversation. Choose the best response.
TCD5, 3

4. Ⓐ   Ⓑ   Ⓒ

5. Ⓐ   Ⓑ   Ⓒ

GRAMMAR: Choose the correct answer to complete each sentence.

6. After Mary _____ the report, she sent it to Doug.
    A. finish   **C.** finished
    B. finishes   **D.** will finish

7. Paul _____ many workshops since he started working here in 2007.
    A. attends   **C.** is attending
    B. attended   **D.** has attended

8. Jennifer _____ the conference call as soon as she left the meeting.
    A. joins   **C.** has joined
    B. joined   **D.** is joining

9. Tina will have her performance review before she _____ home.
    A. goes   **C.** has gone
    B. is going   **D.** went

10. Carl took the workshop on managerial skills, and Debbie did, _____.
    A. either   **C.** so
    B. too   **D.** neither

11. Juneau doesn't have tall buildings, and _____ does Rome.
    A. either   **C.** so
    B. too   **D.** neither

12. Karen has attended three workshops, but she _____ gotten her certificate yet.
    A. has   **C.** had
    B. hasn't   **D.** have

13. Jack was very organized and _____ his time well last year.
    A. managed   **C.** has managed
    B. manages   **D.** will manage

14. Kate _____ leadership skills this year. I've been very impressed.
    A. shows   **C.** has shown
    B. showed   **D.** will show

15. Ed becomes 30 percent vested in his retirement fund next month, and _____ does Ashley.
    A. either   **C.** so
    B. too   **D.** neither

Name: _____   Date: _____

READING: Read the performance reviews. Choose the best answer.

Human Resources Annual Performance Review 2008

Andrew Robinson—Andrew has been in the marketing department for three years. Andrew has been impressive this year. His coworkers have told me that he is very communicative and dependable. His supervisor says that he always meets his deadlines and organizes his time well, although another supervisor said Andrew seemed a little overwhelmed at times. Andrew worked on two big projects this year. With both projects, he was creative and added a lot to the design of the advertisements. Andrew has shown good leadership skills this year. I think he should attend the managerial skills workshop next year. Andrew is a strong candidate for a job as a supervisor.

---

16. Why should Andrew attend a managerial skills workshop?

 A. He shows good leadership skills.

 B. He is overwhelmed at times.

 C. He is creative.

 D. He worked on two big projects this year.

17. Andrew's coworkers would probably agree that _____.

 A. Andrew is uncooperative

 B. Andrew is punctual

 C. Andrew is helpful

 D. Andrew is burned out

18. How long has Andrew worked in marketing?

 A. two years   C. this year

 B. three years   D. since December

19. If Andrew works on his leadership skills, he may get _____.

 A. certification in marketing

 B. more projects

 C. a promotion to supervisor

 D. creative ideas

20. One supervisor thinks Andrew is _____.

 A. creative   C. dependable

 B. a good candidate   D. overwhelmed

VOCABULARY: Choose the best word to complete the sentence.

21. After the meeting, Ivy checked her _____ to see if anyone had called.

 A. schedule   C. conference call

 B. voicemail   D. project

22. Jim is very _____. He comes to meetings on time.

 A. burned out   C. punctual

 B. overwhelmed   D. creative

23. Since the beginning of the year, Kim has attended three _____.

 A. schedules   C. workshops

 B. deadlines   D. promotions

24. Matt didn't get the job because the interviewer thought he was _____.

 A. likeable   C. reliable

 B. disagreeable   D. capable

25. In two more months, Julie is likely to get a _____.

 A. workshop   C. qualification

 B. deadline   D. promotion

Name: _____   **Date:** _____

🎧 **LISTENING:** Listen to the question. Listen to the conversation. Listen to the question again.
TCD5, 4   Fill in the circle for the correct answer.

1. Ⓐ   Ⓑ   Ⓒ

2. Ⓐ   Ⓑ   Ⓒ

3. Ⓐ   Ⓑ   Ⓒ

🎧 **LISTENING:** Listen to the conversation. Choose the best response.
TCD5, 4

4. Ⓐ   Ⓑ   Ⓒ

5. Ⓐ   Ⓑ   Ⓒ

GRAMMAR: Choose the correct answer to complete each sentence.

6. By the time Jill got to the restaurant, her friends _____ their food.

   A. order   C. ordered

   B. are ordering   D. had ordered

7. Estella had never spoken English in class before she _____ to Miami.

   A. moves   C. moved

   B. move   D. had moved

8. Before Josh _____ to the museum, he had read about the exhibit.

   A. went   C. goes

   B. had gone   D. is going

9. Ava had never _____ Romeo and Juliet before last night.

   A. sees   C. saw

   B. see   D. seen

10. Ethan _____ to a lot of countries before he was 20 years old.

    A. goes   C. had went

    B. went   D. had gone

11. Karen _____ when the electricity went out.

    A. is studying   C. had studied

    B. had been studying D. studied

12. _____ the bus arrived, we had been waiting 20 minutes.

    A. Until   C. By the time

    B. After   D. By then

13. The play had been going on for only a few minutes when the fire alarms _____ off.

    A. go   C. went

    B. had been going D. had gone

14. How long _____ George been working before he received a promotion?

    A. has   C. had

    B. is   D. was

15. How long had you been driving before you _____ to rest?

    A. stop   C. was stopping

    B. stopped   D. had stopped

Name: _____   **Date:** _____

READING: Read the paragraph about Clint Eastwood. Choose the best answer.

> **Clint Eastwood: Actor and Politician**
>
> When most people hear the name Clint Eastwood, they think of his starring roles in movies or of the Academy Awards he won for directing movies such as *Unforgiven* and *Million Dollar Baby*. Many people do not think of his political career. However, for the past 25, years Eastwood has been active in California politics.
>
> Eastwood was born in San Francisco on May 31, 1930. He served in the U.S. Army after he had graduated from high school. After serving in the army, Eastwood moved to Los Angeles to be an actor. In the 1960s, Eastwood became famous for playing the hero in westerns. In the 1970s, he starred in many action and comedy movies. He also started directing. In 1992 and 2004, Eastwood won Academy Awards for best director.
>
> In 1986, Eastwood was elected mayor of Carmel, California. While he was mayor, Eastwood worked to improve communication between the business community and the local residents of Carmel. In 2001, Eastwood was appointed to the California State Park and Recreation Commission. The commission protects all of California's state parks. In 2004, Governor Schwarzenegger reappointed Eastwood to the commission.

16. What did Eastwood do right after high school?
   A. He joined the army.   **C.** He starred in movies.
   B. He ran for mayor.   **D.** He directed movies.

17. How old was Eastwood when he became a mayor?
   A. 45   **C.** 56
   B. 50   **D.** 60

18. What type of movies did Eastwood first star in?
   A. comedy   **C.** action
   B. romance   **D.** western

19. When he was mayor, Eastwood wanted to improve relations between the people who lived in Carmel and _____.
   A. actors   **C.** business leaders
   B. tourists   **D.** directors

20. In 2001, Eastwood was appointed to a commission which is in charge of _____.
   A. national parks   **C.** city parks
   B. state parks   **D.** skateboarding parks

VOCABULARY: Choose the best word to complete the sentence.

21. When we got to the auditorium, the _____ showed us to our seats.
   A. hostess   **C.** street vendor
   B. usher   **D.** body builder

22. Michelle's parents went to the concert to see her _____.
   A. reservation   **C.** exhibit
   B. brochure   **D.** debut performance

23. Tommy got really scared when he watched the _____.
   A. cartoon   **C.** TV game show
   B. horror movie   **D.** comedy

24. James and Kevin went to the _____ to watch the football game.
   A. stadium   **C.** auditorium
   B. amusement park   **D.** street fair

25. Mario is a really fast swimmer. I think he should enter swimming _____. I think he could win.
   A. tests   **C.** competitions
   B. exhibits   **D.** festivals

Name: _____   **Date:** _____

🎧 **LISTENING:** Listen to the question. Listen to the conversation. Listen to the question again.
TCD5, 5   Fill in the circle for the correct answer.

1. Ⓐ Ⓑ Ⓒ
2. Ⓐ Ⓑ Ⓒ
3. Ⓐ Ⓑ Ⓒ

🎧 **LISTENING:** Listen to the conversation. Choose the best response.
TCD5, 5

4. Ⓐ Ⓑ Ⓒ
5. Ⓐ Ⓑ Ⓒ

GRAMMAR: Choose the correct answer to complete each sentence.

6. I can't find my wallet! I _____ lost it somewhere.
   A. must have   C. should have
   B. must not have   D. should not

7. You paid $40 in interest this month? You _____ paid off your credit card and saved the money.
   A. must not   C. must have
   B. shouldn't have D. should have

8. We _____ bought a new car this year. We can't really afford the payments. I wish we had kept our old car.
   A. should have   C. must not have
   B. shouldn't have D. must have

9. Celia got a penalty on her electric bill. She _____ paid it on time.
   A. should not have C. must not have
   B. shouldn't   D. must

10. I never seem to have any money when I need it. I should make a monthly budget, _____?
    A. don't it?   C. should I?
    B. shouldn't I?   D. won't I?

11. This is the bank where you have your personal account, _____?
    A. isn't it?   C. is it?
    B. aren't you?   D. don't you?

12. Michael has a lot of debts to pay. He shouldn't spend so much, _____?
    A. shouldn't he?   C. has he?
    B. did he?   D. should he?

13. Roberto had his credit card information stolen. He didn't shred his personal documents when he threw them away, did he?
    A. No, he shouldn't. C. Yes, he must have.
    B. No, he didn't.   D. No, he did.

14. They've requested their credit reports, haven't they?
    A. No, they haven't. C. Yes, they did.
    B. No, they didn't.   D. No, they shouldn't.

15. I don't have to balance the checkbook today, do I?
    A. No, you do.   C. Yes, you do.
    B. Yes, you don't. D. No, you should.

Name: _____   Date: _____

READING: Read the email that Jacob wrote. Choose the best answer.

> Hi, Mom. I found out why the bank didn't give me a loan for a new car. The loan officer showed me my credit report, and my credit score was awful! I didn't understand how that could happen, because you know I don't even have any debt. My credit report shows three credit cards that I don't have. More than $10,000 has been charged to those cards in the last two months. Someone must have stolen my personal information. It must have happened when I was in France. Most of the charges were made in Paris. I called the credit bureaus right away and filed an identity theft report, so I won't have to pay the $10,250. But my credit score may take years to straighten out! What a nightmare!

16. Why did the bank refuse Jacob's loan?
    - A. He didn't pay his bills on time.
    - B. He had a bad credit score.
    - C. His loan officer didn't like him.
    - D. They didn't have his credit report.

17. How much debt does Jacob have now?
    - A. none
    - B. $10,000
    - C. $250
    - D. $10,250

18. Why does Jacob think his personal information was stolen in France?
    - A. He doesn't like French people.
    - B. He didn't enjoy his vacation to France.
    - C. The charges were made in Paris.
    - D. He hasn't used his credit card anywhere else.

19. When Jacob discovered the charges, he _____.
    - A. called the credit card companies to complain
    - B. called the credit bureaus to file a report
    - C. asked the bank to help him fix his credit report
    - D. paid the $10,250 to the credit card companies

20. Why does Jacob want to get a loan?
    - A. He wants to buy a house.
    - B. He needs to pay for school.
    - C. He wants to buy a new car.
    - D. He wants to start a business.

VOCABULARY: Choose the best word to complete the sentence.

21. My checking account is _____. I need to deposit some money and pay an insufficient funds fee.
    - A. outrageous
    - B. overdrawn
    - C. balanced
    - D. delinquent

22. Miho scheduled _____ on her bank's website. She didn't want to forget to pay her mortgage.
    - A. an automated payment
    - B. a credit card offer
    - C. a monthly allowance
    - D. a credit report

23. We shouldn't eat out for the next two weeks. Our _____ is very tight right now.
    - A. mortgage payment
    - B. monthly budget
    - C. credit score
    - D. automated payment

24. Raul and Natalie's _____ helped them make a plan to pay off their credit card debt.
    - A. teller
    - B. loan officer
    - C. bank officer
    - D. financial advisor

25. I'm glad I invested in a _____. I'm making some money, and it's safe, too.
    - A. checking account
    - B. certificate of deposit
    - C. credit card
    - D. mortgage loan

Name: _____   **Date:** _____

🎧 **LISTENING:** Listen to the question. Listen to the conversation. Listen to the question again.
TCD5, 6   Fill in the circle for the correct answer.

1. Ⓐ   Ⓑ   Ⓒ

2. Ⓐ   Ⓑ   Ⓒ

3. Ⓐ   Ⓑ   Ⓒ

🎧 **LISTENING:** Listen to the conversation. Choose the best response.
TCD5, 6

4. Ⓐ   Ⓑ   Ⓒ

5. Ⓐ   Ⓑ   Ⓒ

GRAMMAR: Choose the correct answer to complete each sentence.

6. The Supreme Court _____ that the tax was illegal.
   A. decide
   B. decides
   C. is decided
   D. decided

7. The new election law _____ by the Senate.
   A. was approved
   B. approved
   C. approve
   D. approves

8. The students' schedules _____ out by the faculty.
   A. handed
   B. were handed
   C. are handing
   D. hand

9. My teacher _____ on a jury last year.
   A. is served
   B. serves
   C. served
   D. was served

10. Megan _____ the problem with her landlord many times.
    A. is discussing
    B. discusses
    C. discussed
    D. is discussed

11. Was Dylan _____ to the City Council?
    A. electing
    B. elected
    C. elects
    D. elect

12. An attorney _____ for the defendant if he doesn't have one.
    A. appointed
    B. is appointed
    C. appoints
    D. is appointing

13. Were your tax forms _____ by an accountant?
    A. preparing
    B. prepare
    C. prepares
    D. prepared

14. How much federal tax _____ from your paycheck?
    A. deducted
    B. deducts
    C. has deducted
    D. was deducted

15. Why didn't Charlie _____ animal control?
    A. call
    B. calls
    C. called
    D. calling

Name: _____ **Date:** _____

READING: Read the paragraph about Presidents' Day. Choose the best answer.

The only federal holiday in the month of February is Presidents' Day. The first president of the United States, George Washington, was born on February 22, 1732. In 1832, the federal government decided to honor Washington, making February 22 a holiday.

Abraham Lincoln, the sixteenth president, who ended slavery and the Civil War, was also born in February. Lincoln's birthday, February 12, was celebrated as a holiday after his death. However, Lincoln's birthday was never declared an official federal holiday.

In 1971, Congress officially combined Washington's and Lincoln's birthdays into Presidents' Day. At that time, it was decided that Presidents' Day would always be celebrated on the third Monday in February.

Presidents' Day is a holiday that allows Americans to think about how much both Washington and Lincoln did for the country. It is also a day to honor the memory of all of the country's presidents.

16. How many federal holidays are there in February?
- **A.** 0
- **B.** 1
- **C.** 2
- **D.** 3

17. When was the first Presidents' Day?
- **A.** 1832
- **B.** 1731
- **C.** February 12
- **D.** 1971

18. When is Presidents' Day celebrated?
- **A.** February 12
- **B.** February 22
- **C.** the first Monday in February
- **D.** the third Monday in February

19. What is Lincoln known for?
- **A.** being the first president
- **B.** ending the Civil War
- **C.** being the fifteenth president
- **D.** being born in February

20. Who declared Presidents' Day a federal holiday?
- **A.** Congress
- **B.** the President
- **C.** all the people
- **D.** Lincoln

VOCABULARY: Choose the best word to complete the sentence.

21. The leaders of city governments are called _____.
- **A.** governors
- **B.** mayors
- **C.** senators
- **D.** representatives

22. Citizens may be called to _____ a jury.
- **A.** serve on
- **B.** approve
- **C.** accuse
- **D.** arrest

23. The jury declared the defendant _____. He has to spend 11 years in prison.
- **A.** arrested
- **B.** accused
- **C.** innocent
- **D.** guilty

24. After he was arrested, Robert hired a good _____.
- **A.** jury
- **B.** trial
- **C.** judge
- **D.** attorney

25. The government _____ taxes from everyone's paycheck.
- **A.** withholds
- **B.** files
- **C.** assigns
- **D.** employs

Name: _____   **Date:** _____

🎧 **LISTENING:** Listen to the question. Listen to the conversation. Listen to the question again.
TCD5, 7 Fill in the circle for the correct answer.

1. Ⓐ   Ⓑ   Ⓒ

2. Ⓐ   Ⓑ   Ⓒ

3. Ⓐ   Ⓑ   Ⓒ

🎧 **LISTENING:** Listen to the conversation. Choose the best response.
TCD5, 7

4. Ⓐ   Ⓑ   Ⓒ

5. Ⓐ   Ⓑ   Ⓒ

GRAMMAR: Choose the correct answer to complete each sentence.

6. We found a problem in the bathroom. But _____ problem isn't serious.
    A. an   C. the
    B. a   D. some

7. _____ weak signal can be a big problem.
    A. An   C. The
    B. A   D. Some

8. The cable company made _____ mistakes on my bill.
    A. an   C. the
    B. a   D. some

9. The plumber gave me _____ estimate for fixing the sink.
    A. an   C. the
    B. a   D. some

10. Which cell phone company is _____ best?
    A. an   C. the
    B. a   D. some

11. Do you know _____?
    A. where the repairman went
    B. where went the repairman
    C. where did the repairman go
    D. where did go the repairman

12. I don't know _____ the policy is.
    A. why   C. whether
    B. if   D. what

13. Can you tell me _____?
    A. how I do file a complaint
    B. how do I file a complaint
    C. how I can file a complaint
    D. how can I file a complaint

14. Do you know _____ the landlord is?
    A. whether   C. where
    B. if   D. when

15. I don't know _____.
    A. why didn't he get the apartment
    B. why he didn't get the apartment
    C. why did not he get the apartment
    D. why not he got the apartment

Name: _____   **Date:** _____

READING: Read the paragraph about June's apartment. Choose the best answer.

> June just moved into a new apartment. She is not sure if she likes it. The rent is only $800 per month. The apartment is very large with big windows. There is a big kitchen table where she can do her homework. The apartment is in a good location near June's school and some really nice restaurants. June really likes cats, though, and the lease says that she can't have a pet. The kitchen appliances are all very old, and the carpet is worn and stained in a few places. The floor in the kitchen is cracked, and the paint in her bedroom is peeling. The landlord is going to fix the kitchen floor, but he isn't going to replace the refrigerator or stove. June doesn't know if he'll repaint the apartment.

16. How does June like her new apartment?
    A. She doesn't like it at all because of the problems.
    B. She really likes it a lot because of the low rent.
    C. She doesn't know whether she likes it or not.
    D. She doesn't know if the landlord will paint it.

17. What does June like about the apartment?
    A. The rent is low. The kitchen and bedroom have new paint.
    B. The location is good. She can get a cat. She can repaint the bedroom.
    C. It's beautiful with big windows, nice carpets, and new appliances.
    D. The rent is low. The apartment is big and in a good neighborhood.

18. Which of the following is NOT a problem in the apartment?
    A. The bedroom has peeling paint.
    B. The refrigerator and stove are very old.
    C. The apartment doesn't get much light.
    D. The carpet is very old and worn out.

19. What does June do?
    A. She is a teacher.   C. She is a student.
    B. She is a painter.   D. She is a landlord.

20. What does June not know?
    A. She doesn't know if the rent is too high.
    B. She doesn't know if the landlord will paint.
    C. She isn't sure whether the landlord will fix the kitchen floor.
    D. She isn't sure if the landlord will replace the kitchen appliances.

VOCABULARY: Choose the best word to complete the sentence.

21. My phone is _____. I can't hear anything.
    A. connection   C. signal
    B. dead   D. power outage

22. The _____ on my cell phone is weak.
    A. signal   C. error
    B. dead   D. leak

23. A _____ is very dangerous.
    A. ugly stain   C. weak signal
    B. Internet connection   D. gas leak

24. I'm going to _____ against my landlord because of the broken toilet.
    A. sign a lease   C. discriminate
    B. file a complaint   D. break my lease

25. What are the tenant's _____ in the lease? Do I have to repair the appliances?
    A. access   C. obligations
    B. agreement   D. property

Name: _____   **Date:** _____

🎧 **LISTENING:** Listen to the question. Listen to the conversation. Listen to the question again.
TCD5, 8   Fill in the circle for the correct answer.

1. Ⓐ   Ⓑ   Ⓒ

2. Ⓐ   Ⓑ   Ⓒ

3. Ⓐ   Ⓑ   Ⓒ

🎧 **LISTENING:** Listen to the conversation. Choose the best response.
TCD5, 8

4. Ⓐ   Ⓑ   Ⓒ

5. Ⓐ   Ⓑ   Ⓒ

GRAMMAR: Choose the correct answer to complete each sentence.

6. The woman _____ the computer was arrested.
    A. who steals   C. which stole
    B. that steals   D. who stole

7. Did you read about the cat _____ a man from drowning?
    A. that saved   C. whom saved
    B. that helped   D. it saved

8. The man _____ $500 received a thank-you card.
    A. who donates   C. that is donating
    B. who donated   D. which donated

9. The woman _____ the child was not injured.
    A. who rescued   C. that rescues
    B. which rescues   D. she rescued

10. The flu epidemic _____ our school was really terrible.
    A. that hits   C. that hit
    B. who hit   D. it hit

11. The movie _____ was based on a true story.
    A. whom we saw   C. we see
    B. that we saw   D. which we see

12. Dr. Harrison is the man _____ last week.
    A. who Don visited   C. Don visited him
    B. whom Don visits   D. which Don visits

13. The blog _____ yesterday was on our newspaper's website.
    A. who I read   C. I read it
    B. which I will read   D. that I read

14. The classified ad _____ is for a job at the hospital.
    A. Allison circled it   C. whom Allison circles
    B. that Allison circled D. that circled Allison

15. That's the man _____ on the local news.
    A. I heard about   C. whom I hear
    B. that I hear about   D. I heard about him

Name: _____   **Date:** _____

READING: Read the newspaper article. Choose the best answer.

The Parent-Teacher Association for Shadyside Elementary School met last night to discuss children and health. Many parents expressed concern that their children are not getting enough exercise at school. In recent years, recess and physical education classes have been shortened to give more time to other subjects. Parents at the meeting said that their children have so much homework, they don't have time to exercise after school. Many ideas were discussed to help children get fit and stay healthy. Lana Peterson, mother of three students at the school, suggested fund raisers to help pay for sports fees so more children could play. Mitch Jackson, the physical education teacher, said that students should have gym class every day, instead of just twice a week.

16. What was the main topic of the meeting?
   A. children and health
   B. after-school sports
   C. how much homework is given
   D. how to stay healthy

17. Parents think that their children are getting _____ exercise at Shadyside.
   A. too much   C. too little
   B. enough   D. the wrong kind of

18. Why were physical education classes shortened?
   A. because students don't like physical education
   B. to give more time to other subjects
   C. because the classes are too expensive
   D. because the teacher wanted to work fewer hours

19. Who suggested fund raisers to help pay fees?
   A. the physical education teacher
   B. the principal of the school
   C. a student who attended the meeting
   D. a mother of students at the school

20. How often do students have gym class?
   A. every day
   B. two times a week
   C. two times a day
   D. three days a week

VOCABULARY: Choose the best word to complete the sentence.

21. Amina is a great _____ for kids because she volunteers at the shelter.
   A. role model   C. officer
   B. demonstrator   D. politician

22. Three people were injured in the _____ on Highway 38.
   A. crime   C. epidemic
   B. collision   D. rescue

23. The article was on the _____ of the newspaper.
   A. section   C. classified ads
   B. column   D. front page

24. The _____ today was about a man who sailed around the world alone.
   A. local section   C. top story
   B. URL   D. columnist

25. Do you know the _____ for Missy's blog?
   A. headline   C. top story
   B. URL   D. investigator

Name: _____   Date: _____

🎧 **LISTENING:** Listen to the question. Listen to the conversation. Listen to the question again.
TCD5, 9   Fill in the circle for the correct answer.

1. Ⓐ   Ⓑ   Ⓒ

2. Ⓐ   Ⓑ   Ⓒ

3. Ⓐ   Ⓑ   Ⓒ

🎧 **LISTENING:** Listen to the conversation. Choose the best response.
TCD5, 9

4. Ⓐ   Ⓑ   Ⓒ

5. Ⓐ   Ⓑ   Ⓒ

GRAMMAR: Choose the correct answer to complete each sentence.

6. Diane is nervous about _____ lost.

   A. get   **C.** getting

   B. to get   **D.** got

7. Nathan was serious _____ going to China.

   A. of   **C.** about

   B. in   **D.** for

8. Sue believes _____ protecting the environment.

   A. of   **C.** about

   B. in   **D.** for

9. They were afraid _____ flash floods.

   A. of   **C.** about

   B. in   **D.** for

10. My boss was _____ in learning about natural disasters.

   A. interesting   **C.** interests

   B. interest   **D.** interested

11. The EPA _____ on removing toxic waste.

   A. helps   **C.** cares

   B. believes   **D.** focuses

12. The NRDC cares _____ finding a solution to global warming.

   A. of   **C.** about

   B. in   **D.** for

13. The American Red Cross helps _____ disaster relief after tornadoes.

   A. on   **C.** for

   B. about   **D.** with

14. We _____ on volunteering with the Red Cross next month.

   A. plan   **C.** help

   B. believe   **D.** care

15. She was concerned about _____ in the thunderstorm.

   A. driving   **C.** to drive

   B. drive   **D.** driven

Name: _____   Date: _____

READING: Read the paragraph about Mark. Choose the best answer.

> Mark is a college student in San Francisco, California. He is studying biology, but he may change his major to environmental science. He has taken one class in environmental law and may eventually go to law school. He is very concerned about protecting the environment, especially regarding pollution. He is upset about the amount of pollution in the air because he has asthma, a medical condition that sometimes makes breathing difficult. He believes in planting trees to clean the air and take carbon out of the air. On weekends, he volunteers with Friends of the Urban Forest, a local organization that plants trees all over the city. Recently, there was a terrible wind storm that knocked down a lot of trees. Mark is helping with cleaning up the fallen trees in the park. When he graduates from college, Mark is interested in working for the Natural Resources Defense Council. He might also apply for a job at the Environmental Protection Agency. It works on removing toxic waste and keeping the air and water clean.

16. What is Mark's major right now?
   A. biology
   B. plants
   C. environmental science
   D. environmental law

17. What happened in San Francisco?
   A. Many of the plants are dead because of a blizzard.
   B. A mudslide knocked down a large part of the forest.
   C. A tornado destroyed many of the buildings.
   D. Many trees fell down because of strong winds.

18. Who does Mark want to work for after graduating?
   A. The EPA or the NRDC
   B. Friends of the Urban Forest
   C. The American Red Cross
   D. FEMA or the EPA

19. What issue is Mark especially worried about?
   A. global warming
   B. air pollution
   C. environmental laws
   D. deforestation

20. What does Mark do to reduce air pollution?
   A. He rides a bicycle.
   B. He removes dead trees.
   C. He plants trees.
   D. He studies biology.

VOCABULARY: Choose the best word to complete the sentence.

21. It hasn't rained in several months. We've having a severe _____.
   A. hurricane
   B. drought
   C. blizzard
   D. mudslide

22. The National Weather Service _____ a tornado warning.
   A. advised
   B. evacuated
   C. stayed
   D. issued

23. The Federal Emergency Management Agency (FEMA) _____ victims of natural disasters.
   A. plans on
   B. volunteers
   C. believes in
   D. evacuates

24. Greenpeace is concerned about environmental problems like _____.
   A. severe thunderstorms
   B. global warming
   C. precautions
   D. torrential rain

25. The American Red Cross provides _____ for victims.
   A. global warming
   B. toxic waste
   C. disaster relief
   D. natural disasters

Name: _____   Date: _____

🎧 **LISTENING:** Listen to the question. Listen to the conversation. Listen to the question again.
TCD5, 10 Fill in the circle for the correct answer.

1. Ⓐ Ⓑ Ⓒ

2. Ⓐ Ⓑ Ⓒ

3. Ⓐ Ⓑ Ⓒ

🎧 **LISTENING:** Listen to the conversation. Choose the best response.
TCD5, 10

4. Ⓐ Ⓑ Ⓒ

5. Ⓐ Ⓑ Ⓒ

GRAMMAR: Choose the correct answer to complete each sentence.

6. The law requires all school buses _____ before crossing railroad tracks.

   A. stopping   **C.** stop

   B. to stop   **D.** stopped

7. Rita had her car _____ today.

   A. wash   **C.** washed

   B. to wash   **D.** washing

8. Felicia's mother _____ driving her to school when she was 16.

   A. stopping   **C.** stop

   B. to stop   **D.** stopped

9. The driver education teacher let Johnny _____ on the highway.

   A. driving   **C.** drive

   B. to drive   **D.** drove

10. The traffic officer had all the cars _____ so that the ambulance could pass.

    A. stopping   **C.** stop

    B. to stop   **D.** stopped

11. The city doesn't allow drivers _____ turns on that street during rush hour.

    A. make   **C.** making

    B. to make   **D.** made

12. Ashley will never forget_____ her road test. It was a scary experience.

    A. taking   **C.** take

    B. to take   **D.** took

13. Ben remembered _____ his extra set of car keys to the repair shop. Last time he forgot them at home.

    A. bringing   **C.** bring

    B. to bring   **D.** brought

14. A wheelchair lift _____ handicapped passengers get on a bus.

    A. helps   **C.** helping

    B. to help   **D.** help

15. The crossing guard made the cars _____ while the children crossed the street.

    A. stopping   **C.** stop

    B. to stop   **D.** stopped

Name: _____   **Date:** _____

READING: Read the paragraph about a snowstorm. Choose the best answer.

> **Unusual Snowstorm Causes Big Accident**
>
> San Francisco, CA—Police allowed drivers back onto Highway 101 this morning after a big traffic accident. Late last night, 23 cars crashed into each other after a rare snowstorm hit San Francisco. Although drivers are required to drive no faster than 55 miles per hour on Highway 101, many people drive over the speed limit. Unfortunately, at around 12:15 a.m., this unusual snowstorm created dangerous driving conditions. Cab driver Harold Smith said he had stopped to help the drivers of two cars when a large truck hit the cars and jackknifed. "After that, cars and trucks started to pile up on top of each other. I'll never forget the sound of all those cars hitting each other." Amazingly, no one was seriously hurt. Fourteen people were taken to General Hospital with minor injuries. Most of them will be released later today.

16. How many cars were in the accident?
    - **A.** 14
    - **B.** 23
    - **C.** 34
    - **D.** 101

17. When did the accident happen?
    - **A.** around midnight
    - **B.** around noon
    - **C.** around 1:00
    - **D.** around 3:40

18. When did police allow drivers to go back on the highway?
    - **A.** late at night
    - **B.** around 12:15 a.m.
    - **C.** in the morning
    - **D.** in the afternoon

19. What happened to the large truck?
    - **A.** It jackknifed.
    - **B.** It was going too fast.
    - **C.** The driver stopped to help the injured.
    - **D.** It had minor injuries.

20. What caused the accident?
    - **A.** a turned-over truck
    - **B.** an unusual snowstorm
    - **C.** people driving too late at night
    - **D.** a cab driver

VOCABULARY: Choose the best word to complete the sentence.

21. The visually impaired man has a _____ to help him get around town.
    - **A.** wheelchair lift
    - **B.** guide dog
    - **C.** crossing guard
    - **D.** tow truck

22. You can't park here. It's a _____.
    - **A.** parking meter
    - **B.** parking space
    - **C.** school zone
    - **D.** tow-away zone

23. Michelle wanted a map of downtown and a bus schedule, so she went to the _____.
    - **A.** Visitor Information Center
    - **B.** Department of Motor Vehicles
    - **C.** post office
    - **D.** hardware store

24. Jennifer parked her car and put four quarters in the _____.
    - **A.** fire hydrant
    - **B.** parking lot
    - **C.** tow-away zone
    - **D.** parking meter

25. Rick stopped at the post office to pick up a _____.
    - **A.** road test
    - **B.** proof of insurance form
    - **C.** change of address form
    - **D.** tow truck

Name: _____   **Date:** _____

🎧 **LISTENING:** Listen to the question. Listen to the conversation. Listen to the question again.
TCD5, 11 Fill in the circle for the correct answer.

1. Ⓐ Ⓑ Ⓒ

2. Ⓐ Ⓑ Ⓒ

3. Ⓐ Ⓑ Ⓒ

🎧 **LISTENING:** Listen to the conversation. Choose the best response.
TCD5, 11

4. Ⓐ Ⓑ Ⓒ

5. Ⓐ Ⓑ Ⓒ

GRAMMAR: Choose the correct answer to complete each sentence.

6. Melanie said, "I'll come with you to the safety class." Melanie said _____ with us to the safety class.
   A. she is coming
   B. she will come
   C. they would come
   D. she would come

7. Carol said, "My friends weren't at the first aid class." Carol said that her friends _____ at the first aid class.
   A. haven't been
   B. weren't
   C. hadn't been
   D. wouldn't have been

8. Jim said, "John, your house isn't safe." Jim told John that his house _____ safe.
   A. isn't
   B. hadn't been
   C. wasn't
   D. wouldn't be

9. Mary said, "You can have our baby gates. We don't use them now." Mary said that we _____ her baby gates.
   A. could have
   B. can have
   C. would have
   D. could have had

10. Terri _____ a walking group she wanted to join.
    A. gave up
    B. found out about
    C. paid off
    D. used up

11. Harry didn't _____ for the gym, so he can't attend the aerobics class.
    A. follow his application through with
    B. follow through with his application
    C. follow through his application with
    D. follow through his application

12. I had to _____ salt because I have high blood pressure.
    A. sign up
    B. use up
    C. count on
    D. give up

13. We _____ have smoke detectors in our house, but now we do.
    A. didn't use to
    B. wasn't use to
    C. aren't used to
    D. used to

14. Janet _____ lifting weights, so it was difficult for her to start.
    A. didn't use to
    B. isn't use to
    C. wasn't used to
    D. wasn't use to

15. Alex _____ play the piano, but now he's forgotten how.
    A. was use to
    B. was used to
    C. used to
    D. use to

Name: _____ **Date:** _____

READING: Read the story about Miles. Choose the best answer.

Life as a paramedic sure is exciting! I love getting into the ambulance and racing to help people. We have saved the lives of many people, and that's a great feeling. Last week, a man called us because his son was having shortness of breath. We got there just in time! The boy had asthma and didn't know it. We helped him breathe again and took him to the hospital. We were really happy to help that little boy. But sometimes, people call us when they don't really need us. Once, we arrived at a woman's house to find that her "emergency" was a little rash on her leg. It was just poison ivy, and it wasn't serious at all. People shouldn't waste our time unless it's really an emergency.

16. What does Miles do for a living?
    A. He's a doctor.
    B. He's an ambulance driver.
    C. He's a nurse.
    D. He's a paramedic.

17. What does Miles like about his job?
    A. It feels good to save people's lives.
    B. He meets many nice people.
    C. The work is easy and low-stress.
    D. He makes a lot of money.

18. What does Miles dislike about his job?
    A. the fear of making a mistake
    B. helping scared children
    C. people calling when it isn't an emergency
    D. spending time in the ambulance

19. What was wrong with the little boy?
    A. He was dizzy and nauseous.
    B. He was having trouble breathing.
    C. He was vomiting and couldn't stop.
    D. His eyes and lips were swelling.

20. Who had poison ivy?
    A. Miles
    B. the little boy
    C. the woman
    D. the ambulance driver

VOCABULARY: Choose the best word to complete the sentence.

21. Jenny used _____ so her children wouldn't get an electric shock.
    A. outlet covers
    B. smoke detectors
    C. carbon monoxide detectors
    D. handrails

22. The school has a _____ once a month..
    A. safety device   C. child-safety lock
    B. fire drill   D. smoke detector

23. Yolanda moved the _____ to a high shelf..
    A. toxic cleansers   C. electrical outlet
    B. child-safety locks   D. burn hazard

24. When I'm in trouble, I know I can _____ my sister to help me.
    A. fall for   C. count on
    B. show up   D. give up

25. We don't have any tissues because Marge _____.
    A. came back   C. looked them up
    B. thought it over D. used them up

Name: _____   Date: _____

🎧 **LISTENING:** Listen to the question. Listen to the conversation. Listen to the question again.
TCD5, 12 Fill in the circle for the correct answer.

1. Ⓐ   Ⓑ   Ⓒ

2. Ⓐ   Ⓑ   Ⓒ

3. Ⓐ   Ⓑ   Ⓒ

🎧 **LISTENING:** Listen to the conversation. Choose the best response.
TCD5, 12

4. Ⓐ   Ⓑ   Ⓒ

5. Ⓐ   Ⓑ   Ⓒ

GRAMMAR: Choose the correct answer to complete each sentence.

6. If Ryan sells five cars this week, he _____ a big bonus.

   A. would get   **C.** was going to get

   B. will get   **D.** got

7. If I don't finish this today, my boss _____ me.

   A. is going to fire   **C.** has fired

   B. would fire   **D.** fired

8. If Stella doesn't hire an assistant, she _____ her work.

   A. wouldn't finish   **C.** hasn't finished

   B. couldn't finish   **D.** won't finish

9. If Janet gets up early, she _____ her email before work.

   A. is checking   **C.** checked

   B. checks   **D.** would check

10. I _____ nervous if my boss calls me.

   A. felt   **C.** feel

   B. had felt   **D.** am feeling

11. If Will found a better job, he _____ his current job in an instant.

   A. would quit   **C.** quits

   B. will quit   **D.** would be quitting

12. Megan _____ her parents for Easter if she had more vacation time.

   A. visits   **C.** is visiting

   B. will visit   **D.** could visit

13. If Shelly _____ a conference to go to, she could play golf this weekend.

   A. couldn't have   **C.** isn't having

   B. didn't have   **D.** will have

14. Paul _____ a good impression with people if he wore nicer clothes.

   A. is making   **C.** would make

   B. makes   **D.** has made

15. If my coworkers lived in my neighborhood, we _____ to work together.

   A. would drive   **C.** are driving

   B. drive   **D.** have driven

Name: _____   **Date:** _____

READING: Read a reference that Gina wrote for Raj. Choose the best answer.

> I first met Raj at a networking event last year, and I was very impressed by how friendly and professional he was. Since we met, Raj has completed several freelance projects for our company, so I know that his technical skills are excellent. His level of education is outstanding, since he has a master's degree and has taken several continuing education courses in the last two years. The only concern I have about Raj is his dislike of teamwork. Raj gets along with everybody, but he prefers to work alone. He can also be impatient with people who don't work as quickly as he does.

16. Where did Gina meet Raj?
    A. in college   C. through work
    B. at a conference   D. at a networking event

17. How does Gina know about Raj's technical skills?
    A. Raj showed her a portfolio of work.
    B. Raj has done freelance work for the company.
    C. Raj has several good references.
    D. Raj and Gina worked together before.

18. When did Raj take continuing education courses?
    A. two years ago   C. in the last two years
    B. last year   D. during college

19. Why doesn't Raj like teamwork?
    A. He would rather work by himself.
    B. He doesn't get along with people.
    C. He is not friendly and doesn't like to talk.
    D. He thinks he is always right.

20. How could Raj improve his people skills?
    A. He could be friendlier with people.
    B. He could be more patient with people.
    C. His people skills are perfect the way they are.
    D. He could work harder than his coworkers.

VOCABULARY: Choose the best word to complete the sentence.

21. That training course is expensive, but I'm pretty sure I can _____.
    A. evaluate my credentials
    B. get feedback
    C. conduct a job search
    D. cover the costs

22. Steve got some great _____ about his new ideas for the company. The boss was really impressed.
    A. opportunities
    B. feedback
    C. professional development
    D. teamwork

23. Larry never impresses his interviewers because he always looks _____ when he arrives.
    A. sloppy   C. assertive
    B. prepared   D. professional

24. Clara is really unhappy as an accountant. It's time for her to _____.
    A. make a career change
    B. negotiate better benefits
    C. have good connections
    D. make a better impression

25. I love my company, but I'm getting bored doing the same thing all the time. Maybe I should _____.
    A. make a better impression
    B. work on my people skills
    C. transfer to a different department
    D. encourage teamwork

Name: _____   **Date:** _____

🎧 **LISTENING:** Listen to the question. Listen to the conversation. Listen to the question again.
TCD5, 13 Fill in the circle for the correct answer.

1. Ⓐ   Ⓑ   Ⓒ

2. Ⓐ   Ⓑ   Ⓒ

3. Ⓐ   Ⓑ   Ⓒ

🎧 **LISTENING:** Listen to the conversation. Choose the best response.
TCD5, 13

4. Ⓐ   Ⓑ   Ⓒ

5. Ⓐ   Ⓑ   Ⓒ

GRAMMAR: Choose the correct answer to complete each sentence.

6. Martin _____ his boss to the conference this year.
   A. will be accompany
   B. will accompanying
   C. won't be accompanying
   D. is going to accompanying

7. You _____ classes for next semester soon, right?
   A. are going to be selecting
   B. will going to selecting
   C. are going to be select
   D. had been selecting

8. Next month, I _____ on a beach in Rio de Janeiro.
   A. am going to lying   C. will be lie
   B. will be lying   D. get to lying

9. _____ the workshop on Tuesday or Wednesday?
   A. Will she giving   C. She will giving
   B. When will she giving   D. Will she be giving

10. Why _____ the online course next semester?
    A. don't you be taking   C. you won't be taking
    B. won't you be taking   D. are you won't taking

11. The company is sponsoring a Quit Smoking Day _____ better health for its employees.
    A. to promote   C. to enhance
    B. to keep   D. to avoid

12. Janice does yoga every day _____ stress.
    A. to balance   C. expand
    B. to minimize   D. emphasize

13. Michelle rode her bike to work _____ the traffic on the freeway.
    A. to lose   C. to keep
    B. to save   D. to avoid

14. It can be difficult _____ a new job.
    A. to expand   C. to start
    B. to find out   D. to address

15. I was surprised _____ that Rich was promoted.
    A. to emphasize   C. to improve
    B. to find out   D. to decide

Name: _____   **Date:** _____

READING: Read the paragraph about Beth. Choose the best answer.

> Starting my own business has been a lot more work than I thought it would be. I like to make pottery, and I love kids, so I opened my own shop, Pots for Tots. I thought I would give lessons to kids and sell my own art to their parents. Simple, right? Wrong! My life is hectic now. I spend so much time doing business that I rarely get to make pots anymore. The only relaxing I've done for six weeks has been taking my two daughters fishing on Sundays. Next week, I'll be filing the paperwork to make the business a corporation. And in the next month, I'll be teaching three pottery courses for kids. I had no idea how many pots kids could break in just two hours. I lost a lot of money on my first workshop, but I sure learned some good lessons.

16. Who are Beth's main customers at Pots for Tots?
    A. children who want to make pottery
    B. people who like to fish
    C. assistants who work with children
    D. parents who don't like art very much

17. Beth thinks running her own business is _____.
    A. awful because she hates working with kids
    B. great because she has time to make pots now
    C. more difficult than she expected
    D. much easier than she thought it would be

18. What does Beth do to relax?
    A. makes pottery
    B. takes her daughters fishing
    C. plays with the children in her classes
    D. sells her art on the Internet

19. What will Beth do in the next month?
    A. file paperwork to pay her taxes
    B. make a special line of pottery for girls
    C. teach a parent-child pottery course
    D. teach three children's courses

20. In Beth's first kids' course, _____.
    A. the kids broke a lot of pots
    B. the kids wouldn't pay attention
    C. her assistant wasn't very helpful
    D. parents complained about the cost

VOCABULARY: Choose the best word to complete the sentence.

21. Our teacher was in a serious car accident, so a new teacher is _____ next week.
    A. running
    B. taking over
    C. coordinating
    D. selecting

22. I can't wait to go _____ in Europe this summer!
    A. enjoying
    B. accompanying
    C. quality of life
    D. sightseeing

23. Mayor Whiteside's _____ has been excellent so far. He has made some good speeches.
    A. issue
    B. balance
    C. campaign
    D. efforts

24. The city is opening a new park downtown to enhance the _____ for residents who live there.
    A. stress
    B. enjoying
    C. quality of life
    D. sightseeing

25. The company president posted a huge calendar in the office _____ the importance of deadlines.
    A. to minimize
    B. to emphasize
    C. to avoid
    D. to coordinate

Unit 1

1. A; 2. B; 3. A; 4. C; 5. B; 6. A; 7. C;
8. D; 9. A; 10. B; 11. D; 12. C; 13. A; 14. B;
15. D; 16. B; 17. A; 18. C; 19. B; 20. A;
21. D; 22. B; 23. C; 24. D; 25. A

Unit 2

1. B; 2. A; 3. C; 4. B; 5. C; 6. C; 7. D;
8. B; 9. A; 10. B; 11. D; 12. B; 13. A; 14. C;
15. C; 16. A; 17. C; 18. B; 19. C; 20. D;
21. B; 22. C; 23. C; 24. B; 25. D

Unit 3

1. B; 2. C; 3. A; 4. A; 5. C; 6. D; 7. C;
8. A; 9. D; 10. D; 11. B; 12. C; 13. C; 14. C;
15. B; 16. A; 17. C; 18. D; 19. C; 20. B;
21. B; 22. D; 23. B; 24. A; 25. C

Unit 4

1. C; 2. B; 3. B; 4. A; 5. C; 6. A; 7. D;
8. B; 9. C; 10. B; 11. A; 12. D; 13. B; 14. A;
15. C; 16. B; 17. A; 18. C; 19. B; 20. C;
21. B; 22. A; 23. B; 24. D; 25. B

Unit 5

1. B; 2. A; 3. C; 4. C; 5. B; 6. D; 7. A;
8. B; 9. C; 10. C; 11. B; 12. B; 13. D; 14. D;
15. A; 16. B; 17. D; 18. D; 19. B; 20. A;
21. B; 22. A; 23. D; 24. D; 25. A

Unit 6

1. C; 2. B; 3. B; 4. C; 5. A; 6. C; 7. B;
8. D; 9. A; 10. C; 11. A; 12. D; 13. C; 14. C;
15. B; 16. C; 17. D; 18. C; 19. C; 20. B;
21. B; 22. A; 23. D; 24. B; 25. C

Unit 7

1. B; 2. C; 3. A; 4. A; 5. B; 6. D; 7. A;
8. B; 9. A; 10. C; 11. B; 12. A; 13. D; 14. B;
15. A; 16. A; 17. C; 18. B; 19. D; 20. B;
21. A; 22. B; 23. D; 24. C; 25. B

Unit 8

1. C; 2. A; 3. B; 4. C; 5. A; 6. C; 7. C;
8. B; 9. A; 10. D; 11. D; 12. C; 13. D; 14. A;
15. A; 16. A; 17. D; 18. A; 19. B; 20. C;
21. B; 22. D; 23. D; 24. B; 25. C

Unit 9

1. B; 2. C; 3. C; 4. A; 5. B; 6. B; 7. C;
8. D; 9. C; 10. C; 11. B; 12. A; 13. B; 14. A;
15. C; 16. B; 17. A; 18. C; 19. A; 20. B;
21. B; 22. D; 23. A; 24. D; 25. C

Unit 10

1. B; 2. C; 3. A; 4. B; 5. A; 6. D; 7. C; 8. C;
9. A; 10. B; 11. B; 12. D; 13. A; 14. C;
15. C; 16. D; 17. A; 18. C; 19. B; 20. C;
21. A; 22. B; 23. A; 24. C; 25. D

Unit 11

1. A; 2. B; 3. B; 4. C; 5. C; 6. B; 7. A;
8. D; 9. B; 10. C; 11. A; 12. D; 13. B; 14. C;
15. A; 16. D; 17. B; 18. C; 19. A; 20. B;
21. D; 22. B; 23. A; 24. A; 25. C

Unit 12

1. C; 2. B; 3. B; 4. A; 5. C; 6. C; 7. A; 8. B;
9. D; 10. B; 11. A; 12. B; 13. D; 14. C; 15. B;
16. A; 17. C; 18. B; 19. D; 20. A; 21. B;
22. D; 23. C; 24. C; 25. B

Unit 1

LISTENING: Listen to the questions. Listen to the conversation. Listen to the questions again. Fill in the circle for the correct answer.

1. What is Anna doing on Thursday?

    Maria: Anna, can you come for dinner on Thursday night?

    Anna: Sure, Mom, I'd love to. My business class was cancelled for that night.

    What is Anna doing on Thursday?

    A. She is having dinner with her mother.

    B. She is going to class.

    C. She is reading a business book.

2. What classes will Brian take next semester?

    Female: What are you registering for next semester?

    Male: English and history. I wanted to register for geography, too, but the course was full.

    Female: Aren't you taking any business classes?

    Male: Oh, yes, I forgot. I'll have accounting on Mondays.

    What classes will Brian take next semester?

    A. English, history, and geography

    B. English, history, and accounting

    C. geography and accounting

3. When can Maria study with her friend?

    Male: So can we get together on Tuesday to study?

    Female: Yes, I think so. I have to work in the morning, and in the evening I have my continuing education course. But I'm free in the afternoon.

    When can Maria study with her friend?

    A. Tuesday afternoon

    B. Tuesday morning

    C. Tuesday evening

LISTENING: Listen to the conversations. Choose the best response.

4.

    Male: I heard you got a promotion at work.

    Female: Yes, I did. I'm an assistant manager now.

    Male: That's great! You work so hard, you really deserve it.

    Female:

    A. That's terrific!

    B. Yes, it's really interesting.

    C. Thanks, I appreciate that.

5.

    Female: I can't believe you quit your job! Why did you do it?

    Male: I just wasn't happy there. The boss was always rude to me and accused me of stealing, which I didn't do.

    Female: Are you kidding? That's terrible.

    Male: Yeah, I couldn't work there anymore. So I marched right into his office and told him I quit. I'm so glad I don't work there anymore. And I already got a new job—a better one!

    Female:

    A. I'm sorry to hear that.

    B. Well, good for you!

    C. Thanks, I'm really happy about it.

Unit 2

LISTENING: Listen to the question. Listen to the conversation. Listen to the question again. Fill in the circle for the correct answer.

1. What are the people talking about?

    Female: Hello, Mr. Nelson's office. May I help you?

    Male: Hi, Barbara. It's Glen. Did you send Mr. Wilkes the report yet?

    Female: Yes, I sent it right after lunch.

    What are the people talking about?

    A. lunch

    B. a report

    C. Mr. Wilkes

2. What did Gary do?

    Carlos: Hey, Gary. I'm glad I found you.

    Gary: Hi, Carlos. What can I do for you?

    Carlos: Did you pull together the materials for today's meeting?

    Gary: Yes, I put a folder on your desk last night around 5:30.

What did Gary do?

A. He gathered information for a meeting.

B. He found Carlos.

C. He went to a meeting last night around 5:30.

3. Why is Rita happy?

Male: Wow, Rita. You look really happy.

Female: I am. I asked Donna to cover for me next week and she said okay. Now I can go to my cousin's wedding.

Male: That's great.

Why is Rita happy?

A. She's getting married.

B. She's going to work for Donna next week.

C. Donna is going to work for her next week.

LISTENING: Listen to the conversation. Choose the best response.

4.

Female: Robert, have you finished the project you were working on?

Robert: Not yet. Mr. Morris wanted me to add the sales figures for 2006. I'll finish it as soon as I get back from lunch.

Female:

A. Oh, that's too bad.

B. You're so organized.

C. That's not very helpful.

5.

Female: Hi, Laura. What's wrong?

Laura: I've got an important deadline tomorrow, and I scheduled a meeting this afternoon. I'm afraid I won't have time to finish the assignment.

Female: I could stay after my work is done and help you.

Laura:

A. You're so organized.

B. I'm not glad to hear that.

C. Thanks. That's very helpful.

Unit 3

LISTENING: Listen to the question. Listen to the conversation. Listen to the question again. Fill in the circle for the correct answer.

1. What happened at the concert hall?

Tina: I never got to see the symphony concert on Friday.

Male: Why not, Tina?

Tina: When Paul and I got to the concert hall's box office, the tickets were already sold out.

What happened at the concert hall?

A. Tina and Paul saw a symphony concert.

B. Tina and Paul couldn't get tickets.

C. The symphony concert was cancelled.

2. Where did they meet?

Male: This sidewalk café is a great place to meet.

Female: Yeah. I can't believe how convenient it is to the museum.

Male: I had never been to the museum before today.

Female: Really? That's too bad. They have some great exhibits.

Where did they meet?

A. the museum

B. the exhibits

C. the sidewalk café

3. Why was the baseball game cancelled?

Female: Mark, I thought you had tickets to the baseball game today.

Mark: I did, but you won't believe what happened. First, there was a delay because it was raining. I had been waiting for an hour when they cancelled the game.

Female: Because of the rain?

Mark: No. It started to snow!

Female: Really? That's too bad.

Why was the baseball game cancelled?

A. It started to snow.

B. It started to rain.

C. It was too late to start.

LISTENING: Listen to the conversation. Choose the best response.

4.

Female: How was dinner at The Four Corners?

Male: We didn't get to eat there. It was too crowded.

Female:

A. What a shame. Didn't you make a reservation?

B. That's too bad. Didn't you ask the usher to seat you?

C. Oh, that's awful. Didn't you buy tickets in advance?

5.

Male: Did you have a nice lunch with Ron?

Female: Not really. There was a TV on in the café. He watched the basketball game the whole time.

Male:

A. Oh, that's great.

B. I'm glad you had a good time.

C. Oh, how rude!

Unit 4

LISTENING: Listen to the question. Listen to the conversation. Listen to the question again. Fill in the circle for the correct answer.

1. What does the man buy?

Male: What is the interest rate on the six-month certificate of deposit?

Female: It's three percent. But you can get a higher interest rate if you buy a twelve-month certificate of deposit. The interest rate is four percent.

Male: That sounds good. I think I'll buy that one.

What does the man buy?

A. a six-month certificate of deposit

B. a certificate of deposit with a three percent interest rate

C. a twelve-month certificate of deposit

2. How will the couple pay for their groceries?

Female: Let's use our debit card to buy the groceries.

Male: We can't do that. I just balanced the checkbook, and we don't have enough money.

Female: All right, let's use the credit card.

How will the couple pay for their groceries?

A. cash

B. credit card

C. debit card

3. When is the mortgage payment due?

Male: What's the due date for our mortgage payment?

Female: It's due on the first of May. That's five days from now.

Male: We should pay it right away, then.

When is the mortgage payment due?

A. May 3

B. May 1

C. May 5

LISTENING: Listen to the conversations. Choose the best response.

4.

Male: I need to open a retirement account, but I don't know what to do.

Female: You should see a financial advisor.

Male:

A. That's a great idea! Thanks.

B. I could get a certificate of deposit.

C. I'll call my credit card company.

5.

Female: I don't know how I'm going to pay all of these bills.

Male: You could use your credit card.

Female: I don't want to do that. I already have too much debt.

Male: Why don't you get a second job? You could work part-time in the evenings.

Female:

A. My credit score is too low.

B. I could make an online payment.

C. I never thought of that.

Unit 5

LISTENING: Listen to the question. Listen to the conversation. Listen to the question again. Fill in the circle for the correct answer.

1. What happened?

   Male: Animal Control. How can I help you?

   Female: Hello. My name is Laura Brown. My daughter was bitten by a dog. She seems okay, but I'm going to take her to the hospital just in case. I think someone should come and catch the dog.

   What happened?

   A. Laura Brown's daughter bit a dog.

   B. A dog bit Laura Brown's daughter.

   C. Laura Brown caught a stray dog.

2. What does the Community Center provide?

   Female: Franklin Community Center. May I help you?

   Father: Hi. My son is starting summer camp at the center tomorrow. Are lunches provided for the children?

   Female: No, your son should bring his lunch from home. We do give the campers snacks in the afternoon.

   What does the Community Center provide?

   A. snacks

   B. campers

   C. lunches

3. How often are free hearing tests given?

   Female: Mission Street Free Clinic. How may I direct your call?

   Male: Hi. How often do you give free hearing tests?

   Female: We have free tests twice a month, on the first and third Saturdays. Would you like to make an appointment?

   How often are free hearing tests given?

   A. The tests are given every Saturday.

   B. The tests are given once a month.

   C. The tests are given twice a month.

4. Why are they sending an ambulance?

   Operator: 9-1-1. What is the emergency?

   Caller: I'm watching a soccer game, and one player was accidentally kicked in the head. He fell to the ground and hasn't gotten up.

   Operator: We'll send an ambulance right away. Where are you?

   Why are they sending an ambulance?

   A. The caller kicked a soccer player in the head.

   B. The caller was kicked in the head.

   C. A soccer player was kicked in the head.

5. When is the garbage collected?

   Male: Public Works Department. How may I help you?

   Female: Hi. I live at 933 Scott Street. It's Tuesday and my garbage wasn't collected today. Do you have a new schedule?

   Male: Yes, the new schedule took effect this month. Your garbage is collected on Thursdays now. We sent out notices last month.

   When is the garbage collected?

   A. Garbage is collected on Tuesdays.

   B. Garbage is collected on Thursdays.

   C. Garbage is collected this month.

Unit 6

LISTENING: Listen to the question. Listen to the conversation. Listen to the question again. Fill in the circle for the correct answer.

1. What is Harry's problem?

   Female: Harry, there's a strange smell in your apartment.

   Male: Yes. It smells like a gas leak. We have to call the gas company right away!

   What is Harry's problem?

   A. His apartment smells bad.

   B. There is an error on his gas bill.

   C. There is a gas leak in his apartment.

2. What does Karen's father think of her apartment?

   Father: Karen, the carpet is stained.

   Karen: I know, but it's not so bad.

   Father: And the paint is peeling. This is a terrible apartment!

Karen: Oh, Dad. It's okay. I'm comfortable here.

What does Karen's father think of her apartment?

A. He thinks that it's not such a terrible apartment.

B. He thinks that it's a very bad apartment.

C. He likes Karen's apartment a lot.

3. What's Mary's problem?

Employee: Good afternoon. Central Gas Company. How can I help you?

Mary: I'm calling because there are three errors on my gas bill for this month.

Employee: I'm sorry about that. I'll be glad to take care of those mistakes.

What is Mary's problem?

A. There is a mistake on her gas bill.

B. There are three errors on her gas bill.

C. There are three errors on her electric bill.

LISTENING: Listen to the conversations. Choose the best response.

4.

Female: Are you okay? You look upset.

Male: My landlord is trying to evict me.

Female: That's terrible! Why?

Male: He wants his daughter to move in. I wonder if I should get a lawyer.

Female:

A. I'm really sorry about his daughter's problem.

B. I'm glad that you found a solution to the problem.

C. Yes. You should definitely get a lawyer quickly.

5.

Female: Okay, so you read the rental agreement. Do you have any questions?

Male: Yes. I like the apartment, but can I have a pet?

Female:

A. Yes. You can have a cat or a small dog.

B. No. You can't sublet the apartment to anyone.

C. There is a deposit of $1000.

Unit 7

LISTENING: Listen to the question. Listen to the conversation. Listen to the question again. Fill in the circle for the correct answer.

1. What happened to the skier?

Male: Did you hear about the skier who got lost at Snowy Mountain?

Female: Yes, I read about it in the paper this morning. He was rescued, wasn't he?

Male: That's right. He skied off the trail and couldn't find his way back. The ski patrol took a helicopter up the mountain to find him.

Female: He shouldn't have been skiing by himself. That's dangerous!

What happened to the skier?

A. He went skiing off the trail but then found his way back.

B. He got lost and was rescued.

C. He lost his friend while skiing.

2. What has been banned in the park downtown?

Female: Where were you this morning?

Male: I was at a demonstration that was held in the park downtown.

Female: Really? What was the demonstration for?

Male: People are angry because dogs have been banned from the park. We should be allowed to play with our dogs there and take them for walks.

What has been banned from the park downtown?

A. demonstrators

B. walks

C. dogs

3. Where did the woman find exercise equipment to buy?

Male: Where did you buy your exercise equipment? I really need to get in shape, but I hate to go to the gym.

Female: I found my treadmill in a classified ad. It was very cheap, and the owner brought it to my house.

Where did the woman find exercise equipment to buy?

A. in a classified ad

B. at the gym

C. at her house

LISTENING: Listen to the conversations. Choose the best response.

4.

    Male: Did you hear that a 90-year-old man went into space?

    Female: Are you serious?

    Male: Absolutely. I saw a video on the news this morning.

    Female:

A. I can't believe it!

B. I don't know yet.

C. Sure, why not.

5.

    Female: Mark, my parents are coming to visit next month.

    Male: Oh? How long will they be here? A few days?

    Female: Um, three weeks, actually.

    Male:

A. It's true.

B. Really?

C. I heard about that!

Unit 8

LISTENING: Listen to the question. Listen to the conversation. Listen to the question again. Fill in the circle for the correct answer.

1. Why is Martine going to the gym?

    Male: Martine, are you going to go running with us? We're going down by the lake.

    Female: No, not today. There's a smog advisory, so I'm going to the gym instead.

Why is Martine going to the gym?

A. She doesn't know how to swim.

B. She doesn't want to run.

C. The air quality is bad today.

2. What is Harry worried about?

    Male: Have you heard the weather report?

    Female: Yes, I did. It's going to be really hot this summer.

    Male: We live in a forest. I'm really concerned about having a wildfire.

What is Harry worried about?

A. There might be a forest fire in the summer.

B. The weather might be too hot for him.

C. There might be a serious drought.

3. What are June and Sam afraid of?

    Male: I can't see anything. I'm really nervous about driving in this storm.

    Female: I know. I'm worried about getting lost.

    Male: There's a place to stop. Let's just sit and wait until the rain stops.

What are June and Sam afraid of?

A. Being late getting to a party

B. Getting lost in torrential rain

C. Having a car accident

LISTENING: Listen to the conversations. Choose the best response.

4.

    Female: Joe. How are you doing?

    Joe: Fine thanks. Just really busy.

    Female: Hey! What's going on with this weather? It's freezing today.

    Joe:

A. It's raining cats and dogs!

B. I know. I hate this heat!

C. It sure is. I'm really cold!

5.

    Male: You work for Greenpeace, don't you?

    Female: Yes, I do. I've been with them for about two years.

    Male: What does that organization focus on?

    Female:

A. We work on protecting the environment.

B. My job is to remove hazardous waste.

C. We're really worried about forest fires.

Unit 9

LISTENING: Listen to the question. Listen to the conversation. Listen to the question again. Fill in the circle for the correct answer.

1. What does the student ask to do?

   Female: Mr. Jackson, I passed my learner's permit exam last week. May I try driving on the highway?

   Male teacher: Do you think you're ready? It's a lot different than driving on streets.

   Female: Yes, I think I'm ready.

   What does the student ask to do?

   A. Practice driving on the street

   B. Practice driving on the highway

   C. Practice for the learner's permit exam

2. What is the man looking for?

   Male: Excuse me, I need to find the Town Hall. Do you know where it is?

   Female: No, I don't. Why don't you stop to ask someone at that gas station? They might know. Or you could stop to get a map at the Information Center.

   Male: Okay. Thanks very much.

   What is the man looking for?

   A. A gas station

   B. A map

   C. The Town Hall

3. Why should the driver slow down?

   Female: Would you mind slowing down? You're driving too fast.

   Male: Why? I'm going the speed limit. It's 35 on this street.

   Female: Don't you see the crossing guard over there?

   Male: Oh, you're right. I'm in a school zone.

   Why should the driver slow down?

   A. There is a crossing guard.

   B. He is driving the speed limit.

   C. He is driving in a school zone.

LISTENING: Listen to the conversation. Choose the best response.

4.

   Female: I always remember to turn off my car lights, but today I forgot. Now my car won't start.

   Male: Hmm. Is the battery dead?

   Female: Yes, I think so.

   Male:

   A. Let's try calling a tow truck.

   B. What's the problem?

   C. You might as well drive home.

5.

   Wife: I can't believe you're this late. We missed the movie.

   Husband: My boss made me stay to finish the monthly report.

   Wife: And he didn't allow you to call me?

   Husband: I'm sorry. I didn't notice the time.

   Wife:

   A. Good idea.

   B. Well, why don't we get something to eat?

   C. Would you mind if I call you?

Unit 10

LISTENING: Listen to the question. Listen to the conversation. Listen to the question again. Fill in the circle for the correct answer.

1. What happened to the girl?

   Boy: What did the doctor say?

   Girl: She said I would be fine in two weeks. My ankle isn't broken; it's only a sprain. Next time I'll make sure there aren't any toys on the stairs. I don't want to fall again.

   What happened to the girl?

   A. Nothing. She's fine.

   B. She fell and sprained her ankle.

   C. She fell and broke her ankle.

2. Will the man take the home safety class?

   Female: You should take the home safety class with me on Tuesday evening.

   Male: I really want to, but I can't. I have to watch the kids that night.

Female: You could leave the kids at my house with my daughter Joanie. She's old enough to watch them now.

Male: I'd really like to, but I don't know . . . Joanie's only 13. Do you really think that's old enough?

Female: Absolutely! She's very responsible.

Male: Well, let me think about it. I'll tell you tomorrow.

Will the man take the home safety class?

A. Yes. He'll leave the kids with Joanie.

B. No, he can't. He has to watch the kids.

C. Maybe, if he decides Joanie is old enough to watch the kids.

3. How often does the family test their smoke detectors?

Male: I'm really glad we test our smoke detectors every month. Last night, we forgot to blow out a candle, and the tablecloth caught on fire.

Female: Really? Where were you?

Male: We were in the family room watching a movie and didn't smell the smoke. If the smoke detector hadn't sounded, the whole house might have burned down—with us inside!

How often does the family test their smoke detectors?

A. every month

B. every night

C. every week

LISTENING: Listen to the conversation. Choose the best response.

4.

Male: There's a great party tomorrow night at Brian's house. You shouldn't miss out on the fun.

Female: I hate to turn down a good time, but I have so much homework to do.

Male: Come on, you can do your homework on Wednesday.

Female: Well, okay. I'll see you there.

Male:

A. Fine, I'll call him and ask.

B. I'm looking forward to it.

C. That's terrible!

5.

Female: I had to drop out of my yoga class.

Male: Why? Didn't you enjoy it?

Female: No, I loved it! I just don't have the time for it right now. I'm taking two classes, and I work full-time.

Male: Yes, that's too much to do. You can take the class later, or do yoga at home when you have time.

Female:

A. That's a good idea.

B. It has really paid off!

C. He talked me into it.

Unit 11

LISTENING: Listen to the question. Listen to the conversation. Listen to the question again. Fill in the circle for the correct answer.

1. What does the man think about Dan?

Male: I'm not sure Dan is the right candidate for this job.

Female: Why not? His technical skills are excellent, and he's got good people skills.

Male: That's true, but he doesn't have much job experience.

What does the man think about Dan?

A. He doesn't have enough work experience.

B. He has excellent technical skills.

C. He would be great for the job.

2. What does the woman want to do?

Female: I really need to build a stronger résumé.

Male: What do you plan to do?

Female: I think I'll get more professional development. There's a training workshop coming up in Chicago. Maybe I'll attend.

Male: Well, I went to that workshop last year, and actually it wasn't very good. It might be better for you to take night classes instead. When you're finished, you can look for new job opportunities to pursue.

What does the woman want to do?

A. take night classes

B. go to a training workshop

C. pursue new job opportunities

3. How does the woman offer to help the man?

Male: It's time for me to update my résumé.

Female: Why? Are you going to conduct a job search?

Male: No, but I want to get a promotion at my company. I need to take the initiative so the boss will notice the good work I do. I think I'll get my credentials evaluated, too.

Female: That's a good idea. Let me know if you want any feedback on your résumé.

How does the woman offer to help the man?

A. She offers to evaluate his credentials.

B. She offers to look at his résumé.

C. She offers to help him conduct a job search.

LISTENING: Listen to the conversation. Choose the best response.

4.

Male: I really want to quit my job.

Female: Well, I wouldn't quit now if I were you. We're in the middle of a big project. You won't get a good reference from the company if you leave all that work for someone else to do.

Male: Hmm. I didn't think about that.

Female: The project will be over in two months, and you could leave then without making anyone angry. And besides, you can conduct a job search during those two months.

Male:

A. I'm going to learn a new skill.

B. I need more time to relax.

C. Good point. You're probably right.

5.

Male: You're busy all the time lately. Do you ever take time to relax?

Female: Not really. You know that I'm taking classes at night. If I finish my degree, I'll get a promotion.

Male: I know, but you work too hard already. You always seem tired and you've been getting sick a lot more since you started taking classes. Maybe all the extra work is wearing you out and making you ill.

Female:

A. I like to relax by playing soccer and walking in the park.

B. You're right. I need to update my résumé if I want a promotion.

C. I hadn't thought of that. Maybe I should take a break next semester.

Unit 12

LISTENING: Listen to the question. Listen to the conversation. Listen to the question again. Fill in the circle for the correct answer.

1. What's the mayor's plan for schools?

Male: Mayor Richards, what is your plan for improving our schools? Will you veto the budget cuts that have been proposed?

Mayor: I plan to raise salaries for our teachers. Without good teachers, we can't have good schools. We also need to hire more teachers, because we have more students than ever.

What's the mayor's plan for schools?

A. She will hire fewer teachers to save money.

B. She will veto the proposed budget cuts.

C. She will pay the teachers more money.

2. Who is coordinating the charity auction this year?

Female: Brad, did you know that I'm going to be coordinating the charity auction this year?

Brad: You don't sound very excited about it, Mandy.

Female: I'm not. Tina coordinated it last year, and she did such a great job. It will be hard to follow in her footsteps. Besides, Tina was always complaining that the auction took too much of her time.

Brad: You're right. It's a lot of work for just one person. I'd love to help, Mandy, but I'm going to be teaching summer school so I won't have the time.

Who is coordinating the charity auction this year?

A. Brad

B. Mandy

C. Tina

3. Who will get into the zoo free for the company picnic?

Male: I heard that the company picnic this summer is going to be happening at the zoo.

Female: That's right. The picnic committee decided it would minimize stress for everyone if we have the picnic away from the office this year. Last year, it was a lot of work to set up for the picnic and clean up afterwards.

Male: The zoo sounds like a great idea. Can we bring our families?

Female: I think so, but only employees will get in free. Family members will need to pay the zoo entrance fee.

Who will get into the zoo free for the company picnic?

A. only the picnic committee

B. all employees

C. family members

LISTENING: Listen to the conversation. Choose the best response.

4.

Male: Did you hear that the company is going to promote telecommuting?

Female: Yes, I did. You must be pretty happy about that. I know you've had problems with your schedule because you're a single dad.

Male: Definitely. I want to be home when my son comes back from school every day. It's been difficult to find babysitters for him in the afternoon.

Female:

A. I'm really happy for you.

B. I'm looking forward to it.

C. I'll ask the boss for more information.

5.

Female: So how do you like all the travel that comes with your job?

Male: I'm thrilled to see new places, but I've also had to miss a lot of family events like birthdays and parties.

Female: I'm sorry to hear that.

Male:

A. Yes, it's fantastic.

B. That sounds like fun, thanks.

C. That's okay, so far it has been worth it.

Daily Book Scanning Log

Name: _Darianny_____ Date: _____ # of Scanners: _____

BIN #	BOOKS COMPLETED	# OF PAGES	NOTES / EXCEPTIONS
Bin 1	49	10454	
Bin 2	45	10006	
Bin 3	40	9718	
Bin 4			
Bin 5			
Bin 6			
Bin 7			
Bin 8			
Bin 9			
Bin 10			
Bin 11			
Bin 12			
Bin 13			
Bin 14			
Bin 15			
Bin 16			
Bin 17			
Bin 18			
Bin 19			
Bin 20			
Bin 21			
Bin 22			
Bin 23			
Bin 24			
Bin 25			
Bin 26			
Bin 27			
Bin 28			
Bin 29			
Bin 30			
Bin 31			
Bin 32			
Bin 33			
Bin 34			
Bin 35			
Bin 36			
Bin 37			
Bin 38			
Bin 39			
Bin 40			

(BOOKS / LIBROS) TOTAL:_____ / 600

(PAGES/PAGINAS) TOTAL:_____

SHIFT:_____ STATION #:_____